Performing Science and the Virtual

This dazzling new book from Sue-Ellen Case looks at how science has been performed throughout history, tracing a line from eleventh-century alchemy to the twenty-first-century virtual avatar.

Theatre and science are deeply interwoven in the European tradition, both in historical development and in strategies of representation. As science and new technologies become more pervasive in the social world, whilst at the same time retreating into their own specialized disourses, performances of their power provide a familiar, active interface with them. *Performing Science and the Virtual* reviews how these performances borrow from spiritualist notions of transcendence, as well as the social codes of race, gender and economic exchange.

In this daring and wide-ranging book we encounter Faust, glimpse Edison in his laboratory, enter the soundscape of John Cage and raid tombs with Lara Croft. Case looks at the intersection of science and performance in a way that unsettles our assumptions across these disciplines.

Sue-Ellen Case is Professor and Chair of Critical Studies, Theater UCLA, where she also directs the Center for Performance Studies.

Performing Science and the Virtual

Sue-Ellen Case

Routledge
Taylor & Francis Group

NEW YORK AND LONDON

First published 2007
by Routledge
270 Madison Ave, New York, NY 10016

Simultaneously published in the UK
by Routledge
2 Park Square, Milton Park, Abingdon, Oxon OX14 4RN

Routledge is an imprint of the Taylor & Francis Group, an informa business

Typeset in Baskerville by Taylor and Francis Books
Printed and bound in Great Britain by Antony Rowe Ltd, Chippenham, Wiltshire

Library of Congress Cataloging in Publication Data
Case, Sue-Ellen.
    Performing science and the virtual / by Sue-Ellen Case. – 1st ed.
       p. cm.
    Includes bibliographical references and index.
    1. Science—History—19th century. 2. Science—History—20th century. 3. Science—History—
    21st century. 4. Technology—History—19th century. 5. Technology—History—20th century.
    6. Technology—History—21st century. 7. Science and the arts. 8. Technology and the arts. 9.
    Science—Social aspects. 10. Technology—Social aspects. I. Title.
    Q125.C3837 2006
    500—dc22   2006020716

British Library Cataloguing in Publication Data
A catalogue record for this book is available from the British Library

ISBN10: 0-415-41438-5 (hbk)   ISBN13: 978-0-415-41438-8 (hbk)
ISBN10: 0-415-41439-3 (pbk)   ISBN13: 978-0-415-41439-5 (pbk)
ISBN10: 0-203-96716-X (ebk)   ISBN13: 978-0-203-96716-4 (ebk)

For Susan Leigh Foster, divine choreographer

Contents

List of illustrations   *x*
Acknowledgments   *xi*

Introduction   **1**

Prologue   ***Theater's rebirth***   **7**
All the world's a theater: war and science   10

Act One   ***Alchemy***   **15**
From mercurial change to monetary stasis   18
Coding and decoding: Isaac Newton, alchemist   20
Gender and sex in alchemy   26
Alchemy's antagonist: Ben Jonson   27
The gender divide: The Roaring Girl   30
Faust: the new paradigm of alchemy   32
    Faust I: the fall from Goethean science   35
    Proliferation of virtual spaces   39
    Faust II: transcendent gender and money   41
    Virtualizing the feminine gender   45
    The apotheosis of gender   46
    Eurythmy: erforming Goethean science   49

Entr'acte   ***The price of admission***   **51**

Act Two   ***Grassroots performances of science***   **58**
Accessing the virtual plane   60
The advent of the avatar   62
A sometimes man: fleshing out the gendered avatar   64
Embodied geography: Tibet   66
Mme. Blavatsky's phenomenal physics vs. the theater of Darwin   70

The Gothic medium of matter 75
Gothic ghosts haunt Marx 77
The medium of invention: Edison and G.B. Shaw 80
Tortured alchemy meets Darwinism: Strindberg 82

Act Three   *A century of science*   **86**

Scene One: the early years   **89**
Expressionist schematics 90
Between typewriter and electric chair: Machinal 92
Vampiric typewriters 95
Revue-ing sewing machines: Pins and Needles 96
The Adding Machine 98
Animating the machines: the robot 99
Factories of death: Gas 101
Expressionist futures 103

Machine-love: the Futurist embrace 104
Futurist futures 107
Engineering Soviet science: Aelita Queen of Mars 108

Scene Two: mid-century modern   **114**
Cold War alchemy 117
Grassroots sightings of science: UFOs 119
Alien abductions 122
The mechanics of memory: Samuel Beckett and tape 123
Songs of infidelity: Pauline Oliveros and John Cage 128
The theremin and the Cage 131
Virtual closet 137
Out of the sonic closet 138

Scene Three: under-modern: trash   **142**
Queer and cyber trash 145
Queering trash 147
Trash as dramatic universe: Jack Smith 148
Cyberpunk trash 149
Biospheres and bioreserves 151

Scene Four: neo-nature   **152**
Virtual Tibet 152
Harmonic Himalaya effect 155
Critical Art Ensemble vs. Frankenature 157
Doing Dolly: cloning and Caryl Churchill 159

Act Four   *The avatar*   **163**

Twentieth-century Fausts 166
  Rocket science and satanism 166
  Church of Science 167
  Heaven's Gate 168
  Faust is Dead 170

Staging scientists 171
  Fleshy physics: Galileo 172
  Darwin 177
  Heisenberg 181
  Einstein on the Beach 182
  Cyber-Darwin 185

Avatars of synth-race 185
  Sun Ra: Pharoah from Outer Space 188

Channeling New Age avatars 193

Composing the cyber-avatar 196
  The avatar as credit 199
  Logo-centric avatars 201
  The digital diva: Lara Croft 203
  Waitingforgodot.com 206
  Stelarc 208

The other avatar: neo-minstrels meet Cyber-Vato 209
  Transgender avatars are Virtually Yours 215
  Transgender express: the Brandon website 218

Notes   223
Bibliography   228
Index   236

Illustrations

1 Frontispiece from Johann Gottfried Kiessling, *Relatio practica*,
   Leipzig, 1752   16
2 Emblem of Solomon's Temple sketched by Isaac Newton   25
3 "David Garrick is Abel Drugger in Jonson's *The Alchemist*"   55
4 Madame Blavatsky   59
5 *Dr. Caligari*   91
6 Ruth Snyder execution   94
7 *Aelita: The Queen of Mars*, "All Power to the Soviets"   110
8 *Aelita: The Queen of Mars*, telescope   111
9 *Aelita: The Queen of Mars*, set design   112
10 Pauline Oliveros at the Tape Music Center Opening   129
11 *Variations V*   134
12 *Lunar Opera*, Tibetan Monks, and Moonstrels   141
13 Final scene from Philip Glass's *Einstein on the Beach*, 1976   183
14 Sun Ra from *Space is the Place*   189
15 *Lara Croft Tomb Raider: Legend*   204
16 *Waitingforgodot.com*   207
17 Kate Bornstein in *Virtually Yours*   216
18 *Big Doll*   219
19 *Roadtrip*   221

Acknowledgments

First, I would like to thank my editor, Talia Rodgers. During this project, I experienced several crises of confidence and Talia was always wonderfully supportive, assuring me that a more "horizontal" organization was viable, and leading me to other books with similar approaches. Several UCLA graduate students have helped with research, writing, and thinking through some of the issues: Nikki Eschen, Ayan Gangopadhyay, Jason Farman, Heidi Miller, Yael Prizant, Kaitrin McDonagh, Cheryl Lubin, and Chantal Rodriguez. My thanks to Candace Moore and the UCLA Center for the Study of Women for last-minute help with illustrations. For questions of historical accuracy, I asked Marvin Carlson and Simon Williams to read early drafts of certain sections. Their responses were helpful and supportive. But most of all, my partner, Susan Leigh Foster, endured the long, summer months of obsessive writing with humor; choreographed the time so that I could work on this project; read numerous drafts; supplied insights and additions, and corrected my awkward grammar. Moreover, she helped to create a rich life together that could afford this project.

Introduction

Although I have seen it inscribed on some of the older buildings at some of the better universities, replete with its capital "S," the grand, singular noun Science has lost some of its power to summon. Without the capital inscription, the sciences join the ever-more-multiple postmodern pluralities of once singular notions such as globalisms, genders, and feminisms. Yet those of us in academic disciplines clustered in the Humanities continue to feel the economic and institutional sting of Science, as do many in the mediatized realm of documentary reportage. While the sciences and their technologies, proliferating wildly, seem to assimilate more and more of our social, economic, ecological, and aesthetic reserves, they have also increasingly withdrawn into their own specialized styles of articulation, consorting exclusively with their chosen forms of so-called facts and figures and actively rejecting any "humanistic" tracking of their ideas as "uninformed." Thus, Science both impounds the social in effect and affect and retreats from its critical articulation. This book tracks performances inspired by the reclusive, transcendent status that Science seems to hold in the cultural imaginary, from performative rites of its technologies to fearful expulsions of its machines and ideologies.

My first encounter with the seductive spectacle of new technologies occurred when I was approximately ten years old. The only entertainment my working-class parents could afford was Friday nights at the Sears Roebuck department store. With popcorn in hand, we strolled past the performances of new blenders and power saws, but the performance that always caught me up in its power and radiance was the chromed, wailing vacuum cleaner whose reverse air flow held multiple balls high in the air. While the other apparati simply performed their intended functions, the vacuum cleaner invoked an invisible power to elevate those colored orbs into the air, spinning beautifully above the racks of clothes. Not only did its chrome sheath seduce and its power of transcendence amaze, but its ability to keep many balls in the air had a deep influence upon my writing—as this project will demonstrate.

As I grew older, the Sears Roebuck performances were amplified by school field trips to local laboratories and observatories and enforced participation in science fairs. The science fairs required me to devise a "winning" demonstration of my own little research projects and to note, competitively, how many other students from other schools were demonstrating their own. Meanwhile, my parents gave me chemistry sets and telescopes for Christmas, which kept me busy performing various science-oriented tasks as entertainment, and Hollywood served up science-fiction films with scientists as heroes. The darker side of science and technology appeared in various forms: we practiced hiding under our desks at school in case of a nuclear attack; sonic booms split the skies above our backyards as test pilots broke the sound barrier over nearby air fields; and, at school, we were brought into the auditorium to listen to a radio countdown of an execution in the electric chair.

At the time, I was not aware that these performances of science with its technological victories and threats had derived from years, even centuries of imagining Science. Similar demonstrations of apparati had already been performed in the nineteenth century, notably, in this study, by Thomas Edison; the science fairs devolved from a century or more of museums of science and the practices of display; fears of the darker side were as old as Faust legends, and the performance of machines had inspired numerous playwrights, electronic composers, and grassroots rites throughout the twentieth century. In order to review the performance of science, I realized I needed to look to the apparatus of theater and beyond to what I am calling grassroots performances that have played out the psychic affect of the ever-imposing rise of science in various invented rites and social organizations. From the canonical *Faust* by Goethe to decoder rings in cereal boxes, then, a variety of performances have served to locate and define the scientific discoveries of their times. However, the performance of science is not simply a matter of the stage or adepts imagining science. Theater and science are deeply interwoven in the European tradition, both in historical development and in strategies of representation. As these few examples illustrate, if theater staged science, science also staged itself as theater.

My studies have revealed two major strategies of representation that have worked across the fields of science and performance: constructions of virtual space and the avatar. Both the laboratory and the stage construct a space that is organized as alternative to the ubiquitous, pedestrian realm. Acting within that space requires particular codes of behavior, traditions of costuming, and training in specialized gestures or functions. In order to imagine how that space can be set apart from quotidian spaces and how behavior in that space might be recognized as "special" or "specialized," both theater and science have deployed notions of the virtual and its avatar that are as old as *The Upanishads* and as new as cyberspace and online avatars. One way to perceive the particular meaning of the term "virtual" is to review its definition in the *Oxford Dictionary*. Usage of the term in English spans at least four hundred years, referring to both science and philosophy. "Virtual" is first defined as "Possessed of certain physical virtues or capacities;" in 1660, it refers to herbs as "possessing certain virtues;" in 1683 it is a power "capable of producing a certain effect or result; effective, potent, powerful"; in 1654 it "is so in essence or effect although not formally or actually"; in 1704, it refers to optics "applied to the apparent focus or image resulting from the effect of reflection or refraction upon rays of light;" and, finally in 1883 from "Dynamics" "of velocity or momentum." As for "virtuality," the dictionary offers three usages: "the possession of force or power;" "Essential nature or being, apart from external form or embodiment" (1646), and "a virtual (as opposed to actual) thing, capacity, etc; a potentiality" (1836). Thus, the English usage of the terms "virtual" and "virtuality" moves across the fields of moral philosophy, optics, physics, and ontology. This mix of immaterial and material referents that all somehow display a sense of power and "otherness" is crucial to the application of virtual space in producing theater and science. It is at once the effect of an apparatus and a potent realm of essence, apart from function.

Today, one can experience Virtual Reality through new technologies and even buy virtual property on eBay, finally turning the cyber-virtual realm into real estate. The economic uses of the virtual do play into this concoction; however, they are augmented by a crucial addition, one that I will here call "spiritualism." Although this term has certain nineteenth-century associations, which do pertain here, I want to broaden "spiritualism" to include various practices that participate in alternative imagined spaces inspired by or in resistance to the reception of science and technology. These notions are sometimes practiced by religions, sometimes cults, sometimes eccentric individual inventions, and sometimes by the scientists themselves. Celebrating technologies as transcendent surely participates in the tradition of elevated spaces and avatars as invented by spiritual movements; performing spiritual spaces and avatars against science as a fallen materialist practice also ironically recreates some of science's own claims; and perceiving discoveries as "damnable," as against God and Nature repeats the Faustian parable, even in the twenty-first century.

As noted above, costumes and specialized systems of gesture and function are necessary for action in the virtual spaces of science and performance. The virtual must somehow be made manifest. The tradition of avatars has been made to represent the somehow "othered presence" in these virtual realms. From actual scientists in lab coats manipulating their various apparati to Sun Ra with antennae and Egyptian religious symbols performing the "Pharaoh from Outer Space," costumes and behavioral codes are required to mark the dimensions of these techno-virtual spaces. Reading these codes, I begin with the alchemist, who purposefully invoked the cosmological in the laboratory, and conclude with the celebrated cyber-avatar of Lara Croft, who seems to belong solely to the corporate world of entertainment. Along the way, I hope to show the ways in which, from alchemist to Lara certain borrowings from among scientific, spiritualist and performance practices continue to produce the performance of science through the avatar and the virtual.

While the materials of the book are organized in roughly chronological order, I have subsumed them under headings that imitate the performative structure of acts and scenes. My turn to the traditional structures of the play was caused by several factors. First, as I have already argued in *The Domain-Matrix* (1996), I believe we are caught in an historical era that mixes the customs and beliefs of print culture with the more performative and episodic spaces of the cyber. Caught between books and the World Wide Web, ambivalent practices of writing and reading suggest to me that I could not continue to frame my research in a strictly print tradition. Thus, not strictly adhering to the confines of print culture, I have not sought to develop one long sequential argument. While similarities and resonances do prevail among these centuries-long practices, they are not developmental. So I have assembled them under various rubrics. As the critic Carolyn Allen remarked, this book might be read as a narrative of tropes. Contemporary readers may want to read the book as they read the web, seeking out certain examples of interest and ignoring others, or they may follow links, in this case tropes that appear in various places throughout the text. I have listed most of the examples in order to make that opportunity easier. Acts, meaning, really, performative critical actions, inscribe sets of examples within the temporal tropes of centuries in the same way that gestures and encounters are caught up in the temporal form of a theatrical Act.

Even popular computer games have moved from narrative, linear forms to topological ones, for example *The Sims* or the *Grand Theft Auto* series. In both, players can freely roam the virtual spaces of the game. *Grand Theft Auto: San Andreas*, the latest game in a series almost ten years old, even offers an entire state to explore. Although some narrative form lingers in the game, in that the user takes on a character and needs to accomplish missions set by the bosses, she or he may decide to climb a mountain, play various betting games in the casino, get a tattoo, eat, go to the gym, listen to music, and even have cyber-sex.[1] Would that I could provide these alternatives here, although during the time the reader peruses this text, all of those activities might occur. With sales of over five million dollars, what author wouldn't envy this game?

Second, research today has been radically altered by the internet, particularly when it concerns popular culture and specifically techno and internet cultures. While my own training in print scholarship has led me to include a number of traditional citations, much of the material has been derived from the internet and may be considered specious by more traditional readers. Hanging on to the authoritative power of print is becoming more and more anterior to contemporary searches though, and while print does continue to offer some assurance to the reader, it may actually be just as profligate as the digital. Error and plagiarism are not unique to the internet, nor indeed is the cache of documents deemed "original." For example, there is no better archive of materials than on the website of The Newton Project (http://www.newtonproject.ic.ac.uk), funded by the English Arts and Humanities Research Board and hosted by the Centre for History of Science, Technology and Medicine at Imperial College London, in collaboration with Cambridge University. Researchers have uploaded onto the website an amazing number of Newton's alchemical manuscripts, which had previously been very difficult to access. The powerful Google search engine provides links to many contemporary and historical practices, including images, bibliographies, critical articles, fan websites, production histories, etc. I cannot imagine why any researcher would ignore its offerings. So net research and net reading have become ubiquitous in my academic endeavors as well as in the lives of many of my colleagues and students. Thus, I have attempted to provide some of the opportunities afforded by the web, while still "appearing" in print.

Finally, I have repeatedly asked myself why I wrote this book, since I have dedicated the majority of my academic career to work on feminist, or lesbian approaches to performance, and to politically-oriented productions by German playwrights. Why now, in the fullness of my career, would I turn to the performance of science? And what has become of the campy writing style that has been my signature? Well, the last question is the easier one to answer. There is one kind of camp irony that is displayed in the writing style and another kind that is deeply embedded in the choice of topics and the treatment of them. This book partakes in the latter. For example, the choice of the grand Mme. Blavatsky and my insistence upon her title—my serious critical treatment of her as one worthy to set against those giants of the nineteenth century, such as Darwin or Strindberg, is as deeply campy as it is legitimate. Likewise, the discussion of canonical, serious movements, such as Expressionism, set alongside considerations of the harmonic convergence or channeling brings a campy negotiation of the avant-garde and those practices generally regarded as "wacky." Or to situate Samuel Beckett's *Krapp's Last Tape* in proximity to Pauline Oliveros's *Lunar Opera* once again ironically tests the literal "lengths" auteurs have gone to imagine recursive technologies. Without a campy approach to performance, I would never have discovered some of these personages, or known how to approach their work.

As for the deeper question about the object of my research, I can only reply that I believe I have witnessed The Great Upload in my time. Previous practices of gender, sexuality, materiality, community, and corporeality have been uploaded into various new technological zones. While I will confess that this upload has provoked considerable nostalgia and anger in me, it has also driven me to witness new forms of performance and sociability—new "cultural life forms"—as Jordy Jones put it. The damnable collusion between the military and the corporate in the development and deployment of new technologies has also inspired many sophisticated forms of resistance. The privileged, highly-capitalized, removed practices of science have awakened new grassroots performances critical of science and its long reach into our micro and macro worlds. Whatever the outcome, the very assembling of large groups of people at different sites in the world to meditate on peace in a time of armament is the kind of performance that brings me hope. So I have composed a set of examples that I hope can illustrate historical practices of collusion and resistance, in order to amplify the perception of how the performance of science is shaping social and economic forces in our contemporary world.

So let's pretend that we are in the state of performing science. We meet a variety of fascinating characters, including the aristocratic Goethe, the imposing orientalist fakir Mme. Blavatsky, the brooding, reclusive Strindberg, and catch glimpses of Newton and Edison in their laboratories. We visit stage productions of robots, Einstein and Darwin, enter the soundscape of John Cage, play a computer game with the digital Lara Croft, and become a transgendered cyber-Brandon.

Theater's rebirth

The curtain opens on the traditional history of theater's rebirth in Europe. This story is familiar to most of us who have endured standard coursework in theater history. The following is a retelling of the myth, or history we have received, narrated from a different perspective, and with a different emphasis. Here, it will serve to illustrate the myth of origins deployed in the displacement of performances designed to induce transformation, or transmutation with a theater of representation. Hopefully, revealing the specific cultural investment in this displacement will help to clarify how theater, and its cultural partner, the "new" science have served to construct a strictly European tradition of the mode of representation. The ironic tone of this revised narrative has been encouraged by the omissions and subjugations embedded in the traditional history of origins, particularly as they have affected the participation of women in cultural production and the construction of "othered" cultural ethnicities. It will be argued that two basic strategies of extraction were deployed to displace sciences and rites dedicated to change: the special role assigned to the human subject and the notion of a virtual space that was designed for exclusive access.

As the curtain parts, we discover a gathering of men in vestments, near the altar in the Christian Church, on Easter day, performing the story of the god's resurrection. This is the site traditional histories of European theater will insist upon as the resurrection of theater itself. As the story goes, after centuries of Christian censure in Western Europe, theater's rebirth took place, propitiously, around the performance of the *quem queritis* (*Visitatio Sepulchri*), or the liturgy surrounding Christ's own resurrection, in the tenth century. While certain transformational practices still remained in the liturgy, such as the transubstantiation of wine and bread into the body and blood of Christ, the liturgical tropes identified as those that encouraged theater were tropes concerning the narration of the life of Christ, celebrated at specific times in the Christian calendar, particularly at Easter. Cut off from its association with other rites, what would become theater took its cue from the Christian history, re-imagining its own roots as from an ancient source, Greece, (from around the same period and geographical location as Christianity's), along with its own birth, death, and resurrection—the latter happily coinciding with the liturgical representation of Christ's own.

Church and Theater commingled their strategies. The chronology of the god's life was fashioned to fit the now-traditional elements of a plot. Its ultimately happy ending fashioned the god's life into a comedy. As Dunbar Ogden (2002: 24) describes it in his definitive study, *The Staging of Drama in the Medieval Church*:

> The action of our first medieval play embodies a quest which comes to a successful conclusion in discovery. . . . The structure we may call comic in that the play moves from complication to happy revelation, turning climactically on the two-phase revelation: the angel says, "He is risen," the women reacting with an *Alleluia*. . . .

At its rebirth, theater emulated the Christian narrative, emerging from its liturgy. It did not spring from transformational rites, but as a plotted narrative with certain specific characteristics of change resulting in a happy ending.

The notion of an actor, or performer, in the European tradition was not derived from the priest's ritual of the transformation of the wine and bread. Had acting been understood as ritualistic and transformative, it might have found consonance with different traditions in the world and different cosmologies. It might have remained embedded in ritual, music, and dance and dedicated to transformation. But the extraction of "theater" from the fusion of change, dance, and music actually displaced those performances of transmutation. This extraction constituted one of the major contributions of European culture—a kind of historical dentistry that produced careful divisions among the arts, leaving dancers mute and actors less mobile. The success of the extraction depended on theater's participation in narrative and representation. The structure of theater would not be the celebration of a god who corporealized through ritual; instead the focus was shifted to a man-god who was *represented* as an absent figure and whose absence evoked the presence of actors in the Easter liturgy: the two Marys. Not to linger on the seductive theories of presence and absence as many have done, the point here is merely that these first "actors," took on the representation of Biblical figures: they acted out a written story. The shift of focus, from rites of transubstantion to representation ultimately differentiated theater from liturgy.

In this model of theater, the god did not corporealize through, say, trance dancing, nor was he somehow embedded in transmutating materials. In fact, as we will see, this sanctioned form of representation was designed to *displace* transformative rites and discourses, such as alchemy. The only transformation in the story theater would tell was expressed through the narrative, not the enactment of the resurrection. It was a story that promised *deferred* transformation to the spectator/believers. Transformation would be an effect of spectatorship rather than a performative action. This promise of resurrection, deferred to the end of one's life, became the central promissory note in the Christian economy and created the sense that spectatorship could finally pay off. While transformational rites of the period, such as alchemy, or witchcraft, were designed to enhance the participant, theater promised a pay off for the audience. Later, theater would demand payment up front for its performance of deferred transformation, albeit aesthetic rather than religious.

Although transformation was deferred in this new form, a particular form of exchange was practiced in the casting. It seems that the two Marys were primarily played by men, except, perhaps, in some convents (Ogden 2002: 143). While Ogden and others, such as myself, have expended much energy to reclaim those early performances by women, still, what is marked here, is how representation was founded, in this tradition, on a gender exchange.[1] At first glance, such an exchange might be construed as an aberration in a form designed to displace transformation. Could gender exchange be the one remaining element, so to speak, of alchemical practices that imagined a debased metal transmutated into gold? Could a man be changed into a woman through performance? Perhaps. But this exchange, though, in one sense, an unstable element, actually stabilized the rite of *representation* as belonging to the exclusive all-male realm of men in vestments. As theater became extracted, vestments became costumes, music an accompaniment, and the all-male realm stable in marking places of privilege.

Enter the "new" science, also designed to displace, say, alchemy. These new performance practices also carried over into the laboratory. Access would be limited to men in robes, experimenting through equations of stable and unstable elements, perceived through an iterative rather than transformative lens. Although, by now, these observations belong to an obvious, overworked interpretation of the traditional history of theater and science, they may prove useful in an examination of rise of the "new" theater and the "new" science as contingent practices in Europe. The uses and discoveries of theater and science may be seen to found a kind of social realm that would extend between their sites of practice.

Moreover, the sites of the laboratory, the Church, and the stage claimed to provide an architecture of the virtual that would become crucial to the ways in which they would inform one another. The medieval cathedral purported to provide an architecture of the virtual space of heaven, where the "spirit," or the actor/character was cast as an effect of that space. The grandiose effort and effect of the cathedral exclaimed the virtual as a transcendent space, appropriating communal labor, investment, and a dominant place in the social and natural landscape. David Wiles argues, this "sacred" space articulated "a complete value system" outside of which, the participating nun, or priest, had no identity (2003: 49). Thus, the architecture of a space that claimed the virtual not only offered a structure of meaning, it also bestowed meaning upon the performers it encased. In her book *The Pearly Gates of Cyberspace* (1999), Margaret Wertheim emphasizes the promises of such virtual space to the exclusion of decay and the embrace of the universal, relating these earlier, Christian claims to the promises of the new, technological virtual in the late twentieth century. Thus, as Wertheim and others argue, technology borrowed its sense of the virtual from the Church architecture. Theater also borrowed the claims to these powers and promises in the construction of the stage, organizing a later claim to ascendance as "art," and to the universality of representation. As we will see, the notion of the primacy of a constructed virtual space, transcending the structures of what lay outside its envelope, practiced by the Church, science and theater will also wreak havoc on social and natural environments that lay outside their perimeters.

All the world's a theater: war and science

As an emblem of structural organization and investment, theater helped to organize a variety of representations, making its specific construction of elements operative in science as well as in war. In her book *The Theater of Nature*, Ann Blair argues that "the metaphor of theater conveyed the bringing of a vast topic under a single, all-encompassing gaze" (1997: 157). Thus, science could organize both the terms of its practice and the nature of its object through the paradigm of theater. The early modern notion of "nature as a theater, in which the human is the spectator rather than the actor looking out at the world as to a stage" helped to shift the sense of agency to the spectator (153). Theater signified a space in which a potent observant spectator could subject a field or a bounded space to its gaze. Space, as a stage, organized elements for view and created a unified field of objects, separated out from their social or natural environment. An object of the gaze thus became available for isolation and study as an effect of its staging. Perhaps this claim seems all-too-familiar, especially when reviewed from a contemporary perspective. After all, the subject/object binary is the central point of poststructuralist criticism. But for theater scholars, it is important to assess how theater and science historically linked together to create this partition; how the success of the model known as theater worked together with the new science to suppress other available structures of perceiving and knowing. As a result, the role for humans in this natural philosophical "theater of the world" "is not to take part in the show, but to watch and contemplate . . ." (154). The construction of the spectator position in science set humans apart from the elements they would study, creating a category called "nature" as an object of the gaze.

As a result of this binary, a special role was assigned to "man" as the spectator, or knower of this vast organization (157). This special role set "him" apart from animals, plants, stones, and metals—a separation that would later prove deadly to many species and environments. The power of the subject as spectator resided, partially, in a certain sanctity, wafting like incense from the Church tropes. Walter Benjamin, in his *Reflections*, attacks the vitalism that partially composed this special status for the human and its seemingly sacred origins:

> However sacred man is . . . there is no sacredness in his condition, in his bodily life. . . . What, then, distinguishes it essentially from the life of animals and plants? And even if these were sacred, they could not be so by

virtue only of being alive, of being in life. It might be worthwhile to track down the origin of the dogma of the sacredness of life. Perhaps, indeed probably, it is relatively recent, the last mistaken attempt of the weakened Western tradition to seek the saint it has lost in cosmological impenetrability.

(quoted in Hanssen 2000: 133)

Borrowing, then, from the virtual powers of the saint, the "liveness" of the human seemed to raise "him" above the elements. As we will see, the "old" science of alchemy provided a different epistemology, in which a shared subjectivity extended across "man" and elements.

The slow development of the notion of "man" as superior subject occurred in both the philosophies and sciences of the European tradition. In his book *The Open*, Giorgio Agamben traces this development of "man" as an exceptional subject noting that, at first, "in the Ancien Regime the boundaries of man are much more uncertain and fluctuating than they will appear in the nineteenth century after the development of the human sciences" (2002: 24). Even so, Agamben points to Linnaeus, the great taxonomer, as establishing "man" as a special species. Through discursive strategies of self-recognition, "man" established himself as a category (26). God-like, Christian notions of "man," and his special status as "live" were buttressed up by his participation in virtual systems, such as language and self-consciousness. "Man" could appropriate the virtual as a product of his own nature, rendering his powers as unique. If god was in his heaven, it was man that had imagined him there. Although, at first, the "new" science simply claimed this special role for "man" the observer, later Darwinian notions of his origin from among the animals challenged his virtual and saint-like genealogy and, in the twentieth century, his role as special subject, the knowing observer, was both challenged and maintained by physics.

Nonetheless, as special spectator, "man" claims a vitalistic dynamism for "his" gaze, which renders the object as static. Blair notes how the seventeenth century scientific deployment of the paradigm of theater displaced qualities of change with the condition of stasis: "Renaissance natural philosophical authors" observed "the static qualities of the theater of nature—its vast expanse . . . and elaborate construction . . . " (1997: 155). Tranformation, or transmutation, so central to alchemy, was eschewed by the "new" science. Blair, like Agamben, amplifies her argument by referring to the later development of the taxonomic system by Linnaeus in 1785, which assigned organisms to fixed places within a system of classification. The space of nature, then, as examined, would be one that was enclosed, static and calibrated for isolated integers. The great furnaces of the alchemists, firing up the transmutative essence of elements would be displaced by apparati designed to reveal and record their static properties. The objects of study would be static in their location, and self-referential in their attributes. The emphasis is on regularity, not dynamism—iteration, not transmutation. Representation.

A prime example of how this paradigm of the theater literally "operated" as science may be found in the amphitheater of anatomy, constructed in 1593 at Leiden University, where scientists gathered around to observe a corpse. The scientists were situated as audience and the corpse was on the operating stage. This practice recalls that scene of the opening act of theater's rebirth, in the *Visitatio Sepulchri*, where the two Marys stood before the empty tomb. However, in the theater of anatomy, the doctors actually discover the corpse, enhancing their mastery of the living body through the observation of the dead. The promise of transformation is no longer even deferred, but displaced into the acquisition of knowledge. The spectator benefits immediately from his observation of the dead body. The performing body has reached perfect stasis, while the spectators experience their receptive recompense. The scientific adoption of the theatrical model secured the success of the art as the preferred cultural rite, insofar as it could perform the new epistemological paradigm. Art and science worked together to fix into the cultural imaginary the properties of vital subject and static object bounded by a virtual that could iterate their essence and their promise for future enhancement.

The essential stasis inherent in the theatrical/scientific model also defined the conditions of wealth, or economic value. The paradigm of the static object and the external, dynamic subject informed notions of agency and appropriation for centuries to come. Not surprisingly, Mao Tse Tung, an activist/philosopher invested in direct social and economic change theorized how the stasis central in this scientific model also establishes material and social relations. In his revolutionary work, "On Contradiction," he begins by describing this mode of perception: "perceiving things as isolated, static and one-sided. . . . regards all things in the universe, their forms and their species, as eternally isolated from one another and immutable." Therefore, he reasons, the cause of change is perceived as "*not inside things but outside them, that is, the motive force is external* [emphasis added]" (2002: 45). Mao continues, "In Europe, this mode of thinking existed as mechanical materialism in the seventeenth and eighteenth centuries and as vulgar evolutionism at the end of the nineteenth and the beginning of the twentieth centuries." Mao, proposes, instead, a new science or an old one if we think back to alchemy, perceiving:

> The fundamental cause of the development of a thing [as] not external but internal. . . . There is internal contradiction in every single thing, hence its motion and development. . . . Thus materialist dialectics effectively combats the theory of external causes, or of an external motive force. . . . Simple growth in plants and animals . . . is likewise chiefly the result of their internal contradictions. Similarly, social development is due chiefly not to external but to internal causes. . . . (46)

Combining cultural, social, and scientific operations, Mao insists that change is an inherent part of the composition of a plant, animal, human, or social entity.

Mao portrays a dynamic universe in which change is the essence rather than the external engine of things. Thus, the so-called attributes of all elements are actually attributes of the dynamics of essential change rather than properties that define a single, bounded element: they serve as adverbs, not adjectives. In this way, it is possible to imagine a materialist critique that might move toward the integration of social and ecological elements and away from the kind of static partition Mao eschews above.

In spite of Mao's utopian model, what theater stages, instead, is change through an external force. In the theater of plots and characters, the human subject, or "motivation," causes change in the world and among elements. In as much as later political theater practitioners, such as Brecht, would hope to put theater in the service of change, their dramaturgical force still resides in the human subject as if separate from and vitally transcendent to the elements. The function of change remains located solely within the character.

To emphasize this perception of nature as a theater, as a space managed and observed, is not to suggest that earlier European practices embraced some Nietzschean notion of nature as wild, or even posited an origin of the "real" and "pure" nature. "Nature," in England, had already been managed through various sorts of enclosures long before those parcels of private property would begin to appear in the eighteenth century. The management of natural spaces that were set aside and demarcated for specific uses were at least as old as the New Forest—the *Nova Foresta*—founded by William the Conqueror in 1079 for his deer hunting. The royal management of the woods both protected them and devastated them. The woods were designed for the needs and pleasures of the special human subject. Certain species were decimated in favor of those that were useful to the humans. Rules and dispensations governed hunting and woodcutting to conserve the young game and the saplings for further use. An even more severe appropriation of the woods was exercised once they became a supply for the Navy's ships. Elizabeth I had begun "encoppicing" enclosures of forest with the idea of supplying timber for her Navy. Thus, the woods, first designed to supply heat and game for the royals and the locals became a factory for the production of ships sent out to expand and protect the Empire. For these ends, the woods, the forest, the trees—the undergrowth and the canopy—were highly planted, cut, and managed through practices of ownership and surveillance, even becoming a supply terminal for imperialist ventures.[2]

Science and theater offered an organization of knowing and managing as a viewing apparatus, a lens, through which the appearance of the object was translated, with the assumption that its translation would provide a more accurate vision of it. If science emulated theater, theater also emulated science. In "The Artificial Eye: Augustan Theater and the Empire of the Visible," Joseph Roach enforces this notion, interpreting "the Augustan theater as an instrument, closely analogous to contemporary optical instruments, especially suited to the magnification of behavior" as well as to classification (1991: 143). Further, this drive to classification was a kind of inventory, familiar to what Roach, like Mao, perceives as a mechanism of representation and economic value. For Roach, theater offers a "multinational corporate vision" of trade (138–139). Theater is the apparatus that intercedes between subject and object, yielding a vision of its essential elements, whether they be physical or behavioral.

Act One

Alchemy

To fully situate the operations of theater and "new" science in the seventeenth century, it is necessary to understand how they functioned as interdictions against the occult sciences and arts. Within this general era, as imagined by traditional histories, the occult science most at issue was alchemy. Although alchemy continued to inform both performance and science, it was sufficiently debased by this new collusion to lose any institutional power it might have gained in earlier centuries.

Part of the reason that alchemy has been constructed as the fallen "other" of the rites of representation and the new science has to do with its social and political associations. Alchemy came into Europe from Islam, taking its name from the Arabic *al-kimiya*. The founder of alchemy was identified as the possibly-mythical Egyptian, Hermes Trismegistus. Alchemy was part of what R.W. Southern describes as a "one-way traffic in ideas" in the twelfth century, radiating out from the major Muslim centers in Spain and Sicily. Southern notes the central role the sciences played in this influx, particularly mathematics and astronomy, from 1150 onward and he describes the complex reception this influx encountered, as the developing sense of "Europe" began to be formed (1963: 64–66).

An anxiety of influence within Europe, alongside the fear of the growing territories of Islam to its South and East, catalyzed the need to establish a notion of "Europe" that could compete with the political and intellectual spread of Islamic influence. Edward Said, in *Orientalism* emphasizes that orientalist discrimination is never far from the idea of Europe, which established its base upon the notion of a superior cultural identity (1979: 7). Said further clarifies this position, noting that discrimination in the form of orientalism actually operates through its "distribution" into aesthetic and philological texts, by organizing "orthodoxies and canons of tastes, texts, and values . . . " (12). In the face of such a major intellectual and practical influx of ideas from Islam, Europe required the construction of an "intellectual authority" that could be identified as its own (19). The displacement of alchemy by the "new" science was key to establishing a new European "intellectual authority."

In part, alchemy was made esoteric, or driven into secrecy by prejudices against it based upon superstitious reactions to its contents as associated with

Figure 1 Frontispiece from Johann Gottfried Kiessling, *Relatio practica*, Leipzig, 1752
(A049. http://www.alchemywebsite.com © Adam McLean 2002)

Islamic beliefs. If alchemy was indeed superstitious, its reception was also superstitious. As Said notes, during the middle ages it was not the knowledge of Islamic thought and practice that became more accurate, but the *ignorance* of it that became more refined and complex (62). Indeed, that ignorance was lent a certain moral value. Said illustrates how, instead of inquiry into Islamic sciences and literature, they were constructed through a "narcissistic" approach that made them into a mirror of European practices, but a bad, evil one (67–70). As we will see, Goethe imagines the alchemist to be in league with the devil—the practice to be the opposite of Christianity.

Alchemy, philosophy, and religion were all intertwined with medical and arithmetical discourses, coloring their reception, while also establishing their worth. Astronomy and astrology as well as chemistry and alchemy were directly linked to philosophical traditions. As Christianity tied its discursive power to the Latin tradition, a language elevated against Arabic, it needed to assimilate what it could from these findings, while actively suppressing large portions of the learning. Christian/Latin Europe devised a way to extract the findings, or the data, as we would say today, from its embedded location within cosmological, philosophical and occult dimensions. This extraction would "color" how scientific knowledge was constituted. The isolation of elements for study, the sealed-off isolation of the laboratory is a consequence of this mode of extraction.

Set against belief systems, the "new" science claimed empiricism as its difference from these ancient practices. Yet Adelard, in twelfth-century England, recorded methods of inquiry practiced by the Arabs that suggest they may have routinely practiced a similar experimental approach (Daniel 1979: 271). In fact, it is easy to imagine that the Latin studies, based on disputation and iteration, were less open to those experimental methods than the Arabs, whose science was allied with the practical arts of metallurgy, pharmacy, and astronomy. Arguing for the adoption of Arabic sciences with his nephew, who was ensconced in the Latin tradition, Adelard notes: "from the Arabic masters I have learned one thing, to be led by reason, while you are caught in the image of authority" (qtd. in Daniel, 270). Alchemy was a science of experimentation. What knowledge was passed down in the great emblems and poems was a result of the findings in the labs. No alchemist was without his laboratory, or furnace. Alchemy was a practice that fused methods derived from the various trades of metallurgy and embalming with philosophy. Hands-on processes were well developed, alongside the figurations of astrology. In working with the basic structures of matter, alchemy sought to understand those structures as in consonance with those of philosophy. While these sciences were experimental, they were not extracted from philosophical inquiry. The emphasis on the extraction and isolation of empiricism was the force with which the new European intellectual authority installed itself. This European form of cultural dentistry was operating on several fronts at once, then, in terms of theater and the "new" science.

As the active construction of Europe was proceeding through identifications with the Latin and Chrstian traditions, it was deemed necessary to make these

Islamic influences appear not only as "foreign," but as threatening. Prohibitions against Arabic astrology arose in 1277, and manuscripts were burned (Daniel 288). These negative characterizations of Islamic sciences and literatures continued up through nineteenth century reconstructions of the period, allying themselves with theories of "race" that would bind certain forms of knowing to certain peoples. Along with suppressing and displacing the roots of Arab scientific knowledge, a new genealogy was invented to re-imagine where the knowledge was formed. Martin Bernal, in his study *Black Athena: The Afroasiatic Roots of Classical Civilization*, argues that a suppression of the Egyptian influence in medieval philosophy resulted from a nineteenth- and early twentieth-century racist bias that wanted to establish what Bernal calls "The Aryan model." Bernal argues that the collective, self-conscious project of substituting Greek roots for the Levantine mix of African and Semite practices was an attempt on the part of historians of the period to move the origins of European culture onto an Aryan, Greek base. Bernal identifies several lasting traces of Egyptian practices throughout the medieval period, particularly the Hermetic traditions of esoteric or secret practices such as alchemy. He goes to great lengths to describe the specific moves made by historians to suppress the Egyptian roots of these beliefs (1987: 130–138). In contrast to the substitution of Greek roots for "neo-platonism," the emergent philosophy of religion, Bernal illustrates how it was actually the esoteric traditions that promoted the structures of philosophy. The Jewish and Islamic diasporas brought these philosophical structures up into Spain and further north, along with the majority of scientific knowledge and practices (145–149). The association of alchemy and the occult sciences with Levantine, particularly Arab societies helped to make them unacceptable to the establishment of a history and identification of the European.

By the fifteenth century, the process of ethnic cleansing expelled the Jews and Muslims from Spain and the Arabic manuscripts were burnt. The esoteric traditions had been banned and their practitioners were tortured. The rebirth of the "new" science, then, was part of an ethnic cleansing. As this intellectual and social purge exerted its influence on the imagination of the cultural producers, an image began to appear in performance that portrayed the shrunken, isolated, wrongly-motivated individual through the image of the alchemist. His image, although not associated directly with Jewish or Arab characteristics, nonetheless suggests a familiar mercenary, double-dealing stereotype. The alchemist is a form of the cheating money-lender, perceived as a money-creator.

From mercurial change to monetary stasis

In contrast to the model of stasis, the base of alchemical practices was the notion of internal change. Charles Nicholl describes the centrality of change in *The Chemical Theatre*:

> There are two directions in which alchemical mercury leads us. On the one hand, it is a complex elaboration of a chemical substance. . . . But there is

another direction ... that transformation is something intrinsic and contained inside matter. . . . Each stage of this self-devouring, self-generating process bears the name "mercury."

(quoted in White 1997: 141)

In alchemy, change, represented by the fluidity of mercury, was considered to be the *prima materia*, or the basis of all matter. One of the documents central to the science of alchemy, indeed also to Hermetic philosophy in the early modern period, the *Corpus Hermeticum* by Hermes Trismegistus sets up the second "law" of nature as "all things are changeable."[1] In other words, at the center of this occult tradition is the kind of internal dynamic of change that Mao found missing in later successors of the "new" science. Heralded as both a proto-science (chemistry) and a fake science, alchemy offered a paradigm in which the scientist takes part in the dynamic of change in all things, rather than remaining an observer of static elements. Although alchemy was debunked by the institutions of church and the "new" science, it continues even today to draw a following, as illustrated by the numerous websites dedicated to its study and practice.[2]

Yet in spite of alchemy's practice of the broad base of change in all things, its reception in the seventeenth century often reduced the worth of its practice to the production of gold. The attempt was to convert the investment in change to one in stability. The seventeenth century was an age of crisis concerning money in England, as well as in several other countries. Major banks were founded in Amsterdam, Barcelona, Hamburg, and the Bank of England. These were institutions designed to protect gold, money and jewels, and to establish archives of economic value safe from counterfeit. The creation of these institutions intervened in a circulation of economic value that was, one might say, mercurial. In addition to gold and silver, a dizzying array of substances newly traded as money, such as tobacco in Virginia and tulip bulbs in Holland began to complicate the understanding of how value might be maintained and traded. "Wampum," seashells collected by Native Americans, was made legal tender in Massachusetts; goldsmiths' notes were exchanged as if money; the Massachusetts Bay Colony issued paper money, etc. A search for central issuance and value in the early eighteenth century led theorists such as John Law to publish treatises on the viability of bank notes rather than coins. Moreover, coins themselves, the traditional metal representatives of value, had degenerated, both physically and in terms of issue. Fears and uses of counterfeit money, led to a major recoinage in England in 1696. This crisis in coins, based on their relation to gold was managed, in part, by one of the leading alchemists of the age, Isaac Newton, who was in charge of the mint from 1699–1727.[3] In England, the province of money was moving from the exclusive hold on it that the royalty had enjoyed for centuries to provincial banks. The royalty, desperate for funding, resorted to extreme measures, usurping all the holdings in the mint at one time, and levying steep taxes to draw money made from labor and substances into its coffers. All of these forces of change were forming the beginning of the modern money market. Maintaining value was a driving anxiety hostile to local and counterfeit vagaries of exchange.

In this time of anxiety about monetary value it is small wonder that alchemy was perceived as primarily a science for turning "base" metals into gold. In the popular imagination, the alchemists became the magi of "real" money, who could transform other materials into the substance of ultimate value. The alchemists were used, then, not to celebrate the rites of the potential for change, but to mint the stability of absolute value. Alchemy, as the science of the production of gold, was reconstituted as a conservative rather than as a radical practice of change. Yet, although many alchemists were employed by the crown to provide it with gold, the alchemical tradition established a long history of the esoteric and theological management of money outside the control of the crown and state. For example, the Knights Templars, an esoteric, international Order served as financial agents, while the monasteries and even some convents enjoyed rights to coinage.[4] Alchemy maintained a relation of monetary value to esoteric philosophy; it could be managed by philosophers, alchemical scientists, and even nuns rather than by those exploited by the crown. But, at a time of the differenti- ation of value into different substances, the perception of alchemy seemed to reverse the process, transforming things into the one single sign of ultimate worth—gold. As we will see, the theater partners these projects with plays such as Jonson's *Alchemist* and Goethe's *Faust*, which stages these anxieties between the uses of alchemy, paper money and the crown as a conflict directly connected to the powers of heaven and hell.

Alongside this panic over money, the plague was inducing a panic over the sustainability of the human body. Thus, alchemy seemed also to be focused on producing the elixir of life, which could both bank and issue a longer youthful, continuance of the human body. Perhaps this notion was derived from the earliest Egyptian influences on the art, which were related to the embalming practices—the preservation of the body. Thus, security in value and vitality seemed to be the worthwhile promise of alchemy, and the radical core of alchemy, mercurial change, and the transmutation of materials was put to a conservative use, in producing the essential substance of value, gold, while money was on the way to becoming more and more virtual. The cosmology of change was assimilated by the science of iteration.

Coding and decoding: Isaac Newton, alchemist

Traditionally, Isaac Newton has stood as one of the inventors of the "new" science, instituting a mechanistic and rationalistic approach to matter. His accomplishments as a practitioner and theorist seem to situate him in the lineage of Galileo and Descartes. This reputation was based, narrowly, on his theory of gravity and his *Opticks*. His "other papers," which constituted the most complete collection of alchemical writings of his time, were not published until the twentieth century. In 1936, a collection of his papers "with no scientific value" was purchased at a Sotheby auction by John Maynard Keynes, the eminent economist, who bequeathed them to King's College. In 1942, Keynes spoke to the Royal Society Club, deconstructing the image of Newton as the prime mechanist and rationalist of his time, in order to regard him as "the last of the magicians, the last of the Babylonians and Sumerians . . . " (qtd. in White 1997: 3). Indeed, attention to these papers has already produced a popular new reception of Newton, as illustrated by the recent biography entitled *Isaac Newton: The Last Sorcerer* and the online Newton Project, which is uploading facsimiles of the Keynes collection onto the web, making his alchemical work available to critics and others.[5]

In contrast to the common perception of alchemy as merely a process for the production of gold, Newton's work included the study of the most of the major treatises available to his age in order to discover the master plan of change in the world. Betty Jo Teeter Dobbs, in *The Foundations of Newton's Alchemy*, asserts that "Newton went on . . . to probe the whole vast literature of older alchemy as it had never been probed before . . . " (1975: 88). With a library of more than 109 documents, Newton had the resources to create an overview of the practice (51). Alongside his library, Newton began installing the great furnace of alchemy in his laboratory as early as 1668. Historians conclude that he actively pursued experiments until roughly 1696, when he devoted his energies to decoding alchemical and biblical texts, finally composing his major alchemical treatise entitled, appropriately, *Praxis*. His job, as he saw it, was to decode the writings and drawings of other alchemists, perform the experiments that had been handed down through them, and to reconstruct, from fragments, the whole of the historical process and the formation of the future.

Newton's face was turned to the ancients, as Keynes expresses in his reference to the Babylonians and Sumerians, rather than to what might be termed the "early moderns," or to futuristic projects. In this practice, Newton was closer to Mme. Blavatsky in the nineteenth century, who would reread the ancient occult texts against Darwin, than to the kind of science that emerged, seemingly, from Newton's own highly edited and reconstructed tradition. Dobbs argues, in fact, that Newton represents an even earlier alchemical practice than the one of his time. She stresses that, among those who would be scientists, alchemy was chemicalized and mechanicalized in the latter half of the seventeenth century, to be claimed later as the practice of reason and experiment that would lead to chemistry (80–83). Ironically, this is not the alchemical practice of Isaac Newton, who worked in the analogical, coded manner of the ancients. While he might have taken over the reforms of the minting process of official currency, making gold was the least of his investments in alchemy. Instead, he invested in the "philosophical mercury" of change.

Remembering that the appellation "scientist" did not appear until the decade of the 1830s, we can better understand Newton through the terms of his time, as a "Philosopher of Nature" (Shanahan 2002: 11). As a philosopher, Newton's approach implemented experimentation by decoding philosophical texts. The drive to decode is a familiar one to critics and technologists in the late twentieth century. Widespread software inventions/controls and online communications have also inspired an obsession with decoding, from serious books like *Code*, to popular science fiction novels such as *Cryptonomicon*. In the late twentieth century, this decoding is related to conspiracy theories based on the seductive corporate structuring of appearances that might not match real economic and social relations (as troped in the film *The Matrix*). For Newton, in the late seventeenth century, decoding was likewise perceived as revealing the structure of things, but in the more positive tradition of regarding the codes as inspired, prescient models. In these studies, Newton strove to discover the principles of structure embedded in theoretical/performative writings (Dobbs 1975: 175). In his time of counterfeiting, Newton sought truth in the codes; in ours, we seek the structure of the lie.

Newton's fame is based upon his discovery of the notion of gravity by watching an apple fall. In fact, Newton's "discovery" of gravity has been received as the paradigm of empirical knowledge. Yet, when situated alongside his alchemical practices, his discovery of gravity may be understood as a byproduct of alchemical decoding. Some critics suggest that his discovery emanated from his study of one of the major emblems of alchemy: the *star regulus* (Dobbs 1975: 148–149). In this star, the power flow of the emblem is understood to draw from the points in toward the center, through attraction, rather than emanating out through the points. The emblem of the force of attraction, drawing in, in contrast to the common notion of star light as radiance, projecting out, may have inspired Newton to be able to imagine the attraction of gravity upon the apple. My point, here, is not to discover an actual cause and effect relationship in Newton's work, but to excavate a mode of knowing through a familiar and significant example of Newton. His thought contributed much to his alchemical operations, as to the foundations of the empirical process.[6] In other words, the emblem provided a model of perception that could inform an empirical discovery. If one could imagine the forces of attraction, one might actually perceive them at work.

To further understand how alchemical decoding, or coding worked, we can access a simple example on the web by "Eirenaeus Philalethes" or George Starkey. Newton was greatly influenced by Philalethes in his most alchemical period. Starkey (1628–65) immigrated to London in 1650, where he immediately erected a laboratory and became the teacher of a man who would go on to acquire fame as "the father of modern chemistry," Robert Boyle (also an alchemist). At the same time, Starkey wrote numerous alchemical treatises under the nom de plume of "Eirenaeus Philalethes" (a peaceful lover of truth). These works were read with interest by such other theorists as Locke and Leibniz. His decoding of one rather simple poem (in contrast to other alchemical texts and emblems) has been uploaded onto the alchemy website.[7] Two lines of the poem, followed by the decoding are downloaded here to illustrate how alchemical images represented experiments and theories alike. In the following passages,

Philalethes decodes a poem by George Ripley, an English alchemist from the fifteenth century. Philalethes compares the writing to "Hieroglyphicks," which combine the visual and written image:

The poem: Toad full ruddy I saw.

Philalethes' translation: Here we have a Toad described, and in it the whole secret of Philosophers: The Toad is Gold; so called, because it is an Earthly Body, but most especially for the black stinking venemosity which this operation comes to in the first days of its preparation, before the whiteness appears; during the Rule of Saturn, therefore it is called the ruddy Toad.

The substance, gold, is figured as animated. In Benjamin's terminology, it would be "vital." Here, it is as an animal with an "earthly body." Thus, the notion of an element as "living," or "vital" is not limited to animals, but extended to metals. More, what the poetic line inscribes is not "gold" as a static element, but the smell and color of substances changing into gold. The nomenclature of the element is really a metaphor of its aspects during the process of change. In the process of the transmutation into the metal, the ruddy Toad, like certain animals, has a venomosity, a resident poison it extrudes when molting. And it responds to the Rule of Saturn as if all things are animated, situated among affective relations to one another—even to the "heavenly bodies." Again, this "Rule" is a figure of temporality, a register of change rather than, say, a fixed constellation. But the alchemical process is described through an adjectival description, "ruddy," rather than through an arithmetical measure.

The deployment of emblems and poetry as lab instructions created the first version of "science fiction," in which science and literature share a discourse. Verse and image communicate the processes of experimentation and change by articulating their *qualitative* relationships, rather than their *quantitative* ones. Metaphor and analogy figure the process of transmutation as a porous interface among different orders of things, through transmutable and affective relations. Although this approach was later abandoned in favor of the numerical and algebraic representation of relationships, it never really disappeared from science. Einstein's metaphor of the elevator falling through space in the earlier twentieth century illustrates how contemporary physics can still be guided by metaphor into a formula for the structures of space.

But to continue with the alchemical poem/formula:

The poem: With drops of poysoned sweat, approaching thus his secret Den.

Philalethes: The following two Verses then are but a more Ample description of this work; of volatilization which is an ascension, and descension, or circulation of the confections within the Glass. Which Glass here called the secret Den, is else-where called by the same Author, a little Glassen-tun, and is an oval Vessel; of the purest White Glass, about the bigness of an ordinary

Hen-Egg, in the which about the quantity of an ounce of 8 drachms of the confection, in all mixed is a convenient proportion to be set, which being Sealed up with Hermes Seal, the Glass having a neck about 6 fingers high, or there-abouts, which being thin and narrow; is melted together Artificially, that no Spirits can get out, nor no Air can come in, in which respect it is named a secret Den.

In this passage, the specific apparati and effects required for the chemical process are described as actions, "sweat," and place, "den." The toad is moving and changing, both externally and internally. The tube in which the chemical effects take place is a "den" where the toad lives. The alchemist is interacting with a vital substance, rather than manipulating one that has a mere object-status. The subject itself is changing, within its environment, rather than representing properties within an external force of change. Alchemical discourse does not read as an address to the alchemist, such as "now add a drop of mercury, " evoking him as the subject who acts, but figures the actions in terms of the elements themselves.

Emblematic practice included more than the decoding of alchemical poems. Newton's projects, like the lines above, sought to think through experiments of conjunction rather than through the isolation of elements. Using Pythagoras, he sought a consonance among the lengths of strings and the distances among planets. He spent many years of his life endeavoring to reorganize fragmentary references to Solomon's temple in order to compose a pattern, a mandala (in New Age speak) of space that would organize all of history as well as the future. He reconstructed its floor plan as an emblem of the world's change through time.[8] Even his renowned anti-trinitarian stand, dangerous in terms of the collusion of church and state, refused the partition embedded in the notion of the trinity. In his era, this conjoining of practice and poetry, of science and art, of rite and experiment within the emblem was being partitioned into discrete and sometimes opposing practices. Finding the "big picture," an integrated sense of the world across species and elements, through history and future, was abandoned for smaller and more tightly focused projects. Charting movement and change became numerical.

Even though the sense of the emblematic expresses the alchemical science in figures more suitable to its sense of a shared, changing universe than the language of numbers, there still lingers the sense that the practice of experimentation has been encoded into these emblems. So the question remains, to what end? This question prompts some consideration of alchemy as an esoteric, secret practice. Part of what the esoteric tradition is designed to effect is social protection surrounding the knowledge of potential transformations of power—a hermetic hermeneutics, if you will. As the twentieth century would witness, the unleashing of transformative power, as in fission, can be threatening to the whole planet. While the *Faust* legend individualized the dangers of that power, rendering them a moral risk for the soul, alchemy, as esoteric, claims to shield the social rather than the individual from the misuse of such powers. In its coded

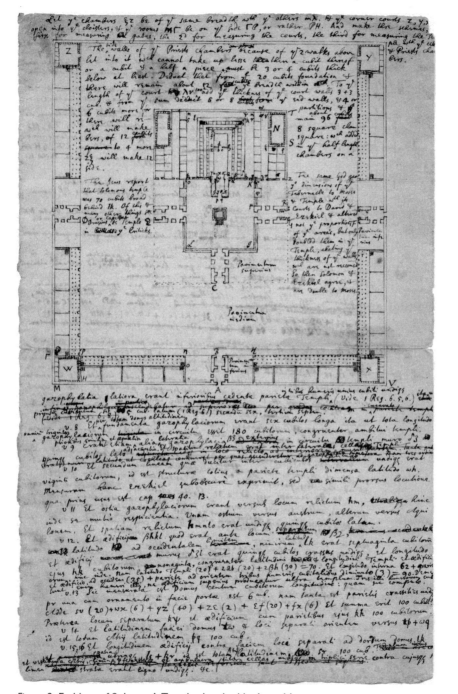

Figure 2 Emblem of Solomon's Temple sketched by Isaac Newton
(http://www.world-mysteries.com/awr_8sbynewton.gif)

exchange of knowledge, it forms an exclusive "brotherhood" as do contemporary, elite practices of science. Yet alchemy's exclusions were meant to remain underground, never to become official or institutional, in league with states, or churches. As the Royal Academy of science began to gain prominence in this era, espousing those values now identified as early modern, this secret brotherhood sought to maintain ancient practices of power that were hermetically sealed off from nation building. The alchemists sought to hide the great powers of change from those who would deploy them for base motives. Moreover, this esoteric protective barrier required ethical behavior of the practitioner, in order to remain within the secrets of the practice. The success of the experiment and the true understanding of its goals were available only to those who were initiates into the right uses of transformation. Famously, Newton applied these strict codes of behavior to himself as part of his overall alchemical practice. The scientist was not separate from his science—both operated within a code of ethics. In the twentieth century, the project of imagining the ethics of scientific discoveries and of the scientist will become an urgent, but difficult project.

Gender and sex in alchemy

As far as we know, alchemy was a secret fraternity of men. For women, at least publicly, the rites of transformation were related to witchcraft, which had more to do with herbs and remedies, perceived to be more like cooking than experimenting. As we will see, Goethe would proximate the witches' kitchen to the alchemist's study in his *Faust*, reproducing the gender codes that determined the perception of these occult practices. Yet within alchemical discourses, gender appears as an element of change, assigned across substances. Within the paradigm of alchemy, it is possible to imagine gender not as a code controlling human action or confining human identificatory processes, but operating more in an adverbial manner to animate substances in their transformation. Those animations are specifically sexual in nature, so to speak.

In working from Philalethes, Newton describes an experiment in this way: "Another secret is that you need the mediation of the virgin Diana" (quoted in Dobbs 1975: 182). Diana's virginal, gendered status indicates how the elements will change. Her qualities figure silver interacting with other substances as a form of embodiment, replete with aspects of gender and sexuality. In Philalethes' full description below, which describes the production of "true philosophical mercury," we can see how this virgin enters into a mode of elemental change that is understood as a sexual relationship:

> Grind the mercury . . . the doves of Diana mediating, with its brother, philosophical gold, from which it will receive spiritual semen. The spiritual semen is the fire which will purge all the superfluities of the mercury, the fermental virtue intervening.
>
> (quoted in Dobbs 1975: 182)

The virgin Diana is not anthropomorphized here, made into a woman who would receive sperm; instead, her "doves" serve as mediators of germination. Her gender, her virginal status, is thus more adverbial than adjectival. Her doves, her virginal gender, mediate the cleansing fire of sperm, to produce the base material, the essential, at once both the philosophical and natural ferment of change.[9]

Traditionally, such examples are read as a kind of "primitive" understanding of matter, merely emulating the human condition. More radically, one can read attributes of gender and sexuality as aspects of transmutations across substances rather than codes of strictly human behavior. "Diana," her virginity, and the actions of "sperm" are not attributes of regulated gender identification, nor of prescribed sexual practices. They are figures that ferment the action of transmutation, momentary and progressive in their functions. As adverbs rather than adjectives, gender and sex can be perceived as attributes of change across a field of elements and processes.

The understanding of gender that grew up with the "new" science accompanied its observance of elements as discrete units, with properties that help to describe and bind them. Gender ceased to operate across elements as a dynamic of change and became, instead, a fixed attribute of humans. As we will see, the same year in which the alchemist took the stage as a character in *The Alchemist*, the staging of gender as strictly human, and its change as strictly adjectival appeared in *The Roaring Girl*. As an attribute that bounded identity, gender became one of the most crucial and most socially devastating codes of partition that accompanied the rise of science and theater.

The assignment of gender exclusively to the human subject accompanied the general enhancement of the human subject. "Nature," or the world of elements became the object of the human subject: the "new" scientist. New Historicists have brilliantly transcribed the empowering of the agency of the human subject in this early modern period. In fact, they have focussed "new" history on studies of human agency. What was lost, as the alchemical papers of Newton document, was the ascription of that agency to any other substance.[10] The scientific laboratory was cleansed of such a sharing of agency across materials. Theater's contribution to the partition resides in how it could preference motivation over transformation, character rather than magus, and the stage as the virtual space. Theater became the social mechanism of the new science, installing human agency at the center of virtual space.

Alchemy's antagonist: Ben Jonson

Alchemical practices were literally character-ized by performance. *Faust* playlets were puppetized in popular gathering sites, Jonson satirized the alchemist as a con man, and Goethe set Faust's own initial "fallen" experiments on the day of the liturgical celebration of the corrective *quem queritis*. As the human was installed as singular subject, the perception of alchemy was shifted from practice to character, from alchemy to the alchemist. The transmutation of elements, the dynamics of internal change, were exchanged for an eternal motive, as Mao would phrase it. The engine of motivation, devised as a character-istic of character, was fired up in the portrayal of the alchemist. Motivation is a key strategy for representing the individual as subject, disconnected from the fabric of an essential integration with so-called nature.

The technology of staging was designed to throw focus on this singular subject. Design, a favored term in emblematic discourses no longer connoted the symbiosis of all things, but the arrangement and concealment of devices that focused human optics on the actor. "Theater" then connoted both a space for scientific presentation and the representational playing of the human engine—motivation.

Alchemy served Ben Jonson well—not as a practice, but as an object of his theatrical satire and his scripting of apparati. Jonson treats alchemy fully in two pieces—a masque and a play. Masques had established a showcase of technology through performance. Belonging primarily to the court, they linked new technologies with the performance of privilege—a link that would endure. Masques exhibited technology as an engine of power, primarily as the showcase of royal power. Coding became concealment with curtains, flats and wings to conceal the engines of show, and emblems were downgraded into allegories. Masques served as an entertaining laboratory for the frivolous, luxurious reproduction of nature as the mirror of power, an accessory of the privileged. Inigo Jones, the leading engine-er, designer of the masques, worked together with Jonson to stage these inventions. Jones arranged illusion into perspective, aligning representation with human optics and thus installing the observing subject as the definition of the space. The masque, then, was well-suited to the representation of alchemy, or rather, the character of alchemy.

Jonson's masque *Mercury Vindicated from the Alchemists at Court* (1616) focuses on the alchemical notion of Mercury as a subject of change. Mercury, now a character, escapes from the alchemical furnace to pronounce a witty monologue to the court. He portrays his central role in alchemical experiments:

> It is I that am corroded and exalted and sublimed and reduced and fetched over and filtered and washed and wiped; what between their salts and their sulfurs, their oils and their tartars, their brines and their vinegars, you might take me out now a soused Mercury, now a salted Mercury, now a smoked and dried Mercury, now a powdered and pickled Mercury: never herring, oyster, or cucumber passed so many vexations. . . .
>
> (1970: lines 47–55).

It seems that Mercury is less the catalyst of change than the object of the alchemist's machinations. In fact, his description of his ordeals suggests cooking, the fallen practice of chemistry and pharmacy, rather than laboratory experiment. The wit resides in bending the high-minded practice to a base one. This

Mercury is a fragment of court wit on its way to the bawdy joke: "Get all the cracked maidenheads and cast 'em into new ingots; half the wenches o' the town are alchemy" (lines 92–94). Alchemical terms offer a metaphoric discourse for the expression of sexual peccadilloes. This Mercury is not a figure of elemental change so much as a fickle lover. Through the form of the masque, Jonson uses alchemical figures to flirt, concluding with a pleasurable and, hopefully, promising dance for those who participate. Alchemy is made to seem antique, while theatrical engines of illusion would appear as "early modern." Moving Mercury into character overlays alchemical scripting of transmutation with theatrical representation.

Jonson's play *The Alchemist* (1610), however, deals a more serious blow to the perception of alchemy, leeching out its internal dynamics to firmly establish a different order of change—motivation. As the title of the play suggests, the focus is displaced from the practice of alchemy to the alchemist. Whatever seems to appear in the way of transformation is undercut by revealing the cheating motivations of the characters. Moreover, the characters are merely animations of social taxonomies, catalogued, like elements in the "new" science, within a taxonomy of characteristics, with names like Subtle, the Alchemist; Dapper, a lawyer's clerk; Abel Drugger, a druggist who sells tobacco; Sir Epicure Mammon, a voluptuary; Pertinax Surly, a doubting Thomas; and Dame Pliant, a widow. The adjectival overcomes the adverbial in a form that portrays characters as representatives of static qualities. So, while the identity or identification of the character is static, his or her motivation provides the engine of the plot. In this way, motivation is foregrounded as the single element of change within the otherwise static qualities of the characters.

Yet this motivation is a base one. In a lengthy argument about alchemy in Act Two, Surly characterizes alchemy as "Tricks o' the cards, to cheat a man/With charming" (Jonson 1967: lines 181–182). "Charming" and "cheating" are the focus of the play, illustrated through alchemy but referring to motivation. In one sense, all change is debased as it becomes only the illusion deployed to cheat others out of money. One can imagine how the theater worked its charm to socially discredit the alchemical rites.

In *Mercury Vindicated*, the alchemical furnace is something to escape from, out into the society of the court. In *The Alchemist*, the mythical alchemical lab is tended by squatters in a house vacated by those who fled the plague. Staging the fallen lab in a house may reflect, as David Noble suggests, the taint of the domestic on the scientific, as the "new science" begins to form its special, removed space, free of women (quoted in Shanahan 2002: 45). We have already observed how the culinary terms for Mercury's change in the masque are used to denigrate the methods of alchemical experiment, but in *The Alchemist* their domestication is also made illicit. The house does not even belong to the con artists who pose as alchemists.

In Jonson's *The Alchemist*, change itself is indicated through its association with subterfuge. Alchemical practice is portrayed as a mere farcical trick—a mystification designed for profit. Mathew Martin, in his article "Play and Plague in Ben Jonson's *The Alchemist*," refers to the play's "anti-transformative poetics" indicating that the corruption in the play furthers only character motivation, but founders any possibility for social or material change (2000: 401). Remembering Mao once again, the potential for internal change in the make-up of matter, as Martin points out, accompanies the possibility for social and economic change as well. Martin goes on to describe the lab as the space of "unlicensed theater," surreptitiously performed in a temporarily vacated house. Martin summarizes the effect of the play: "Jonson offers no external, stable vantage point from which illusory existence might be distinguished . . . only equally illusory and groundless epistemologies competing in the theatrical marketplace" (407). In the era of an economic crisis over value, filled with anxieties of the counterfeit and the simulations of the money market, the alchemist, who was thought to produce gold, that ultimate value, is really only a con, a performer, an illusionist.

However, the price of the ticket has changed the operations of access. Illusion extracts a cost, while delivering little. We will attend to the practice of licensing later, but for now, it may suffice to note how many details of the play point to a satire of its own theatrical conditions of production: the audience pays to see a two-hour show which concerns two hours of con work through a fake experiment; the house in which the play takes place is located in Blackfriars, where the theater itself was located, and the epilogue addresses the audience directly to articulate the pleasures of illusion, inferring that perhaps they, too, have been gulled.[11] Mercury has truly jumped out of the fire into the frying pan, where he will be served up to the paying public. He no longer catalyzes baser metals into gold, but exchanges money for illusion. Like city comedy, of which *The Alchemist* took a part, the virtual becomes a space designed for for-profit illusion. As the alchemists were employed to make gold, theater will be licensed to make money, and the "new" science will be turned toward invention and product.

The gender divide: *The Roaring Girl*

Meanwhile, in another theater in London, at approximately the same time, *The Roaring Girl* (1608–11) represented how gender attributes that in alchemy were distributed across elements, could be singularly and definitively assigned only to the human agent. As Jonson set up a stage that worked its illusion against rites of transformation, Middleton and Dekker staged the operations of gender as definitive of human identity. Even Jonson's alchemist still offered up some of the discourse of the dynamic, adverbial play of gender across substances that the traditional alchemy practiced:

> . . . mercury is engender'd;
> Sulphur o' the fat and earthy part: the one,
> (Which is the last) supplying the placed of male,
> The other of the female, in all metals.

Some do believe hermaphrodeity,
That both do act, and suffer. But these two
Make the rest ductile, malleable, extensive.

(Jonson 1967: 160–166)

The "malleable" and the "ductile," however, would delve underground with the
esoteric practices and "hermaphrodeity," a figure of the fusion of sexual difference, would become a utopic fantasy, perhaps corporealized in the human. In
contrast to this dynamic muddle of matter, Middleton and Dekker staged Moll—
a woman dressed as a man. Moll's gender exchange operates as a counterfeit
crossing. She appears to some in the play as one who "strays from her kind/
Nature repents she made her" (The Roaring Girl 2001: 211–212). Sex/gender,
which, in alchemy were an aspect of nature's dynamism are Moll's iteration of
social codes. Insofar as her performance of gender is malleable, she "strays." She
is a counterfeit. Note how the term "nature" here functions as an attribute of the
human condition.

Moll character-izes how gender appears as a property of a human subject,
locating it within strictly social relations. Rather than an element of natural
philosophy, as it operated in alchemy, gender becomes a key definitive element in
the organization of the social, displacing the aspiration to conflate matter with
metaphysic. As Jonathan Dollimore, in his book on the era, *Sexual Dissidence*,
describes it: "The metaphysical is displaced by, and then collapsed into, the
social" (1991: 295). If Jonson foregrounded the virtual as illusion, Middleton and
Dekker portray it as the social sphere—a space of partition and conflict.
Dollimore (280):

> The early modern view of identity . . . was also, and quite explicitly, a
> powerful metaphysic of social integration. . . . Metaphysics here underpins a
> discursive formation of the subject, of subjection.

As gender attains the status of a regulatory code, rather than an aspect of transmutation, its properties become fixed and fix the location of the subject. The
imagined construction of the virtual realm is signified as the social. As character
and motivation take center stage, the remains of the perception of a unified field
of the virtual are gradually sucked into the construction of individual interiority.
Gender will become key to what Dollimore characterizes as the era's "quest for
authenticity: underpinning and endorsing a philosophy of individualism" (284).
The seventeenth century, according to Michel Foucault, established the discourse
of sexuality as it installed gender.[12] Change is no longer the nature of the fabric
of matter and the social, but a disruption of it—*Sexual Dissidence*, as Dollimore so
aptly termed it. Theater and the new science thus initiate humans into the exclusive rights of the subject position, taking the stage for their machines and
machinations of the illusory and the social for the virtual realm of their conflict
and wedded harmony.

Faust: the new paradigm of alchemy

Said's argument that medieval notions of Islam did not originate in knowledge about its beliefs, but were constructed as an evil imitation of Christianity seems particularly resonant in Goethe's version of alchemy in *Faust*. The experiments in metallurgy and ur-chemistry so central to alchemy are not represented in the play; rather, *Faust*, the alchemist, practices a form of devil worship. The prime emblem in the play, the pentagram, is designed to hold the devil in its space and Faust begins his journey to damnation on the day of the *quem queritis*. Unlike Jonson, who still retained some of the actual terms of alchemy in his play, Goethe's sources are more from the philosophy of religion, with fragments of Latin rather than Arabic. Goethe organized a new paradigm for the "fallen" scientist in his Faust plays, not only by overwriting the Arab traditions, but also by locating the scientist within a binary metaphysical space of transcendence/damnation.

In overwriting the Arab tradition, Goethe was in sync with the restrictions of his age. By the beginning of the eighteenth century, even an interest in Islamic texts was a liability. In 1709, William Whiston, Newton's successor at Cambridge, was expelled from his post for his scholarly interest in Islamic texts (Said 1979: 76). Goethe succeeds in untying the depiction of the alchemist from these censored Islamic roots, even though he was well familiar with Islamic writings. Once he had successfully claimed alchemy as within the Latin discourse in *Faust*, Goethe could overwrite, in a more celebratory fashion, an original Islamic text. In 1819, he composed a poetic meditation based on the fourteenth-century Muslim poet Shams-od-Din Muhammad Hafez entitled *West-östlicher Divan*, or the *West-Eastern Divan*. (Note: the term "Divan" means a collection of poetry, and the name "Hafez" means "Koran memorizer.") This work is the very definition of orientalism, dreamily portraying an "araby" of symbolic and aesthetic remove, but the invention of such an orientalist fantasy could come only after the real inheritance of the Islamic sciences had been successfully displaced.[13] Once untied from its deep scientific and philosophical roots, "araby" could be extremely useful in charting exactly that remove, through floating significations that represented the "pure" aesthetic realm.

From this perspective, one can view the complex and numerous appearances of the ancient Greeks in *Faust II* as an insistence upon the sort of displaced "roots" that Martin Bernal traces in his book, *Black Athena*. While *Faust I* situates the medieval alchemist securely within the Latin tradition, scripting none of the contest of cultures the practice incited, *Faust II* stages the inherited intellectual and cultural traditions of Europe as Greek, Greek, Greek. Thus, the Arab and Jewish traditions become philosophically mute and ethnically unfixed. The godless results of alchemy are writ large in these two plays, while the sociopolicital referent of that godlessness, Islam, is subsumed into the Protestant realm of individual moral motivation.

Nonetheless, Goethe did not invent the Faust legend. The historical Faust was known, both by his contemporaries, and by those who followed, to be "the most accomplished alchemist that has ever lived."[14] Numerous puppet plays and fragments inspired by his legend had enacted the story for more than a century. Perhaps these shows offered one of the first examples of grassroots performances of science. Alchemy, the science of the day, was imagined in this popular realm through puppets.

However, one *Faust* commentator, Erich Trunz, figures Paracelsus to be the more persuasive model for the character of Goethe's Faust than Faust legends. Some critics contend that Goethe actually read Paracelsus during his convalescence in 1768 (Zajonc 1998: 21). So perhaps Goethe's source for the character was an alchemist who practiced and taught as a medical expert. In other words, a scientist. Paracelsus was a leading medical innovator and alchemist of his time (1493–1541), a recalcitrant practitioner, who was rewarded for his medical innovations and shunned for his direct challenges of the Latin tradition. His discoveries and his biography haunted the intellectual traditions that followed, making him a rich historical figure from which Goethe could derive the character of Faust (Trunz 1976: 461). If Goethe was ruminating on Paracelsus, then his suppression of the Islamic origins of the practice is even more obvious, for Paracelsus traveled extensively through Egypt and other non-European sites and brought back his alchemical discoveries to Switzerland and beyond. His success derived from the inventive, one might say the experimental, hands-on tradition of the Islamic and alchemical practices. In the idiomatic language of an enthusiast, Manly P. Hall, a contemporary chronicler of esoteric traditions, describes how Paracelsus gained his knowledge in *Paracelsus, His Mystical and Medical Philosophy*: "not from long-coated pedagogues but from dervishes in Constantinople, witches, gypsies, and sorcerers, who invoked spirits and captured the rays of the celestial bodies in dew."[15] Successful in treating medical problems with new techniques learned on his travels, Paracelsus was made chief medical officer and lecturer at the University in Basel. However, he became so agitated about the iterated practices of medicine unquestionably received from Galen, that he publicly burnt the manuscripts. Of course, the public spectacle caused the demise of his employment in public office and he hurriedly fled Basel to wander through much of Europe. His biography resounds with the combination of great medical innovation and a dedication to alchemy and astrology. On the one hand, he was respected for his experimental approach to maladies, and on the other, he was regarded as suspect for his public reliance upon alchemical texts such as the *Corpus Hermeticum*. Trunz interprets Goethe's turn to this figure as characteristic of his age, when, in Germany "Die paracelsische Sehnsucht nach Erkenntnis ist religiös" ("the Paracelsian longing for knowledge is [was] religious"; 1976: 461). Thus, the reception of the figure was, by then, less focused on his introduction of medical techniques, such as cauterizing a wound, than in the philosophies within which these practices were located. An adept, Paracelsus was re-translated into one who "longed" for knowledge—was unsatisfied by his expertise. The opening scene of *Faust* illustrates this shift.

Two maneuvers are evident in this eighteenth-century reception of Paracelsus: first that the practice of science and medicine can be extracted from the system of natural philosophy and second, that the ideological contest Europe staged with Islam could be transcribed into a strictly moral battle, in which the sociopolitical referent is embedded in the cosmic figure of the devil. Ironically, then, the intimate connection alchemy enjoyed between experimentation and philosophy, the practice of science and ethics, as Newton demonstrated, once severed, was depicted as devoid of both.

For Goethe, as for Jonson before him, the character on the side of alchemy is a con artist. Goethe's Mephistopheles is the supreme trickster, ever intent upon conning Faust through illusions. Jonson's Mercury is Goethe's Mephistopheles. Yet, in *Faust*, the use of astrology and alchemy in the quest for knowledge is translated as an anti-religious impulse, rather than as a seductive form of court play. Moreover, the religious act is caught up in forms of economic transactions. Faust "sells" his soul through a written contract for un-earthly delights and is finally condemned to hell. He writes a promissory note to the devil for his soul. In *Faust II*, the issue is literally paper money, which Mephistopheles proffers to the Emperor.

Prior to Goethe's scripting of the story, puppet plays depicting Faust's fall circulated throughout the fairs, staging the story in the very venues of barter and exchange. The performances of *Faust*, then, originated in a space coincident with the marketplace. Its dialogue and narrative worked in an atmosphere of barter. The negotiations between Faust and the devil concerned the exchange of goods for a soul, animating the commercial process into the virtual realm of absolute value for the entertainment and instruction of the traders. The devil lures Faust into a bad bargain, in which he exchanges "goods," or the good, for counterfeit payment. The scenario must have resonated, both comically and tragically among the negotiators at the fairs and beyond, in an age that was anxiously creating new forms of material value and money itself.

In Goethe's *Faust*, the metaphysical barter is expressed through references to the two metals popularly associated with alchemy, gold and mercury, as if metallurgy and transformation were now somehow embedded in market trading. Faust rhetorically asks the devil what materials he has to trade, gold that doesn't hold its value and quicksilver that runs through your hands (lines 1679–1680). These metals are not part of a laboratory experiment, but part of a bartering process. While the play transcribes the traces of the marketplace, it also demarcates a tension between theater and the marketplace by setting up a spiritual/virtual realm, as theater set up a distinct, removed, theatrical space that seems to be in contrast to the material. The notion of the transcendent virtual space will become an effect of this barter. Once Faust sells his soul, he is given access to virtual travel.

The written pact can also be perceived as the issuing of a kind of letter of credit, which will become the literal referent in *Faust II*. While Goethe is widely received as an artist, in the Romantic sense, he was also a lawyer, and, appointed in the early 1780s to the post of minister of mines, war, and finance in Weimar. Surely aware of the spirit of his time, he observed the world of contracts and financial obligations of his time and perhaps did not find them completely divorced from theater and the metaphysical. Laura Brown summarizes the dynamics of the age in *Fables of Modernity* (2001: 97):

> The early eighteenth century was the first age to live the immediate intensity of credit, loans, discounts, shares, futures, national debt, deficit spending . . . An international money market and a futures commodity market were established in the first decade of the Restoration.

Although Brown is discussing England, the practices were widespread, including the notion of mortgage, which plays an important role in the scene of Faust's bargain. The discussion concerning the elements of the promise of payment is one of the most dramatic in the play. These haunting lines suggest the broader anxiety of the age: "a parchment alone, inscribed and stamped is a specter, from which all shrink" (1726–1728). Signing one's name as a mortgage of the soul, a line of credit, with a distant due date, is, in itself, a terrifying event. Something about a promise, an aspiration caught in a promissory note resounds with cautionary rhetoric. Although resonant with the relation of alchemy to gold, Goethe returns the depiction of alchemy to the frame of the liturgical inheritance of theater, relocating transformation within a promissory note of salvation. Paracelsus, the alchemist/scientist must somehow account for his practices through economic forms.

Faust I: the fall from Goethean science

Goethe was a practicing scientist for most of his mature years. While his literary works have earned him continued veneration, his scientific work inspired only a few somewhat esoteric practices, until the past two decades when his work gained a new acceptance among phenomenological and ecological approaches to science.[16] Goethe's scientific studies spanned such diverse fields as geology, meteorology, botany and plant development, morphology and embryology, and, perhaps most influential, the nature of color and vision. Reading his version of *Faust* with his theories of science in mind helps to chart the way in which the play is in dialogue with his own notions of science and the portrait of the scientist.

In his youth, Goethe was introduced to the studies of alchemy, from which he derived certain principles he later combined with the practices of the new science to create his own version of what constituted scientific knowledge. While he was not an alchemist *per se*, he wrote in a letter as late as 1770 that "Alchemy is still my veiled love" (quoted in Zajonc 1998: 21). Goethe shared Newton's alchemical desire for integration, inventing a scientific method that would combine observation with integration. He termed his approach a "delicate empiricism." In his *Maximen und Reflexionen* (*Maxims and Reflections*) Goethe suggests that "There is a delicate empiricism, which identifies itself with the object" (quoted in Cottrell 1998: 259). In other words, in Goethe's paradigm, the scientist would not act as a removed observer, but one who would somehow share the subject position with the object, if only through identification. From a shared sense of the experience of the object, as in alchemy's notion of a qualitative not quantitative measure, the scientist would come to better understand the object of study. In this way, Goethe's scientific practice was dedicated to this principle of interaction, as exemplified by the title of one of his essays, *The Experiment as Mediator Between Object and Subject*. The research experience, for Goethe, was positioned as a binding one. Moreover, the translation of the observed into language also troubled the immediate, bonded apprehension of the living: "Yet how difficult it is not to put the sign in the place of the thing; how difficult to keep the being (*Wesen*) always livingly before one and not to slay it with the word" (quoted in Zajonc 1998: 24). Understood as a version of phenomenology, Goethe's notion of observation, if that's a suitable term, is one that "accedes with one's intentionaliy to their [the subject/objects'] patterns . . . " (Amrine 1998: 37). As Frederick Amrine puts it, in "The Metamorphosis of the Scientist" (38):

> In direct contrast to prevailing scientific methodology, Goethe's ideal scientist tries consciously *not* to reduce phenomena to a schema but, rather, to remain inwardly mobile. . . . Thus, while mathematical formalism may be the most appropriate *Vorstellungsart* [type of representation] for mechanics, it may well be entirely inappropriate for chromatics. Goethe felt this, and it was the real basis for his polemic against Sir Isaac Newton.

Goethe understood his scientific practice and findings on color and light to be in direct contradiction to Newton's. Around 1666, Newton began a study of color by using light and prisms, publishing his *Opticks*, in 1704. He divided the white light into the seven colors of the prism that composed it. The problem, as Goethe saw it, was that Newton studied light in isolation, extracting the understanding of it from other forces, most importantly, the human perception of it. In his *Theory of Color*, Goethe finds that the perception of color is related to optics, the eye itself, which both perceives and produces color, thus co-constituting the process along with light and substance. Color, then, is not an entity, a bounded zone with properties, as in the prism, but as Goethe describes it in the opening remarks to his 1810 edition, "Colors are the deeds of light; its deeds and sufferings . . . " (quoted in Zajonc 1998: 19). For Goethe, colors are actions, not things. As he phrased it, more generally, the "objects" (*Gegenstände*) of nature are better viewed as "acts" (*Tätigkeiten*) (Fink 1991: 44). For this reason, Goethe preferred the classical Greek discourse of color to the German. In the Greek, color is not fixed as a noun, with properties and differences; instead, it acts as a verb: yellow can "redden" and red can "yellow" (Fink 1991: 47). Goethe also criticized Newton's omission of the role of darkness in the production of light, calling it a "light darkness polarity." Light could only appear in a dialectic with darkness—a dialog, if you will, invoking the Faust/Mephistopheles duality.

While color presents a more obvious example, Goethe located dynamic change in all substances—even granite. He perceived a "play of elements" (*Spiel der Elemente*), in which all things enjoy an "inner development" over time (quoted in Fink 1991: 18). Goethe's paradigm of knowing, then, is an active one in which the researcher enters into an ongoing relationship with changing substances, altered by and co-constituted with the substances involved. While it is not exactly alchemical, it is certainly reminiscent of its basic assumptions.

For Goethe, "delicate empiricism" contested both the overdetermined scientific empiricism and the philosophical abstractions of his era. He disagreed with Hegel's dialectics because, he argued, they were conceptualized as operating apart from continued direct observation, and he wrote against the received tradition of Newton's mechanistic universe. He also opposed what he termed "mathematical formalism," arguing against "Mathematics [that] must . . . declare itself independent of everything external, must proceed according to its own spirit and laws" (quoted in Heitler 57). Rather than these paradigms of removed reason, or causal chains, or quantifying mathematical equations, Goethe sought an empiricism combined with an interrelational dynamic. Experience and change were categories of knowing within these bonded relationships.

Reviewing *Faust* from the perspective of Goethe's scientific studies, we can perceive, most obviously, the scripting of the interaction of dark and light (Mephistopheles and the Christian God) as necessary to what Goethe believed to constitute the structures of appearance. Recalling Mao's sense of contradiction and dynamism as the essential make-up of the elements, Goethe's dialectic mode of the production of appearance seems to invoke this more potentially alterable universe. The prelude in the theater initiates the virtual space of representation, where one can actively observe appearance through the dialectic/dialogue of opposing forces. In viewing Creation, the god welcomes a wager with Mephistopheles that makes the dramatic conditions occur. Contradiction is the apparatus of appearance. Instead of the moralistic message that most readings of Goethe presume, the play may actually be staging the conditions of Goethean optics.

Faust could be understood as the alienated scientist, whose distanced, withdrawn relation to the object of learning is signified by his remove in his study. Although he longs for a more dynamic relation to the world, he maintains a strict division from it in his study. The esteemed German critic, Georg Lukacs, puts it this way: "Faust longs for the same thing for which the young Goethe longs: a philosophy [and we might add practice] which transcends the solely contemplative, dead objectivity, and the disunity between the knowledge of nature and human activity" (1968: 168). Faust's fault resides in his resistance to an active engagement with what he would know, preferring, instead, to peruse the contemplative texts. Goethe writes this against "pure" contemplation:

"Know thyself" has ever seemed suspicious to me—a cabal on the part of secretly conspiring priests . . . wanting to seduce mankind away from activity directed toward the outer world into an inward-directed, false contemplation. Man knows himself only to the extent that he knows the world; he becomes aware of himself only within the world, and aware of the world within himself.

(quoted in Cottrell 1998: 257)

Although Lukács understands the world to be strictly social, Goethe, the scientist includes the very construction of matter and light to adjoin it. Thus, the cosmos, mostly received as a Christian sphere of moral division, represents a holistic interaction in the production of appearance. As the scientist is drawn into an active relationship, a shared subjectivity, with what would be known, its appearance, both philosophically and empirically will occur.

In the beginning of the play, Faust expresses the familiar the desire to understand "was die Welt/Im Innersten zusammenhält." (Goethe 1965: I, lines 382–383), or what integrates the world in its deepest structures. He is tired of mere words, "te' nicht mehr in Worten kramen" and desires to discover the activating alchemical semen, "Samen" (in most translations rendered as "seeds") of change and production (I, 384–385). For Faust, even the moon, the light of the natural world, merely illumines the pages of words, and then only through the painted, or tainted lens of the window (I, 400–401). The word, the sign, for him, has overcome the living, changing interaction with the world. Faust desires to know nature without the dead intermediary, the remove of the prism. Faust: "You instruments, you mock me, I can see,/With wheel and pulley, cylinder and cords. . . . you were to be the key/But cannot lift the bolts" (I, 668–671). Nature will not yield to become a passive object of the apparatus. The scientist cannot successfully try "To torture out of her with screw or lever" her secrets (I, 675).

In his *Sprüche* (*Sayings*) Goethe claims that "the greatest misfortune of physics is precisely that the experiment has been separated from the person, so to speak, and nature is apprehended only through what is shown by artificial instruments, yes—and one would limit and prove in this manner what nature produces" (quoted in Hegge 2003: 18). Yet this is the world Goethe stages in Faust's study. It is mediated by contemplation and apparati, cut off from an active, participatory knowing. Even Faust decries the traditional paradigm of nature as perceived through the conditions of theater: "What glorious show! Yet but a show, alas!" (I, 454). At various times in the play, even Mephistopheles suggests that Faust give up his remove, and become active in the world. For example, in the first scene in the witches' kitchen, Mephistopheles suggests: "Go out into the fields, today,/Fall to a-hoeing, digging. . . . spurn not chores unsung. . . . This is the best resource, you may be sure," to which Faust replies, "I am not used to that, it goes against my marrow." Mephistopheles then concludes "So back to witching after all" (I, 2352–2365). Clearly, "witching" is the counterfeit double of labor and of interaction with nature. Faust's remove from any interactive process of knowing, and his insistence upon his privileged exclusivity as subject, damns him.

And yet, this reading ignores the position of Mephistopheles, which makes something even more dynamic appear. Perhaps Goethe is scripting what he understood to be the dynamics of experiment, the active knowing that must be co-produced between dark and light, the representation and the observer. Goethe begins his play with a reflexive prelude because it is about theater as a science, a laboratory, an experiment in the structures of perception. It is difficult to decide whether theater marked Goethe's science, or his science marked his theater. But since, in his lifetime, he worked as a lawyer, a poet, a novelist, a minister of roads, a playwright, and a scientist, he did not care for the careful distinctions among these roles, but rather what could appear in the areas in which they could be seen together. After all, the further division of knowledge and practice is part of the tradition of extraction that isolated, in the first place, theater from other rites. Like Newton before him, Goethe was working on the great emblem, such as, for Newton, the Temple of Solomon, that could, together with the observer, make the conditions of change appear.

Proliferation of virtual spaces

That great temple of Solomon, common to alchemical studies, was a virtual space, the design of which would reveal historical and elemental change. In contrast to the singular structure, Goethe's *Faust* stages a variety of virtual spaces that seem to design the probable consequences of their dynamics. *Faust II* is a veritable cornucopia of the virtual. As the cultural friction around transformation is registered in the play, so, too, the design and use of virtual space that accompanies it. Virtual spaces introduce the play and it is access to those spaces that drives the narrative. Let's rehearse again the opening of the play, this time to review the construction of the virtual. The play opens with a "prelude in the theater." Returning, for a moment, to the practice of orientalism, it is interesting to note that Goethe was inspired to construct this scene by his reading of the classical Sanskrit text of *Sakuntala* by Kalidasa, which begins with a similar prelude. Yet again, he displaces the ancient text with the Christian paradigm. The character of the Director initiates the dialogue, expressing his anxiety about pleasing a well-informed, sophisticated audience, who has paid admission. The Poet, however eschews such considerations, invoking a more transcendental space of inspiration and contemplation. Note, however, this space is one that is interior to the poet. But the Merry Actor also disagrees with the Poet, insisting that the "now" of performance must grip the audience. The Director then outlines the structures of theatrical success, such as the plot, which the Poet calls charlatan's tricks. Hence, alchemy and the theater are aligned as inhabiting virtual spaces of illusion. Like the Witches' kitchen, the Director advises that theater must offer a "potent brew" (*stark Getränke*) (223) with stage machinery and special effects such as fire and thunder. The desired result of the theatrical concoction is not so different from that of the witches' kitchen. Yet, while these virtual spaces are depicted as debased sites, similar to those accessed through Mephistopheles, they also design the overall space of the transcendent quest, as revealed in the line: "So, on this narrow stage the circle of Creation will appear" (239–242).[17] The stage conjures, then, both the heavenly and the debased virtual space. The action of conjuring, however, belongs only to the dark side.

The prelude is followed by a "prologue in heaven." One might imagine theater as the "double" (as Artaud put it) of the metaspace of the spheres, which houses the more transcendent moral disputation. Or, perhaps Goethe has made heaven in theater's image. The angel Raphael opens the scene by describing the music of the spheres, which is punctuated by thunder, so heaven seems to have its own special effects, not too unlike those of the stage. Otherwise, heaven seems to serve as a vantage point from which the angels and the god can observe creation. Goethe lends it no description of its own. Interestingly, he gives the stage direction at the end of the scene that "heaven closes" (*der Himmel schliest*), leaving Mephistopheles alone on the stage. Heaven has a curtain, then, like the stage, or somehow, like the stage, closes its scene.

The prelude in the theater and the prologue in heaven lead to the discovery of Faust alone in his study. Here, the potential access to the virtual will hinge on motivation. At once, the space of alchemical research is matched by the interior space of Faust's ruminations. Unlike Jonson, however, the alchemist is not a simple fraud, but rather a philosopher of the fraudulent. In *Faust I*, Goethe maintains these doubling procedures among the spaces of the trancendental virtual and the interiority of the subject. Now, either away from Faust's study, or as illusions conjured within it, Faust and Mephistopheles access numerous other virtual spaces, as well as "real" ones. For example, Faust and Mephistopheles fly to Auerbach's tavern in Leipzig, then, they vanish from there to discover the Witches' Kitchen. After drinking a potion, Faust finds himself on the street where Margarete walks past. Presumably, the so-called Gretchen tragedy, the ruination of Margarete by Faust, takes place in a "real" space with actual consequences, somehow participating in a different order of space from the Witches' kitchen.

The stage is one of constantly-shifting scenes. Faust's access to these "other" spaces is the payoff to the bargain he struck with Mephistopheles. Their proliferation is presumably the "riches" he gains. This whirling vortex of virtualities that Goethe constructs, from the prelude in the theater, to heaven, to semi-mythical witches' haunts, to the room of a "real" woman suggests the earlier, Christian medieval sense of the gradated space between heaven and hell, which, in literature, had been illustrated by Dante and, in the plastic arts, through numerous religious paintings. Yet, in contrast to the medieval sense of space, Margaret Wertheim, in *The Pearly Gates of Cyberspace*, asserts that the eighteenth century received the Newtonian notion of "absolute space" as an empty backdrop or frame for the universe (1999: 168). Space appeared as a Euclidean-type space, in which everywhere is the same. Perhaps this would be the "absolute space of heaven," for which the Poet longs in the Prelude, but which is confounded by heaven as theater. Wertheim argues that this absolute space was the only one with the "sanction of scientific authority" in the period, so perhaps the appropriate aspiration for a poet/scientist such as Goethe (133). Yet, for Goethe, this absolute space is not empty, as in heaven, but established as dynamic.

Should this proliferation of virtualities be seen as Goethe's portrait of medieval time and space, suitable to his subject, or a staging of other experiences of virtuality contemporary to his own time? Perhaps the cultural investment in travel in the eighteenth century, in which Goethe participated, could be imagined as organizing some sense of a virtual space for the visiting travelers—a space which they share, but from which they are removed. Goethe's travels in Italy were certainly formative to his writing, so perhaps these visits to other realms are an inscription of the experience of tourism. Tourism is the removed space of observation. Travel and the distant will certainly inform nineteenth-century grassroots imaginings of the virtual plane, as we will see. Yet the virtual spaces through which Faust travels are not virtualities of dynamic contradiction. They are spaces that are observed by Faust and Mephistopheles, and by extension, the audience that represent a given situation. They are almost what will later become the tourist's photograph—an image caught by a removed observer that catches the nature of a culture as if static. What makes these virtual sites hellish in *Faust* is the division between observer and observed—one of the central principles of science that Goethe the scientist disputes. Thus, the friction between the dynamics of appearance, and the distanced observation by the "traveler," Faust, makes the spaces hellish; whereas heaven, the site of wager, or contradiction, is, well, heavenly. Because of a bad bargain, an inverted promissory note that brings damnation, not transcendence, Faust, the alchemical scientist, is forever separate from that which he observes.

Faust II: *transcendent gender and money*

Completed much later, in 1832, *Faust II* stages the economic and material business of the empire as the context for a dizzying array of virtual worlds. Because of the difference in structure, tone, and content, completed much later in Goethe's life, I will retain the treatment of the play as separate, as *Faust II*, rather than simply *Faust*. Here, rather than Faust in his study, the play depicts the emperor in his court. In this play, the counterfeit is not a result of the paradigm of scientific research, but the social relations tied to the issuance of paper money. Hans Christoph Binswanger, in his book *Money and Magic: A Critique of the Modern Economy in the Light of Goethe's Faust* (1994), argues that paper money is the alchemy of *Faust II*. If the devil seduces through alchemical magic in part one, he seduces through paper money in part two. The two are structurally parallel.

Mephistopheles suggests to the Emperor that he issue paper money to relieve his debt. He convinces the Emperor that, as if by magic, issuing paper money can be made into real compensation for debts.

Mephistopheles: Such currency in gold and jewels' place,
Is neat, it bears its value on its face,
One may without much bargaining or barter
Enflame oneself with Bacchus', Venus' ardor;
If metal's wanted, there's the banker's pile,
If he falls short, one digs a little while.
Gold dish and jewelry are auctioned off,
The paper validated soon enough,
They ask for nothing else now, it's a habit.

(*II*, 6119–6130)

The literal meaning of the lines is clear. It has now become a habit to accept paper money, or promissory notes with only loose requirements that it be amortized (literally *amortisiert*). National banks were increasingly distributing these notes, which were payable in gold upon demand. Thus, the economy worked through the promise of gold, rather than through the exchange of the actual metal. More than once, Mephistopheles assures the Emperor that no one will ask for the payment behind the paper. The emperor signs a contract with Mephistopheles for the issuance of the bill, duplicating Faust's compact in part one. However, rather than extracting a promise of ultimate value, the gold of the soul, for which he will demand payment, Mephistopheles seduced the Emperor into writing a pact of non-payment. Since the monetary promise is not really secured, the trick only works in the short term; it eventually leads to severe inflation, a collapse of credit, and finally, warfare (*II*, acts I and IV). These results were comparable to what was happening in Europe at the time, and were to become commonplace in the following centuries of capitalist development.

Binswanger also contends that the play illustrates how the issuance of paper money creates surplus value. A realm of imaginary needs must be created in order to be capitalized by the surplus of imaginary money (10). Mephistopheles suggests that such money can be used to "enflame oneself" with drink or love. In other words, surplus money subsidizes surplus states of consciousness. Heralding surplus as ultimate value, transcendent emotional and psychic states that emulate surplus will also assimilate value. This is a different sort of remove than that of contemplation. Rather than the active engagement with things and conditions that accompanies Goethe's scientific method, Faust will literally ascend to great heights of emotion and transcendent vision atop the Alps. Ecstasy is a celebration of surplus, after all. Georg Lukács supports this understanding of the interplay between the dynamics of paper money and self-amplification by citing Karl Marx's reading of Mephistopheles's lines: "If I can pay for six stallions,/are not their powers also my own?" Marx interprets the lines this way: "What exists for me through the medium of money . . . is what I am as the possessor of money" (in Lukács 1968: 198). In this way, as Lukács observes, "the dominion of money over conditions" provides a virtual amplification of self and of resources, which satisfies as it seduces" (199). Surplus value takes on an ontological status.

What "I am," my identity, is a possessor of money and self celebrates its own amplification. Thus, not only is the observer removed, but s/he a surplus/transcendence celebrates the distance.

However, rather than a simple condemnation of these new economics, Goethe employs a dialectical attitude toward paper money, recognizing both its power to "really" amplify capital reserves, its allied ability to induce virtual, surplus extensions of social economies and to reveal how the "empty" promise of payment, the lack of ultimate value behind the transaction robs the collective whole. As Lukács notes, Goethe could not imagine anything outside of capitalism, so instead of creating alternative systems in his virtual realms, he literally character-izes its fluctuating values and its boom and bust economies. At times, Mephistopheles signifies the "primitive accumulation" of capital that was a signature of the period. Yet, as Lukács cautions, Mephistopheles is not the simple representative of the evil side of capitalism (1968: 200). Large pools of capital also made industry and, for Goethe, worthy national projects possible. As the production of paper money increases, so do the products of its capitalization.

As alchemy had instituted the single furnace in its laboratory of transformation, the nineteenth century witnessed the introduction of the great blast furnaces for smelting ore, produced through the pools of capital that financed the industrial age. In 1814, Duke Karl August wrote enthusiastically to Goethe about his visit to Birmingham, England, where he saw two hundred and fifty such furnaces. By 1827, Goethe was likewise enthusing about the project of the Panama Canal, which would cut through continents and redirect waters (Binswanger 1994: 105–106). signifies at once the promise and damnation of industrial production and new, major projects in relation to the environment. It seems that, for Goethe his "delicate empiricism" became overshadowed by the possibility of the mass production of technological products and their ability to design ecological conditions. Speculation, after all, is the economic form of amplification. Goethe stages these new possibilities in depicting Faust's enthusiasm for a major land reclamation project. Faust's final speech outlines his plan for draining marshes to build houses for the "millions" of future "free" inhabitants. He foresees great housing projects on what we might now call wetlands. He celebrates himself as the great designer/entrepreneur, who will alter the course of continents:

> The master's word alone imparts his might.
> Up, workmen, man for man, arise anew! . . .
> Sieze spade and shovel, each take up his tool!
> Fulfill at once what was marked off by rule.
>
> (11503–11510)

In one sense, Faust takes up the hoe Mephistopheles offered in *Faust I*, but in another, he passes on that hoe to the hundreds of laborers whose sweat will actually fulfill his plan. The shared subject of nature has disappeared, leaving the sense of land as dominion and science as its agent.

Goethe ironizes any sense of collective labor in these circumstances by depicting the workers as Lemurians, spirits of the evil dead, depicted as skeletons on a bas-relief discovered in southern Italy and familiar to Goethe. These creatures who dig the great channel, and lay the dikes, are referred to by Faust as "die Menge, die mir frönet" ("the crowd that is enslaved to me"). He is not a man of the people, then, who works with them toward a better future for humankind, but the removed designer who assumes the traditional position of a nobleman. He is not planning the future of the land as one who lives on it, but one who plans its future for others. Faust, here, offers a dark depiction of the land developer—the ecological and social nightmares that will come of the developer's dreams, or the alienatede engineer—a figure the Soviets will take up in the early twentieth century. Moreover, Faust is merely dreaming of a future. He imagines a utopic project that does not exist in the present. Goethe is testing such the industrial, nationalist imaginings in *Faust II* as he had the virtual territories in *Faust I*. Such virtual plans for the future are dramatically contrasted to Faust's imminent death.

Binswanger notes that Goethe was familiar with the German translation of Adam Smith's *The Wealth of Nations*, in which Smith sketches a happy partnership between capital and labor (1994: 103). Capital supports productive labor, and then deservedly takes its profit. In *Faust II*, combining capital and productive labor with service to the common good seems to promise Faust redemption. Redemption, in this play, is staged as amortization and the positive actualization of capitalized projects. Faust dies with these great plans, these boasts upon his lips. Many critics, including Lukács, locate Goethe's "final solution" in these lines. However, as stated above, one must read in the interstices between Faust's projections and Mephistopheles' in order to fully accede to the structures of the staged experiment. At Faust's death, Mephistopheles expresses this profound insight:

> No joy could sate him, no delight but cloyed,
> For changing shapes he lusted to the last;
> The final moment, worthless, stale, and void,
> The luckless creature, he would hold it fast.

> (11587–11590)

To Mephistopheles, and in the dialectic of capitalist value, Faust's exploitation of laborers and natural resources seems like just another one of his witcheries.

As value swings wildly between the virtual and the real, the binary realms seem to find some consonance in one another. The virtual becomes the site of celebration in its very surplus. Virtual realms proliferate wildly in *Faust II*, filled with temporal conjunctions. Money and masquerade drunken the emperor and elevate Faust into the ecstatic realm of vision. Paper money belongs to the empire, to the devil, and, finally, to the essentializing of codes.

According to Antonio Negri, "subjectifying" the workings of money and value, as *Faust* accomplishes, is a way to "personify" the crises of capitalization

(1991: 111). Rereading Marx's *Grundrisse*, Negri posits capital as an "overdetermination of a separation" or, in the terms of this study, a dramatic conflict (115). To follow Negri's argument, the issues of surplus and paper money, while literally represented by Goethe in the plot, are subjectified through the characters of Faust and Mephistopheles. As the production of value is untied from labor, a byproduct of the production of paper money, capital becomes social capital, inhabiting the subject position in the social ecology.

Virtualizing the feminine gender

Surplus essence is also the code of gender in *Faust II.*

At the same time, the portrayal of gender becomes more and more as a virtual space. In the first play, the initial virtual realm that Faust visits is a kitchen—a witches' kitchen. There, Faust encounters all the virtual apparati of transformation, derived from the domestic technologies of women and portrayed as the "fallen other" of the laboratory. It's almost as if the kitchen is a feminization of Faust's study, where apparati make research monstrous. Nonsensical language emulates a discourse of performative power and cooking is a counterfeit of experimentation. The witches' kitchen stages an inter-species environment where marmosets speak and work—fully anthropomorphized and subjugated as laborers. In other words, nature has been wrenched and tortured into the object position by the culinary, domestic apparati these witches wield. The laboratory of the "new" science had long been celebrated as a similar spectacle of apparati, as Joseph Glanvill from the Royal Society described it in 1665: "'tis . . . a pleasant *spectacle* to behold the shifts, windings, and unexpected *Caprichios* of *distressed* Nature, when pursued by a close and well-managed Experiment" (quoted in Shanahan 2002: 3). For Goethe, the wrenching of natural things into objects of observation and distressing them in the laboratory to produce knowledge is monstrous. The virtual space of the lab extracts itself from the environment and thus the processes of change are fixed into compounds, like the marmosets.

Scenes of witches bound the Gretchen Tragedy: on one side, in the kitchen, and on the other, in the witches' celebration of *Walpurgisnacht*. The centerfold of this monstrous virtual is Gretchen, a "real" woman, whom Faust, tainted by his illicit encounters with the virtual, socially ruins. In other words, a scenario of heterosexual intercourse punctuates the virtual community of witches, interpellating a brief encounter in the bourgeois Christian virtual of morality into the more pervasive virtual of monstrous remove. The Gretchen story simply models the familiar seduction of an innocent and its ruinous consequences for the woman, which had formed Lessing's *Emilia Galotti* (1772) and would later inform Hebbel's *Maria Magdalena* (1844). But again, within Goethe's scientific paradigm of "knowing," the ruination is the result of Faust's remove and his unwillingness to interact with another subject. Virtual gender, in the form of witches, abounds in a virtual space. These virtual women seem socially, collectively bound to one another in a gender-specific, exclusive community. However, the feminine, as

Gretchen, when snared by the exclusive, removed knowing subject, is extracted from the binding solution of her social realm and ruined. Her extraction/isolation is finally complete in her cell, where she cries out in agony, as if pinned to the examination table. The two scenes of witches and the Gretchen tragedy compose a triptych of potential gender relations in which the virtual space affords some agency for the observed, when still cavorting in its natural environment, while the remove of the subject (Faust) that operates on the object (Gretchen) causes devastation. But witches provide only part of the paradigm of the feminine. In *Faust II*, beautiful women, who walk the virtual of classical landscapes, including even Helen of Troy, will help to catalyze the feminine out of its adjectival role, subjected to the human, and into its own virtual space, as money itself takes a virtual form.

The apotheosis of gender

Faust is first led into the virtual realms of *Faust II* by the Homunculus—the synthetic man made in a test tube. Already there is a form of masculinity that is produced, in a semi-virtual state, within the laboratory. Whereas the play will celebrate the apotheosis of the feminine gender, it condemns virtualizing the form of the masculine. The setting for the production of the Homunculus is an alchemical laboratory and the notion of the Homunculus is a figure actually borrowed from the alchemical writings of Paracelsus, but in this play, the Homunculus serves strictly as a product of the "new" science Goethe sought to correct. Faust's assistant, Wagner, brags about the inception of the Homunculus: "What we extolled as Nature's deep conundrum,/We venture now to penetrate by reason,/And what she did organically at random,/We crystallize in proper season" (6857–6860). Wagner celebrates the substitution of human reason for nature's probabilities. The synthetic man is created by the kind of self-determining reason Goethe rejected in the autonomous workings of mathematics. Born of an alembic, the Homunculus figures the lab of the new science. Without a "real" body, the Homunculus cannot really "own" himself. On the cusp of the eighteenth century, John Locke, in *The Second Treatise*, articulated the association between ownership and one's "own" body by stating: "Every man has a Property in his own Person. This no Body has any Right to but himself" (quoted in Tierney 1999: 241). From this perspective, the Homunculus has no property—he is merely the manifest of abstract reason. Like paper money, he attains value only by the promise of a material value that is yet to come. The Homunculus ultimately plays out the melancholy and lost promise of abstract reason, who will, however, eventually lose his battle to become material and dissipate himself into the sea. In the play, this virtual techno-being is a failed man.[18]

The Homunculus, composed of pure reason, provides Faust access to an impressive database of history. Through him, as though accessing a database, virtual worlds appear, full of scrambled animations of historical, mythical images. Like a software "agent," who guides the researcher through internet sites, the Homunculus is Faust's guide to the "Classical *Walpurgisnacht*" and beyond, to Helen of Troy. As the synthetic form of reason, he figures the masculine subject who can transcend into virtual spaces, at the price of the corporeal. Access to the multiple virtual realms is through the failed corporeality of this masculinized reason. Ultimately, however, it is also this synthetic man who provides the access to the essential feminine.

Helen of Troy first appears onstage as an imitation of her role in the Euripidean play. She appears on a classical Greek set and alongside a classical chorus. All vestiges of the "real" that constituted the representation of desire in the earlier Gretchen tragedy are now completely swept up into the virtual. Helen is a character in a classical Greek play and a creature of myth, with whom Faust can converse and whom he can accompany to other virtualities. The stage cites its own tradition, here, producing a kind of second-level of reference to its own virtual potential. The feminine gender can be perceived through, rather than in, Helen, who is obviously an animated cipher—an avatar. For, if the witches were the fallen other of invention, Helen's referent is a purely abstract one. She represents the ideal of the feminine, not even really incarnated, since she is a figure literally from the classical stage, who can animate beyond its limits, somehow appearing, by assuming the rites of theatrical representation.

Helen is an animation of the code of the feminine gender. She is not really an historical creature, caught in the context of her time, but a figure who travels through various eras, abstracting her from her original situated signification. Through typical Mephistophelian smoke and mirrors, Helen is moved from her Greek stage to a medieval castle where Faust, as a medieval knight, woos her. Unlike Gretchen, Helen is not the victim of Faust's seduction, but his lover. They dance, speak in matching and intersecting lines of verse, which rises up in a crescendo of virtual bliss. But Helen is represented as only a "restored shade;" she cannot quite come to "life" in the traditional sense. Lukács writes of Helen that she is "postulated as real, but only postulated, not empirically real" (1968: 188). She is more than a ghost, but less than a "real" woman. Try as she might, she cannot attain "real" life. Up to a point, she resembles the synthesized masculine—the Homunculus. But then, unlike the Homunculus, Helen undergoes an apotheosis. Rather than a melancholy ending, she is transfigured. She rises up into the air. A cloud formed from her remaining garments transports Faust to the high rocky peaks of the Alps, where he is able to view the apotheosis of the Ideal Feminine:

> The essence forges eastward in compacted train
> The admiring eye pursues it, in amazement lost,
> It parts in floating, undulating, changeably;
> Yet would adopt a shape . . . Yes! I am not deceived!
> On sun-gilt holstery in wondrous splendor laid,
> Of titan size, indeed, a godlike female form.
>
> (*göttergleiches Frauengebild*; 10044–10049)

A mist hovers, seemingly filled with Gretchen or her love, "And, undissolving, wafts aloft into the ether" (10065). Gender has appeared, as code, free from any specific character. The "Feminine" appears as an essence, something which is installed in characters, but which can bear Faust to great heights and there, transcend into the appearance of the code itself. The code and the virtual meet here. The character as agent and the virtual as space are finally confounded as the character becomes code.

In *Faust II*, gender's apotheosis is situated within the emplotting of paper money and dreams of great capitalized projects of nature's soon-to-be-despoiled shores. Both the theater and the laboratory can produce synthetic, essential codes, within the business of the empire and the economics of paper money. Multiple, compelling virtual worlds are accessible, where all of history and the future are comprehensive databases available for animation. Grand capital projects can fashion nature into human habitats and fantasies, and the codes are available for uploading. But is all of this wealth, as Mephistopheles pronounces at Faust's death, merely shape-shifting—a formalist morphing? Has transformation, change, been entirely uploaded into the distanced, abstract space of illusion? Is all of this merely the staging of a Weimar, a courtly remove from a failed (in Goethe's time French) revolution? And what about the by-product of the virtual transcendence of the human subject—devastation and waste?

Goethe, in *Faust II*, answers these questions by staging how *one form of surplus is waste*. The play foreshadows what land reclamation can become, when designed outside a more ecological, holistic framework—a "foul morass"—because there is no outflow for the stinking water. In the play, the dyke silted up the drainage channels and algae is thriving. *Faust II* imagines how the accumulation of industrial waste and the channeling of seas will devastate: how the huge slagheaps accumulated from those glorious blast furnaces will smother the soil with arsenic and chromium (a cancer producing agent), be carried as dust on the winds, seep into the ground water, and flow to rivers and lakes through storm water run off; how there would be slagheaps of more that one million tons of waste, some of them more than twenty stories high. As for the great project of the Panama Canal, how it would constitute a freshwater zone, supplied by rainforest runoff; how every ship that makes the crossing would waste 52 million gallons of fresh water: multiply that figure by 30 to 40 crossings a day—roughly 13,000 a year; how the rainforest in that region would be diminished by over 50 percent; how this water, needed for drinking by the local inhabitants, will be wasted; how the fish will be killed. Just as the inhabitants of Faust's great land reclamation project will be uprooted and even die, with the region devastated, these same capitalized projects, hastened by developers, both national and private, and designed by distant, privileged designers, will bring ruin to living spaces.

All of this devastation is proliferating wildly amidst the capitalist dialectic of boom and bust. This is the devil's alchemy, indeed, that swings between virtual profits and natural waste; the mercury of human and natural waste, still beloved by Faust before he died. It bears repeating, in Mephistopheles' own words:

No joy could sate him, no delight but cloyed,
For changing shapes he lusted to the last;
The final moment, worthless, stale, and void,
The luckless creature, he would hold it fast.

(11587–11590)

This addictive morphing will be anchored to development in the nineteenth century before it will find its true, mercurial apotheosis in cyberspace. Industry will proclaim progress, as Faust had begun to do before he died. Progress will become the moniker of change—the scion of transformation. Nature will be the dominion ruled by the exclusively human subject. Motivation will be grounded in development—character in plot.

Eurythmy: performing Goethean science

Many different schools of thought claim a kinship with Goethean science. A physicist, Tom Mellet, perceives a relationship between chaos theory and Goethean science,[19] David Seamon, a professor of architecture, argues for a phenomenological base to Goethe's epistemology, and some claim his work with plants is applicable to herbal medicine.[20] Yet perhaps the most widespread influence is through a movement called anthroposophy, which focused on Goethean science as principles of architectural design and movement in space.

Goethean science was claimed as the inspirational base for the new, popular esoteric practice that began in the late nineteenth century. In 1886, Rudolf Steiner (1861–1925) published *Grundlinien einer Erkenntnistheorie der Goetheschen Weltanschauung* (*A Theory of Knowledge Implicit in Goethe's World Conception*), working directly from research into Goethe's writings. After years of studying and editing Goethe's scientific papers, Steiner emphasized the unifying features in Goethe's system and the interplay between observation and intuition. Steiner's interest in movement in space, termed eurythmy, inspired him to construct an architecture, a sense of space that would be based on Goethe's paradigm of the virtual, derived from his theater and his science. Steiner called the building the Goetheanum and deemed eurythmy a spiritual science which would be performed within it.

Steiner combined Goethe's sense of theatrical space in *Faust* and his science to invent a performance of what he termed "spiritual science"—a spiritual, scientific, and performative system that enacted an observant, intersubjective relationship to the social and to the environmental. David Wiles, in his book *A Short History of Western Performance Space* offers the best and possibly only study of the Goetheanum in performance studies. Wiles describes Steiner's architectural principles as set against the transcendental Gothic impulse that "moved away from the earth" in its architecture and performance. Instead, Steiner sought a form that would incarnate rather than abstract, producing what he called a "larynx for the speech of the gods" (Wiles 2003: 56). The rites and their spaces were co-productive. "Eurythmy" flows through the walls and the bodies of the performers alike. The Goetheanum was designed so that "Every column should speak in the same way that the mouth speaks when it gives voice to anthroposophically oriented spiritual science. . . . quite distinct from all other architectural styles" (qtd in Wiles 55).

Built in the 1920s, Wiles describes Steiner's Goetheanum as a break with the modernist sense that the theater building is a passive container for the performance. For Steiner, the architecture and movement were co-producing a flow, an exchange of energies. As Goethe staged heaven, staged classical mythology, staged the realms of witches and virtual travel, Steiner incorporated the sense of the stage into his co-production of a scientific and spiritual practice. The style eschews geometry for flow, and the foregrounding of building materials for color.

Steiner began his work as an official of the Theosophical Institute, in the tradition of Mme. Blavatsky, who will be subject of the next chapter. His "spiritual science" was one of spiritual evolution, combining Darwin with the tradition of his interlocutor, Mme. Blavatsky. Steiner's work greatly influenced Michael Chekov, who used some of the principles in his method of actor training. Thus, a tradition was founded that would continue Goethean principles into acting training as well as architecture and movement. Waldorf schools, elementary schools built on Steiner's beliefs, put movement and theater at the heart of early learning, rather than as adjuncts to the "three r's."

The price of admission

The institution of theater formed its own value system concerning the ownership of its virtual space, inventing its own paper money: the ticket and the patent. Closing off the theater space from the public space, theater privatized the virtual space of the stage and of the audience, displacing "free" improvisatory performances. Iteration, its strategy against the rites of transformation, also became its means of commodification. Investment depended on the art of repetition.

Both theater and the "new" science issued patents on their products. Although performance was not a physical product, capable of generating income in the same way an invention might, the ownership of the virtual space and its performances began as early as the seventeenth century, when theaters in England were issued shares in their venues and in their companies. Actors and managers invested in their own creative potential, which they could somehow "own." Forms of paper money secured the ownership of the performance space as a way to develop the privatization of the public domain. Commodifying performance itself was also beginning to be put in place, in spite of its fleeting status.

If invention produced the commodity of science, iteration produced the commodity of performance. The repetition, in the same venue, not only of the plays that were produced, but of the acting techniques that performed them established the basis of investment. The state licensing of the space of performance supported these efforts by limiting the public domain of performance to certain contained spaces. The government censure of outdoor, improvisatory performance and its licensing of a limited number of "private" properties created a sense of value by setting specific limits on space and production. In England, the Licensing Act of 1737 granted the government the power to license plays, players, and venues, when they made money. As to performers, the Act states: "all fencers, bearwards, common players of interludes, and other persons therein named and expressed, shall be deemed rogues and vagabonds" (quoted in Fowell and Palmer 1913: 368–369). The virtual space of theater, both in its production and its reception was no longer "free" to improvisation, vagrant wanderings, or even village life, nor could it proliferate wildly among people. The "magic" of theater and its space of public gathering were strictly limited to only a few venues, a few playwrights, and a few players. The Act served as a kind of round-up of performance into the iterative structures of the theater, installing the structure of script/actor/theater as the legitimate form of performance.

These practices of ownership, so central to the development of theater and science produced an elite, private realm that secured its entrance through various economic means. Access to the virtual was not the devil's work, as Goethe portrayed it, but the work of the state and private investment. This act, which essentially remained in effect in England until 1968, has been much discussed in terms of censorship. As a result, those who did not have access could only imagine, in other grassroots forms, these privatized acts of invention and performance. Without sanction and support, their performances, if not censured, were relegated to the status of amateur, or, in the case of science, the outlawed magician or alchemist.[1]

Alongside the Licensing Act, debates over copyright law filled the galleries in the English courts, forming the base for contemporary Anglo-American legislation concerning intellectual property. In the eighteenth century, court cases concerning copyright laws for printed texts were bringing competing notions of how to value creative production. The project was to determine how creation, be it scientific or performative, could be inscribed in some manner, stabilized, in that sense, bounded, and thus "private" property. Together, copyright law, and the legacy of the Licensing Act have informed the Anglo-American juridical construction of intellectual property and the notion of the public domain. Theater marks the intersection of the two. Virtual space and virtual performance now exhibit boundaries, where "infringement" can occur. In his article, "Nine-tenths of the Law: the English Copyright Debates and the Rhetoric of the Public Domain," Mark Rose (2003: 76), one of the foremost experts in the history of the copyright, points out that:

> Copyright and the public domain were born together. They were formed in the course of the long social process that Jürgen Habermas identifies as the emergence of the 'public sphere.' This process involves the circulation of cultural products as commodities rather than as displays of aristocratic magnificence, and it involves a sense of civil society as collectivity distinct from either the private realm of the family or the public realm of the state.

Thus, the public domain was created by capitalization—investment supported by the state, but not owned by it, a virtual space "up for grabs," for speculators. This is particularly crucial for theater, in which the audience, as addressed, is a form of social affiliation, reflecting the civil and public notions of its time. The space where it gathers and the stage it observes are secured through a form of ownership.

Distinct from the "private realm of the family" and somewhat, though less distinct from "the public realm of the state," the audience's relation to the stage and its regulated reception reflects a juridical and economic, rather than ecclesiastical or aristocratic formation of collectivity. The audience was an organized node of the "public," in that it was not bound by kinship relations, but, it was somehow bound by an economic relationship to the theater itself. The paying audience purchased some rights to the virtual, while forfeiting others. *The theater ticket was a promissory note, issued at the entrance into the virtual space of illusion.* In the theater, the notion of the public and the civil were based upon purchase. The audience could be "gulled" as Jonson suggests, or inducted into the elect, as the elevated notions of art would suggest.

However, not everyone joined in this move toward privatization. On the other side of the debate, the notion of a "free" space of invention and creation continued to challenge these practices of privatization. Lord Camden, addressing the House, perceived, interestingly, the twin contributions of science and art in his determining the debate. In his article, Rose notes that Camden's speech was widely circulated in newspapers and magazines, defining the notion of perpetual copyright. Camden:

> If there be any thing in the world common to all mankind, science and learning are in their nature *publici juris*, and they ought to be as free and general as air or water. . . . Why did we enter into society at all, but to enlighten one another's minds, and improve our faculties, for the common welfare of the species? Those great men, those favoured mortals, those sublime spirits, who share that ray of divinity which we call genius, are intrusted by Providence with the delegated power of imparting to their fellow-creatures that instruction which heaven meant for universal benefit; they must not be niggards to the world, or hoard up for themselves the common stock.
>
> (quoted in Rose 2003: 80–81)

A sense of free, collective access to the world of the virtual still operates here, in spite of the speculation in the public sphere. Unlike the practice of shareholding in the theater, the sense of benefits to the public good opens the borders of the virtual and cancels the notion of trespassing, or vagrancy.

Rebutting Camden's thesis, Rose cites Thomas Noon Talfourd, in the early nineteenth century:

> When the opponents of literary property speak of glory as the reward of genius, they make an ungenerous use of the very nobleness of its impulses, and show how little they have profited by its high example. . . . The liberality of genius is surely ill urged as an excuse for our ungrateful denial of its rights. . . . Do we reward our heroes thus? Did we tell our Marlboroughs, our Nelsons, our Wellingtons, that glory was their reward, that they fought for posterity, and that posterity would pay them? We leave them to no such cold and uncertain requital; we do not even leave them merely to enjoy the spoils of their victories, which we deny to the authour; we concentrate a nation's honest feeling of gratitude and pride into the form of an

endowment, and teach other ages what we thought, and what they ought to think, of their deed, by the substantial memorials of our praise. Were our Shakespeare and Milton less the ornaments of their country, less the benefactors of mankind? (83)

Since these debates concerned books, the static object status of art seems to help to define its role in the public domain. It has properties, in the sense of the "new" science, which enjoy some stability. Iteration, then, needed to be secured for these considerations to apply to theater.

More than private space and script, the more ephemeral nature of performance troubles the rights of ownership. Carefully disassociated from "magick" and transmutation, the iterative and isolatable qualities of theatrical performance were installed as economically viable and legitimate. Actor/managers such as David Garrick invented ways to secure their commodity status. Shortly after the Licensing Act was passed, Garrick rose to fame in London. Garrick carefully constructed a focus on the actor, rather than acting as an entity of value. In several ways, Garrick was invested with and invested in what we would now call his "star quality." Certainly, the restrictions on performance and venues narrowed the field, helping to produce individual success. Garrick worked in the only two licensed houses (Haymarket case aside for a moment), Drury Lane and Covent Garden, investing in and managing the former. Garrick encouraged and circulated images of the actor himself, as actor, to secure his value. The portrait of Garrick as Abel Drugger in *The Alchemist* illustrates how the actor himself became the subject of representation, rather than the character. As *The Alchemist* served to displace transmutation with motivation, the new investment in the actor and the legitimate theaters created a new form of value that would be individualized and even self-referential. The value lent to the self-referential role of the actor was the beginning of the commodification of theater. Etchings, another form of paper money, also reproduced the actor's image, caught in a gesture playing the role that brought him to prominence. Garrick's portrait as Richard III was etched by William Hogarth (1745) into both a promissory and perpetual form of paper valuation.

Part of Garrick's invention of himself as a "star" commodity resided in his break with the more traditional acting techniques, offering something "new" and decidedly his "own." Ironically, his investment in iteration and ownership was based on an acting style considered "spontaneous" in contrast to the old rhetorical style of delivery. Installed in a bounded and licensed virtual space in London, employing scripts securely distinct from village improvisations, Garrick created the impression of spontaneity on the stage as his signature, his image, his "own" acting style. The assimilation of spontaneity as an effect of acting colonized the attraction other improvisatory practices had worked in the village greens and put them to work in the private venues.

Yet, in spite of the illusion of improvisation, Garrick founded his acting approach on a sense of the "new" laboratory science and its methods. In 1769,

Figure 3 "David Garrick is Abel Drugger in Jonson's *The Alchemist*" (http://www.clipart.com)

Garrick, responding to another's acting, reveals how this simulation of spontaneity was actually based on the practices of the "new" science, particularly its own theater of vivisection: "Your desection of her [the character] is as accurate as if you had open'd her alive. . . . " (quoted in Roach 1995: 95). Once again, we are brought back to the corpse, whose absence inspired the two Marys in the church, and whose presence inspired the sense of theater in science. But here, the corpse is resurrected, as Garrick notes how vivisection enlivens the performance of character.

In spite of the illusion of spontaneity, the sense that one could reproduce the image of Garrick's acting, that, indeed, Garrick reproduced his own acting of the role, is his legacy to the juridical future of intellectual property. His playing of the part, his "own" image of the character overtook the process of playing and the mutable dynamics of acting to offer iteration to a possibly improvisatory art. Busts of Shakespeare (one installed by Garrick) and portraits of Garrick (by Reynolds and Gainsborough, among others) promoted the general sense of actor over acting, and playwright over scripting. In other words, these images promoted the sense of an object to be admired, invested in, licensed, and offered up as talismans of national identification. They were emblems of the property owner of the art.

The question of just how performers do own their performances and the effect of characterization has continued to haunt the courts. As Hogarth "coined" Garrick's role of Richard, others have argued that they own the character they create, even in perpetuity. In the twentieth century, Bela Lugosi's familiar portrayal of Dracula helped to form the juridical tradition of assigning ownership to acting. In 1972, after his death, Lugosi's widow and son brought suit to enjoin Universal Pictures from exploiting the actor's likeness in Dracula movies. In other words, not only did Lugosi own his portrayal of Dracula, but his ownership could even succeed his death. The court upheld the claim (Lange 2003: 464). Lugosi's performance, like Dracula, remained as the undead, to be claimed by legitimate heirs.

This sense of entitlement, of owning the acted image has its detractors. Some argue that the "public realm," could also be understood as a general realm of influence, acting upon the performers who exist within it. One participates in the realm of illusion, as a member of the public and cannot be fined for responding to its influence. Within the realm of performance, the actor can, consciously or unconsciously, incorporate elements that constitute the fashion of the times. Anthony Liebig, prompted by litigation between Nancy Sinatra and the Fifth Dimension wrote:

> From the standpoint of performers . . . the right to perform in the popular genre or style is essential. Freedom of a performer to earn a living by adopting—either consciously or because he is "influenced" or simply "with it"—current modes and styles which may be widely or even uniformly demanded is, indeed, imperative. How else can he support himself and develop? *Any* limitation upon absolute freedom of performance—while it might result in short-lived bonanzas for one or two performers—would self-evidently be stultifying to performers as a class.
>
> (quoted in Lange 2003: 467)

How can the fleeting, public realm of gesture, intonation, and expression become affixed to a single person? Presumably, in the case of Garrick, he played Richard III in the same manner each night, making that particular image of the character his own. In the twentieth century, film re-produced the process of acting through its apparatus.

As we will see in later sections, all of these issues will continue to "haunt" the contemporary debates over intellectual property, raised to crisis levels in the digital age. Securing boundaries against piracy through digital reproduction and distribution is now a defensive position. After rehearsing the major contributions to the formation of the public domain, Mark Rose (2003: 85) chillingly concludes:

> That the English lawyers were able to develop a strong discourse of property rights but not an equivalent discourse of public rights should not be very surprising. As the adage has it, possession is nine-tenths of the law—or, as I would like to understand it, the law is mostly about property. The eighteenth

century common lawyers had a much easier time thinking about copyright in terms of property rights—either pro or con—than they did in thinking about how to formulate the claims of civil society. The conclusion that one is forced to reach, then, is that in the early period in which modern copyright was forming in England, the legal discourse related to the public domain was feeble when compared to the strong arguments for authors' property rights.

If the sense of a shared virtual space of production has been weakened by the infringement of property rights, how can one retain it? Who will own cyberspace and its digital representations?

The question remains, historically, juridically, and ideologically, how best to formulate this virtual space of the public domain in order to provide access to it. Is it a space like real estate? James Boyle has suggested that a comparison to the notion of the commons, or common land and acts of enclosure might be one way to understand it (2003: 37). Using the English tradition, Boyle's metaphor is a spatial one, invoking an almost nostalgic sense of a once-common shared space of land. David Lange suggests that the public domain is like a status: "A better metaphor than place, I think, is status. . . . Let us envision the public domain as if it were a status like citizenship, but a 'citizenship' arising from the exercise of creative imagination rather than as a concomitant of birth" (2003: 474). In Lange's case, the domain would be more an effect of production or participation, working from, perhaps, labor issues. Mark Rose suggests that "a defense of the public domain on the model of the environmental movement seems promising" (2003: 87). Rose has identified the public domain with a movement central to the latter part of this study, when the sense of environmental politics and later, ecological ones, will help to inform the sense of the internet. As we will see, these debates play directly into considerations of cyberspace and its production. Indeed, in what Naomi Klein (2001) identifies as "the brand canopy," the incursion of corporate ownership into all space, once open, or municipal, or even national tests the possibility of any space outside of that which is deemed for-profit.

Grassroots performances of science

In Act Two, the curtain rises on a melodrama. In the nineteenth century, a worthy antagonist of theater and science took the stage, costumed in the robes of the ancient traditions that had been cast off by Enlightenment rationality, the success of Empire-building, and modernist Christianity. This practitioner of ancient and invented rites was characterized as a spiritualist, or a praciitoner of the mystic sciences. Shut out from the privileged discourses and laboratories of science, and purposefully turning away from stage traditions bound to them, this practitioner nonetheless adopted a theatrical style of the times, fashioning a melodramatic struggle with the "new" science, in which science was cast as the demon of rank materialism and privilege. While alchemy had become an object of ridicule or moral condemnation in earlier periods, in the nineteenth century, spiritualism attacked science on similar grounds. The interpretation of the Faustian pact was reversed. As we will see, the curtain-ringer for this age will appear in the figure of the tormented alchemist, in retreat from the theater of the "new" science: Strindberg.

Since spiritualism and science share a similar goal, it is not surprising to find them organized through complementary or contestatory roles. The noted mathematician, Stephen Hawking, describes the goal of science in language that is also reminiscent of spritua list movements: "The eventual goal of science is to provide a single theory that describes the whole universe" (2005: 14). Moreover, Hawking continues, the success of the theory, or theories is based on "prediction." One major contest ensues over the mode of prediction. Do these predictions more correctly emanate from numerical calculations, or from the interpretation of other, more performative signs? Other contestations between science and spiritualism arise over the proper training of the practitioner, the designated elements of proof, and, finally, the social and spiritual effects these approaches produce. At the same time that the two practices are caught up in this agon, they also partner one another, by borrowing from the language of the other and emulating the public performance of their inventions.

Helena Blavatsky, Mme. Blavatsky as she came to be known,[1] invented new forms of the avatar and virtual space that would continue to inform various grassroots traditions throughout the nineteenth and twentieth centuries.[2] The figure of Mme. Blavatsky offers an icon of an intellectual, powerful, independent woman in the nineteenth century, who took on the new science and the interpretation of ancients texts, and who invented a tradition of grass-roots, corporeal performances of gender crossings, orientalist imaginaries, and technologies of phenomena. She is a complex figure whose practices invoke many terms of

Figure 4 Madame Blavatsky, courtesy of the Theosophical Society in America and the Adyar Archives

chastisement, including "Orientalist" and "faker" among others. The congruence between Mme. Blavatsky's practices and these claims recommend her to this study as a paradigmatic figure of her time. In her historical context, she could be called the P.T. Barnum of global(izing) mysticism, given the spectacular nature of her promotion of the virtual and sense of self-aggrandizement.

At a time when Romantics were imagining a singular, pure Greek origin, including the late Goethe, Mme. Blavatsky was inventing a wildly synthetic history of origins, beginning with a kind of science-fiction idea of the beginning of the species, drawn fully through the "other" classics. She also invented corporeal and literary performances of the virtual, to unseat the dominance of the privileged discourses of knowing and believing in her time: Christianity and laboratory science. Mme. Blavatsky's inventions of virtual performance have recommended her to many as the "mother" of New Age practices and beliefs. In this way, she provides a monumental model of the grass-roots struggle to understand and appropriate the virtual from an exclusive and distant scientific practice. Mme. Blavatsky reclaimed the power and scientific accuracy of ancient texts, censored by the "new" science and Christianity as impediments to "civilization," and she practiced the rites of transformation that had been deferred by the Church and displaced by the theater. Her monumental corporeality, her eccentric lifestyle, and her showpersonship, offered a "broad" antithesis to the "modest witness" of laboratory science, or the iterative actor on the stage. The composition of elements could be performed rather than observed, and performance was an improvised affair that took place in the drawing room, or even on the Indian subcontinent.

Mme. Blavatsky's invention of a mythical, spiritual Tibet, or Himalayan region, would also resonate in grassroots communities throughout the following years. Ironically, this great virgin, whose body could seemingly assimilate distant regions and even male adepts, associated with Tibetan Tantric traditions that are rich in sexual couplings and animated geographies.

Accessing the virtual plane

In the Fall of 1875, Mme. Blavatsky first accessed the Astral Light. She was beginning to write the first volume of her erudite and complex work on the occult sciences entitled *Isis Unveiled*. Writing in Ithaca, at the home of Hiram Corson, a professor of English at Cornell, Mme. Blavatsky produced twenty-five pages a day. Professor Corson reported that she was

> quoting long verbatim paragraphs from dozens of books of which I am perfectly certain that there were no copies at that time in America, translating easily from several languages. . . . She told me that she wrote them down as they appeared in her eyes on another plane of objective existence, that she clearly saw the page of the book, and the quotation she needed. . . .
>
> (quoted in Cranston 1993: 154)

The Astral Light provided a luminous textbase for Mme. Blavatsky roughly a century before the digital script of the internet began to appear to many others.[3] Although Mme. Blavatsky put the astral script to the use of print, she perceived it as a source of knowledge, accurate and sustained by physical and psychic properties "beyond" those practiced within print culture. Moreover, this fund of knowledge, like the World Wide Web of electronic technology, could be accessed from anywhere, including Ithaca, to be written into rigorous and scholarly accounts without the warranting that print culture or actual books were constituted as bestowing. It could be said that Mme. Blavatsky revealed a world wide web of information outside of modern modes of production and access. Even a professor of English at Cornell could be convinced of an astral accuracy that did not reside in a local print library. Indeed, Mme. Blavatsky managed to convince people across many nations, including India, of the veracity of her discoveries.

Mme. Blavatsky continued to draw her sources from the Astral Plane while living in New York, where she completed the two-volume text. One volume was entitled *Science* and the other *Theology*. As the title *Isis Unveiled* indicates, Blavatsky sought a new epistemology that would reveal how the ancient occult traditions navigated between the two fields. Rather than invoking the new in order to imagine the virtual, she invoked the ancient and the metaphysical, a tradition that would continue to struggle to perform access to technologies outside of modernist science and religion throughout the nineteenth and twentieth centuries.

The "modern," in Mme. Blavatsky's day and perhaps lingering on in ours, was embedded in Western incursions into the Asian subcontinent, where partnerships formed among Christian missionaries and colonial agents. Mme. Blavatsky and her Theosophical Society went against the tide of this "modern," pursuing, instead, an access to the indigenous ancient scripts. For that pursuit, they were honored by many, including the XIVth Dalai Lama, for reviving access to texts that Christianity sought to overwrite (Cranston 1993: 85). Mme. Blavatsky revealed how ancient texts and practices, deemed superstitious and detrimental to the processes of modernization, could be perceived as accurate and useful. The ancient figures of mantras and hieroglyphs could be set against the arcane symbols of Western science and economics to empower local nationalist movements against colonial rule, as in the case of India, or as an alternative science. This fusion will later be termed, among other things, a "mythscience," that suggests a universe structured by forces other than rational, empirical ones.[4] The use of these ancient symbols and traditions in themselves is not progressive. Only when used as strategies against other imperialist and oppressive forces do they produce an effective form of resistance. Even as progressive movements, however, the lasting value of their intervention may be debatable, since we now recognize the destructive potential fundamentalist versions of these beliefs can unleash against practices of social tolerance and cohesion.[5]

This complex set of tensions around the claims of the "new" and the indigenous association with the "ancient" has generated conflicting social, epistemological, and performative claims that continue to proceed into the twenty-first century. Not only, as we will see, does Tibet become the symbol for such conflict, but more recent global tensions around the region continue to illustrate how deadly the conflict has become. The figure of Mme. Blavatsky can begin to character-ize this tension in her time, animating the competing practices of scripting, embodi-ment, and performance as they partner with the virtual in the culture, in both productive and nonproductive ways. She is a harbinger of the ever-increasing synthesis and rupture between science and popular perceptions of the virtual.

The advent of the avatar

In addition to scripting the astral light, Mme. Blavatsky practiced a particular form of embodiment, or corporeal performance that accompanied her access to the astral plane. She corporealized an avatar within her own body. In one sense, she invented a new practice of the avatar. Her use of the avatar was derived from Hindu texts, most generally familiar in the text of the *Bhagavad-Gita*—the first epic story of avatars (Parrinder 1997: 19). In Sanskrit, the term means descent, or a "downcoming." Etymologically, the term *Avatara* is formed by the verb *tri*, meaning to cross over, or save, with the prefix *ava*, which means down. Hindu theological discussions of the term raised issues that continue to haunt the appearance of online avatars. For example, the eighth-century philosopher, Sankara, raised the problem of dualism in the notion of the avatar. Sankara argues that if Brahma is only One, how can he be two—both Brahma and his incarnation, or avatar? Sankara solved this seeming contradiction by insisting that the manifestation of the god is not a "real" incarnation, but merely another image within *Maya*—the veil of illusion (Parrinder 1997: 50).[6] Mme. Blavatsky resolved this dualism by maintaining the avatar in her body.

She records that several months before she began writing *Isis Unveiled*, she underwent a physiological change. In her memoirs, she describes the events that took place in the spring of 1875:

> And just about this time I [began] to feel a very strange duality. . . . I never lose the consciousness of my personality; what I feel is as if I were keeping silent and the other one—the lodger who is in me—were speaking with my tongue. . . . I know that I have never been in the places which are described by my 'other me' but this other one—the second me—does not lie when he tells me about places and things unknown to me, because he has actually seen them and known them well. . . . In the night, when I am alone in my bed, the whole life of No.2 passes before my eyes and I do not see myself at all, but quite a different person—different in race and different in feelings.
>
> (quoted in Cranston 1993: 149)

This man of "another race" is referred to as a "Hindu man" who resides some-where in relation to the Himalayas. Mme. Blavatsky embodies him, but he often appears outside of her as well: "I see him every day, just as I might see another living person. . . . Formerly I kept silent about these appearances, thinking that they were hallucinations. But now they have become visible to other people as well." Yet, at other times Blavatsky notes: "he overshadows the whole of me, simply entering me like a kind of volatile essence penetrating my pores and dissolving in me. Then. . . . I begin to understand and remember sciences and languages—everything he instructs me in, even when he is not with me anymore" (qtd in Cranston 1993: 150).

When Blavatsky shared her corporeality with this man, she could be seen to "twirl invisible side whiskers" or tug at an invisible moustache. Her voice changed, and some said her curly hair would become black and straight (Fuller 1956: 49). Mme. Blavatsky's transgender, transcultural performance of the "Hindu man" did not overcome her continued performance of her own persona. She could embody both personae at once, transferring new data across the gender and race divide. This "man" could appear entirely separate from her, accompanying her journeys, or could be embodied within her as a "lodger" who had traveled from afar, permeating her pores, incarnating his secret knowledge within her brain. In this way, she celebrated the dualism between the virtual and the carnal, the avatar and the self. Moreover, she wrote that the Astral Light, itself was "androgyne . . . double in nature," so her corporeal performance suited the structure of its source (Blavatsky 1994: xxvi). She corporealized her access to esoteric knowledge, as if the database animated itself and lodged with her, replete with gendered and raced characteristics. The "Hindu man," corporealized what Goethe's Homunculus, Helen, and the Ideal Feminine could not. The "Hindu man" maintained an existence, an ontological state, somewhere between pure abstraction and "life." He was sometimes incarnate, but not necessarily; more, he could incarnate within the character, or self, as well as without. Whereas Goethe imagined virtual realms that Faust might visit, Mme. Blavatsky imagined a porous relation among those realms and the "real," inventing a corporeal interface that was untroubled by the encounter. Thus, mimesis and alterity form a dual subject position for the other and the self through an imagined space of a special kind of carnal knowledge.

Aside from her more radical transgender performance, Mme. Blavatsky's incorporation also performed the Orientalism of her age. As the colonial imagination became increasingly obsessed with India and the Himalayas in the nineteenth century, she moved ever more eastward, both in her imagination and literally. After performing the "Hindu man" in the United States, she imported him back into India. In 1880, when she visited A.P. Sinnet in Simla, in Northern India, she even established contact by correspondence between Sinnett and her master, who was known then as Koot Hoomi. Indeed, she even facilitated a letter from "K.H." to A.O. Hume, a Government Official in Simla and the founder of the Indian National Congress.[7] These letters from "K.H." were offered as proof of her relationship to him and constituted the most hotly-debated issue in the allegations concerning her "fakery." In contrast, Mme. Blavatsky's claim to relations with this master also helped to establish her popularity in India and convinced many to support the Theosophical Society there. Thus, the colonial power of this performance was convincing in the colonies as well as in New York, where the invocation of the ancients served to fire the imagination of those who would find a form of subversive social affiliations in the reception of such incarnations. Performing orientalism, then, offered a way to recolonize the imagination and to decolonize it, to some extent, as, in India, where these masters and their Theosophical colleagues were virulently pro-nationalist.

Although Mme. Blavatsky was dedicated to embodiment, she was not involved in any notion of acting. Hers was not a *portrayal* of an "other." She was embodying, without craft, an extant creature alongside herself, who, although "he" might display himself through empirical data, did so only as a side effect of his presence. In the examples above, it is clear that these performatives were not intended for an audience, but happened to her when alone, or noted only by her. She eschewed the scientific base of observation and empiricism, so an audience would not prove or disprove the veracity of this phenomenon by observing it.

All in all, observation was a fraught issue in Mme. Blavatsky's epistemology and her practices. Mme. Blavatsky perceived the belief in observation to be the basis of the scientific fallacy. She felt the exclusive use of deduction without induction would produce false results. She argued that Geometry, for example, proceeds from universals to particulars and that the Pythagorean theory of numerals was learned from the Egyptian hierophants, so that numbers and figures could be situated at the intersection of matter and energy (Blavatsky 1994: 7). The very extraction of the observed and the desire for iteration seemed lifeless to her, without the experience of transmutation. Her own body, then, was in a continual state of transmutation of both gender and race.

A sometimes man: fleshing out the gendered avatar

Lest her encounters with the "Hindu man" be perceived as heterosexual fantasies of a single, mature woman, let us review how Mme. Blavatsky's penchant for cross-gender roles had begun before her encounters with the Astral Plane. At age 17, she escaped from her new husband by riding alone on horseback through the mountains of Russia rather than submit to his "conjugal rights," as they were termed. Her journeys began, then, with a flight from the heteronormative order, which carried with it a gender hierarchy that would make her dependent. She made it to Odessa, where she sneaked aboard a ship, sailed to Constantinople, and there began traveling as a companion to a certain Countess Kisselev (Cranston 1993: 37–38). Mme. Blavatsky reported, when preparing her memoirs, "Suppose I was to tell you that [in India] I was in man's clothes. . . . I was in Egypt with the old countess who liked to see me dressed as a man student" (quoted in Cranston 1993: 42–43). These images of the young cross-dressed Mme. Blavatsky, traveling through countries redolent with mystic wisdom, evoke subversive practices of gender in the midst of the search for the occult. It's as if "crossing the bar" of gender also morphed geography and wisdom into her fleshly form. Moreover, if her male student drag was designed to please Countess Kisselev, evocations of same-sex desire might also emanate from the image. Given her penchant for cross-gender drag and her flight from conjugal rights, Mme. Blavatsky's Hindu male "lodger" takes on a different affect than if she were prone, so to speak, to seek male affirmation. Instead of staging a sort of devotion to a man, Mme. Blavatsky's performance of the "Hindu man" brought mastery and knowledge to her. As a single woman, which she remained all of her life, she could attain the spiritual status traditionally granted only to men. Travel and tropes of transcendence offered her an independence that was not generally afforded to women of her time. Mme. Blavatsky's world wide web of luminous script and masters lent her an agency and relief from discipleship that other women who were attracted to the religions of the subcontinent would not find.[8] She remained an independent woman and the leader of a movement, without assuming any subordinate relationship to a guru. Flying in the face of the all-male traditions in Buddhist and Hindu theocratic hierarchies, she embodied the "Hindu man" and claimed his adept powers.[9]

Beyond her excursions into transgender fashion and behavior, Mme. Blavatsky also claimed special physiological constructions that set her apart from normal gender and sexual identities. In 1885, when accused of promiscuity by some of her detractors, she took herself to a certain Dr. Leon Oppenheim, who verified a diagnosis of *anteflexio uteri*. She made public his report by adding this letter, which she sent to Olcott:

> Here's your stupid new certificate with your dreams of virgo intacta in a woman who had all her guts out, womb and all, by a fall from horseback . . . And yet the doctor looked, three times, and says what the professors Bodkin and Pirogoff said at Pskoff in 1862. I could never have had a connection with any man, because I am lacking in something and the place is filled up with some crooked cucumber.
>
> (quoted in Washington 1993: 407, n. 6)

Her description of the "crooked cucumber" that fills her vagina is a unique one, not covered under the medical description of *anteflexio*. It suggests an amazing feat of a woman penetrating herself through her own anatomy. She did elevate the hermaphrodite in several of her writings and even, in *The Secret Doctrine*, posits it as the origin of the human race. But this image of the plenitude in her own vagina is different from that of a hermaphrodite. She has so filled herself that no man can gain access. She is sexually/anatomically complete unto herself. Like her dual performance of self and "Hindu man," she most certainly offers a corporeal transgender and sexual performance.

In positing the hermaphrodite at the origin of the race, Mme. Blavatsky installs her own transgender dynamics back through her reading of ancient, esoteric texts. Clearly, the hermaphrodite stands against the heterosexual couple of origin—

Adam and Eve. In fact, it is part of her argument that genealogy need not be based on relations established through intercourse, using "scientific" examples, drawn from botany, etc. (*The Secret Doctrine* 1999: 646–660). She is clear that both science and ancient texts that predate the Pentateuch contain evidence that this was simply a later misconception. Indeed, she offers her own *Origin of the Species*, candidly insisting upon a polymorphous, polysexual lineage of the human race (648).

While Mme. Blavatsky may have accessed a luminous script through a world-wide-web of masters, she did not participate in the shredding and redistribution of abstracted data. In her historical context, she deployed the notion of ancient wisdom specifically against Darwin's project of de-animating the past through empiricism. Wittily, she kept a stuffed baboon in her parlor, as an icon of Darwin's limited and fallen project that would insist upon only one form of knowing.[10] In other words, Mme. Blavatsky set possession against science.

Mme. Blavatsky cannily reinterpreted the notions of reincarnation she found in both the Hindu and Buddhist beliefs to house the regions where they were practiced inside of her as a man. But in these earlier traditions, avatars were for life, whereas her "Hindu man" was a sometime thing. Borrowing the notion of the Hindu "avatar," or the Tibetan *tulku*, as a lifetime reincarnation of a past master, Mme. Blavatsky invented, instead, a "lodger," who came and went.[11] Mme. Blavatsky oscillated between all woman and part man, flashing masculinity while she wrote, then receding back into the secondary sexual characteristics of a woman. The tradition of corporealizing avatars for only brief periods that Mme. Blavatsky invented would later be termed "channeling." Although the term "channeling" is more suited to the TV/computer imaginary, some histories of the practice refer specifically to Mme. Blavatsky as the founder of these performances.

It could be argued that these incorporations of Mme. Blavatsky assimilated and revised one "seminal" image in traditional Tibetan practices. The image of the copulating heterosexual couple figures one of the most important tantras—the Kalachakra. The image represents unions of all sorts, both abstract and material through the sexual act. Much too complex to summarize here, nonetheless, the image may be helpful in perceiving how Mme. Blavatsky translated the male-female union into her own virginal practices. Rather than practicing the Kalachakra rite of initiation, through meditation on the mandala, Mme. Blavatsky performed the union within herself.[12]

Embodied geography: Tibet

Mme. Blavatsky's interest in the ancient also invents a way of inhabiting, through being inhabited, the uncharted, "mystical" regions of India and Tibet. Although working against a modernist colonialism in one way, her assimilation of a mystical "elsewhere" nonetheless participates in the nineteenth-century sense of adventure and expedition. The "Hindu man" was considered to be a link to the circle of "masters," as she called them, who existed in different parts of the world, or the "brothers," as they came to be known within Theosophical circles. She claimed that their wisdom and their actual being proceeded from somewhere near India, or Tibet, but the region of the Himalayas was often "beyond" national borders in her mind. Moreover, "Hindu" seemed to connote more a spiritual locus somewhere in the region of the Himalayas than a national or religious tradition.[13] In fact, the full name of Mme. Blavatsky's "Hindu" man was Koot' Hoomi Lal Singh, a Sikh name, confusing religious traditions, but adhering to the general geographical location. Similar to Goethe's staging of the Alps as an elevated locus for the apotheosis of the code, Mme. Blavatsky imagined the Himalayas as a locus for ancient wisdom. However, Goethe's imaginary apex was centered in his own national consciousness, while Mme. Blavatsky's connoted an "other" origin to the virtualized realm.

Koot' Hoomi animated within Mme. Blavatsky at about the same time as Europeans were discovering the lure of the Himalayas. High mountains were beginning to inspire the European cultural imaginary through the growth of mountaineering as a sport of conquest, combined with a new sense of their heights as divine (Schevill 149–161). The Romantic painters had already celebrated summits as subjective, as in Turner's depiction of Mont Blanc. Yet the Himalayas were reputedly higher than other mountains, thus signifying greater heights in every sense. Mme. Blavatsky's sense of Tibet as the remote spiritual center of the world was both a break with her European context and in keeping with her times, as Tibet was beginning to emerge as the mythical center of occultism and exoticism in the late nineteenth century. This tradition of imagining a spiritual Tibet proceeded into the twentieth century, from James Hilton's novel/movie *Lost Horizon* figuring the fabled land of Shangri-la in the 1930s, to the public persona of the Dalai Lama and the tradition of *tulkus*. *Virtual Tibet*, by Orville Schell (2000), traces this imagined Tibet through numerous films and practices.

The actual mapping of such regions by geographical societies, particularly the mapping of Tibet, was not of any interest to Mme. Blavatsky. The basically all-male geographical societies and agencies were measuring distances among points, which the map user could observe, inhabiting an unmarked position while gazing. These scientistic approaches were directly tied to transnational commerce and Empire. In *Mapping an Empire*, Matthew Edney points out that the "East India Company undertook a massive intellectual campaign to transform a land of incomprehensible spectacle into an empire of knowledge. At the forefront of this campaign were the geographers who mapped the landscape" defining a "spatial image of the Company's empire. The maps came to define the empire itself, to give it territorial integrity and its basic existence. The empire exists because it can be mapped; the meaning of empire is inscribed into each map"(1997: 2). "India," Edney notes, became a notion in the eighteenth century, through the borders drawn within the maps. South Asia appeared through the publication of the nineteenth-century *Atlas of India* "as a single space structured by a common geometric framework"(1997: 236). In other words, the translation of these cultures and visions became data—integers of knowledge—for the mapmakers, who were intent upon constructing commercial and national ownership practices as space.

Of course, the Indians who lived there were not perceived as a source of knowledge, unlike the omiscience Mme. Blavatsky ascribed to her "Hindu man." The cartographers and surveyors came from Europe, while the Indians served primarily as their guards and bearers (Edney 1997: 308). Unlike Mme. Blavatsky, these orientalists did not lend any special knowledge or mastery to the indigenous. In fact, the seeming inability of the Indians to "master" these geometric notions of space was perceived as the result of their "superstitious" religious beliefs and practices. The kind of mysticism that Mme. Blavatsky found enabling was perceived as disabling for the necessary foundations of Enlightenment pursuits. According to Edney, the practice of mapmaking was based on the "Enlightenment's ideal of archival knowledge creation"(122). The gathering of data and its organization was aimed at the construction of an archive of data. Unlike Mme. Blavatsky's astral plane, accessing this archive presumed a hierarchical order. The surveyor, or data collector, was merely an observer and recorder of the local, while the cartographer, removed from the field, served as the rationalizer of data and the archivist. The knowledge base was hierarchically structured, then, by function, situating the most abstract and purely formal practices at the top of the ladder. As the cartographers strove for a uniform map of India, a centralization and consolidation of information and its interpretation, the process increasingly became a matter of bureaucracy and even the courts.[14]

Obviously, the Himalayas presented a formidable challenge to the surveyor. Their sheer heighth and difficulty of passage made it an impossible task to measure them on foot. The Himalayas were pereived as both a border of the Empire and an invitation to cartographers to sketch out the arc of the North-East Longitudinal Series. Determined solely by abstract geometric measure, the mountains became pure data in the Enlightment system. What was later called Mt. Everest, after one of these cartographers, was first known, in the early nineteenth century, as Peak XV, deemed the highest mountain in the world (Edney 1997: 265). As its name suggests, such peaks were represented as numerical figures in a computational victory of Empire. Certainly, these Himalayas were not the location of knowledge-producing adepts, nor of the adventures and secret practices Alexandra David-Neel would record. Neither corporealized through David-Neel's wanderings, nor through Mme. Blavatsky's mystic transformations, the Himalayas, to the mapmakers of the Empire were instances of trigonometrical relationships. The Enlightenment domination of such heights inspired the founding of exclusive, all-male geographical societies in Paris in 1821, Berlin in 1828, London in 1830, and New York in 1851.

The imposition of a rational, measured system that installed a universal viewpoint hierarchicized and de-corporealized what Mme. Blavatsky would corporealize and subjectify. Rather than an Empire, her own ample body was capacious enough to corporealize the grandeur of these regions.[15] She swapped a personal, corporeal notion of space for the impersonal Euclidean one. In a contemporary essay, "Breadcrumbs in the Forest: Three Meditations on Being Lost in Space," Vivian Sobchack (2004) sets up a relationship between embodiment, gender, and the structures of location that might help to illuminate Mme. Blavatsky's strategies. Wittily reviewing Freud's essay on the Uncanny, Sobchack observes how the masculinist anxiety of being lost in a "foreign" city composes Freud's sense of the uncanny. Sobchack extends this masculinist requirement of being "found" and never lost to structures of mapping and geography. She argues that the universal perspective from which the map is seen is really the disembodied, invisible site of the masculinist ego anxiety, securing a navigable location for itself. Sobchack illustrates how this new system resolved the anxiety by elevating the "man" who viewed the maps: "the representation sets up a *triangulated* relationship with the unseen spectator positioned at the *apex* in relation to a *flat* horizon line." Sobchack identifies the relationship to this space as one that has been "disciplined" and "sized" (2004: 20). So the great mapping ventures of the nineteenth century and the maps they produced of new "uncharted" territories such as the Himalayas and Tibet, can be understood as the result of a masculinist anxiety that angled the world as if through a disembodied, disciplined gaze.

In contrast to this process, Sobchack sets up a corporeal space-ing, which she terms a "carnal phenomeno-logic" (13). Sobchack cites Yi-Fu Tuan's notion that "In a literal sense, the human body is the measure of direction, location, and distance," which has been signified through folk measures of distance such as "an arm's length" or "feet" (18–19). Rather than the apex inhabited, or uninhabited by the distant, Euclidean engineer, the body in space can organize a local sense-making set of proxemics and distances. Embodied space marks the direction of intent—a radiating space emergent from subjective factors: "Both 'direction' and 'geography' seemed to me discontiguous and arbitrary systems of others rather than projected possibilities for the fluid orientation of my own being" (35). With an experiential, phenomenological base in space, direction and distance can be related to aim and desire. A carnal sense of space begins to emerge.

From Sobchack's perspective, we can see Mme. Blavatsky's performance of the Hindu "lodger" offers a woman's resistance, in the nineteenth century, the age of great mapping expeditions, against the installation of Euclidean, engineered space. Her embodied geography of the Himalayas can be perceived as another version of a "carnal phenomeno-logic" of geography. Yet, while Sobchack would "lodge" spacing in experience, Mme. Blavatsky envelops the distance of space into her own intimate body as a "lodger." Perhaps this carnality is imperialistic in its embrace, but it is also a performance of contiguity, proximity, and cooperation in the making of geographical difference. It enacts a mutable, temporary, and specifically cross-gendered invocation of geography that reveals, both literally and figuratively a "woman of size" whose girth is global and agential, in contrast to the increasingly corseted and dis-abled embodied practices by the women of her time.

Along with her study of the classical literatures, this form of embodiment helped to construct Mme. Blavatsky's cross-geographical agency, warranting her right to set up Theosophical sites in India. While in India, she enjoyed a frequent interface with the "Hindu man," who also seemed to materialize more and more as letters with the signature of Koot' Hoomi Lal Singh, which were delivered to her through the Astral Plane. His letters detail his interest in the political issues of India as well as the machinations of the Theosophical Society in the region. Through contact with him, the Theosophical Society was advised about the growing movement toward national independence which they then supported.

Mme. Blavatsky's embodied geography inverted traditional Tibetan Buddhist traditions of perceiving geography as a body. Rather than assimilating a distant place into one's own body, traditional beliefs perceive geographical sites as locations upon the body, specifically of female demons and deities. Ian Baker's *The Heart of the World* describes how temples on the Lhasa plain were built to "stake the heart of a malevolent demoness, the Srinmo." Baker reveals how these temples architecturallly and geographically map and bind the virtual female body. For example, a temple near the Tsangpo gorge "immobilizes the Srinmo's right elbow," while another structure in Powo "decommissions her left palm" (2004: 89). A geography of spiritual bondage provides the sites for the all-male lamasaries to contain and control the female demon.

Further, pilgrimages to difficult-to-reach sacred sites may provide the enlightened sojourner with a vision of geography and a godess at once. The wisdom deity Dorje Pagmo's limbs and chakras "form Pemako's esoteric geography." When the adept completes a journey, made arduous by elevations and leeches that reflect his own inner blockages, he might, upon reaching, say, Dorje Pagmo's throat chakra in a precipitous gorge, open her and his chakras at once (Baker 2004: 257). Thus, rather than an arithmetical/geometric measure of mountains and lakes, the Tibetans themselves believe their own territory to extend the virtual presence of the body of the gods. Mme. Blavatsky merely inverted the model through her colonial and personal arrogance.

Mme. Blavatsky's phenomenal physics vs. the theater of Darwin

Mme. Blavatsky performed her physics, not as experiments, but as revelations of the structures of matter and energy. She termed these manifestations "phenomena." These performances garnered much attention, both positive and negative, as she seemed to make objects appear or disappear. They were calculated to convince those believers in the modern uses of science and reason, such as Thomas Edison, to join the Theosophical Society. Before Einstein's famous equation or Philip Glass and Robert Wilson's *Einstein on the Beach*, Mme. Blavatsky staged the relative transformations of matter and energy. Her detractors accumulated evidence to disprove her transformations, while others remained convinced by them. Most of her performances of phenomena occurred between 1859 and 1882, during the popularity of scantily-clad women on the burlesque stage and the causal forms of melodrama, realism, and naturalism in the theaters.[16] Even though some actors, such as Edwin Booth, attended her performances, she remained aloof from the stage.

Whereas the stage celebrated the deterministic evolution of human relations in the forms of realism and naturalism, Mme. Blavatsky performed the transformability of matter and the accessibility of the virtual. Like the alchemists, she was dedicated to transmutation as the organizing principle of matter. She founded a performative practice that was designed to illustrate how material transformation is always and everywhere available. Her performances were derived from occult texts on the constitution of matter. As the naturalist plays forged change into a chain of irreversible, causal events, Mme. Blavatsky enchanted her audiences with unlikely, unseasonal, and unbelievable (to many) discoveries. While the stage demonstrated a modernist, Darwinian logic, Mme. Blavatsky demonstrated how the ancient texts—some of the same ones that inspired Newton—could be animated in her time (Ryan 1937: 47).

Acting methods at the time were experimenting with codes and techniques of reproducing the expressions of emotion based upon the writings of Darwin. In other words, acting was associating itself with the principles of the "new" science. As Joseph Roach notes in *The Player's Passion: Studies in the Science of Acting*, Darwin's theory of *The Expression of the Emotions in Man and Animals* lent a scientific or perhaps scientist discourse to the methods of expression (Roach 1991: 177). Modern science, using its mode of observation was penetrating the conscious and unconscious realms, extending its empire into the very structures of human feelings. The stage was once again perceived as providing a kind of social laboratory for these forays, lending an authorizing cultural practice to the hypotheses.

Roach, working from the late nineteenth-century writings of William Archer, reveals how Darwin's notion of "innervation," which denoted the "physical preparation of the animal's muscular system for violent exertion, combat, or display," could be understood as an explanation of an actor's warm-up technique for displaying emotion. Darwin: "He who gives way to violent gestures will increase his rage; he who does not control the signs of fear will experience fear to a greater degree; . . . These results follow partly form the intimate relation which exists between almost all emotions and their outward manifestations; and partly from the direct influence of exertion on the heart, and consequently on the brain." Archer cites a warm-up Macready used to play Shylock by shaking "a ladder violently before going on for the scene with Tubal, in order to get up 'the proper state of white heat'" (quoted in Roach 1991: 181).

In the example above, masculine aggression seemed to figure the technique and the principles of Darwinian acting. So the science of acting was about the expression of heightened emotion. The naturalistic stage was bolstering the primacy of the human subject, in contradistinction to its newly-discovered "origins," and using Darwin to authorize it. The playing of heightened emotion radically asserted human subjecthood through what it claimed to be the expression of its motive force. Shylock's anger, for example, will run the scene and define the playing of his character in it. Mme. Blavatsky focused performance on objects that changed rather than the human subject. Her fakery, or her ability, depending on one's perspective, was an *unemotional* affect, lending credibility, or not, to her knowledge of the ancient sciences. She aimed to illustrate the shared composition of matter more than her own agency to transform.

While Mme. Blavatsky sought to dispel rumors of her fakery, Jane R. Goodall, in *Performance and Evolution in the Age of Darwin*, traces another form of cultural struggle in the period, a resistance against Darwinian science that took the form of an "alert skepticism, a sense of the ludicrous, a desire to play the game of knowledge-making too, but under the anarchic rules of humbug" (2002: 7). To Goodall, freak shows and circuses both demonstrated the so-called natural order and demonstrated its limits—its exceptions. She establishes P.T. Barnum as one of the masters of this performance practice, both in his work in museums, which mounted the principles of such science, and in circuses which hum-bugged scientific demonstration. Goodall offers Barnum's mid-century "Grand Scientific and Musical Theatre" as a trajectory for the development of such resistance (21). More generally, Goodall demonstrates a "shared involvement in the culture of exhibition" between science and show business, beginning with the foundation of the Royal Society in 1660 and proceeding through the nineteenth century (26). Goodall identifies an entire culture of scientific demonstration, from the founding of museums of natural history to sideshows. The museums provided tableaux of the classificatory system of the normative as a form of "infotainment," while the sideshows provided the fun of satirizing it (28).

Mme. Blavatsky's performances partook in this cultural atmosphere of scientific demonstration and performance. Once again, the anxiety over the counterfeit prompted cultural and material invention, but this time, rather than counterfeit coins, counterfeit exhibitions and counterfeit science, evoked the need to establish codes of verification. After all, Archer's attempt to tie acting techniques to Darwinian theories was a mode of verifying the art of acting as a scientific exhibition of emotion. The stage, once again, sought the licensing that science enjoyed. Goodall, however, provides a resistance to this quest, in P.T. Barnum's "hum-buggery" of such demonstrations. Mme. Blavatsky's spiritualist type of performance was designed to humbug the procedures of empirical proof. Her performances suggest that if matter and energy are actually exchangeable, then the exchange can be available without the mechanics of instruments and the application of autonomous discourses of physics. Transmutation can happen in the drawing room, not just in the laboratory. Whether her "phenomena" could be verified by empirical means or not, her insistence upon the agency of those outside the growingly exclusive club of science is clear.

Both Mme. Blavatsky and P.T. Barnum challenged the construction of the scientist as a "modest witness", as Donna Haraway identifies him in *Modest_*

Witness@Second_Millennium.FemaleMan_Meets_Oncomouse. As the "new" scientist emerged, a certain style of behavior emerged with him—one suited to the presentation of so-called empirical objectivity. If P.T. Barnum's discourse displayed a plenitude of exaggeration and metaphor, the rhetorical style of the "modest witness" was "unadorned," and "factual." Haraway's notion of "modest" scientific behavior includes "naked writing," in which "the facts shine through, unclouded by the flourishes of any human author" (1997: 26). Haraway aligns this behavior with an emerging performance of masculinity, associated with the scientific: "Female modesty was of the body; the new masculine virtue had to be of the mind. This modesty was to be the key to the gentleman-scientist's trustworthiness; he reported on the world, not on himself" (30). Haraway goes on to cite David Noble's description of the behavior encouraged by the Royal Society as clerical: "As an exclusively male retreat, the Royal Society represented the continuation of the clerical culture, now reinforced by what may be called a scientific ascesticism" (quoted in Haraway 1997: 31). In other words, the hermetic practice in the laboratory consisted of the quiet, inexpressive mode of the cleric. The style of "modesty," then was designed to support the credibility of the laboratory's findings. The all-male ascetic remove signaled its distance from "the madding crowd" by its claim to an ascetic transparency in its style of writing and its rites (termed "experiments"). Mme. Blavatsky's fulsome style, both corporeal and rhetorical, broke with this performance of the "real." She insisted that such remove served only its own exclusivity. As Koot Hoomi (perhaps Blavatsky herself, as many insisted) put it in his letter to Hume: "And what, in its proud isolation, can be more utterly indifferent to every one and everything, or more bound to nothing but the selfish requisites for its advancement, than this materialistic science of fact?"[17] Modesty, to her, was actually arrogant indifference.

Yet Mme. Blavatsky's theories of the nature of matter and its relation to the virtual borrowed from the discoveries of the "new" science. Eschewing any idea of magic, yet insisting on transformation as one of the laws of nature, Mme. Blavatsky proclaimed that "Our Society believes in *no* miracle, divine, diabolical or human, nor anything which eludes the grasp of either philosophical and logical induction, or the syllogistic method of deduction . . . " ("Magic", 1879: 32). Straddling binaries attested to her intellectual fortitude, as she formulated her approach. She proceeded vehemently (as is her style) to distance her performances from those of "magicians," who were the spiritualist mediums of her time, comparing herself instead to Thomas Edison, who, she argues, would have been consigned to the rack or the stake for his inventions in an earlier age (33). She also associates herself specifically with Paracelsus and the alchemists, who she situates in a direct line with Edison, re-visioning the history of science (36). While claiming logic, she slaps the "brutal hand of Positivism" and its traditions of European medicine, which she found to be merely opportunistic, concerned more with the "business" of disease rather than public health ("An Old Book and a New One"). At this point in the history of biomedical commodification, that characterization certainly seems to be a prescient one.

But how did Blavatsky's "transcendental physics," as she called it, describe the nature of matter? She imagined that one dimension, as she called it, of matter "must be permeability. ... the passage of matter through matter. ... " ("Transcendental Physics," 1881: 16). Through the agency of this property, matter was changed. She perceived an active, accessible set of relations of "Electric and Magnetic Affinities Between Man and Nature" (reminiscent of Goethe's *Elective Affinities*) as she titled one of her articles (*Collected Writings* 2: 21). She thus perceived in matter a permeable and binding property with psychic, psychological, or experiential elements, as if these elements were not of different orders, but of the same order. If relations were struck among people, they were also formed among minerals, matter, and living organisms. This permeability, or potential for change was inherent in the very composition of matter itself, as earlier alchemical findings had also insisted. Nothing was fixed or stable, and more, nothing in the basic structure of elements was inaccessible to participation—cut off from experience and the subjective.

Participation in the dynamic structure of matter defines the standpoint of her performances of phenomena. An ancient mode of elemental change could be practiced by the adept ("Precipitation," 1883–4: 118). She comments that in her performances "Never were the phenomena presented in any other character than that of instances of *perfectly natural though unrecognized forces* ... " ("What of Phenomena," 1888: 49). Since "all matter is animated" ("Misconceptions," 1887: 72), no claim to the special status of vitalism could be made for humans. Mme. Blavatsky performed a shared subject position among forces and materials. She once explained to Colonel Olcott, who observed many of her performances while sharing an apartment in New York, that she could make objects appear because "infinitesimally small particles of the object to be reproduced are detached and become the nucleus around which others are drawn ... " (Fuller 1956: 48–49). In other words, the atomic structure of elements allowed for simple exchanges of particles. Each nucleus did not operate as an exclusive property owner of its parts, but as a potential site for dynamic bonding.

Alexandra David-Neel, another woman traveler who went to Tibet and translated secret documents, explains the transcendental physics behind appearances in her book, *The Secret Oral Teachings in Tibetan Buddhist Sects*. David-Neel, the first European woman and possibly the first European to reach the sacred Tibetan city of Lhasa, wrote numerous manuscripts translating Sanskrit texts into a Western tongue. Between the years of 1921and 1924, at age 54, she walked over a thousand miles through Mongolia and Western China in order to reach Lhasa. In the tradition of Mme. Blavatsky, David-Neel sometimes disguised herself as a man, but sometimes also as a possessed, old Tibetan woman by smearing burnt cork on her face, braiding black yak hair into her own, and darkening her face and body with Chinese ink and crushed charcoal (Foster 1986: 205). Unlike Mme. Blavatsky, David-Neel used transgender, transcultural impersonation for purely functional purposes—to "pass" through Tibet. Her record of her journey, *My Journey To Lhasa*, combines geographical and anthropological interests with spiritualist ones.

David-Neel records that she witnessed many of these performances of transformations of matter in Tibet that proceeded from the Tibetan Buddhist
understanding of "phenomena." In *The Secret Oral Teachings in Tibetan Buddhist
Sects,* David-Neel offers the following situation as an illustration: you are on a
large plain and see a fleck of green in the distance. The green fleck is the size,
say, of your finger. However, memory creates meaning, so, through the memory
of other green spots you have seen, "ratiocinations," as she calls them, rather
than information from the senses, you translate the green fleck into the image of
a distant tree. Probability joins memory to convince you of your image. So basically, you assign rationalized memories as attributes to sensations (1967: 17–18).
However, as David-Neel explains it, Tibetan Buddhist physics argues that there
are actually no objects *per se,* but only "movement which, through repetition,
constitutes sensations construed as objects" (19). Thus, what seems to be an
object is really what David-Neel terms an "event," meaning a confluence of
dependencies caught temporally and translated, through memory and learned
rational processes into an object (20–21). Transforming objects, then, is neither a
trick nor a byproduct of special human agency, it is merely an active participation in a shared, active energy commonly perceived as objects.

Cognizant of these basic Buddhist tenets, Mme. Blavatsky made things
appear and disappear at will. She claimed to grasp the cohesive power that
attracted atoms into forming objects, however unstable. "The profound art is to
be able to interrupt at will and again restore the atomic relations in a given
substance" ("Precipitation," 1883–4: 176). Mme. Blavatsky gave public performances of her adept strategies in her parlor and in the homes of others. These
were invited performances, in which she exemplified the particle nature of
matter and its instability. She practiced physics in the domestic environment of
her drawing room. Obviously, these performances soon drew wide attention to
Mme. Blavatasky's occult knowledge and skill, as well as supplied most of the
material for attacks upon her as a charlatan. The status of "fake" provided the
greatest breach with the modernist dictum of empirical fact. Mme. Blavatsky
violated the role scientists and their apparati were performing in relation to so-
called observation, rather than the manipulation of matter. And if she knew
what she knew through ancient emblems and writings, this, too, was an impossible resource for scientific knowledge. The efficacy of metaphor, or image, or,
indeed, seeing visions would not resurface within science until Einstein's vision of
falling elevators inspired his understanding of even more distant space.

The Gothic medium of matter

Although she worked at the time of the rise of spiritualism and mediums in the
United States, Mme. Blavatsky was not in the tradition of the medium, who
could interface with a once-living spirit. Mediums communicated with those who
had "passed over," often by interpreting mysterious knockings and other signals
from those souls. They functioned, literally, as a medium through which commu-

nication could pass. Ghosts, or spirits, found some consonance with them and could bridge the divide with the living through them. The Gothic, Romantic interest in ghosts and other undead creatures had found its own performance tradition in the Gothic stage, from the later eighteenth century onward, moving out into the nineteenth-century parlors as it retained popularity on the stage.

In the theater, ghosts of wronged women haunted members of their family. The family transcendent, George Haggerty, in his study of Gothic drama, demonstrates how the wronged dead actually catalyze the subject position into action through their appearance. It's as if ghosts are the motive force for human action. Haggerty also establishes the conventions of the Gothic drama and its imaginary as a family drama. Wryly, Haggerty terms the Gothic as staging "the erotics of the family" as a horror story, offering *The Castle Spectre* (1797) as a case in point. In the play, the story of fratricide sets off a series of revelations which culminate in the mother's ghost interpellating the daughter into the narrative—a kind of female Hamlet. Haggerty cites the stage directions for the popular scene in which the specter appears: "*In its center stands a tall female figure, with white, flowing garments spotted with blood; her veil is thrown back, and discovers a pale and melancholy countenance; her eyes lifted upwards, her arms extended towards heaven, and a large wound appears upon her bosom*" (Haggerty 2003: 24).

From this most popular gothic example, one can see the marked difference from the grassroots practices Mme. Blavatsky, who resembled Gertrude Stein more than the pale, wounded, melancholy mother of *The Castle Spectre*. Mme. Blavatsky was never, in any way, perceived as a member of a family unit. Ever distant from Russia, her role as a daughter plays no role in her writing and Theosophical work, and there is certainly no perception of her as domestic or maternal. Peter Washington, in *Madame Blavatsky's Baboon* describes her lifestyle in New York, where she had an apartment adjacent to her collaborator, Colonel Olcott (a subject of gossip). "Her drawing room was littered with manuscripts. . . . in the evenings they worked at adjacent desks. . . . There were occasional parties in the apartment, usually for the purpose of discussing occult matters, but the chums were resolutely undomesticated. Casual visitors, though welcome, were bidden to make their own tea or coffee and to find themselves a corner among the piles of books and papers" (1993: 44).

Along with their entertainment value and grassroots assimilations of science, mediumistic effects were also a matter of study for some scientists. A Nobel-prize-winning, husband-and-wife team, who were pracitioners of the "new" science named Marie and Pierre Curie studied the Italian medium, Euspasia Palladino for two years. On April 14, 1906, Pierre wrote to the physicist Georges Gouy: "We had a few new 'séances' with Eusapia Paladina (We already had séances with her last summer). The result is that those phenomena exist for real, and I can't doubt it any more. It is unbelievable, but it is thus, and it is impossible to negate it after the séances that we had in conditions of perfect monitoring." (See http://www.grahamhancock.com/forum/MACremo1.php?p = 2).

Along with Mme. Blavatsky's "phenomena," these grassroots performances of the virtual drew leading "new" scientists of the time, from Edison to the Curies. This connection between those who were pioneers in new technologies that produced virtual sounds and sights, such as the telephone and the x-ray, and those who perform the virtual through rites and mysteries will continue throughout the twentieth century. It is difficult to know whether the kind of open attitude and broad interest that led these scientists to seriously investigate these performative experiments with the virtual also aided in their scientific discoveries, or whether the nature of their discoveries led them to explore other forms of virtual images and sounds. More radically, one might consider whether both forms of virtual realms, technological and metaphysical share certain attributes. More conservatively, one might imagine that the discourse, the language of discovery, beyond strictly technical terms, can only articulate the nature and experience of the technological virtual by borrowing from the metaphysical/mystic traditions, or that the spiritualist practices are only grassroots attempts to capture the exclusive scientific discourses and discoveries.

In the earlier nineteenth century, the Gothic stage was a showcase for the technical apparati of mood. The stage organized an early technology of subjectivity, in which the illusory veils of vision and traps were used to produce fear and dread in the spectator. Technology's capacity to invoke or represent an internal subjective state, which, when distributed through these effects was called mood, and the mood was one of fear and guilt. This sense of the manifest virtual as a haunting has a long tradition that continues today. Within the Gothic imaginary, it seems that when virtuality is invoked through the apparatus, it sets the scene of fear and recrimination. Does this continue the guilt, first characterized through Faust, for invoking the virtual? Is the effect that any form of conjuring up the virtual is bound to lead to a bad end? Or does it play out some Luddite fantasy of recrimination for consorting with machines? Can the technological apparatus, when producing mood, only reproduce, like Faust, the work of the bedeviled? Or does the Gothic stage install a bourgeois concept of the apparatus? Does a bourgeois stage of special effects necessarily locate them within a retributive domestic morality, in contrast to the fabulous technical displays of the stage of the aristocrats?

Gothic ghosts haunt Marx

Ghosts strayed beyond the stages and parlors devoted to them, even into the social sciences. Karl Marx and Friedrich Engels installed a ghost into the beginning of their revolutionary document, the *Manifesto of the Communist Party*, which they published in 1848. The document that has been associated with massive social changes in the nineteenth and twentieth centuries begins: "A spectre is haunting Europe—the spectre of Communism. All the powers of old Europe have entered into a holy alliance to exorcise this spectre: Pope and Czar . . . French Radicals and German police-spies." (11) (More literally translated "All the powers in Europe have joined together for a holy crusade against this spectre.") Looking back at the figurative language that opens this document, it seems ironic to discover such allusions to ghosts and religious crusades in the midst of a sociological treatise. As a manifesto, however, it sets the socio/political analysis within performative language. It is an exhortation, or perhaps, as Jacques Derrida (1994) suggests, a conjuration.

Coral Lansbury, in "Melodrama, Pantomime, and the Communist Manifesto," argues that Marx and Engels actually derived their sense of a specter from the melodrama: "The idea of the ghost as moral conscience and protagonist comes directly from Gothic melodrama" (1986: 6). She even offers *The Castle Spectre* as the prime example of the kind of Gothic melodrama that the *Communist Manifesto* mimics. Several aspects of the melodrama suit the communist analysis, Lansbury emphasizes, particularly class retribution, which is an essential part of the melodrama's *denouement*. The form of melodrama relies, in general, on class oppression and retribution, linking the representation of class relations in melodramas to those in the *Manifesto* (7). Citing Michael Booth, a leading commentator on the melodrama, Lansbury argues that the "dramatically essential" elements of the "profligacy and savagery of the ennobled and proper-tied classes to the dogma of the melodrama" are the same aspects of class relations that provide the fervor of the *Manifesto* (quoted in Lansbury 9). Thus, the *Manifesto* stages a kind of mid-nineteenth-century melodrama of class rela-tions, partaking in many similar motifs and dramatic strategies of representation. It partakes in the very essence of the Gothic stage, in its invocation of specters who plead for retribution.

Jacques Derrida offers an even more complete explication of the *Manifesto*'s ghosting in his *Specters of Marx*. Describing the opening lines of the *Manifesto*, Derrida writes that this specter, "described or diagnosed a certain dramaturgy of modern Europe." He even goes so far as to refer to this document as "a Marxian theatricalization" (1994: 5). Derrida seems to agree with Lansbury in finding a dramatic shape to the *Manifesto*, but Derrida goes even further to suggest that the case of "modern Europe" is analyzed, or "diagnosed" through a form of dramaturgy. The specter, for Derrida, is a kind of transient, phenomenological apparition of the "spirit," as he calls it, or one could say, in terms of the argu-ment in this work, the virtual. The specter is the virtual as "thing," or an avatar, of sorts (6–7). Rather than turning to the Gothic plays more historically proximate to the writing of the *Manifesto*, Derrida turns to *Hamlet* for the theatrical appearance of a ghost, often conflating the nature of Shakespeare's ghost with the referent of Marx's specter. Although the ghost in *Hamlet* offers Derrida the figure of the father, so redolent with deconstructive promise, he argues that Marx's specter is not a once-living return of the past. Rather, Marx's specter is a ghost of the future. This specter of communism that was haunting Europe in the mid-nineteenth century, was a specter of communism to come, rather than the apparition of a thing past, or gone (37).[18] The specter, a being-there and a not-being-there signified the notion of communism and the future of its effective practice. All the powers that feared it formed a "holy alliance" or "crusade" against it, in order to reassure themselves that it did not actually exist and more, that it would not. Marx's specter resembles an avatar of agency. It is an avatar of an ideology, or a knowledge-producing agency that manifests praxis in its very "being." Yet, shrouded in a fearsome aspect, a figure of violent promise, it inspires dread and fear in those who would defeat it, as the Gothic ghost frightened its audience.

Derrida continues to develop the notion of Marx's specter in terms of money and even alchemy: "As is well known, Marx always described money, and more precisely the monetary sign, in the figure of appearance or simulacrum, more exactly of the ghost." Now the specter of the *Manifeso* has ceased to signify communism, but one of the conditions that necessitates its rise: economic value abstracted from labor. Marx begins to resemble Goethe, in his performative setting for the apparition of paper money. Turning to *The Critique of Political Economy*, Derrida includes passages such as "The body of money is but a shadow [nur noch ein Schatten]." And futher, noting that when the state issues paper money, it is like "magic" as it transmutes paper into gold by its stamp. In Marx's own words; "It seems like magic when its stamp turns paper into gold [scheint jetzt durch die Magie seines Stempels Papier in Gold zu verwandeln" (quoted in Derrida 1994: 45). Thus, we can read the *Manifesto* as we read *Faust II*, in which the alchemical powers of paper money are run by Mephistopheles with the promise of future capitalist calamities.

Marx's "hoarder" is the Faust of his *The Critique of Political Economy*. He is, as Marx writes: "the holy ascetic seated at the top of a metal column. He wants commodities in a form in which they can always circulate and he therefore withdraws them from circulation. He adores exchange-value and he consequently refrains from exchange. The liquid form of wealth and its petrification, the elixir of life and the philosophers' stone are wildly mixed together like an alchemist's apparitions" (quoted in Derrida 46). Interestingly, Marx articulates the relationship to commodities through alchemical terms. Alchemy, here, is the mystification of money and the hoarder wanders through fantasies of commodity's delights, like Faust, wandering in the riches of his many, virtual realms. Moral values and economic values conflate in these theatricalizations. Spirits haunt the social, material world, garbed in religious and alchemical tropes, while dramatic actions are prescribed for their undoing. Faust and Gothic melodramas combine to represent moral and economic degradation. Later, in the *Manifesto*, Marx warns that "a society that has conjured up such gigantic means of production and exchange is like the sorcerer, who is no longer able to control the powers of the nether world whom he has called up by his spells (20)."

Thus, Gothic ghosts and flashes of alchemy haunt the new social science Marx and Engels practiced. Although stolidly grounded in causality and observation, the possibility of social transformation conjures the culturally-available figures of transmutation. The *Manifesto*, one of their more vernacular articulations of theory, dramatizes, through traditions of representing transformation, its promise and its threat.

The medium of invention: Edison and G.B. Shaw

If the science of alchemy was pressed into the service of making gold, or, in *Faust*, of producing paper money, "new" science inventions sought the paper money of the patent. During roughly the same period as Mme. Blavatsky's free performances of phenomena, others were racing to patent their inventions. In 1877, Edison filed a patent for the phonograph—the record of the human voice. In 1876, Bell's invention of the telephone created a public sensation at the Centennial Exposition in Philadelphia, but it was Edison who filed several patents on his elements within the telephone. It seems Edison could "own" the mode of transmission and archive of the voice.

In fact, Edison invented a new sort of lab, different from the labs being developed at MIT and the Smithsonian, which were dedicated to "pure" research. Edison made the decision not to pursue inventions unless there was a market demand, completely subordinating invention to commerce (Josephson 1959: 137–138). He referred to his lab as a factory, performing "the combined work of manufacturing and inventing" (quoted in Josephson 1959: 132–133). In his book, *The Formation of Modern Capitalism* (*Die Enstheung der Moderne Kapitalismus*), the eminent German economist Werner Sombart identifies Edison as *the* example of the capitalist scientist: "Mr. Edison was, perhaps, the outstanding example of a man who *made a business of invention itself*" [sic] (quoted in Josephson 1959: 137).

The interest in profit drove Edison toward public spectacle, unlike the "modest witness" of the "new" science. For example, he publicly performed the new apparatus of the phonograph as a character with whom he carried on a dialogue, asking the phonograph "Well, old phonograph, how are we getting on down there?" to which it would answer in metallic tones and scraps of several languages (Josephson 168). Edison was speaking to a data archiving apparatus and it was sounding back at him. However, Edison was not acting out the archival function of the machine, but the inscription process, which sounded out the noise of its articulated functions. As Friedrich Kittler hypothesizes in his associational, brilliant book, *Gramophone, Film, Typewriter*, "Ever since the invention of the phonograph, there has been writing without a subject" (1993: 44). Later, Kittler notes that "Thanks to the phonograph, science is for the first time in possession of a machine that records noises regardless of so-called meaning" (85). Edison, acting out a dialogue with the meaningless sounds of the apparatus evoked the sound of the subject-less reply. This effect of the new technology was received and, indeed, as we find in this example, promoted, as a kind of technological virtual. For what was that noise made to represent, set in the context of dialogue, if not the sound of a virtual order of things? Perhaps this sense of the other order also inspired Edison to join with Mme. Blavatsky in the practice of Theosophy.

Interestingly, George Bernard Shaw performed some of the earliest demonstrations of the phonograph. He was employed in the Edison London office from 1878–1880. In the preface to his novel about an inventor, *The Irrational Knot*, Shaw describes the new form of dedicated, industrial labor practiced by the Edison employees he had witnessed: "They worked with a ferocious energy. . . . they insisted upon being slave-driven . . . " (quoted in Josephson 1959: 153–154). One year after the publication of this book, Shaw penned the play *Major Barbara*. Perhaps the new form of labor devised by the industrialist Undershaft was based on this experience with Edison's "skilled proletariat." They were well-paid, grateful, and dedicated. As Shaw described his co-workers: "They adored Mr. Edison as the greatest man of all time in every possible department of science, art and philosophy . . . They were free-souled creatures . . . sensitive, cheerful, and profane" (quoted in Josephson 154–155). Shaw's portrayal of the worker's condition as one of free contentment and even pride, in *Major Barbara*, offers a striking comparison to his descriptions of Edison's own men. While this may appear to be only an interesting little tidbit of theater history, it is hopefully more.

Shaw's reflections portray a new kind of faith and dedication to the labor involved in industrial invention, its production and promotion. These workers do not belong to the brotherhood of the "modest witness," partaking in the privileged class and access of those who inhabit the research laboratories. Yet their almost clerical dedication and faith constitute the attitudes required to produce and promote the new link between science, invention and product orientation. Thus, a replication of social formations around the virtual, derived from the church, continue to inform these fraternities of science, and now industry. They would never induct a large, candy-eating, phlegmatic woman, who attacked such preserves with hyperbolic accusations of privilege and narrow self-interest—even if performed in the form of a distant, Hindu master.

As suggested above, Edison was well aware of the virtual aspects of his inventions and their resonances with esoteric practices. His hopes for some future developments move in the direction of mediumistic practices, but from the perspective of an inventor:

> I have been at work for some time building an apparatus to see if it is possible for personalities which have left this world to communicate with us. If this is ever accomplished, it will be accomplished, not by an occult, mysterious, or weird means, such as are employed by so-called mediums, but by scientific method. . . . I am engaged in the construction of one such apparatus now, and I hope to finish it before very many months pass.
>
> (Edison 1948: 233–234)

So Edison himself may have been inspired by the associations surrounding the disembodied voice to imagine an apparatus for communicating with those who have "crossed over." Kittler accounts for this conflation of the new inscriptive machines with the virtual as a result of the innovative mode of re-producing pitch. He reviews the break with Pythagoras's traditional notion of pitch determined by the length of the string. If Pythagoras's fractions, termed *logoi*, led to the structuring of a "harmony of the spheres," then, surely, he reasons, the new inscriptive mode of frequencies would lead the nineteenth century to re-imagine the relations pertaining to the structure of its world (Kittler 1993: 24). Certainly, as we will see, in the twentieth century, the recursive looping of tape inspired phenomenological and ontological claims by musicians and playwrights alike.

Edison's work provoked science-fiction-type sightings by some of his neighbors. They reported seeing meteoric lights blazing in the lab and mysterious figures gliding in the fields with lights and equipment, seemingly on secret, mystic missions (Josephson 1959: 170). The nature of his inventions incited scenarios of virtual illuminations and creatures in his neighbors—both the space and character of another world. They created little theaters of the alien to figure their imagination of just what his inventions might produce. These imagined scenarios marked the distance of his neighbors from the specialized skills of the laboratory. They attempted to stage for themselves the influential new modes of social communications that they could neither comprehend nor duplicate. Well, one might argue, images of saints work the same way, or, as early critics of rituals conjectured, so do rites. These are merely the commonplace explanations of all rites and images of faith, after all. Perhaps this is true, but it doesn't matter. Explaining the objective truth "behind" performance is not the goal of this exploration. What does appear, at this invocation, is the conjunction/disjunction of performances of the virtual in the convergence of scientific and mystic discourses. Even though the "new" science attempted to distance itself from the old sciences of rites, runes, and transmutations, it still sometimes understood itself and was understood in forms haunted by the liturgical and spiritualist discourses of the time. As new forms of communicating and archiving created technological, virtual spaces, the articulation of how they worked, or the performance of their functions often employed the more familiar tropes of the "other world."

Tortured alchemy meets Darwinism: Strindberg

Adrift in Paris in 1896, having severed marital relations with his wife and with the theater, the playwright August Strindberg set up his alchemical laboratory in his small apartment. He describes this turn to alchemy in his work *Inferno*:

> Night fell, the sulfur burned with hellish flames, and towards morning I observed the presence of carbon in what had hitherto been supposed a pure element, sulfur. And with this observation I supposed myself to have solved a great problem, destroyed the prevailing chemical theory, and won the only immortality allowed to mortal man. But by then, the skin of my hands, roasted by the intense heat of the fire, was peeling off . . . and the pain caused by the simple act of undressing was a constant reminder of the price I had paid for my triumph. Alone in my bed, still smelling of woman, I felt myself blessed and happy. Conscious of the purity of my soul, male virginity, I looked back on my married life as something unclean. . . .
>
> (1968: 121)

This complex string of thoughts reveals the equation within which alchemy resided for Strindberg: pain, self-torture, ambivalent feelings about his divorce and his wife, a desire for transcendent fame, and a contradictory evaluation of his own sexual identification. Strindberg offers a portrait of an alchemist at the turn of the century, in which the practice of alchemical, metallurgical experimentation is totally in league with self-reflexive psychological processes; serving not so much as a shared subjectivity across elements as an extension of psycho/physiological formations out into the social and ecological topography.

It seems ironic to find Strindberg, the playwright most traditionally known for bringing the deterministic model of naturalism to the stage, turning to transmutative alchemy. His play *Miss Julie* (1888) is traditionally understood as a classic example of naturalistic drama and his preface to the play as one of the central, discursive documents of the style. The naturalist school may be situated as an exact contradiction to principles of transmutation. Adopting aspects of Darwinism, the naturalists staged hereditary, environmental, and psychic processes as deterministic forces upon the formation of individual actions. Darwinian evolution is, after all, the long arm of determinism, extending back into the distant past and forward into the future. Sexual practices provided the naturalist playwrights with an exacting compound of the reproductive, hereditary, environmental and psychic processes with which to portray the deterministic workings within the human subject. Strindberg mixed this compound in *Miss Julie*. In his preface to the play, he insists that his "treatment has not been one-sidedly physiological nor obsessively psychological" mixing the two in an "abundance of circumstances" including "the influence her fiancé's suggestions had on her weak, degenerate brain," along with her period, her mother's bad instincts, her improper upbringing, the influence of flowers and the midsummer equinox, and the "boldness of the aroused man" (1998: 58).

Strindberg is careful to denote several principles of a desired staging for his play in the preface. As is his want, the innovations are mostly expressed in the negative: if the women actors didn't paint their faces so much, if the lighting didn't make them roll their eyes upward, if the set were simpler and without obviously phony devices, and if the auditorium were darker without intrusive orchestra lighting, the actors could better appear as a part of their environment, better able to reveal its determining effects. Jane Goodall relates these aims in naturalistic acting to the influence of Darwin, particularly, again, his *The Expressions of the Emotions in Man and Animals*. Darwin's interest in the control, or lack of control that humans exhibit in the small sets of muscles involved in facial expression informed the idea of how to best design the productions for an intimate play of emotions on the stage (2002: 174). Goodall notes that Darwin's estimation of good acting, in fact, rested upon the ability to voluntarily control the reflex patterns of expression (175). Goodall continues, however, that Darwin realized there must be "points of abdication," in which any simulation of emotions must "surrender to the animal energies of passion" (175). In other words, the actor swings between instinctual behavior and voluntary behavior, as

does the human species itself. Involuntary behavior was a register of evolution from animal instincts. Thus, the involuntary emotional reaction is determined by its genealogy. Citing Joseph Roach's *The Player's Passion*, Goodall refers to the acting techniques considered by the naturalists André Antoine and William Archer as "zoocentric," and "nurtured from the depths of animal nature" (177). Strindberg embraced Darwinian principles, but insisted upon a more complex surround of influence and change. Strindberg perceived his characters as existing in an "urgently hysterical age of transition" which incurs vacillation and fragmentation (1998: 59). While he recommends Darwinism to the theater, he also sees "modern" technologies and their accompanying ideologies as part of the influence, complicating the simple binarism of instinct and will (59–60).

If the nineteenth century began with Goethe's ode to the ascendancy of the code of the eternal feminine, Strindberg closed it with an adamant suppression of women's potentialities. In his preface, Strindberg deploys Darwinian evolutionary discourse to assert that woman, in fact, is a "stunted form, governed by the laws of propagation, [who] will always be stunted and can never catch up with the one in the lead [man]" (1998: 60). The woman who seeks equality is "degenerate" and is struggling, essentially, against nature itself, becoming a "half-woman" (61). Now, only degenerate men would couple with these degenerate women and when they do, they produce offspring who are "creatures of uncertain sex for whom life is a torment" (61). So, for Strindberg, gender informs heredity, the genetic results of copulation. Gender equality is pathological, both psychically and physiologically and, ultimately, tragic, as he scripts in *Miss Julie*.

Strindberg begins to discover these life principles expressed in pure code—alchemical/chemical figures. However, rather than finding the code on the top of a mountain peak, as Goethe had done, Strindberg found it in the alleyways of Paris. Walking through an alley, he sees a charcoal inscription on the whitewash of a building: "Seeing the letters F and S intertwined made me think of my wife's initials. She still loved me!—The next instant I was illumined by a vision of the chemical signs for iron (Fe) and sulfur (S) . . . displaying the secret of gold before my eyes" (1968: 151). At once, these chemical codes also signify his wife's initials; thus, the material and the subjective conflate into units of a psycho-chemico code. On another occasion, Strindberg sees a statue that reminds him of his wife. When he approaches, he finds two pieces of cardboard at the base with the numbers 207 and 28 on them. He realizes that these numbers are the code for the atomic weight of lead and silicon, supporting the direction of his current alchemical experiments. Soon, codes and images appear all around him. He sees faces, landscapes, animals, on walls, in the clouds, on dishes, on his pillow, almost everywhere. These signs continue to signify both alchemical principles and his wife. In his small laboratory set-up, his alchemical experiments begin to manifest his wife: "I had occasion to amalgamate some mercury, tin, sulfur, and ammonium chlorate . . . when I removed the mixture the cardboard had a face imprinted upon it exactly like my wife's . . . " (184). Perhaps it is not totally surprising to discover that, for a determinist, transmutations would finally inspire fear and horror. Strindberg cycled down through these visions to what is termed a "mental breakdown." His alchemy essentially combined his fear and loathing for women with a sense that the transmutation of metals participated in, what he termed, a "psychology of sulphur . . . " (144). Strindberg descended into a sulphurous hell, where the lifeline of his deterministic model was shattered by proliferating images of transmutative change.

Strindberg was isolated during this time, shunning the company of others and retreating into his small, domestic, alchemical lab. Like Faust, he became a victim of his private, removed illusions. For Strindberg, the virtual did not open out into other realms, as it did for Faust, but was invasive, like a virus. Experimenting with transmutating change, in an age of Darwin, led him to a complete break-down with the social and with perception itself. As Strindberg began to grasp for moral straws to save himself from his terror, he embraced the mystic writings of Swedenborg and finally, Christianity. Yet, while he dabbled in Swedenborgian mysticism, Strindberg had nothing but contempt for Mme. Blavatsky and her movement. In a letter to his friend, Torsten Hedlund, he characterized Mme. Blavatsky as a "great self-deceiver who, with all the suggestive power her sex exercises on the other sex, had succeeded in creating the illusion that she was an exceptionally profound mind" (Strindberg. 1968: 185–186, n. 28). Strindberg's mad mechanism and hyper-misogyny could not entertain the idea of a movement led by the ideas of a woman, even if it embraced some of the same mystic principles in which he found comfort. As in *Faust*, the combination of women and alchemy seemed to lead only to damnation.

These two figures, Mme. Blavatsky and Strindberg figure the bipolar agon of the "new" science and grassroots performances of a scientific imaginary in the nineteenth century. As science receded into specialist discourses and secured laboratories, other practices were invented to perform its principles, either as protagonists or antagonists. The collusion of science with manufacturing, the increasing emphasis on commodities developed from research, and the wealth these products offered to investors drove these relatively poor practitioners into inventions of discovery that promised them access to other virtual realms of power. Strindberg, without funds or opportunities in the theater, sought to find power and recognition through alchemy. At the same time, it shored up his need to feel superior to women—particularly his ex-wife. Mme. Blavatsky, a poor, Russian immigrant, wielded international power and influence through her spiritualist performances. Whereas Strindberg saw himself as a protagonist of science, Mme. Blavatsky fashioned herself into its antagonist. Rather than relegate these two practitioners to the traditional reception of their practices as either fakery, or madness, they can be perceived as in dialogue with the rise of science and theater—the apparati of iteration—in an attempt to retain, somehow, the promise of transmutation, either as a celebration of it, as in Mme. Blavatsky's case, or the effects of its horror, as with Strindberg.

A century of science

The curtain rises on the final act. Deemed by some as the "century of science," the twentieth century launched new scientific discoveries, theories, and inventions that exceeded all the centuries before. The century framed the formation of a "scientific imaginary," in which the discourses and discoveries of scientific research came to dominate the imagined realms of social and cultural organization. This scientific imaginary was articulated through many of the major tropes this book has sought to trace. Peopled by avatars, who dwelt in new, virtual domains, these imagined forms of embodiment managed various modes of exchange, from transformation to the transference of funds. The century began with the dominance of machines, technologies proceeding from the nineteenth-century age of invention. As we will see, the early imaginary was a machinic one. However, the invention of electronic devices and, finally, "smart" machines, that mix the machinic with a sense of porosity, or fields, will mark a major shift in the imaginary in the later years of the century.

The greater influence of science was due, in part, to a shift in its own basic paradigm of time and space, the ruling framework of the scientific imaginary. The science of the "other" Newton, not the alchemist we reviewed earlier, but the discoverer of gravity, had permeated the understanding of time and space up until Einstein's theory of relativity, first published in 1907. There, Einstein drastically revised Newton's theory of gravity, altering, at base, the relationship between time and space, energy and matter. His theory of relativity troubled the stable division between time and space, creating, instead, a third term—space-time. Space-time is not a stable, empty frame, but one that is curved, or "warped" by the distribution of mass and energy within it (Hawking 2005: 38). Abandoning the standard rule of three dimensions, Einstein introduced space-time as a fourth dimension. Relativity revolutionized all applications proceeding from this new paradigm. For example, the great geometries that ruled the nineteenth century map-makers were altered, as straight lines became curved. Einstein's famous metaphor for these relations, the elevator in empty space, illustrated that there is really no "up," no "down" in space (an image that will appear later in Robert Wilson's staging of Philip Glass's *Einstein on the Beach*). If it moves with constant acceleration, you would feel a pull, which is something like gravity,

BUT you would feel the same pull if it were not moving, remaining at rest in a uniform gravitational field. This "equivalence" also alters time, which can be slower and faster, depending upon these factors. Thus, there is no absolute measure of either time or space, but only an interdependent, dynamic relationship.[1]

As these discoveries began to permeate the cultural imaginary, new forms of composition appear in the arts, as if somehow mimetically reproducing the new paradigm of the space-time continuum. Indeed, abstraction, as it was termed, will become a new, contested form of composition, proceeding from the reception of the scientific imaginary. In theater, a new structuring of the mise en scène mimicked the schematic designs of engineering in the early part of the century, while the notion of field theory influenced composition in the later decades. Artistic replications of the research uses of "relativity," "uncertainty," and "field theory" guided breaks with old narrative structures, the "engines" of nineteenth-century modalities. Heisenberg's principle of "uncertainty" was actually staged as descriptive of his own historical situation in *Copenhagen*, and "relativity" became a byword of ethical determinations.

Unfortunately, the new paradigm also led to new modes of weaponry. Transformation, once the alchemical realm of mercury, took on the processual forms of fission and fusion. Anxieties surrounding the development of the atomic bomb haunted the mid-century. Transmutation was raised to the level of a global power of destruction as well as sustenance. The potential destruction of the entire planet fueled mid-century scenarios of the fear of transformation, such as alien abductions, while strategies of survival led to the construction biospheres.

In the late twentieth century, mapping, the great Enlightenment adventure of the nineteenth century, although disrupted by the notion of "curved" space, took an immediate and even individual form in global positioning systems (GPS). The omniscient view of the surveyor ascended into satellites circling the globe. On the one hand, the GPS created a global-positioning cyclorama of surveillance, upon which the sites and figures of citizens appeared before "homeland security" spectators; on the other, performances in these spaces created new entertainment, such as "geocaching," or finding hidden treasures through clues in the GPS.

Money itself became literally virtual—its paper/metal body uploaded to somewhere behind the flickering screens of ATMs and computers. Virtual forms of money enabled fast-moving capital investment across national boundaries and currencies, untying from precious metals and "floating" financial value through rapid trading maneuvers. The rights to intellectual property became the focus of individual and national debate, as digital duplicating and downloading tested the limits of ownership.

The alchemical tradition of emblematic discourse and the numerical discourse of the "new" science conjoined to form a proliferation of codes and a cultural obsession with cryptography, from the very basis of physiological composition in DNA to critical theories concerning attributes of gender and "race," known as cultural coding. While national agencies struggled to decode and encode their instructions to agents, grassroots performances of encoding included code rings in cereal boxes and best-selling novels, such as *The Da Vinci Code* to inspire pilgrimages to art museums and religious sites.

The ascendancy of the human subject continued to combine with new technologies to create earth-threatening levels of pollution, endangering the very survival of all species. Not only did humans lock themselves into biospheres in order to ensure their own mastery of nature, but they also reveled in a new space, apart from "nature" called cyberspace, or Virtual Reality. Performances within this new space sought to demarcate its transcendent, simulated technospace of ascendancy from the "real." Cyber-space was immediately inhabited by a privileged, virtual class, as a secure and profitable realm for business and entertainment. On the one hand, what was once imagined as a spiritual realm, some integral site of vitalist, human difference, was interwoven into corporate networks of software and electronic circuitry; on the other, traditional religious beliefs sought to retain their hold on the definition of virtual space, coming into sometimes violent conflict with the modernist ideologies that supported the transnational, corporate spread of the technological virtual.

Spiritual practices both fractured into innumerable cults and amalgamated with nations into massive movements of the traditional faiths. In the late twentieth century, and into the twenty-first, debates still raged over Darwin's theories, defining one of the contested borders between science and the spirit. At the same time, a New Age dawned in the spiritual imaginary, performing the spiritual affect of new technologies, including the healing, spiritual harmonics of electronic music, and the practice of channeling avatars. On the darker side, the Faustian paradigm continued to inform both real-life and theatrical conflicts concerning the relationship between the human subject and the virtual realms. Avatars appeared through channelers and on the internet.

Moreover, performance itself became an operative term for the interactive relationship emerging between the technological and the social. The elements of performance, from characterization to the mise en scène became useful in the expression of scientific affect. Individual scientists were fashioned as characters of human intelligence and productivity. Images of Einstein were reproduced on postage stamps, T-shirts, and posters and the biography of the scientist stood in for the social and moral dilemmas surrounding the discoveries. Einstein, Galileo, and Darwin literally took the stage at various crisis points in the scientific imaginary to figure the social inter-face with the rational processes of scientific proof and the ethical dimensions of invention. Moreover, new technologies of staging provided high levels of special effects, literally staging a spectacle of new technologies, in rock concerts, Broadway musicals, and even Las Vegas shows.

As the technological surround increasingly enclosed and perforated the postindustrial subject and the interactive relations of the social and the technological became more ubiquitous, the notion of performance came to represent both the mode of participation in the digital realm and an oppositional embodiment of the "live." The construction of the online avatar as actor in cyberspace offered a navigational device that imagined its functions within the electronic realm as a performance. In contrast, the notion of "live" performance came to represent an urgent, rhetorical contradiction to both the archival functions of film and television and to the mediatization of the public sphere. Thus, the forms and potentialities of performance and science melded in several ways: performance created a social interface for the technological, and scientific discourses offered new forms and apparati of proximities, dependencies, and spatialities.

SCENE ONE: THE EARLY YEARS

The early years of the century were still marked by anxieties and hopes surrounding the proliferation of machines. New performance mechanics and narratives arose around the formation of the machinic consciousness. Mark Seltzer terms the anxieties of the machinic as "melodramas of uncertain agency," inspiring performances of "the machinelikeness of persons and the personation of machines (1992: 18)." Early plays by the Expressionists and Futurists both condemned and celebrated the machine and the machine-like. Robots on stage, as in *R.U.R* and *Sexual Electricity* promise either a form of free labor, or the violent displacement of human existence. Taylorism, the schematic organization of factory work and workers as machine-like, produced social nightmares, as in the plays *Machinal* and *The Adding Machine*. Later, mid-century grassroots performances of UFO sightings and alien abductions brought powerful machines into contact with domestic settings, creating scenarios of invasion, on the one hand, and the invention of empowered interstellar personae, on the other. By the end of the century, prostheses and software developments created a cyborg imaginary that troubled the sure boundaries between human and machine, with online avatars such as Lara Croft, replicating themselves in "live" actresses.

The century began with three basic approaches to staging science and new technologies: the Expressionist depiction of scientific developments as oppressive and authoritarian; the Futurists' ecstatic embrace of technological power as enabling and liberating, and the Soviet address to the scientist rather than the technology, testing his goals in terms of the sustenance of the social. These modes of representing science continued to inform the cultural imaginary throughout the twentieth century.

Central to each is a focus on the production of commodities that derive from scientific research. The machines invented in the late nineteenth century are now shown to dominate the economic and social realms. Some plays focus on the laborer at the machine: stenographers and clerks, garment workers, and those responsible for the production line. Others focus on the factory itself, where the machines demand constant tending. The need for more labor-intensive machines drives the growth of capital into its final form: the military-industrial complex. Here, the character of the Engineer emerges as the interface between science and development. He is depicted as power-hungry in the Expressionist plays, and, although tempted, finally responsive to the collective in the Soviet ones. He is the figure who creates the designs that result from research work. He can choose to use them for profit or for sustenance.

Expressionist schematics

Expressionist plays staged the psychic register of science and its visual culture as a dark, twisted, oppressive field that contained and enslaved the human subject. German Expressionist stage design deployed a twisted geometry to depict this force field of oppression. Based on the abstraction of the painted line and the geometric plane, the sets installed a composition of slashing diagonals and colliding planes as the representation of the force field that contained human action. Often rendered in the strict polarity of black and white, this agonized geometry disallowed any fanciful flourish, or organic referent to grace its intersections. Even when the scenes revealed a mimetic impulse, the abstracted nature of the lines suggested that the sites were twisted by the *codes* of oppressive social, psychic, and scientific practices. In other words, the codes could be made visual. The schematic of the codes determined the actions of the human subject, or, more precisely, the human object within them. The referents of this scenic geometry, as in geometry itself, were the postulates of authority that determined their figures. As geometric figures proceed from the authority of theorems that organize space through laws governing straight lines and angles, the Expressionist set offered a rendering of the unseen force field of authority which prescribed the angles of visibility and of social intercourse.

The schematic set participated in the larger visual culture that science and invention were creating. With the proliferation of machines came the proliferation of plans, designs, diagrams, and charts. Not only were schematics the source of machines, but they were also their results, shaping information into diagrams. The geometric lines of the Expressionist set theatricalize this mode of representation, putting the schematic into the service of the psychic and the social. Yet schematics were only the more accessible and active discourse of science. The increasing abstraction of scientific discourses that operated as authoritative codes that affected the subject but were inaccessible to "him" also inspired the Expressionist geometry of authority. The diagram the set offered was an authoritarian one, determining what played within it. While the codes were depicted as oppressive, the revelation of them through this design was considered revolutionary and liberating. The ability to actually make the operations of these codes visible was, literally, a form of revelation. Thus, the Expressionist set was established as counter-cultural—a scenic critique of dominant codes.

Robert Wiene's *The Cabinet of Dr. Caligari* (1919) provides a film archive for the Expressionist mise en scène. The sets in *Caligari* were designed by three artists who had been part of the leading Expressionist painting school known as *Der Sturm:* Walter Reimann, Hermann Warm, and Walter Röhrig. Painted tableaux with flattened perspective represent living spaces, streets, and workspaces as colliding planes and lines. They demonstrate the violent effect of jagged diagonal lines converging in small, claustrophobic locales. The actors share in the maelstrom of the codes, wearing costumes with competing geometric designs.

At the conclusion of the film's story, the nightmare of human relations is laid at the feet of Dr. Caligari, who is revealed to be the director of a mental hospital. The mental institution, as it was once termed, operates as the site of collusion between investigative science and the enforcement of normative social behavior. The newer science of the mind performs the scientific surround that has thoroughly penetrated the human subject, even into the deepest reserves of the subconscious. In the institution, scientific observation has become surveillance, and the scientist in a lab coat is represented by the authoritarian psychiatrist, Dr. Caligari.

The play *Job* (1917) by the painter and graphic artist Oskar Kokoschka offers a Faustian version of the Expressionist portrait of the psychiatrist. The psychiatrist first appears to Job as a poodle, as did Mephistopheles in Goethe's *Faust*. The association, although satirical, is clear—the psychiatrist tempts the mind into a false, contorted state. The psychiatrist spies through a keyhole at Job's wife, a take-off on psychiatric observation. He concludes his study of her through his discovery of the "Erotococcus," a bacillus of sexuality that composes her core. He then becomes infected by this bacillus, obsessively tied to the wife. In other

Figure 5 Dr. Caligari

words, the play of scientific terminology and the science of the mind infects all those who participate in its surround with a literally twisted (Job cannot straighten out) and obsessive need to spy, diagnose, and infect.

These examples illustrate how the Expressionist mise en scène of repressive codes, together with characterizations of scientists as scientists of the mind, made the human actor a porous site, written on by the codes in costume and make-up, corporeally twisted by them, and psychically tortured through their application.

Between typewriter and electric chair: Machinal

Edison's success in tying the scientific laboratory to its commercial products conflated, in the popular reception, science with the machine. Machines, in industry and in daily life, became the most visible effects of scientific research. Their growing numbers signaled the perforation of the social and cultural realms by scientific development, inspiring anxieties concerning their assimilation of human functions. At the same time, the Taylorist organization of labor, which treated human functions as if machinic, inspired the sense that industrial labor made men into machines.

Sophie Treadwell's American Expressionist play *Machinal* (1928) stages the story of a rather innocent young stenographer who is eventually destroyed by the hierarchies and machine-like relations of the office. The title *Machinal* empha-sizes the permeation by machine into the social and individual psyche. Treadwell's dialog imitates the rhythm of the machines, often described as tele-graphic. The adjective "telegraphic" used to describe the curt, spliced dialogue is an apt one, in its invocation of the mechanical transmission of communication.[2] As Marshall McLuhan summarized many decades later, the medium indeed became the message. Take, for example, the opening scene. Stage directions indi-cate that the sound of machines open the scene and accompany all of the dialog, rendering a joint production of staccato rhythms. The characters are identified by their functions and their dialogue is composed of the numeric, machinic discourse appropriate to their function. The adding clerk, as we will see in another play, speaks in numbers. The stenographer in the language of another—one who has dictated language to her.

> ADDING CLERK: (*in the monotonous voice of his monotonous thoughts; at his adding machine*) 2490,28,76,123,36842,1,¼,37,804,23,½,982.
> FILING CLERK: (*in the same way—at his filing desk*) Accounts—A. Bonds—B. Contracts—C. Data—D. Earnings—E.
> STENOGRAPHER: (*in the same way—left*) Dear Sir—in your letter—recent date—will state—

The tone of voice is that of the machine—monotonous and regular. None of the traditions of the grammatical structure of ideas is incorporated into these lines.

The repeated dashes indicate a breakdown in continuity and logic. The scene continues, as the office workers discuss the young woman, using this same type and rhythm of language to describe social relations:

> STENOGRAPHER: She's late again, huh?
> TELEPHONE GIRL: Out with her sweetie last night, huh?
> FILING CLERK: Hot dog.
> ADDING CLERK: She ain't got a sweetie.
> STENOGRAPHER: How do you know?
> ADDING CLERK: I know.
> FILING CLERK: Hot dog.
> ADDING CLERK: She lives alone with her mother.
> TELEPHONE GIRL: Spring 1876? Hello—Spring 1876. . . .
> STENOGRAPHER: Director's semi-annual report card.
> FILING CLERK: Shipments—Sales—Schedules—S.
>
> (Treadwell 1993: 2–3)

The discussion of human relations is fragmented by the language of function. The repetitive "hot dog" foregrounds the displacement of insight and analysis by a machine-like iteration of empty idioms.

The narrative line of Treadwell's play leads from the machinic social space of the office to the ultimate machine of discipline and punishment—the electric chair. The Young Woman, the stenographer who takes dictation from her boss, later kills him for his assimilation of her sexual and emotional resources. In the final scenes of the play, she is strapped to the electric chair, in complete bondage to the machine of social punishment made possible by new applications of electricity. The function of the new machine is at issue to the observers: FIRST REPORTER: Suppose the machine shouldn't work! SECOND REPORTER: It'll work!—It always works! (Treadwell 1993: 82) New inventions and their large-scale production thus determine this young woman's labor conditions, her subjectivity, and, finally, her death. Treadwell stages a frightening, haunting image of the "machinal" social, concluding with the death machine.

Treadwell based her play on the case of an actual woman, Ruth Snyder. Snyder was a telephone operator, rather than a stenographer, who plotted, in a more cold-blooded fashion, the killing of her husband. Her story inspired both *Machinal* and *Double Indemnity*. Snyder was the second woman to be executed in the electric chair. Her execution was actually photographed by Thomas Howard, a photographer for the *New York Daily News*. Howard strapped a small camera onto his ankle and, at the moment of execution, crossed his legs and captured the grisly scene on camera. He published it the next day. This image, burned into the memory of thousands of readers, was later staged by Treadwell.

It was Edison who first demonstrated the effectiveness of electrocution in 1887, publicly killing multiple cats and dogs by luring them onto a metal plate wired to a 1000 volt AC generator. Presumably, the vitalism of other animals has

Figure 6 Ruth Snyder execution. Photograph: Tom Howard
(http://www2.dailynewspix.com)

less value than that of the human subject. As we have seen, Edison was the great showman of invention, creating dramatic demonstrations of the applications of his laboratories. The newspapers fully described this gruesome event for their readers. Following the publicity around the executions, there was even a run on copper wire in the commodities market. After experimenting on various dogs and finally a horse, Edison, however, did not make a "killing" in the execution market. Others discovered that an alternating AC/DC current might better serve the purpose of execution. In fact, experiments in this direction led to the discovery of the alternating current, which put Westinghouse on its feet as a major manufacturer of domestic devices. So, the market and the manufacturers profited greatly by experiments in electrocution, while others were literally sacrificed to them. The Young Woman stenographer in *Machinal*, like so many women from the late-nineteenth through the first half of the twentieth century, was trapped by machines: in her case, between the typewriter and the electric chair.

Vampiric typewriters

In *Dracula's Legacy* (*Draculas Vermächtnis*), Friedrich Kittler wittily deploys the elements in Bram Stoker's novel *Dracula* to image the new relations between women and the machinic technology of typewriters.[3] For Kittler, *Dracula* illustrates the anxieties, possibilities, and repressive strategies that accompany women's emerging role in the use of this new technology as a Gothic horror story. In the novel, Mina Murray is a stenographer who knows the ways of the typewriter. Mina figures the secretaries who will transcribe patriarchal discourse throughout much of the century, transforming the individual writing or speaking of men into an objective script that can bind together the transactions of business and nation.[4] The female secretary will enter the office, the work force, as an adjunct of men, in an unequal relation to their pay, social standing, and salary.

Mina operates what Kittler, in a clever German agglutinate, terms the "discoursemachineweapon" (*Diskursmaschinengewehr*), the Remington typewriter, developed and capitalized by the company that made guns for the Civil War (1993: 29). This "discoursemachineweapon," in itself agglutinates the functions of weapon with machine with the deployment of language. Yet, while it agglutinates, it also disarticulates the traditional links among hand, eye, and letter that writing represents. The push of a key created a letter in a place distant from the hand. As Mark Seltzer argues, in *Bodies and Machines*, "these dislocations radicalize a logic of standardization and a logic of prosthesis. . . . "(1992: 10). In the form letter, the major assignment of stenographers, writing becomes standardized and its transmission machinic. While women enable the transmission of the discourse, they do not create it. They are in the province of the vampire, who leeches both authorship and writing from them.

Kittler explicates the cultural location of stenography through a discussion of Jacques Lacan's seminars on the psychoanalytic critique. Lacan's oft-cited notion of woman as "Lack" was originally delivered as part of his seminars, which were recorded, and later transcribed off tape. Kittler ironizes the transmission of the psychoanalytic lectures about women's desire, or "lack" as transcribed by the husband of his daughter (Jacques-Alain Miller), whom Kittler refers to as the *Tochtermann*, both his daughter's man and his daughter-man (1992: 12). The process of typing these psychoanalytic insights, then, was dependent upon the skill of the stenographer, a role associated with women, and by a man associated with Lacan through his daughter. "Woman" is Other, then, as Lacan would have it, not only in the discourse, but also in its transmission—even in the transmission of the theory itself. "She," or her gendered function provides the link between the iterative technology of tape and the machinic inscription of the oral.

Further along these same lines of thought, Mark Seltzer, in *Bodies and Machines*, argues that dictation is considered a transparent, or somehow immaterial form of writing between speech and page, producing a form of disembodiment (1992: 195). The writing represents he who dictated. The stenographer is made surplus to the referents in the communication. It follows, then, that secretaries should be seen and not heard, attractive and silent. In *Machinal*, the surplus embodiment of the secretary, the Young Woman, is figured through her sexuality, which is likewise appropriated by her boss.

Mina, the stenographer, is proximate to the vampiric, then, by virtue of her labor. Kittler sets the typewriter within a Gothic scene of horror, where the oppressed worker is portrayed in the Expressionist mode, preyed upon by the vampiric forces of industry and dominant discourse.

Revue-ing sewing machines: Pins and Needles

In its earliest years, the role of stenographer was actually a desirable form of employment for women. She was a skilled worker, who worked in offices, with fairly regular hours. The more oppressive conditions for women who operated machines were found in relation to the sewing machine. Although there is no Expressionist play about these conditions, the haunting images of hundreds of garment workers toiling in sweatshops resembled the conditions of the workers in *Machinal*. Their lives were oppressed by labor at the machines. Their conditions were unsafe, their pay low, their labor endless, repetitive, and unfulfilling.

The first patent for the sewing machine was issued to Isaac Singer in the 1850s, providing the base for the Singer Manufacturing Company. By 1890, Singer had produced 9 million sewing machines. Many of these machines were operated in sweatshops in tenement workshops. In 1900, workers formed the International Ladies' Garment Workers' Union (ILGWU) to organize against low wages and unsafe working conditions. A labor union organized by and for women was unique in its protections, emphasizing the gendered practices around the operation of these machines. In November 1909, ILGWU organized the first garment workers' strike, known as "The Great Revolt." The protest brought 60,000 New York City garment workers to the streets to fight for their rights. Women and children on the picket lines were beaten or fired at by the police. Yet ILGWU prevailed, winning wage and hour standards and impartial arbitration of disputes. In 1910, the "Uprising of the 20,000" among women garment workers in New York led to a "protocols of peace" that was negotiated among the workers and their bosses.

In spite of these advances, the image of the sweatshop, as these workshops became known, was fixed forever in the public mind on March 25, 1911. On that day, a fire broke out on the 8th floor of the Asch Building in Manhattan, which housed the Triangle Shirtwaist Co., which made women's clothing. The company employed some 500 workers, most of them women, most of them immigrants from Southern and Eastern Europe, most of them between the ages of 15 and 25. They worked upwards of 50 hours a week, cutting and sewing fabric to make a popular shirtwaist style of blouses. 125 young women were killed in the fire. Investigations revealed that there was only one fire escape in the building, so women were forced to leap to their deaths, ten stories below. The ILGWU soon began more militantly negotiating for safe workplace environments.

Around that time, the ILGWU was using the Princess Theatre as a meeting hall. Several members talked the union into sponsoring an inexpensive revue about the garment trade that would use only two pianos in the pit and a cast made up of ILGWU union members. The workers thus collectively created their own set of performances about their lives. Their actual job conditions may have been as oppressive and frightening as an Expressionist play, but the form their theatrical imagination took was one of humor and satire. Appropriately named *Pins and Needles* (1936), the revue included skits by various authors that spoofed everything from Fascist European dictators, to "Lessons in Etiquette," to bigotry in the Daughters of the American Revolution (DAR), an organization for women who could claim bloodlines back to the American Revolution. Some of the leading artists of the time joined the project, including Marc Blitzstein, author of *The Cradle Will Rock*, who composed a skit on the Federal Theater Project, and the composer-lyricist Harold Rome, including his song "Sing Me a Song of Social Significance."

Because of their jobs, rehearsals had to be held at night and on weekends, and performances could only be set on Fridays and Saturdays. The show ran on and off for four years, enjoying 1,108 performances. In other words, it was a hit. The revue kept changing, deleting some numbers and adding others. In 1939, the skit "Bertha, the Sewing Machine Girl," was added with the dance by the first African American woman to become a noted dancer and a choreographer, Katherine Dunham.[5] The success of the show illustrates the central role this machinic labor played in the social environment of New York.

In spite of the strength and talent of the ILGWU at the beginning of the twentieth century, the large-scale deployment of sewing machine sweatshops continued to oppress immigrant women in the U.S. throughout the twentieth century, as well as outsourcing its exploitive conditions into other countries in order to take advantage of cheap labor there. For example, Guess Jeans, once one of the largest apparel manufacturers in the U.S., moved 75 percent of their production to Tehuacan, Mexico in 1998, where their wages range from $25 to $50 for a forty-eight to sixty-hour work week, with forced (unpaid) overtime.

Within the U.S., modern-day slavery was practiced in one of the hidden sweatshops. In August 1995, inspectors of the California Department of Industrial Relations and the U.S. Department of Labor arrived at a small apartment complex in El Monte, California, near Los Angeles. They discovered that inside the complex, surrounded by razor wire, was a garment factory. Locked inside the factory were 72 Thai workers, mostly women and mostly illegal immigrants. The workers told the officials that they worked up to 20 hours a day, 7 days a week, for 70¢ an hour. When not working, they slept ten to a small room. They were prevented from leaving, they said, by locked gates, barbed wire, threats of physical punishment, and their status as illegal aliens.

These oppressive labor practices hold women to poor conditions for luxury clothing lines, from designer jeans to high-end sportswear. Thus, the profit margin is very high for the businesses employing them. To protest the marketing of these products, women in Athens performed a "sew-in" near the Acropolis during the time of the 2004 Olympic Games. A form of performance art, the production used an Expressionist sense of work at the machines. Wearing white, "faceless" masks, indicating the "faceless" identities of the thousands of women exploited by these practices, the performers sat at rows of sewing machines, with the Acropolis in the background. The familiar image of "high" culture and the so-called democratic origins for the European tradition served as a background for the performance of the faceless labor women garment workers are forced to endure.

The Adding Machine

The title of the play *The Adding Machine* (1923) suggests that the machine, not its operator is the subject of the play. Elmer Rice, an American Expressionist playwright of the period, named his protagonist Mr. Zero. His name, only an arithmetical symbol, suggests both his function and his social status. The quantification of his status, its arithmetical sign, further indicates the proliferation of social discourses that derived their vocabulary from the scientific or numerical ones at play in the new machinic surround. Mr. Zero is defined by the vocabulary of his machine. The stage picture focuses on a single man at the machine, with its paper spilling out across the stage. The stage directions note that the tape from the machine should cover the walls and doors, creating the effect of a suffocating environment, from which Mr. Zero cannot escape. After putting in 25 years of labor, pushing the buttons on the machine that adds up millions of sums of investment, cost, and profit, Mr. Zero learns that he will lose his job to a machine. He has become literally only a middle-man between machines. In a rage, he murders his boss and is executed. In heaven, he learns his next life on earth will be as a mere waste product.

William Burroughs, the grandfather of the novelist by that name, patented the adding machine in the late nineteenth century, securing his fortune. By 1900, over a million machines had been sold and the first two decades of the twentieth century witnessed exponential growth in the use of the machine in banks and major businesses. Rice's play ironizes the gap between the mountain of figures, representing vast amounts of money and the status of the operator, Mr. Zero, whose personal value is so low his next life will be as a waste product. The play is prescient in its staging of a future life as waste, for, as we will see, waste, or trash, human, industrial, and nuclear will become an international issue, ever-growing and contaminating natural sites. To think back to the operator of an adding machine as the prior incarnation of waste draws an interesting through-line across the century.

Mr. Zero works the number machine, in contrast to the feminized labor of the discourse machine, or typewriter. He runs the numbers, the symbols of money, in an isolated environment like a vault, in contrast to the stenographer in the office pool. The access to and production of numerical discourse is masculinized. Mr. Zero's position in the social order is not fixed by his sexuality, as is the Young Woman's in *Machinal*, or his immigrant status, as in *Pins and Needles*, but by his economic value—zero. Gendered characteristics became attached to the varieties of work at the machines and their resulting social practices, as well as to the operations of science and its fraternities in the labs.

These plays that focus on machines notably do not depict them as tools used to better commerce or communication. They focus on the effects on the laborers who run them rather than the successes of the inventor, or industrialist who profits from them. The science of experimentation and research is not even imaginable in the dramatic world of these plays—only the consequences of their products in the lives of the people who tend the machines.

Animating the machines: the robot

Karel Čapek's *R.U.R.* (*Rossum's Universal Robots*, 1920) is arguably the first play to stage robots. It is even credited by some with inventing the term "robot." Čapek sets the play in a factory. In the background, multiple factories can be seen extending into the distance. Industrial production extends across the entire visible topography. The walls are covered with shipping charts and a huge tape machine that prints stock exchange returns stands in the corner. The setting is the economic center of the factory, where costs, profits, and the shipments of goods are literally accounted. The heart of this factory, then, is not its developmental laboratory, nor its production line, but its economics.

The story of the invention of the robot is narrated near the beginning of the play. Apparently, the findings of an old, Faust-like chemist in search of the Homunculus actually led to its invention. As the character Harry Domain describes it: "It was in the year 1922 that the old Rossum, the great physiologist. . . . attempted by chemical synthesis to imitate the living matter known as protoplasm, until he suddenly discovered a substance which behaved exactly like living matter, although its chemical composition was different . . . " (Čapek 1961: 5). It seems old Rossum sought to realize the promise of Goethe's virtual lab in *Faust*, where the Homunculus was revealed. His quest to isolate and replicate the primary element of life is surely a forerunner of DNA research, yet it results, finally in simulation rather than replication. The description of the quest is described in evolutionary, Darwinian terms: "Imagine him sitting over a test-tube and thinking how the whole tree of life would grow from it, how all animals would proceed from it, beginning with some sort of beetle and ending with man himself . . . " (Čapek 1961: 6). Simulated protoplasm, then, will be able to produce a genealogy of creatures like the human, though not human. It is this promise of a genealogy that will define the conclusion of the play.

In this play, Čapek imagined a creature that will haunt the science fiction imaginary of the twentieth century—the Android. The scientific breach of the boundaries of life and death and the ability to create life in a test tube will inspire fantasies, actual experiments, and social debates for decades to come. Although Goethe had staged this same achievement one hundred years earlier, his context, alchemical and strictly virtual, ultimately condemned the Homunculus as one who was ultimately unable to materialize. He remained strictly within the virtual realm. Čapek stages a factory of simulation, where androids, or robots, actually labor, speak, and interrelate. However, as the play reveals, the young Rossum, who inherited this android project, abandoned the research into a protoplasmic substitute. As an engineer, he exchanged the chemical, physiological project for an industrial, engineering one. He manufactured workers who could be produced relatively cheaply and who would have no other desire but to work. His factory, R.U.R., could supply the enormous, ceaselessly-working labor force required for the new compound of industrialization and invention.

Čapek represents the mechanical displacement of the more vitalist experiments as the transformation of a research scientist into a profit-hungry engineer. It's as if scientific research is still somehow engaged with the living and the mutable, in the experiments of the old Rossum, while engineering partakes solely in the economics-driven application of scientific principles to the material and the social. The Engineer will develop into a character that is so removed from change and emotion that he will become the apex of authoritarian power. Both he and his product will ultimately seek dominion over human existence.

Čapek also introduces characters who represent a more liberal response to the working conditions of the androids. They unsuccessfully appeal to management to better the plight of the robotic workers. Management, however, begins to manufacture robots for governments who would deploy them as soldiers, so their conditions become even more tightly controlled. Here, we can observe similarities between *R.U.R.* and Kaiser's *Gas*. Both plays image the consolidation of industry and state in the military-industrial compound. In this play, however, the weapon is in the form of the laborer rather than a chemical substance. The military-industrial compound produces a compound of man and machine. The robots thus become the ways and means of national competition and violence. They are the animated products on the market that compete for their own success and provide their own security. Once they become more sophisticated in their functions, the machines revolt. Soon, uprisings of the robots take place around the world, killing thousands of humans.

Finally, the robots exterminate all of humankind, with the exception of one worker. The problem: the robots cannot reproduce. Although they were made with signs of sexual difference, their design was intended only to fill gender-specific labor roles. It's a deep irony that Čapek constructs, here, with sexual difference and gender fit only for specific roles in labor. Reproductive sex, the other potential of a sex/gender assignment is configured, by the manufacturers, as surplus. So, it seems there will be neither humans nor robots in the future. But wait: the ending of the play sets up a kind of android Adam and Eve, who show signs of love and desire, thus presumably capable of reproduction. The heteronormative solution to the play reveals that no matter how radical the social and scientific perspective of the playwright, the principles of sexual difference and heteronormativity still hold as determining elements.

Čapek's image of a robot take-over haunts the future of the scientific imaginary. As recent as 2004, the Hollywood blockbuster *I, Robot* narrated frightening robot rebellions. Čapek's robots also provide a chilling antecedent to the cyber-avatar. The animation of the product of engineering, able to represent gender and able to perform humanoid operations may provide a mechanistic foretaste of the electronically, software-produced avatar of the late twentieth century. While these early plays stage a division between labor and its products and the social conditions of human existence, later corporate strategies will erase that zone of difference, troubling the very distinction between human social conditions, electronic functions, and the corporate space of the cyber. The electronic, digital form of animation displaces the human while seeming to represent it.

Factories of death: Gas

Not all commodities resulting from scientific research are machines. Some are more ephemeral, unstable chemical and processual compounds. Georg Kaiser's Expressionist plays *Gas I (1918)* and *Gas II* (1920) portray a volatile chemical compound that, unlike the optimistic transmutations of mercury in the alchemical tradition, produces a deadly form of poison. The anxiety that drives this play prefigures later fears of ephemeral, technological threats from fission to germ warfare.

The setting for Kaiser's play is a combination of laboratory and factory, fully mechanized, and financially secured by an immense capital investment by corporate and national funds. In *Gas I*, the son of the millionaire (as he is identified) who founded the factory runs it according to utopic social goals, including the plan to divide the profits of the factory among the workers. However, the gas compound, always unstable, explodes, destroying the factory. The son does not want to rebuild. He realizes that the instability of gas will only continue to cause such explosions. He prefers to divide the factory land among the workers, so that

they could enjoy a better quality of life as settlers, living a "green" life, culti-
vating their gardens. The government, however, needs the gas for warfare and
cannot afford its shut down. So it takes over the factory and begins rebuilding in
preparation for war. The Engineer, a character who revels in the domination that
the production of the destructive agent promises, keeps inciting the workers to
continue their work, in spite of the owner's pleading to cease production.

Gas II opens on a grim scene in the factory. The workers are now in uniform.
They must work day and night to keep up production levels. Even the children
are conscripted into the labor. The men mechanically report on the production
levels of the gas in the various sectors, hysterically reporting when some are
falling below and therefore endangering their position in the ongoing war. They
decide there will need to be overlapping, ceaseless shifts required to continue the
production. Suddenly, some workers, worn down and exhausted, begin to revolt
by leaving their posts. In the end, the Engineer, madly promising complete
dominion and victory to those who will continue to operate the plant, convinces
them that they should hurl a bomb of poison gas against the rebellion at the
gates. Instead, the Billionaire's Son hurls it up into the air above them. It crashes
down, leaving only bleached skeletal remains. The final report on the scene is
made by a Figure in Yellow, who arrives on the scene and is talking on the
phone, transmitting the apocalyptic news:

> Report of effect of bombardment—Turn your bullets on yourselves—exter-
> minate yourselves—the dead crowd out of their graves—day of
> judgment—*dies irae*—*solvet*—*in favil* . . . (*His shot shatters the rest. In the mist-grey
> distance sheaves of flaming bombs bursting together—vivid in self-extermination*)
> (Kaiser 1972: 44)

In these plays, gas is the volatile compound that, at the beginning of the century,
teetered on the brink between socialist hope and capitalist/governmental investment in mass destruction. The hope, installed in the single human subject, fails
before the conglomerate of investors, the arrogance of the Engineer, and the
growing reliance upon the military. Production requires ever higher levels of
labor. The laboratory becomes a factory of destruction, overdetermined by the
profits of the industrial investment in war. As we know, the play was quite
prescient in its dialectic, for, in Germany, the socialist hope was extinguished by
the rise of fascist forces that created gas chambers of death.

Written after World War One, the play reflects the historical association of
new technologies with the implements of war—specifically gas. Poison gases, first
chlorine, then phosgene and finally mustard gas were introduced by the German
Army for the first time in military history. By 1918, the Allies were using mustard
gas as well. The injuries and panic around the use of gas may have lent a
dramatic element to the play. Yet Kaiser's gas is more than a compound, it is an
emblem of the unstable use of new technologies and their potential for self-
destruction. The laboratory and the factory are destined to become an arm of

the state military. The space of science is indeed volatile, prey to militaristic take-overs and ultimate self-destruction. Engineers are power-hungry, profit-takers, who work for the development of the military/industrial compound. They are the only avatars of science in these plays.

Expressionist futures

The legacy of the Expressionist staging is less a theatrical one than cinematic. The Expressionist plays discussed here are rarely produced on contemporary stages. The exile of German Expressionist playwrights, directors, and actors to Hollywood during the Nazi period partially explains this turn. More relevant, perhaps, is that beyond the painted flats of the early plays and the mood lighting, the technology required for producing this style was better suited to cinematic special effects. Moody lighting, fuzzy focus, and strange, threatening angles became the signature of *film noir*. Robots created through motion capture and other animation devices can seem more "alive" on screen than on the stage. The huge, menacing machines that devour human labor and leisure outsize the stage, but can be seen to dominate whole cities on the screen. Nightmarish visions can be better produced on screen, as well as menacing, atmospheric effects.

However, the specifically German tradition of the Expressionist depiction of oppressive conditions that wrench the human psyche into twisted, dysfunctional behavior can be seen in several types of contemporary performance. Elements of it may be seen in the earlier work of Pina Bausch. In Café Müller, Bausch chore-ographs repetitive, violent interactions between people, which seem to find no solution. The productions directed by Klaus Michael Gruber reveal stage images of nightmarish creatures in unreal conditions—monsters of alienation. The late plays of Heiner Müller, such as *Hamletmachine*, or *Medeamaterial* offer fragmented visions of the horrors of waste, for both humans and the social and natural ecologies. *Medeamaterial* will be more fully discussed later in this chapter.

Perhaps an endstation of German Expressionism could be found in the performance entitled *Kunst und Gemüse* presented at the Volksbühne in Berlin in 2005. One of the major characters was a woman who suffers from ALS, or Lou Gehrig's disease. Almost completely paralyzed, she is situated in the center of the audience, attended by a nurse. She can communicate through a camera/software apparatus that translates the movement of her eyes into letters. Thus, by blinking and shifting her gaze, she types a narrative to the audience that is projected above the stage. Her narrative concerns how the medical profession did not want to grant her the apparatus, since she was dying. Below, the stage revolves through various dark and mystifying scenes, with a kind of anarchist aesthetic. As it turns, the scenes begin to agglutinate into a collage of misunderstanding and potential violence. Thus the machinery of science, which enables this woman, also abused her. As the machine continues its illuminated script, seeming unrelated incidents reveal other social distancing and abuse.

Machine-love: the Futurist embrace

The aspects of new technologies that terrified the German Expressionists delighted the Italian Futurists. Filippo Tommaso Marinetti, one of the founders of Futurism published its first celebratory manifesto in 1909, in *Le Figaro*. Unlike the Expressionist nightmarish portrayal of lengthy workshifts, the Futurist manifesto opens with a celebration them: "We stayed up all night. . . . An immense pride was buoying us up because we felt ourselves alone, awake, and on our feet. . . . Alone with stokers feeding the hellish fires of great ships, alone with the black specters who grope in the red-hot bellies of locomotives. . . . " (http://www.cscs.umich.edu/~crshalizi/T4PM/futurist-manifesto.html). Here, the ceaseless stoking required for the sustenance of the machines is portrayed as an exciting energy rather than an oppressive labor practice. Perhaps because, as the manifesto suggests, Marinetti, who was the scion of a wealthy family was not required to work at these jobs, so he could romanticize the labor from afar, as he stayed awake celebrating with his friends. Marjorie Perloff (1986: 36) describes this "Futurist Moment" that Marinetti recounts as a

> brief utopian phase of early Modernism when artists felt themselves to be on the verge of a new age that would be more exciting, more promising, more inspiring than any preceding one. Both the Italian and the Russian versions of Futurism found their roots in economically backward countries that were experiencing rapid industrialization—the faith in dynamism and national expansion associated with capitalism in its early phase.

The manifesto continues to script this awakening. Charged with the energy of the late night, Marinetti and his Futurist cohort hang around Marinetti's own, beloved machine, his car: "I stretched out on my car like a corpse . . . but revived at once under the steering wheel, a guillotine blade that threatened my stomach."

This violent acceleration, this celebration of mechanistic speed produces violent consequences in the environment, which Marinetti celebrates: "And on we raced, hurling watchdogs against doorsteps, curling them under our burning tires. . . . " Speed and destruction partner to form the exhilarating sense of technological power and transcendence. It's as if the machine triumphantly destroys the "lower" animals. It is only a short distance from the celebration of the deadly, speeding car to the broader celebration of the war machine: from "the beauty of speed . . . eternal, omnipresent speed" to "We will glorify war—the world's only hygiene . . . " As his car destroys the lower species, dogs, war purifies the human species for the rule of the super-heroes, certainly in line with the Fascist ideology of Mussolini, which Marinetti will later embrace.

In another "punch" line, Marinetti announces that they will also glorify a "scorn for women."[6] For Marinetti, machines provoke a characteristic combination of a specifically masculinist aggression and feeling of transcendence. In fact,

Marinetti identifies Futurism as "*le mouvement agressif*" (13), which will launch the "violent assault" (14). Moreover, this aggression is marked with erotic desire. The manifesto begins: "*Nous voulons chanter l'amour du danger*" (13) and this "love of danger" leads to a repetition of the term "*l'extase*," or ecstasy. This masculinist embrace of technology is what Vivian Sobchack terms "technophilia." Sobchack applies the term to Jean Baudrillard's postmodernist reading of the now-canonized novel and subsequent film, *Crash*. J.G. Ballard's novel *Crash*, published in the 1970s, takes Marinetti's early celebration of the speeding automobile and its potential for destruction to its logical cultural conclusion. The novel describes literal sexual acts with the mutilated bodies of crash victims at the site of the accident, or in the remains of the car. What Sobchack identifies as disturbing in Baudrillard, one of the central critics of the new cybercultural studies, is his own celebration of "a body commixed with technology's capacity for violation and violence" (quoted in Sobchack 2004: 166). Baudrillard, she argues, "gets off" on a masculinist transcendence from the traditional body which registers pain, to the convergence of "chrome and mucous membranes" and "all the symbolic and sacrificial practices that a body can open itself up to—not via nature, but via artifice, simulation, and accident" (quoted in Sobchack 2004: 167).

Marinetti celebrates his own crash, which he jubilantly describes in the manifesto. As the car rolls into a ditch he raises this invocation: "O Maternal ditch! Fair factory drain!" He "gulped down your nourishing sludge" as if at a teat, remembering his "blessed black" Sudanese nurse.[7] The sexual implications are clear, colluding with racist and destructive fantasies of a body elevated through machinic violence. Sobchack notes that Donna Haraway reviewed her own cyborg manifesto some years later, after this masculinist transcendent surfaced in cyber-publications. Donna Haraway, who once celebrated the cyborg as a new, anti-essentialist border crossing, later "warns against the very 'liberatory' cyborgism she once celebrated . . . insofar as it jacks into (and off on) what she calls 'the God trick' . . . a "transcendentalist move," reports Sobchack. Haraway corrects this transcendental, destructive embrace of new technologies, warning that they "really do wound each other . . . that escape-velocity is a deadly fantasy" (quoted in Sobchack 2004: 170).

Of course, it is important to remember that Marinetti was writing a manifesto. He sought a performative language that would provoke change. Manifestos were in abundance during the early years of the century, including numerous Surrealist manifestos, Dada manifestos, etc. As a provocation, readings of manifestos were designed to incite shock, or outrage in the audience. They were a form of performance art. Marinetti performed this manifesto one evening before the production of his play: *Poupée Électriques* (1909). The title *Electric Dolls* is Marinetti's term for the robot, or android. Ironically, in the same year as he published his manifesto, written in an experimental new form, Marinetti published this play, written in the traditional nineteenth-century three-act structure. His ambivalent position, as one who would both shock the bourgeoisie, and belong to the "haute bourgeoisie" is clear formally, as well as biographically. Act

II of the play was later extracted to become fashioned into one of the short, experimental plays Futurists called *sintesi* (synthetics) under the Italian title *Elettricità sessuale*, or *Sexual Electricity*. The "electric dolls" are situated within an atmosphere of sexual attraction.

In the play, androids are portrayed as taking part in the private, domestic, middle-class lives of a married couple. They perform as domestic laborers and mimics for their inventor, John Wilson. Unlike the Expressionist portrayal of androids in terms of unfair labor practices and militarism, Marinetti depicts them as characters in the familiar form of the French farce, replete with marital disputes and deceits. At the beginning of the act, the androids are animated by the "real" chambermaid and valet in order to demonstrate their mimetic potential. The androids are made to represent a couple named Monsieur Prudent and Mme. Prunelle. When activated by a button, Monsieur Prudent can mimic familiar bourgeois gestures: he wipes his glasses on his handkerchief, puts them on, and reads the paper. His wife coughs politely to gain his attention. As an electrical satire of bourgeois behavior, the androids reduce the science and technology that produced them to mimetically reproducing the most insignificant of human gestures. The humans who design and own these androids are, by extension, also thus reduced. The valet relates that the engineer/inventor John Wilson and his wife spend their evenings playing with these mechanicals (1909: 111).

Later, the "electric dolls" are inserted into a domestic scene between the inventor and his wife. They are psychically and physically inserted between them, engaging their personal pleasures, conflicts, and desires. Metaphors of marital rupture and bliss are literalized in the dolls. Mary says, melancholically, "You think of me as one of your puppets" (131). Enjoying the electrical storm energy in the night air, within which these electric beings animate, John enjoys how "electricity vibrates the nerves as a conductor of voluptuousness" (132). Thus, electricity itself is sexy and the electric dolls only take that charge into familiar marital patterns. Eventually, in order to save their marriage, Wilson and wife throw the puppets out the window, provoking the police to investigate what seems like a murder. This play stages the kind of life Marinetti despises: taming the machine and reducing its potential to domestic squabbling.

However, this satire does not fit the function of "The Futurist Synthetic Theatre" (1915), as that manifesto describes it: "As we await our much prayed-for great war, we Futurists carry our violent antineutralist action from city square to university and back again, using our art to prepare the Italian sensibility for the great hour of maximum danger." Synthetic theater is the form they designed to inspire war. In their characteristic capitals they conclude: "THEREFORE WE THINK THAT THE ONLY WAY TO INSPIRE ITALY WITH THE WARLIKE SPIRIT TODAY IS THROUGH THE THEATRE." Synthetic theater, as it evolved, was a play without logic that staged, instead, "frenzied passion." Its short form imitated "The form of propaganda or, of ads." Hailed as " The language of the future," synthetic theater was celebrated as "THE SCIENTIFIC OUTBURST THAT CLEARS THE AIR" (http://www.

futurism.org.uk/manifestos/manifesto21.htm). In other words, Futurist theater is like a terrorist bomb, or a super-effective commercial, which are somehow similar to one another in the Futurist mindset, exploding into the social space of the status quo. Character and plot are eschewed for the detonation of a sudden single effect. Francesco Cangiulio's *Detonation/Detonazione* is the prime example of this synthetic theater. The entire script reads as follows:

> Character: a bullet.
> Road at night, cold, deserted.
> A minute of silence.—A gunshot.
> CURTAIN

If the Expressionist plays warned that technology could become deadly, a tool of the military/industrial compound, the Futurists hoped it would. Marinetti joined the fascist party that supported the rise of Mussolini and, although he criticized the party, remained active in it. In spite of the common reception of the Futurists as fascist, however, Marjorie Perloff notes that their political associations were more complex than that. Some were members of the communist party and others were anarchists. Perloff also summarizes various political agendas proclaimed in their various manifestos that are not fascist in nature: the abolition of the monarchy, the socialization of land, mineral resources and water, and equal pay for women (1986: 36). Finally, then, it is difficult to parse out a single political ideology of the movement, but it is certainly evident that the potential violence in the new technologies was at the core of their attraction. They launched the violent embrace of the machine in the twentieth century.

Futurist futures

The Futurist legacy proceeded more as notions and emotions concerning the relations among "men" and machines than as a strict theatrical or even cinematic legacy. As noted above, the masculinist celebration of the transcendental powers of new technologies became an earmark of the postmodern reception of new technologies. Not only, as mentioned, in works like *Crash*, but also in myriad computer games, where the excitement of performing the destructive power of new technologies provides the pleasure of the form. Even the academic reception of new technologies, as Sobchack point out, replicates elements of the Futurist embrace. Steven Shaviro, in *Doom Patrols*, depicts it this way: "Postmodern culture is pervaded by apocalyptic imaginings" and "longings" a kind of "restless fascination, a deep yearning that arises in long nights of insomniac vigilance" (1997: 93). Here the "postFuturist" insomnia is replicated by staying awake all night, but instead of the rush of auto tires over dogs, it is filled with longing for the apocalyptic act, in the sense that perhaps it has already happened, or it is happening all the time, in a slower, duller way. Visions of cyberspace also offer the "ecstatic" experience of speed and destruction in games, both in the arcades and in the U.S. Army training programs. Images of cyborg soldiers, armed with full-metal jackets, field-protective masks, infra-red goggles, and grenade launchers, backed up by drone airplanes, heat-seeking missiles, and directed by satellite signals, and internet command signals, valorize the deadly embrace between masculinist aggression and new technologies. The "path of glory" permeates the promise with transcendence.

Engineering Soviet science: Aelita, The Queen of Mars

Science and technology were central to the new society that Socialist Russia hoped to create after the Revolution. The transition from a feudalist to a modernist society was abrupt and extreme, relying on the widespread use of new technologies to communicate the changes to a scattered population and to alter the economic and social structures of both rural and urban Russia. New technologies were embraced for their potential donation to the economic wealth of the nation and the general betterment of the peoples' lives. Machines were perceived as social tools, aimed at greater food production, additional housing, hydroelectric power, and the creation of other resources. For example, images of the tractor, the machine that helped to bring farming into its new collective mode, and those of the tractor drivers were found on posters throughout the country. Likewise, new factories and dams were celebrated as monumental heroic constructions in posters, paintings, songs, and films. Work at the machines was depicted as a form of heroic labor for the collective.

Russia embraced scientific knowledge as if it were less ideologically mystified than more social discourses. Its seemingly empirical structure suggested science as the preferred discourse of a revolution. Coupled with the cultural vocabulary of heroic labor and monumental factories, the Soviet embrace of science and technology made its representations central to the emerging cultural vocabulary. However, issues concerning the proper aim of scientific research, the role of the scientist in society, and the aesthetic style appropriate to the representation of science and technology became core debates in the policies of the new socialist government. Once again, as we have seen in the Expressionist and Futurist movements, the image of the Engineer came to represent the troubled hinge between scientific research and its application. Emerging from a more elitist education, the Engineer was tainted with privilege. His dedication to the collective good would be tested in plays and films of the period.

Debates over the proper style for depicting science and technology were central to the emerging state-sponsored cultural policies. During the period of the New Economic Policy (NEP) in the 1920s changes in economic and social structures accompanied aesthetic ones. Experimentation, in science and in art was both encouraged and discouraged during this time. A partial return of the free-enterprise system, i.e. partial capitalism, was launched along with new, state subsidies. Avant-garde theaters and artists' ateliers proliferated as well as laboratories for scientific research. At the same time, a growing sense that realism was the only style of representation that suited a proletarian society accompanied a notion that science should be aimed only at producing utilitarian products. The enforcement of these modes of production was beginning to displace support for the more experimental forms. In 1925, Fyodor Gladkov's realist novel *Cement* appeared, soon to become hailed as the first, classic proletarian novel. It depicted the heroic rebuilding of the factories after the civil strife and the changes in the social system of relations that communism inspired. The novel treated the role of the heroic factory worker, the problematic role of the bourgeois engineer, and the new liberated role for women in the workplace and at home—themes that are also common to *Aelita*. Although *Cement* dramatized the inherent conflicts in social change, it was its realist style, more than its content that hailed it as the model proletarian form of representation. By the 1930s, socialist realism was installed as the official style of representation in Soviet Russia, while more experimental forms were censored.[8] The film *Aelita: The Queen of Mars* (1924), made during this period, dramatizes the ideological conflicts concerning the uses of science and art in both its narrative and its conflicting styles. The film combines both constructivist spectacle and realist narration in a story that tests the proper role of the Engineer. State ambivalence around these conflicts in the film, particularly those of style, was demonstrated by its lavish production budget and advertising and then its sudden removal from distribution.[9]

Aelita is best known to theater historians for the brilliant costume and set designs by Alexandra Exter. Her designs for the Martian court society have become canonical examples of Cubist-Constructivist stage design. Like the German Expressionist designers, Exter's scenic vocabulary was composed almost entirely of geometric forms and bisecting lines. Her stage was an abstract space through which actors moved with stylized gestures. Although she shared in the early-twentieth-century scientific imaginary, her space was not tortured one, as with the Expressionists. For her, geometric design provided an opportunity for a more interactive environment between actor and space. Before the revolution, Exter had gained prominence in Russian cultural circles for her designs for Alexander Tairov's Kamerny Theater. There, she broke with the tradition of the painted realist set to design spaces and costumes composed entirely of geometric forms. Some critics claim that Exter's designs were the first consistent and complete realization of three-dimensional, volumetric sets on the Russian stage (Kolesnikov 1999: 88). Moreover, her set design for Tairov's *Salome* in 1917 may be the first example of kinetic stage design. Using kinetic apparati and levels designed to bring the actors into play with set elements, Exter introduced a design for the stage in which the set "acted" as an equal and dynamic partner to the actor. Like the designs of Adolphe Appia and Gordon Craig, Exter's staging relied heavily upon stair units and platforms to offer the actors dynamic movements up, away from the stage floor, bisecting the vertical lines of the scenic forms with their actions. An interest in visual dynamism as part of theatrical expression drew away from the text-centered, painterly effects of realism, lending dramatic agency to the design itself. Schematic space was agential, for both the actor and the set.

Exter's costume designs were also highly regarded for their geometric elements, which abstracted movement away from the actor's body. Her choice of flowing silks and satins to be worn beneath the geometric forms created an aesthetic tension with the abstractions, revealing the actor's body and its movement in flowing lines in contrast to the mechanical movement of the geometric exoskeleton. Exter's interest in fabric and color separated her from the more monochromal Cubist exercises she had seen in France, leading her into explorations of fabrics and synthetic materials that could be brought into a dynamic interplay with geometric forms.

So when the new revolutionary Russia decided to produce its first big-budget science fiction film, *Aelita: The Queen of Mars*, in competition with Hollywood for popular entertainment, it was not surprising that Exter was chosen to design the spectacular costumes and set elements for the Martian scenes. *Aelita* is set in Moscow in 1921, the beginning year of the New Economic Policy. It swings between a narrative of the massive economic and social changes occurring in the new revolutionary society and a fantasy of a royalist Mars. The hinge between these worlds is located in the scientific laboratory and the role of the Engineer. Mars is a production of pure science; it both illustrates a world permeated by scientific inventions and a world only imaginable, and, indeed, reachable through scientific advances. *Aelita*'s design swings between the abstracted, constructivist sets for Mars and the realistic portrayal of contemporary Moscow. The film could be viewed as staging the crucial ambivalence between what was later known as Russian formalism and Soviet Socialist Realism. Tellingly, however, the constructivist style was associated with the royalist society of Mars and the realist style with the changes the New Economic Policy brought about in Moscow.

Figure 7 Aelita: The Queen of Mars, "All Power to the Soviets"

Figure 8 Aelita:The Queen of Mars, telescope

The film provides an example of how the debate over cultural policies was tied to the specific material and social practices of science. *Aelita* is the story of two engineers and the social consequences of their research agendas.[10] The film opens on machines in a laboratory flashing a signal composed of three words that cannot be decoded. Engineer Spiridinov, a single man, becomes absorbed in the decoding process, as does his married friend, Engineer Los. They presume the signal originates in outer space—specifically Mars. They begin to work feverishly on designing a space ship to take them there. In socialist traditions, the engineer is a familiar focal character, representing the intellectual who can be directly useful to society or not. Unlike the artist, the engineer works at the point between design and industrial development. In the early Soviet society, the engineers came from the educated, privileged class that the revolutionary society had overthrown. Thus, their challenge was to make themselves useful to the new state, working to develop projects necessary for the betterment of the people, rather than remaining at a disinterested class remove. The notion of a "pure" research agenda, abstracted from utility needed to be abandoned in favor of designing factories and dams. Rather than an individualist agenda in design, the engineer needed to learn to work within the collective structure, responding to the needs of the construction workers and the people who would be using his creation. In *Aelita*, the choice to design a space ship to go to Mars, then, is a removed, abstract project, conceived in isolation by the two engineers. At one point, engineer Los alternates between his obsession with this speculative research and actually working on a dam project. Out of the laboratory, he is depicted drawing designs directly on the construction site. But his designs for the spaceship result in his increasing isolation from others, wasted by fantasies of luxury.

Figure 9 Aelita: The Queen of Mars, set design

While the film portrays the technology of contemporary Moscow as industrial and machinic, the technology of Mars appears as "pure" design without machinery. For example, Gor, the master scientist of Mars, has invented a telescope for viewing other planets. His design/production processes are one, consisting of moving a powered stylus over a translucent surface (now actually possible with stylus and computer screen). His telescope is a tower of transparent isosceles triangles intersected by a curve and a ball—more like a composition by Malevich than an astronomic instrument. All of the Martian architecture is composed of independent geometric units, without representations of any supporting devices, or functional elements such as windows and chairs. All doors are automatic and appear only when required from hidden recesses in the wall. Likewise, there does not seem to be any labor concerning these projects; they move seamlessly from design to use. In other words, design is both the schematic and the product in one. This constructivist vision is seemingly utopic in the beginning of the film. Only later are the repressive police force and the oppressive labor practices that support this design revealed.

In contrast to the world of "pure" design, the wife of engineer Los works at a checkpoint for the immigrants who are pouring into Moscow after the civil war. These are homeless people, who arrive in overcrowded boxcars or by riding on the tops of trains, with no employment opportunities, no housing, food, or clothes. Their lives have been disrupted by the war and the new economics require new assignments for them. They are moved into apartments once inhabited by only one family, given food rations, and some means of employment. Thus, we have the "marriage" between an engineer, who will be more and more given to his "daydreaming" about life on Mars and the woman who confronts the daily needs of the poor, working directly for the state. As the engineer is more and more attracted to the Martian Queen Aelita, he grows more and more distant from his wife. Thus, the Engineer's ambivalence is portrayed by his relationship to two women.

The role of women was at issue from the beginning of the construction of a communist ideology in the nineteenth century. In Engels' founding essay, *The Origin of the Family, Private Property and the State* (1884), gender oppression was perceived as a structural result of the family unit, basic to the capitalist order. The patriarchal family was perceived as a capitalist institution, in which women were oppressed by their necessary domestic servility and sexual monogamy, while the patriarch enjoyed domestic and sexual liberties. Engels suggested that in the new socialist economic conditions, patriarchy would come to an end. Women would enter the workplace and the state would take over some of the basic functions of the family, including communal dining rooms, daycare centers, etc. in order to lighten the burden of domestic labor. The state would displace the private property of women and children organized by the family unit. Escape from the enforced bondage of marriage meant that divorce was deemed a crucial right for women's equality (Goldman 1991: 126–127). Abortion was also legalized.

In *Aelita*, the queen of Mars resembles the bourgeois, or aristocratic woman, who lived in Russia prior to the revolution. Traditionally, she did not work. The Queen is portrayed as lounging about with her maid and playing the harp. The spectacular costumes for Queen Aelita and her maid imitate the "high" fashion of the rich. They combine orientalist harem pants (perhaps a costume concept left over from the production of Wilde's *Salome*) with geometric forms. Both the queen and her maid wear halter tops, revealing bare mid-drifts within the geometric devices. Both sport significant geometric headdresses: Aelita in wires radiating outward from her forehead like antennae and the maid in an upward-spiraling pillbox hat. These are costumes of leisurewear—their design would not enable physical labor of any kind, or, say, safety in a factory. They are extremely gendered and seductive, invoking the practices of the beauty and fashion industries, aimed at the moneyed classes, and constructing desire through design. In one scene, the film cuts from Queen Aelita to the engineer's wife, who wears a modest print dress and is up to her elbows in dishwashing suds. Very simply, the narrative suggests that the traditional figure of desire is really the product of a class-based, oppressive society, while the good woman works modestly for the common good.

Engineer Los finally reaches Mars in his spaceship. The film portrays the gleaming futuristic city through constructivist models. Once there, one of Los' fellow space travelers urges an uprising of the oppressed laborers on the planet. He tells the Martians the story of the Russian Revolution, which is depicted in heroic, monumental, abstract symbols, such as the breaking of chains, and the passing of a torch. The hammer and sickle are forged by a massive worker's arm and for a moment, the movie is taken over by a third aesthetic movement—the soviet monumentality of its public art and architecture and its state parades. It seems a certain form of abstraction could capture at least the originary events of the movement, if not appropriate to contemporary conditions. The comrade urges the formation of the Martian Union of Soviet Socialist Republics. Then, the familiar Russian epic cinematic style shows the spectacle of the uprising, with hundreds of extras and massive battle scenes on the constructivist sets. It's as if realism rises up on the very base of the formalist design, overtaking its composition. Aelita fools the people into thinking she is on their side, only to use the revolution for her own end, slaughtering the workers. Los kills her/flashes on killing his wife. He then wakes from what is revealed as his daydream of Mars and rushes home to destroy his secret designs for his spaceship, committing himself to the building of hydroelectric dams and other useful projects alongside his good wife. The love of the abstract has been shredded, the remove of pure design has been abandoned and the collectively-engaged labor of engineering will determine his future. Perhaps it was this ending, along with the removal of the film from distribution that persuaded Exter to flee Russia right after the completion of the film and to live the rest of her life in Paris.

While the Expressionists created a certain atmosphere of technological oppression surrounding the human agent, and the Futurists lent agency to machines, the Soviets situated science and technology within a set of social decisions. Design, the site where art and practice meet, was tested for its utility in bettering the lives of the poor. The scientist is a figure that is caught up in a revolutionary debate about economic and social conditions. Ethics are not an ancillary part of the consideration of science, but the base for its practice and its representation.

These three movements, then, Expressionism, Futurism, and Soviet depictions of the scientist model basic strategies for the performance of science in the ensuing century. The formation of an abstracted, schematic design, inspired by research and engineering will find various forms in the performance space, particularly presaging a more interactive environment between the actor and the set. The Expressionists warn of a future surround of surveillance and a lethal, authoritarian capitalization of scientific research by the military-industrial compound. The Futurists provide the articulation of ecstasy and transcendence that will accompany the experience of new, immersive technologies, and the Soviets stage the conflicting ethics around the applications of scientific research. The scientific cultural imaginary is launched, through stagings of the scientific surround and its permeation of the social, with the resulting crises in human ethics and the promise of a technological transcendence, where "pure" design can create virtual worlds of leisure and remove.

SCENE TWO: MID-CENTURY MODERN

Away and away the aeroplane shot, till it was nothing but a bright spark; an aspiration; a concentration; a symbol (so it seemed to Mr. Bentley, vigorously rolling his strip of turf at Greenwich) of man's soul; of his determination, thought Mr. Bentley, sweeping round the cedar tree, to get outside his body, beyond his house, by means of thought, Einstein, speculation, mathematics, the Mendelian theory—away the aeroplane shot.

(Virginia Woolf, *Mrs. Dalloway*)

"Mid-Century modern" is a term that generally refers to a style of architecture, furniture, and accessories from the decades of the 1950s–1960s, with substyles demarcated as Danish Modern, Atomic, Space Age, etc. Today, a retro version of the style is highly fashionable in urban centers in the U.S. and parts of Europe for its simplicity of line and its campy allusions to space-age technologies and fictions, such as cathode-ray-tube-shaped lamps. Borrowing from the seemingly sterile environments of the labs, minimalist "clean" lines combined with gleaming surfaces to bring the style of new technologies into fashion and domestic environments. As Allecquere Rosanne Stone details, in her article, "Split Subjects, Not Atoms; or, How I fell in Love with my Prosthesis:"

> the guts of things—the visual apprehension of the way they worked, and the consequent link to a rational comprehension of their function—began to recede inward, and the skin of such devices such as toasters and vacuum cleaners became smooth and shiny. The newly constituted "shroud", described as streamlined, futuristic, and decorative, not only conceals the operation of the device (which had been hitherto implicit in its specularity), thus producing the interiorized space of desire, but also, redirects the gaze to the featureless, shiny screen upon which is projected the new meaning and purpose of technological prosthetics. . . . The surface that in Deleuze and Guattari's words becomes deterritorialized, also becomes **hypertactile** (sic); the ontic quality of touch decouples from the object being touched. . . . the whole arena of machinic surface becomes organized in relation to the gaze . . . the chthonic interior space of technology is heightened in its mystery and allure.

(1995: 398)

The machine is now perceived as an almost formal device that can lend the "aura" of its surface to design. The gleaming surfaces of these techno-shrouds inspired the familiar associations of cleanliness, self-discipline, education, and privileged access to highly capitalized projects. The social reception of these elements borrowed from racist assumptions as well. Lab coats were white, after all, and highly-polished gleaming surfaces, once perceived as belonging to "alabaster cities," were now safely ensconced in the homogeneously-populated suburban tracts. The exodus to the "white" suburbs from what became the ethnic urban centers brought with it particular forms of entertainment that could represent, virtually, the sanitized social space.

Television provided a new medium of the virtual to deliver the sanitized signals directly into the safely-removed domestic sphere.[11] As a machine, with dials and antennae, the TV set represented a new technology that could be operated by the average person, without the need for a specialized education and laboratory environment. Yet it offered up a lab-type screen, with test patterns and reception problems causing distorted images. In the suburban tract house, TV helped to encourage a performance of the domestic as scientific. With its sanitized quiz shows and serials, TV's screen was as clean as its neighboring kitchen. Its glow assumed the place of the fire, around which the presumably happy family gathered in safety. It was the entertainment machine with a screen that presaged all those that followed, from computer gaming, to ipod and cell-phone downloads.

Beyond the ubiquitous performances of science, avant-garde performance practices took up the machinic as a mode of composition. The recursive loop of iteration central to recording devices became a site of emulation and intervention. Such unlike artists as Samuel Beckett and John Cage composed performances around the looping of tape and its reception. Stylistically, these performances withdrew from expressivity, performing as the "modest witnesses" in the labs had done. Emotional excess was assigned to the racially marked "Blues" or to early modernist women dancers, such as Martha Graham, or to the popular stage. Unlike suburban TV, or avant-garde performances that played with and through the machinic, the popular stage provided anxious-ridden portraits of the "live," in alcohol-laced monologs of domestic violence and guilt as in Eugene O'Neill's *Long Day's Journey Into Night*, or to the staged, closeted fantasies of "summer" hothouses, with devouring plants and nativized, sexually targeted "boys," as in the works of Tennessee Williams.[12] While TV created the virtual home space of a family of "modest witnesses"—an audience of suitably-trained pseudo-scientists—the stage was serving up the American Gothic, if you will, portraying the tortured dysfunctional family unit, replete with obsession and sexual longing in the kitchen, living room, and bedroom. The haunted house on the stage was a dark "other" to the bright, happy TV "window on the world" that opened up for the suburban family. One could almost imagine that the audience of an *embodied* performance was marked as somehow prurient in its watching in contrast to the modest witnesses of TVs virtual space, with the exception of the Broadway musicals. The musical opened up its own sanitizing window on the world with all the high-tech specularity of surface, rendering issues of education, political repression, and sexualized performance as "foreign," in *The King and I*, *The Sound of Music*, and *Can-Can*, leaving the home/land secure and sanitized.[13] The glossy, specular surface of the musical will inflate in the coming decades, staging high-tech special effects at the center of the "live" performance.

In contrast to these more celebratory performances of the machinic style, mid-century anxieties around the effects of new technologies inspired perfor-mances of fear and even loathing. Christine Jorgensen's highly-publicized sex reassignment surgery in 1952 imaged, for some, the new potential for medical technologies to decode the strict sex/gender dyad. Susan Stryker refers to the phenomenon as "Christine Jorgensen's Atom Bomb," noting that "the spectacle of transsexuality mushroomed into public consciousness during the early days of the Cold War with all the force of a blistering hot wind roaring across the Trinity Test Site" (Stryker 1999: 160). Bombs and "bombshells" shook the ground of traditional sites of safety. In the case of the bomb, a new technology was introduced that could potentially end life on the entire planet, inducing a fear of large-scale destruction, and encouraging citizens to build and supply "underground" shelters where they could hide from the effects. Testing the bomb in Western deserts endangered the "homeland" with radiation seeping into the ground and carried on the winds. Images from various horror films of the period reveal the anxieties caused by the testing, with giant tarantulas and ants emerging from the contaminated soil. In the case of the "bombshell," Jorgensen's case made the bright, shiny shroud of medical technologies reflect the frightened conservative viewer, who felt that what lay beneath the lights of the operating room could threaten individual forms of sexual identification. Biomedical assimilations of and incursions into "natural" processes threatened the traditional cultural location of the body.

The outbreak of intense surveillance into the private lives of U.S. citizens committed technological devices to search out and file data on so-called communist affiliations and sexual practices. From 1953–1954, the McCarthy hearings filled the newspapers and media broadcasts. Calling over 500 witnesses, Eugene McCarthy and his chief counsel Roy Cohn (a closeted homosexual) searched out "communist infiltrators," profiling people with secrets, such as homosexual liaisons, as "spies and subversives." These investigations served to create a general sense of hidden identities, affiliations and schemes within the public realm. On the one hand, then, machines were playing their role in the specular imaginary as bright, helpful accessories of viewing and cleaning, and on the other, they were peering into the dark, destructive dangers to social cohesion.

Cold War alchemy

Primary to the formation and design of the new high-tech secret government was the founding of the National Security Agency in 1952. No news coverage, no congressional debate, and no press announcement made its installation public, nor was there any mention of it to be found in the Government Organization Manual of the Federal Register, nor in the Congressional Record. The agency's director, its numerous buildings, and its ten thousand employees were invisible to the public. The NSA continues to play a central role in government functions today, with a new public façade erected in the 1990s, behind which most of its functions still remain secret. It is an agency dedicated to making and breaking codes, intercepting signals, and tracing their source. The agency employs what they term cryptanalysts, recruited from many disciplines, from mathematics to computer science. This focus on interception and codes has become a stronghold of secrecy in the government. In terms of technology, its need for the fast, high level crypto-analysis of thousands of messages has led to the development of super computers, with increasing power for data storage and speed. It has also participated in developing new technologies related to aerial reconnaissance and spy satellites. The NSA often works as a silent partner with universities and private corporations, particularly, in the 1950s with IBM, using university labs for secret governmental projects. This practice creates a secret underside to the university as well, and to the open exchange of ideas in the academy. Computers and codes were linked in several ways, then, with secrecy and surveillance and became central to the increasing capitalization and national power of the military-industrial compound, which, even President Eisenhower warned against, in his 1961 farewell address.

In 1950s popular culture, the secret powers of the NSA were playfully performed by children using decoder rings, which were offered on TV shows, in comic books, and on the backs of leading cereal boxes. Such different heroic figures as Captain Midnight, Red Ryder, the Lone Ranger, and Space Patrol all offered secret messages to be deciphered by the owners of these rings. Children also sent and received coded messages from their friends. All the decoder rings worked on the simple coding system of letter repositioning. The letter "A" is no longer One, "B" is no longer Two, "C" is no longer Three, and so on. Over six million decoder rings were sold during this period. Their packaging hinted at the fear, power, and mystery associated with the new technologies and their relationship to government secrets. In this way, children were encouraged to invent new forms of social play through the mechanisms of cryptography. The fascination with the coded exchange between the seen and the unseen played a major role in their cultural imaginary, as children, and perhaps lingered on into adulthood for some, who became the first software designers writing code for the computers. As the adults were drawn into the broadcast trials alleging secret political affiliations of suspected communists, children were knit into that same fabric of codes and secrecy through interactive environments among TV shows, comics, and movies that offered coded messages for their rings to decipher. Thus, the bifurcation between the shiny, clean surface and the secret, dark guts of machines and their codes animated both governmental agencies and children's fantasies. Codes and emblems were still forming secret societies, as they had in the earlier, esoteric sciences, but this time they were linked to national projects and presumed national threats.

Alan Turing might be perceived as an avatar of this new compound of machinic processes of coding and decoding and personal, sexual secrets. In England, Turing had worked as a cryptanalyst during the war as part of a team who broke the infamous Nazi coding machine known as "Enigma." The machine worked, essentially, like the decoder rings in the cereal boxes, but with electrical wiring that amplified the number of encoding possibilities. In addition to his work on decoding, Turing developed the notion of the Universal Turing Machine; one that, when furnished with the number describing the mechanism of any particular Turing machine could perfectly mimic its behavior. In effect, the "hardware" could be translated in software and entered as data into the universal machine, where it would run as a program. Arguably, then, Turing had invented the computer and computer programming. Turing combined the role of "pure" scientist and engineer, when he both imagined and constructed the machine.

In 1950, Turing's paper, *Computing Machinery and Intelligence* became an internationally-known concept for what would become Artificial Intelligence, or the notion of the "thinking machine." Through processes of coding and decoding, Turing was led to the conception of the subjective machine and the machinic aspects of the mind. He bridged machine and mind, both philosophically and practically.

Whereas Turing kept national secrets, he provided the circumstances for "outing" his secret, sexual life. Reporting a petty theft by a boy he had picked up on the street, Turing led the police to further investigate the circumstances of the encounter. In 1952, he was charged on the same 1885 act that had led to the prosecution of Oscar Wilde's "gross indecency." Following public and professional humiliation, Turing committed suicide in 1954 by eating a poisoned apple.

Turing's biography offers a paradigm of the mid-century modern condition. The play *Breaking the Code* (1986) by Hugh Whitemore stages the interface between numbers/machine and the social as a drama of pathos, in which the oft-wounded Turing says things like "When I was a child, numbers were my friends." Presumably, for their stability. The title suggests the lethal mix of mathematical and social codes that Turing broke, but, whereas his professional life is heroicized, his non-normative sexual practices merely offer the portrait of an outsider/intellectual at play. For example, a liaison with a Greek boy, who cannot understand English, provides the opportunity for Turing to expose the complex workings of the Enigma machine. The result is that, in this play, Turing is made into not so much an avatar as an exception. Yet the play proceeds as many in the twentieth century, to stage science through a biography of a scientist, who must confront some troubled interface between his life as a researcher and ethical, social issues. Turing's biography, which has now inspired numerous treatments, both academic and popular, stands as the intersection of secrets and science in the mid-century.

Grassroots sightings of science: UFOs

The UFO and its alien bodies were the avatars of science in the mid-century grassroots imagination. UFO sightings began to occur in the late 1940s, early 1950s, during the era of the public and political emphasis on science and technology, as described above. Along with cryptology, the language of secrets, the U.S. opened secret military bases, for example, in Thule, Greenland. Surveillance reached continental proportions, when the Distant Early Warning system (DEW) was constructed, which consisted of 63 radar and communication systems, extending along the 69th parallel from Alaska to Baffin Island. The combination of the heightened awareness around the influence of scientific developments and the more secretive nature of the research may have inspired the growing number of UFO sightings and reports of alien abductions. People performed sighting when they were not allowed to see.

UFOs resembled aircraft, but, as in *Aelita*, were driven only by design. With only a smooth exterior, they revealed no working parts and no obvious source of energy and drive. They mimicked the smooth, shiny shroud of the machine, but with no internal engine underneath. Like transcendent laboratories, the UFOs floated literally "above the heads" of the populace. Their origins and missions were mysteries to those who were able to sight them. The UFOs were operated by aliens. Like the scientist in the remove of the laboratory, these aliens were denizens of distant spheres. They behaved much like the "modest witness" Haraway (1997) characterizes as the scientific mode. Aliens are almost always expressionless, with smooth facial features and bodies, no obvious gender markings, and able to speak only in an untranslatable, science-saturated language. UFO sightings and alien abductions filled the popular science imaginary of the mid-to-late twentieth century. These sightings are imaginings that empower, through corporeality and ceremony, an access to scientific power, literally grounding it in transmission and reception.

In *The UFO Book*, Jerome Clark offers a brief outline of the UFO phenomenon. He notes that, although the first sighting was in 1947, it was actually in the 1950s that the first big craze hit the U.S. Project Blue Book was a UFO investigation launched by the U.S. Air force in 1952 that supplied much of the data on the phenomenon. The report lists 886 UFO sightings by members of the Air Force and another 800 by the general public in the period from June to October, 1952. In the same year as the image of Christine Jorgensen filled the newspapers, the threat of atomic destruction fueled fears, the hunt for subversives intensified, TV entered the home, and decoding became a profession and a pastime, nearly two thousand people were sighting UFOs in the skies. The UFOS were alien technologies incarnate.

By 1953, Project Blue Book called a meeting between some scientists working on the project and representatives of the CIA. The group concluded that "UFOS might not be a threat to national security, but belief in them is. . . . such belief could cause hysteria and could be manipulated by 'skillful hostile agents'" (quoted in Clark 1997: 467). Therefore, the governmental agencies published a new policy that would debunk rather than research any future UFO sightings in the service of national security. This marks an interesting shift in paranoia—it is doubly paranoid—to fear the fear of the UFOs, shifting the focus from the potential aims of the object itself to those of agents who might make use of the object's reception. Nonetheless, the project still recorded a later wave of sightings in the summer of 1965. By 1969, the Air Force had elected to close Operation Blue Book and to drop all further investigation.

In response to the flood of sightings, C.G. Jung published the book *Flying Saucers: A Modern Myth of Things Seen in the Skies* (1959) to theorize what these sightings might indicate, from his particular psycho/mythological perspective. The shape of the saucer, imagines, argues Jung, "an archetype of wholeness, a balancing of the intellectual and intuitive halves of the psyche. . . . It is a sighted shape that could resolve the growing sense that *something is seen, but one doesn't know what*" (1978: 6; italics his). Flying saucers assume the round shape, Jung adds, functioning like the symbol of the *mandala* (Sanskrit for circle) and participating in the history of magic, protective circles: "the mandala encompasses, protects, and defends the psychic totality against outside influences"(20). Thus, the sightings of UFOs register and resolve at once, the anxieties about the sense that one cannot know, or understand what one is seeing, either because it is disguised, as a communist agent might be, or secret, as in government proceedings, or indecipherable, as in scientific discourse and codes. The virtual space within the magic circle is object-ified. A UFO, in place of a hand-drawn mandala, or the embodied, human form of a saint, Jung observes, is "Characteristic of our time that . . . the archetype should take the form of an object, a technological construction in order to avoid the odiousness of a mythological personification"(23). In other words, the techno appearance also shrouds an avatar.

In 1952, soon after WWII, in which the embodied struggle seemed so heroic and participatory, the increasing indenture of the body to the abstractions of scientific discourse and its machines, no matter how brightly polished, inspired a collective vision, what Jung terms a "visionary rumour" in the U.S. (2–3). Essentially, Jung argues, the sighting is a "psychological projection"—based on a collective emotional tension—that creates a "collective dissociation," by which he means a split between the conscious attitude and the unconscious contents opposed to it: "Precisely because the conscious mind does not know about them and is therefore confronted with a situation from which there seems no way out, these strange contents cannot be integrated directly but seek to express themselves indirectly, thus giving rise to unexpected and apparently inexplicable opinions, beliefs, illusions and so forth" (9). Jung calls the UFOs a "living myth or legend" which we can observe being formed (14). He sums up the relation of the anxiety to its sign: "The threatening situation of the world today (1950s Cold War) is like the times when people saw rains of blood." As he emphasizes, the nuclear threat risked planetary destruction, so the projection soars into the heavens, "where the rulers of human fate, the gods, once had their abode" (10).

One need not accept the details of Jung's explanation to nonetheless perceive how the deployment of psychic, mythic, spiritualist, and ritualistic traditions translate the specialized language and structures of science into esoteric ones; how the two traditions, science and spiritualism, once caught up in a nineteenth-century melodrama are here conflated with one another. Alien bodies can figure the scientist, alien worlds the secret, closed laboratories, and UFOs the technologies of pure research. How these sightings take on meaning relies on the spiritualist notions of myth, visions, and rituals. Performing science, in this period, reveals the distance from its research and discourse and the search for other rites and emblems that would make it available to the layperson.

Alien abductions

Following the major period of these UFO sightings, a spate of alien contacts began to occur. Unlike the distant scientist, the aliens seek interaction with the public, often desiring to amalgamate their technology with domestic lives, and their future with ancient earthly practices. Even though they speak an untranslatable language, they respond to gestures and sign back to the humans, or communicate by mental telepathy—a language completely abstract, with no material signs or sounds, but which requires no special training to understand. Some aliens are evil. They plan to usurp privileges, inseminate virgins with their own species, harvest humans for food, or harvest fetuses and genes for the propagation of their own, dark or dying civilizations. Whatever their goal, they perform together with the layperson, who is somehow needed in their laboratories.

Histories of alien abductions seem to agree that the first contact was recorded in 1945 by a certain N. Meade Layne, in San Diego. The meeting was not a threatening one—in fact, the aliens gave Layne some needed insights. In 1952, George Adamski recorded an encounter in the Mojave Desert with a man from Venus. (It seems that Southern California was conducive to these encounters.) Adamski claimed that his alien remained in communication with him for 13 years, until his death, giving him advice on a variety of topics (Klimo 1998: 51). Both Adamski and Layne are careful to note that these aliens are not from a known physical planet, but an "etheric" one that exists in another frequency or dimension. Like Mme. Blavatsky's astral plane, this special virtual zone provided access between humans and alien life, both bodily and telepathically.

These two encounters remained relatively isolated, but later, a wave of alien encounters occurred between 1964–1973. In the period of the late 1960s, "close encounters" outnumbered aerial sightings (Clark 1997: xi–xiv). It is commonplace now to assign these sightings to the anti-communist anxieties of the period. For example, typical readings of the sci-fi film *The Invasion of the Body Snatchers* (1956) interprets the takeover of normal communities by aliens who look just like your neighbor, as scripting fears of a communist take-over.[14] While this is undoubtedly true in some cases, many of these encounters were considered positive, with aliens providing new solutions to social and material problems, as in the cases of Layne and Adamski. Many encounters had more to do with imagining a contact with other forms of knowledge than to reconfiguring a social threat.

The second wave of alien abductions occurred in the 1980s, with 300 accounts recorded by 1985 and 900 by 1992 (Clark 1997: 3). The encounters were more sinister than the previous ones. These aliens entered the domestic space as invaders, or kidnappers. They were imagined to have the same problem as the robots in *R.U.R.*: reproduction. Unable to reproduce, these aliens mined human eggs, DNA, and other genetic materials to stock their reproductive laboratories. In this period, reproductive technologies were brought to public attention in the media, with reports on endocrine alteration, transplants, genetic alteration, and methods of alternative insemination. Connie Samaras, in her article "Is It Tomorrow or Just the End of Time?" concludes that this wave of alien abductions, with their narratives of abduction from the domestic space, performance of sexual experiments and inseminations reveal contemporary anxieties around the collapse of privacy, the end of traditional forms of insemination, and the contestation of traditional gender roles and sex assignment (1997: 210–211). Abductees were performing a kind of subject/object status regarding new technologies of the body. Taken into labs aboard UFOs, they actually underwent versions of the operations they were hearing about in the media.

If, in the 1950s, people were merely witnessing the technology through sightings, they were now participants in its procedures. These grassroots imagined performances literally encountered scientific procedures in the form of another body that entered their domestic realm and engaged with them in the laboratory. Their own bodies were hailed as necessary for the continuation of alien life and practices. Yet the rites were invasive and sacrificial. They registered a corporeal loss—in eggs, or tissue samples. Their encounters with these new technologies incurred a depletion of their own bodily resources. This anxiety may also be a register of the sense of the upload into the technological virtual that will crescendo during the second half of the century.

The mechanics of memory: Samuel Beckett and tape

Visions of machines that could bind human existence to outer space, to alien transmutation contradicted the ubiquitous experience of machines as iterative— mere recursive archives of past human performances. Phonographs and tape machines recorded performance, archiving its time in an iterative mode. In contrast, UFOs were futuristic machines, traveling in different time zones, entering zones of contact, and marking a time that presaged things to come. They slipped into time warps, lifting people out of earthly time and then delivering them back, while, seemingly, no earthly time had passed. Only recently, in the latter part of the nineteenth century, had time been standardized, dividing up the globe into time zones. This standardization of time enabled the production and distribution of goods as well as long-distance communication across geographic divides. As the industrial time of zones divided up the globe, it seemed that time had come under rational, human control. Likewise, iterative technologies made it possible to repeat the time of performance at will—as if voluntarily managed by the consumer.

Recordings suggested a kind of documentary form of memory—the objectification of a subjective function. Interactions with iterative machines emphasized the experience of the recursive loop, implying the recycling of time. This mechanical recycling troubled the subjective recycling processes of memory. Thus, an "objectified" document archived by the machine could play against "subjectified" memory. At the turn of the century, the degree to which time could be captured or recaptured informed the work of Sigmund Freud, who explored the psychic dynamics of memory; Henri Bergson, who theorized the sense of *durée* or duration, and Marcel Proust, who narrativized the experiences of subjective time in his novel *Remembrance of Things Past*.

Samuel Beckett's first discursive work on time and memory may be found in his early monograph *Proust* (1931). Although a brilliant analysis of Proust's novel, Beckett's critical investment was in his own authorial function rather than in an explication of Proust's text. Indeed, as John Pilling concludes, in his study of *Beckett Before Godot*, "For all Beckett's talk of a 'Proustian equation', it is the possibility of a Beckettian equation which most concerns him" (1997: 37). Beckett identifies two types of memory in *Remembrance of Things Past*: voluntary and involuntary. As he observes: "Voluntary memory (Proust repeats it ad nauseam) is of no value as an instrument of evocation, and provides an image as far removed from the *real* as the myth of our imagination or the *caricature furnished by direct perception*" (Beckett n.d.:4). Two important associations with voluntary memory emerge in this sentence, each of them representing Beckett's, more than Proust's, characterization of it: first, the distancing of the voluntary from the "real" and second, the assertion that direct perception and voluntary memory both provide "caricatures," rather than representations of the "real." Beckett thus associates voluntary memory with empirical functions and marks them both as distant from the "real." In this way, he inverts the traditional relations of perception and hallucination, resituating the "real" within functions of evocation. For Beckett, both the real and the virtual, then, are subject to different modes of evocation than those assumed by the "new" science and its recording technologies.

However, Beckett goes on to complicate this simple inversion. In Proust's paradigm of the Madeleine, he finds that: "the experience is at once imaginative and empirical, at once an evocation and a direct perception, real without being merely actual, ideal without being merely abstract, the ideal real, the essential, the extratemporal." Beckett then pithily concludes: "time is not recovered, it is obliterated" (Beckett n.d.: 56). In these passages, Beckett the theorist conflates the two traditionally binary orders of the real and the ideal through sensate memory. He creates a shared terrain between the empirical and the imaginative, perception and evocation. However, as memory loops back in an attempt to recover time, it ceases to do so within measure and thus obliterates time. The recursive looping of time became literalized in Beckett's work as the machine of iteration—the tape recorder.

According to Martin Esslin, Beckett's fascination with tape began with the production of his first radio play, *All That Fall* (1957) (Esslin 1980: 203). At that time, tape was just beginning to become a medium for recording and broadcasting for the BBC (Zilliacus 1976: 24). Apparently, Beckett's use of tape in *All That Fall* was so innovative that it inspired the founding of a new workshop for the development of tape's capabilities for radio drama, called the BBC Radiophonic Workshop (Zilliacus 1976: 24). The innovative element in *All That Fall* created what Esslin called "stylized realism." Sound effects in the play, such as animal noises and footsteps, which marked the character's reception of them along with their status as "real" needed somehow to be removed from the context of naturalistic reproduction, which most resources provided. Treating these effects electronically with changes in speed, fragmentation, and montage produced the sense that these sounds existed in a more removed space of consciousness or experience. Esslin notes that the stylizing of the acoustic elements positioned the piece "halfway between the objective events experienced and their subjective reflection within the mind of the character, who experiences them" (Esslin 129), thus creating the conflation of dualities Beckett that described in Proust's experience of eating the Madeleine.

Margaret Morse refers to the medium of radio itself as a machine that encouraged listeners to construct personae and environments from "paralinguistic cues" coded as objects and environments—"parallel worlds" as Morse phrases it. These virtual worlds were peopled with virtual subjects through acoustic cues, forming a new technological virtual through the medium of radio (1998: 6). Beckett's radio plays further complicate the virtual space of the medium by distorting, through tape, the sounds that traditionally signified the "real," designing another virtual realm within that of the medium itself. His particular combination of radio and tape, then, exponentially virtualized the realm of performance and help to create a shared space of the subjective both within the medium and in its reception. *All That Fall* lent a new virtual dimension to the iterative function of tape, in highlighting its manipulation as part of a subjective topography. Combined with the broadcast media, which distributed these effects across receiving instruments and listeners, a new kind of virtual space was designed, in which the technical apparatus became part of the dramatic landscape, rather than its archive or its conductor.

Beckett wrote *Krapp's Last Tape* one year after *All That Fall*. In this play, rather than exploring the subjective effect created by the manipulation of tape, he staged the subject effect created in the recursive looping of tape. On the narrative level, tape provides an archive of Krapp's memories, which he recorded at various times in his past. The re-playing of them in the present, along with Krapp's responses to them "obliterates time," as Beckett suggests in Proust, since it ceases to measure past and present, but, instead, through recursive looping, conflates multiple past moments with the present. Tape constitutes a form of voluntary memory, in the sense that Krapp can choose the spool he desires to hear and to start and stop it at will. The tape acts as an objective archive of his voice on a given date. Yet what Krapp had recorded was the memory of an event. So playing the tape, voluntarily choosing the memory, is performing the reconstituted memory of a recorded memory. Further, the break between the listener, Krapp, and the recording of his memory is acted out in a broad gestural style, derived from physical comedy, situating the taped voice at some remove: both invoked by its agent and distanced from him by his very corporeality. The tape as memory, both recalled and resisted thus invokes the hallucinatory quality of the voluntary, ceasing to signify the actuality of the event, but running as an hallucination of the past, which invokes a corporeal distancing from the archived voice. Krapp's voice, then, is uploaded into the recursive looping of memory, while his body corporeally resists it.

In this way, *Krapp's Last Tape* stages the recursive looping of tape and memory as processes that situate the "live" subject. The "live" Krapp is situated in a space dedicated to the storage and indexing of tape. Outside of his proximity to machinic iteration, there is no other order of perception or retention. Beckett specifies: "*Table and adjacent area in strong white light. Rest of stage in darkness*" (1984: 55). Perhaps the stage lighting signifies the radiance of the tape apparatus as fetish, an aura of the machinic produced in the mechanical age, as Walter Benjamin did not quite yet grasp. Krapp listens to the tapes in rapt, motionless attention, evoking their fetishistic affect with the word "spoool." As he corporeally responds to the tapes and the tape recorder, the phallic anxieties that prompt fetish relations are acted out in several ways. For example, one of his actions is to eat a banana. The phallic allusion is marked in the stage directions: "*strokes banana, peels it, tosses skin into pit, puts end of banana in his mouth and remains motionless, staring vacuously before him*" (56). To paraphrase Freud, a banana is not just a banana in this instance, but part of the play of potency and impotency that is embedded in the fetish relations to the technology of tape. But it is not so much the tape itself as the looping of the tape, its recursions, that construct its potency. In the concluding section of the play, Krapp listens to a tape of himself once more remembering an earlier memory:

> TAPE: I lay down across her with my face in her breasts and my hand on her. We lay there without moving. But under us all moved, and moved us, gently, up and down, and from side to side. [*Pause. Krapp's lips move. No sound.*] Past midnight. Never knew such silence. The earth might be uninhabited. [*Pause.*] Here I end this reel. Box—[*Pause*]—three, spool—[*Pause.*] five. [*Pause.*] Perhaps my best years are gone. When there was a chance of happiness. But I wouldn't want them back. Not with the fire in me now. No, I wouldn't want them back. [*Krapp staring motionless before him. The tape runs on in silence.*]
>
> (63)

It is Krapp's LAST tape, as the title indicates and therefore the end of something. The problem of how to end a recursive loop is part of the dramatic design of the play. The title suggests that the play will somehow end the recursive looping, which tape and memory represent in their very structures. The character will cease to move and the play will cease to sound. Krapp no longer desires, and thus no longer desires the recursions. The character and the tape both end together. As there is no running of the tape without Krapp, there is no running of Krapp without the tape. Man and machine are synchronous in their functioning, inhabiting a shared subjective space of recursion that actually defines their functions. Without the recursion, the play, or the playing is over.

This hybrid condition between man and machine that Beckett scripts offers an earlier form of interactivity. Currently, in an era in which tape is passing away, already serving merely as a nostalgic form of acoustic reproduction, we might view this stage picture as fetish of the analog, in the time of the digital. But *Krapp's Last Tape* stages a relationship to tape near the beginning of its dramatic uses, exploring how some of the first encounters of interactivity between the machines of iteration and the live performer may interact, sharing a virtual realm of the subjective.

In the later play *Rockaby* (1980), interactivity displays even more porous borders between tape and human. The character's name has shrunken to a single letter, "w," which, presumably, stands for "woman." She is a mere cipher of gender and of self. The tape again suggests the archived voice of the character on stage, but its role is more definitive than that of simple archive. The taped voice sometimes speaks when "w" does not; sometimes she joins it in unison. This interactive space of tape and character lends an object status to the traditional subject, or character, while amplifying the subjective quality of the tape itself. Krapp controlled the tape and thus, to some extent, the order of events, but in *Rockaby*, the tape runs the performance. As the director Alan Schneider put it: "Once we cut the track, there's no way out of it. The track then becomes the armature for the whole damn thing."[15] The performance seems to emulate the strictly prescribed functions of the mechanical, or of the operations code.

In fact, the character, as cipher, as "w" seems to run like a function in a code, or like a software program in relation to the machine, for not only are the tape segments scripted, but Beckett has specified, down to the second, the actions of the character. Unlike Krapp, who eats, takes pratfalls, and in other ways acts out the exigencies of corporeality, "w" sits nearly motionless in her rocking chair. She does not even rock the chair herself. Beckett is careful to note that the rocking is "controlled mechanically without assistance from w" (Beckett 1984: 274). The almost-mechanized quality of the play is also installed through stage directions that indicate a hyper-precision of cues. Even the blinks of w's eyes are prescribed. The directions determine the blinks to occur "About equal proportion section 1, increasingly closed 2 and 3, closed for good halfway through 4" (273). The voice runs on, as in Krapp, and once again, the conclusion of the play coincides with stopping the taped voice. But in *Rockaby*, the end of the tape is also the end of the character.

"W" (or "woman") is cast in the role of the faithful listener—a role not unfamiliar to women in the traditional social codes. In *Rockaby*, Beckett has staged the condition of the "listener" of the iterative machine as it evolved throughout the twentieth century. "W" is reminiscent of the logo for RCA Victor, which pictures a dog sitting before a speaker, ears cocked, listening to "his master's voice." RCA Victor reported that the overwhelming popularity of the logo was because it was perceived as a figure of fidelity (Taussig 1993: 213). The term "high fidelity" which refers to a type of sound system plays on this notion of a faithful receiver of a faithful reproduction. But the dog, or "w" in this case, is faithfully listening to the recording, aurally bound to its playing, bound to her chair rocked by an external, mechanized force, and bound by split second timing to even the blinks of her eyes. She is the very image of "high fidelity."

One could perceive *Rockaby* as a later version of *Machinal*, with traces of the Expressionist conceit. The psyche and body of the female protagonist is totally overdetermined by mechanization. Treadwell concludes her play with the Young Woman strapped to the electric chair and "w" is strapped to her mechanically-rocked chair the entire play. *Rockaby* stages the regulatory mechanisms of the codes that govern machinic spaces and how they have become partners and even surrogates of subjectivity. Beckett stages how these codes adhere to the character, rocking her chair and regulating the blinks of her eyes. Her fidelity to the codes, as an actress and a character constitute her social semiosis. She is the "user," in computer parlance, whose subjective surrogate is the operations code.

Songs of infidelity: Pauline Oliveros and John Cage

"Experimental" music, as it was aptly termed, began with experiments with tape and other recursive devices. The term "experimental" marked the laboratory/ engineering aspect of this new genre. Events took place in spaces that resembled laboratories more than recital halls and the instruments were either machines, or machinic adaptations of acoustic instruments. The functions and temporalities of apparati displaced the traditional sense of composition that was based upon a strict progression of tones. Intervening in the looping of tape, through time and space, became a major form of composition, leading to new explorations of temporality and place.

One of the pioneers in the field, Pauline Oliveros, co-founded the San Francisco Tape Music Center in 1962, along with Morton Subotnik and Ramon Sende. The collective, inviting nature of the Center helped to launch the more widespread practice of experimental music. In contrast to Beckett's faithful "w," Oliveros created magnetic tape compositions based on the *infidelity* of reproduction. Although her early pieces were composed through the recursive looping of magnetic tape, she invented clever, sonic strategies to sound the gaps and irregularities of frequency and speed. For example, Oliveros stretched the tapes through actual space to alter the time of the looping. Rather than the working the simple off/on function of the recorder, performed by Krapp, Oliveros composed with the accidentals of sound produced by alterations in the apparatus. If Beckett staged the isolated "w" bound to the "machinal," Oliveros encouraged collective improvisation that playfully interacted with the exigencies of the apparati in space. Her compositions encourage "musical potentials" through what she calls "recipes" for sound that leave the participants relatively free to improvise within the overall structure.[16]

In *Tape Delay* (1966) Oliveros combined the recording and rerecording of sound using a tape loop, creating an echo-based dialogue between two tape machines. Thomas Holmes describes the process in *Electronic and Experimental Music*:

Figure 10 Pauline Oliveros at the Tape Music Center Opening.
Used courtesy of the CCM Archive, Mills College

A sound was recorded on the first machine and played back on the second, creating a long delay between the first occurrence of the sound and its repetition on the second machine. If the sound being played back on the second machine was simultaneously recorded by the first machine, an extended echo effect was created with long delays between successive, degenerating repetitions.

(2002: 82)

Oliveros embellished on this concept by threading one reel of tape through two machines, and, finally, three. The composition was created by the delays (maybe eight seconds) caused by the length of the tape and the positions of the machines in space. Rather than retaining the distinction between sounds reproduced on the substrate and the machine itself, Oliveros composed through the exigencies of their relationships. Thus, her interest was less in iteration than in differences obtaining within seeming iterations, including the noise of the machine, as in feedback, and the accumulation of sound. Moreover, often working with long, continuing drone sounds, Oliveros could induce the listener to hear overtones and pulses that are often purposely ignored in traditional forms of composition and reception. Beneath and above and in the sound, one could hear electricity itself.

Like Oliveros, John Cage's experiments began with recursive mechanics. In *Imaginary Landscape No. 1* (1939), he experimented with variable-speed phonographs and recordings of frequency tones. Like Edison, he made it possible to hear the voice of the machine, although altered by the composer. Although this early work marks the human as an active agent in terms of the machine, Cage later scripted the relation of the human subject to the machine strictly in terms of the machine's function. For example, in his piece, *0'00"* (1962) Cage appeared onstage with a cart of vegetables and an electric blender. He proceeded to feed the vegetables into the blender to make juice, with the noise of the blender amplified through loudspeakers. Then, machine off, he drank the juice. The function of the blender determined the sound and performance of the piece. The performer merely runs the machine, finally ingesting its product. The behavior of the performer, here, is merely functional—the mid-century withdrawal from expressivity—the modern "modest witness" of science, who observes and manipulates machines. Unlike the visions of the machine in Expressionist or Futurist pieces, in Cage's compositions, the machine has no affect, but only a ubiquitous function.

Soon, both Oliveros and Cage became interested in the proximities of sound—the sound surround. In order to further develop compositions that extend beyond the simple production of sound, Oliveros developed a craft known as "deep listening." "Deep listening" is a practice that enables one to become an active listener in the environment, in contrast to the faithful listener, who has been disciplined by the European classical tradition to hear only the performed music. In deep listening, one hears more than simply what the machine or instrument produces. Oliveros narrates her discovery of this craft as beginning on her 21st birthday (1953), when she received her first tape recorder. Fascinated by this still somewhat rare device, she began recording all the sounds around her—outside her window, in her bedroom, etc. But as she began listening to the playback, she heard the tape playing within its acoustic environment, rather than as an isolated iteration of other sounds. In line with this discovery, Oliveros crafted pieces in which the sound is co-produced by instrumentalists and the acoustic environment alike. For example, Oliveros and two other musicians played in an underground cistern in Seattle. The closed, resonant space offered an intense focus on the sound surround. They improvised within the sound surround, playing with and off of the traveling pitches and pulses of the work: "As we improvise together, and listen intensely to one another, our styles encounter in the moment, and intermingle to make a collective music. I call the result *deep listening*" (see her deep listening website: http://www.deeplistening.org/).

Cage's early experiments with a sound space were still object-oriented, although they began to compose spatial proximities of sound. For *Cartridge Music* (1960) Cage and David Tudor attached contact microphones and phonograph cartridges to various household objects—furniture, ladders, waste baskets—and replaced their needles with wires, matches, pipe cleaners, feathers and the like, making everyday objects sound, while also registering their spatial relationships. In this way, Cage began to compose the topography of sound through objects in the space. *For Cartridge Music* composed the virtual space of sound as a ubiquitous and domestic one. The acoustic coordinates were simple projections of the objects within a domesticated space.

The interest in acoustical resonances in space led Oliveros to also experiment with the environmental effects of alternating electrical currents. Harking back to the experiments with alternating electrical currents, which led to the invention of the electric chair, Oliveros wrote a piece in honor the inventor who discovered them, Nikola Tesla. However, instead of imagining the murderous or commodified promises of the alternating currents, as Edison and Treadwell had done, Oliveros sought to explore their sympathies. Employing Tesla's discovery that the oscillator could share resonances with the materials that surround it, Oliveros designed a piece for musicians and dancers called *In Memoriam Nikola Tesla, Cosmic Engineer* (1969). She asked the musicians to search for the resonant frequencies of the theater structure in which the piece took place. As she put it: "If the search for resonant frequency has been successful, then the frequency of the generators selected by the musicians can cause the performance space to add its squeaks, groans. . . . Thus the space performs in sympathy with the musicians," and, she might have added, in sympathy with dancers who were performing in the piece (quoted in von Gunden 1983: 64). Oliveros's score invited "sympathetic vibrations," hence her title *Cosmic Engineer*, invoking earlier notions of the sympathetic relations among elements in the universe, popularly referred to as "the music of the spheres."

In this account, we can perceive Oliveros's and Cage's experiments with sound as moving from alterations of iterative archival devices to an interest in the acoustic and electronic surround: from the machinic to the electronic. If the machine suggests the production of sound and an object-oriented spatiality, the electronic suggests a sonic field, which penetrates objects and architecture alike. Ultimately, experimental music will invent a new form called the soundscape, based on the notion of a field.

The theremin and the Cage

The first musical instrument that seemed to acoustically deliver the sound of the electrical field was called the Theremin. Playing the Theremin suggested performing in an electronic field rather than manipulating an instrument. The Theremin consists of two tubular metal antennas: a straight vertical tube on the right, and a horizontal loop on the left. Antennae already suggest a more synthetic relationship between the production and the reception of sound than a classical instrument. The Theremin's sound is elicited by the movements of hands in space. The closer the right hand of the performer moves to the straight rod, the higher the instrument's pitch. The closer left hand moves to the loop, the louder or softer the volume. The Theremin provides opportunities for performance beyond the traditional European instruments, in which the hand and body seem bound to the physical instrument, such as the violin. Waving one's hands in the air to produce the tone, touching no solid mass in order to elicit the sound, and making gestural figures sound actual pitches invites associations of theatricality and virtuality at once. Recalling the magic wand, waving the hands through the air could elicit music. Although the Theremin was invented in the early part of the twentieth century, it was Robert Moog's (developer of the Moog synthesizer) packaging of a do-it-yourself Theremin kit that brought the instrument to the attention of experimental composers and performers.

Here was a musical instrument designed especially to sound the virtual field of electricity that haunted the surround of mid-century-techno culture. Technology was not imagined as a machine, as in the early part of the century, but as a field. Like the UFO, the Theremin was a "clean machine" with no "guts:" only metal antennae in space. The glissando-effect of the sound, in which pitch seems to slide along an invisible, airy axis seemed uniquely modern, compared with the production-by-single-pitch that most classical instruments produced. The Theremin's sound production through a virtual field and its unique timbre encouraged its reception as "otherworldly" by many, associating it with outer space. It was used in the soundtrack of several science fiction movies, such as *The Day the Earth Stood Still* (1951) in which it accompanied the arrival of the smooth metal flying saucer and a featureless, silvery-shrouded robot. The Theremin was the sound of new science.

In fact, electronic music in general seemed a suitable accompaniment to mid-century fantasies of outer space. In 1956, the first completely electronic soundtrack for film was designed for the science-fiction classic *Forbidden Planet*. The "composers," Louis and Bebe Barron, were inspired by Norbert Wiener's *Cybernetics* to begin generating sounds with electronic apparati. Their soundtrack to the film so challenged the institutions and practices of ownership in the traditional production of music that the musician's union blocked them from being credited as "composers" on the film, and thus unable to be considered for an Oscar. They invented the term "electronic tonalities" to represent their score, stressing the origin of the sound as from the apparatus rather than from the "composer's" mind. They were more engineers than composers, designing an acoustic schematic. Their soundtrack drew the attention of others working in experimental music, particularly one of the leaders in the field, John Cage.

Cage organized a definitive composition of the performative soundscape through the use of the Theremin in his piece *Variations V* (1965). Cage commissioned Moog to set up antennae in an experimental space, where they could be activated, like the Theremin, to create percussive noises as dancers moved in proximity to them. Along with choreographer Merce Cunningham, Cage was interested in how the dancers themselves, through their proximity to the antennae could actually co-create a performative soundcape. He also collaborated other experimental composers and cross-over engineers in the piece: composers Gordon Mumma and David Tudor and two engineers from Bell labs, Billy Klüver and Max Mathews (optical light triggers). This combination of engineering and art would be a prescient one. In addition, visual artists Robert Rauschenberg, Nam June Paik (manipulated TV images), Jasper Johns (projections), and the filmmaker Stan Vanderbeek designed a syncretic space of visual imagery. In other words, Cage imagined a field of design in which technical apparati mixed with painting, dance, and video in a non-narrative, non-unitary fashion. One of the composers, Gordon Mumma described the set-up this way:

> The Stage consists of two systems of electronic sensors; the first is a set of focused photocells, the second a group of five-foot-high antennae. As the dancers move about the stage they interrupt the light which falls on the photocells. The vertical antennas are capacitance devices which respond to the distance of the dancers from each other, to the proximity of the dancers from the antennas, and to the number of dancers on the stage. The changes of light intensity on the photocells, and the capacitive responses of the antennas, are both transmitted as electrical signals to electronic music 'trigger' equipment in the orchestra pit. The musicians operate an "orchestra" of tape recorders, record players, and radio receivers which contain the sound materials composed by Cage. Before these sounds are heard by the audience they are fed into the electronic-music "trigger" equipment. The sounds are then released to loudspeakers in the audience by the triggering action of the dancer's movements on the stage.
> (http://www.theremin.info/info-65.html)

So some sounds were triggered by the movement of the dancers and others came from data archiving machines that played original compositions by Cage, Tudor and Mumma. Sounds were produced by both reception and production, emitting from shortwave receivers, audio oscillators, light beams aimed at photocells that could be interrupted to generate sounds, contact microphones on dancers and props—and all fed into a ninety-six input mixer (see Holmes 2002: 128–129). Basically, then, what was produced was an indeterminate field of images, movement and sound.

The visual space of Cage's performative soundscape resembled a lab or an inventor's workshop. Antennae were placed around the dance floor, and cables from the instruments lined the borders of the space. Electric cords, machines, projection screens and other technical apparati, which are often hidden from view in performance, actually compose the visual field. The composers/operators are in full view as well, tending to the apparati in the forespace. They are dressed in suits and ties, resembling the scientists in 1950s sci-fi movies, as they manipulate the machines with seeming precision. Thus, one looks through their technical operations into the space; the composer/operators constitute a lens of sorts that focuses performance through technological experimentation. The

Figure 11 Variations V, courtesy of the Archives of the Merce Cunningham Dance Company

dancers move behind them, through a seemingly "empty" space, since their movements do not relate to the visual field. The dancers' movements do not coincide with either the images on the screens or the nature and rhythms of the sound. The performance space seems like a laboratory for the investigation of movement and the production of sound and image acting independently of one another. Although they share a space, they do not illustrate any sympathetic resonances—except, perhaps, in style. This is apparently an abstract space that can accommodate integers, but is unchanged by them.

If mid-century grassroots performers were imagining technology as alien, Cage imagined it as quotidian. Cage had moved away from expressive music and acoustic instruments to electronic ones and Cunningham had left Martha Graham's company of expressive "modern" dance to found a more eclectic, non-expressive style of choreography. For them, the converse of expression was the quotidian. Like Cage's earlier work with the electric blender, Cunningham's choreography scripts peri-functional tasks. At one point in *Variations V,* Cunningham puts together a prefabricated plastic plant, which a female dancer later waters. He also rides a bicycle through the space. These abstracted functions relate neither to the environment nor to other dancers. The functions appear almost like examples of pedestrian movement dropped into the "empty" space of composition.

A videotape recording of the piece, archived from an early German television presentation of the performance, allows one to view the piece in action.[17] At first, the vocabulary of classical ballet with its traditional partnering and familiar extensions seems out of place in this high tech environment, but then the simple line, although derived from nineteenth-century choreography, appears more as the style of the mid-century modern with its geometric, minimalist aesthetic. The movement, without narrative or symbolic referent, remains abstract. It points to the composition of the field rather than to any determinative narrative. The dance theorist Susan Leigh Foster notes that the movements have no emotional or psychological referent, a point Cunningham makes repeatedly in his program notes. Foster continues: "Cunningham's determination to cultivate the body as a neutral field of possibilities" led to "an equivalence of male and female bodies, and black and white bodies. ... Difference, his dances proclaimed, could only be located in the distinctive physical capacities of each individual body's joint flexibility, bone lengths, muscular mass, speed, or dexterity" (2001: 175). Foster's description certainly fits the sense of a laboratory of movement, with all of the seeming neutrality of field and referent, and a focus on structural composition. The effect is analytic rather than expressive or synthetic. Here are dancers who resemble the "modest witnesses" in the laboratory, or who move as neutrally and functionally as the imagined aliens. As a mid-century modern experiment, any sense of interior expression, or even social relations is evacuated for a focus on the structural, or surface qualities of the dance and the dancer's body.

At first, Cage reacted negatively to the application of the adjective "experimental" to his compositions, but later he embraced it when used to denote a particular aspect of his work. In his book *Silence*, he writes that as long as:

> attention moves towards the observation and audition of many things at once, inclusive rather than exclusive—no question of making, in the sense of forming understandable structures, can arise (one is tourist), and here the word 'experimental' is apt, providing it is understood not as descriptive of an act later to be judged in terms of success and failure, but simply as an act the outcome of which is unknown.
>
> (1973: 13)

Cage's concept of the experimental embraces some of the traditional meanings of the term and rejects others. He would differentiate his experiments from the notion of iteration, so central to the definition and positioning of elements in the laboratory; yet, he accepts the idea that, as an experiment, the outcome is unknown. Rather than serving as a test of a hypothesis, Cage celebrates the element of uncertainty or indeterminacy of the experiment.

However, along with science, Cage derived his sense of composition from a spiritual movement. Cage's notion of silence as a virtual space directly related to a philosophical/religious system that he began to adopt in the 1940s, when he attended lectures by D.T. Suzuki on Zen Buddhism at Columbia University. This spiritual tradition became a structural one in Cage's laboratory of sound. The principles he gleaned from Zen even guided his notion of "experimental" as indeterminate. He described an "*experimental* action" (italics his) as one "generated by a mind as empty as it was before it became one." The action, moreover, is in no way "informed" by knowledge because that would unnecessarily narrow the possibilities of the project (Cage 1973: 15). So for Cage an experiment, as in experimental music, is a Zen action, escaping the determinism of prior conceptions through silence. Cage often substituted the use of the *I Ching*, or the Taoist *Book of Changes* for traditional Eurocentric notions of structure and composition. The fall of the yarrow sticks, or the elements of divination, chance-like, replace sequencing and causality, tempo and signature. In his foreword to the English translation of the *Book of Changes*, Jung describes its basic premise as "a configuration formed of chance events in the moment of observation," or, as he would put it, "a synchronicity" (xxiii). We might consider *Variations V* as composing a performative virtual based on an indeterminate synchronicity in space and duration.

So Zen Buddhism offered Cage one sense of a field of composition through silence, but early twentieth-century field theories, such as electromagnetic field theory, quantum theory of the electromagnetic field, and unified field theory offered him another. If he attended lectures by Suzuki, he also attended lectures by Einstein. These field theories represent one of the most important versions of virtual space peculiar to the twentieth century. While I do not pretend to comprehend these notions, nor the physics behind them, their translation into a popular vocabulary provides some basic sense of how they were imagined. The traditional idea that the world consists of both fields and particles seems familiar to many philosophical systems—even classical Greek ones. But the notion of particles, or atoms became complicated with the understanding of electromagnetic fields and electrons. Rather than particles constituting the basic unit of the composition of the "universe," field theories postulate that fields are the basic units and that particles are just "bundles of energy and momentum" within the fields. (This idea is not too distant from David-Neel's description of Tibetan Buddhist physics described earlier in this work.) As Steve Weinberg, a quantum physicist, expresses it: "In a relativistic theory a wave function is a function of these fields, not a function of particle coordinates. Quantum field theory hence led to a more unified field of nature than the old dualistic interpretation in terms of both fields and particles."[18] A field as a basic compositional unit greatly altered work in the arts, producing new compositions like *Variations V.*

While Cage sought to break with European notions of causality and empiricism at the deepest level, his laboratory space still displayed the familiar fraternity of urban, middle-class, white male experimenters, as Foster suggested above. In other words, though structurally indeterminate, Cage's laboratory space was socially overdetermined. Jazz musician and scholar George Lewis argues that Cage's interpretation of improvisation was as a specifically Eurocentric form of innovation, taking little from expressive popular forms, such as jazz (quoted in

Foster 2001: 163–164). Cage's laboratory was thus bounded by many of the same codes of access that the sciences traditionally enforced according to gender, class, etc. *Variations V* exhibits a strict control of the space's borders. The composer/scientists define the forespace, with the projected images lining the back, and cables defining the sides. The space is not open to intrusion from the outside and the principles of access are exclusive, even if structurally indeterminate.

Virtual closet

Cage's strictly-bounded lab had another function as well—it served as a closet. Jonathan Katz, in "John Cage's Queer Silence; or, How to Avoid Making Matters Worse," ties the closeting of Cage's sexuality to his adoption of Zen the principles mentioned above:

> Zen repositioned the closet, not as a source of repression or anxiety, but as a means to achieve healing; it was not in talking about—and hence not recti-fying—one's troubles that healing began . . . One can hear just this Zen note in Cage's remarks. . . . "You can feel an emotion; just don't think that's so important.". . . . Cage had undergone a remarkable alchemy: his anxiety and pain had metamorphosed into detachment. . . .
>
> (Katz 2001: 45–46)

Cage's flight from expressivity is represented by Katz as a sign of the necessary closeting of his homosexual relationships. The "silenced" homosexual could, through Zen, find structural solace in that silencing. Katz's aim is to "recuperate silence as a means of what I will characterize as a historically specific queer resistance during the Cold War. . . . For Cage, silence was an ideal form of resistance, one attuned to the requirements of the Cold War consensus—at least within its originary social historical context. There is both surrender and resistance in these silences. . . . " (53) Situating Cage's closeting device of removed silence within the atmosphere of Cold War secrecy and revelation, Katz brings social determinism back to the structurally indeterminate principle.

Cage's partner, Merce Cunningham, created a similar structuring of the closet. Susan Leigh Foster identifies a similar way in which Cunningham signi-fied his own closeting practices, specifically in *Variations V.* She notes that even though Cunningham denied the "sexual and gendered referents of the dancing body," his style, in which "men partnered and lifted women" moving with "uprightness and clarity of purpose, the erect, nonorganic movement style, allied his dances with the more masculine ballet tradition than with the feminine modern dance." Cunningham thus produced a masculinized field of operations in which the seemingly non-gendered dancer's moved. Foster's analysis of Cunningham's closet resides in the fine distinction that within this masculinized dance environment "Cunningham circulated as the odd man out" (177). Foster illustrates her point by citing how he works in a space apart with the plastic plant; rides around on the bicycle while the others dance, and does sit ups and a headstand alone on a blanket while three couples perform nearby. Foster concludes that his strategy of "distinctiveness" negotiated a space for him outside of the "matriarchal modern dance" on the one side, through his assimilation of the masculinized tradition of ballet and "vicious" homophobia on the other (178). Like Cage's silence, Cunningham's choreography of "apartness" signified their "other" partnering that could not be expressed. It appeared only in the absences, the vacant spaces that seemed to signify "nothing."

Thus, *Variations V* organizes a complex virtual space of inclusion and exclusion, improvisation and adherence to principle, performativity and that which cannot be performed. It combines the laboratory experiment with Buddhist meditational principles and with a mid-century cryptography that coded "secret" sexual practices in an era of violent homophobia. Technology is a key component in Cage's closet because of its seeming resistance to signification. Although, to some, the song of the machines may sound "other worldly," for Cage, the sound and the intermittent silence resides outside the kind of signification of emotional, psychological, or natural allusions that European classical music invented. The functional sound of the blender making juice, or the self-referential looping of magnetic tape foregrounds the machine in itself. Technology helps to establish the remove of the soundscape while it also secures its inclusion in the electronic surround in the culture at large. Its seeming lack of social signification displaces any sense of secrets that may be lurking in the closet.

Cage's composition was on the way to the later immersive environment of Virtual Reality. The piece seems oriented more toward the practitioners themselves, rather than to an audience. The desire to be totally within the immersive environment of media and sound would later develop into the performative space of VR.

Out of the sonic closet

As an "out" lesbian feminist composer, Pauline Oliveros composes sonic inscriptions that are in synch with their social resonances, rather than distant from them. In 1970, she composed *To Valerie Solanas and Marilyn Monroe In Recognition of Their Desperation* ... for "any group or groups of instrumentalists (6 to large orchestra)" (a short excerpt can be heard at http://www.newmusicjukebox.org./). In several online interviews, Oliveros points to Solanas' *S.C.U.M. Manifesto* as one of the core influences on her work. The manifesto of SCUM, the Society for Cutting Up Men, manifests a very aggressive, angry attitude toward "men" as exemplars of war, of governments, and as perpetrators of violence against women, such as sexual predators, censors, etc. The manifesto calls for women to abandon men, take control of their empires, liberate profits for the people, and finally kill all men who do not belong to the male Scum auxiliary unit. The same year she wrote the manifesto, Solanas gained notoriety by shooting Andy Warhol.[19]

Oliveros' composition to Solanas and Monroe, however, is far from aggressive; rather, it invites improvised sets of very long, meditative tones. The players select different pitches, without consulting with one another, and then play them in a "very soft or long attack and release," with only variations that do not "change the fundamental frequency of the tone." The slow, expansive, and enduring set of tones, played in groups of instruments, both acoustic and electronic, and with singers, makes for a meditative, melancholic continuum of sound. Perhaps the melancholic aspect of the piece relates to Marilyn Monroe, as the object of the kind of male violence Solanas describes. In a performative surround, the music is conducted partially by light cues. The colors of the lights, red, yellow, blue, and flashing white determine the introduction of the different pitches and their return to the originary pitch. Thus, there is a sense of the performative interaction among the elements of performance, keying improvisation in a relay among lights and sounds. While there are no words to articulate the politics of the piece, its title inspires the listener to reflect upon the desperate and tragic conclusions to the lives of Monroe and Solanas and their relationship to powerful, oppressive men: Monroe overdosed and Solanas died in degrading, squalid conditions. Interestingly, Oliveros had the piece played at the ceremony of her marriage to another woman, in 1971. Perhaps she felt that the union of two lesbians performed the kind of sympathetic relationship the piece also sought to compose, in contrast to the violence of objecthood.[20]

Later in her career, Oliveros composed several performance pieces with her partner, Ione, in which she explored ancient and ritual resonances along with her sonic ones. Their operas reflect many of the early feminist strategies in re-creating and claiming liberatory narratives for women, with elements of ritual and shamanism interwoven with historical details. Unlike Cage and Cunningham, whose closet withdrew expression into a neutral, silent style of composition, their partnership celebrates various expressive forms that point directly to lesbian and feminist politics. They openly celebrate the union of their two modes of composition: experimental electronic music by Oliveros and the shamanic performance of rites by Ione. What these two forms have in common is an investment in improvisation—an open form rather than a closed laboratory.

Oliveros and Ione produced one particularly shamanistic piece entitled *Njinga The Queen King; The Return of a Warrior,* which offers a study in transgender identification, feminist historiography and transcultural performance styles. The production is based on a play by Ione, relating the story of Njinga, the seventeenth-century regent of Ndongo, the country that is now known as Angola. The play enjoyed a large international cast of approximately 22 members and opened to critical acclaim in December 1993 at Brooklyn Academy of Music's Next Wave Festival. An essay on Njinga that clarifies the critique of the work appears in a book edited by Cornel West and Rosemarie Robotham, entitled *Spirits of the Passage; The Transatlantic Slave Trade in the Seventeenth Century.* The piece reflects the feminist concern with revising histories and notions of traditions that are inaccurate in terms of gender identification. In general, Ione's vocabulary combines spiritual traditions with UFO imaginings. On her website, she claims to draw upon a synthetic mix similar to the tradition of Mme. Blavatsky: "Senoi, Ancient Egyptian, Greek, Tibetan and Native American dream-ways." Her website links also include SETI, a website for the Search for Extraterrestrial Intelligence and *The Egyptian Book of the Dead* (http://www.deeplistening.org/ione/). Thus, Ione brings these indigenous and science fiction imaginaries in contact with Oliveros's own experimental music.

Their more recent work, the *Lunar Opera*, while not mid-century, brings together many strands of fantasy and experiment from the period in a kind of grand finale. Created as part of the Lincoln Center Out of Doors Festival, from 2–7 pm. on August 17, 2000 (at the time of the full moon), the opera involved a mixture of professional and amateur musicians and performers, who improvised events that took place around Lincoln Center, the Julliard School of Music, the Metropolitan Opera House, the Performing Arts Library, and concluding at the Guggenheim Bandshell. The opera interlaced improvised performances around the major archives of high culture in New York, wittily designating the performance sites as the outer space cities of Lunarus. Re-nominating these sites through tropes of science fiction intervened in the authority these institutions command in the classical training of music and performance. According to the script, the land of Lunarus is situated on the far side of the moon Anomaly, which orbits a planet "like earth." The opera was based on the trope that at this particular conjunction of time and place; the people of Lunarus could be seen by the people on earth. The wandering Moonstrels, Ambassadors, and Atchetypal Beings of Lunarus thus populate the performance, improvising dialogue, music, and action within loosely described outlines. The mythical setting draws on a synthetic imagining of outer space and indigenous practices that are familiar to New Age forms in the late twentieth century.

Three hundred performers represented various types of experimental composition from experimental theater and music practices to those of shamans and leaders of rituals. A sampling of participants includes the performance artist Linda Montano, the popular feminist vocalist Linda Tillery, the online theater performer Marlena Corcoran, the poet Trudy Morse, who had also worked with Sun Ra, the experimental musician/composer Stuart Dempster, an Argentinian music collective called Reynols, and a vocal trio of improvised sound called Comma. The performance commenced with Drepung Loseling Tibetan monks singing an eleventh-century invocation, followed by their form of dialog— Buddhist disputation. Participants then formed a procession, with collective sound-making to the various sites, where improvised dialogue and music-making took place. Moonstrels prowled the area with their original bits of dialog and other people participated online. Thus, the Tibetan forms of the nineteenth century, the virtual Tibet of the twentieth century began the opera with traditional performance traditions, which then led into a science fiction imaginary, experimental music, poetry, and performance art.

Oliveros organized the opera through a website, where she posted the score of events and the sites. A two-day walk-through constituted the only "real-time" rehearsal. Linda Montano described the event as feminist: "Why was it a feminist, memorable event? You have to have been there really. It was so circular and continuous and multi-focused and collaborative and visual and sonic and magnanimous and full bodied and outrageously incorrect in its process and comment on the paradigm of doing the right thing that the place will never be the same" (http://web.ukonline.co.uk/n.paradoxa/define2.htm). It is not difficult to imagine the difference in composition and affect this piece organizes in contrast to *Variations V,* or *Rockaby.*

Oliveros and company formed a complex notion of the virtual through this performance. A rag-tag mixture of unlike elements, invoked through production and the receptive device of deep listening come together through the trope of outer space and ancient ritual, suggesting that the virtual carries with it resonances of both esoteric and "alien" referents. Still maintaining the virtuality of aesthetic performance, the opera casts a receptive space around the institutions of privilege, where capital endowment and exclusive, rigorous training take place, inviting the sound of traffic to join the garden hose, chanting monks, snatches of Moonster's songsounds, and short scenes. There is no canonic exclusionary tradition of sound or performance. The machinic and the embodied come together in this social space and online through a collective, improvisatory

Figure 12 Lunar Opera, Tibetan Monks, and Moonstrels, courtesy of Pauline Oliveros

receptivity to the space in which they meet. The social is made part of the performance rather than excluded from its parameters. Consorting with machines is playful and resonant, partaking in civic life and its critique.

The Lunar Opera thus recycled mid-century fantasies of outer space along with Tibetan traditions of improvisation, a synthesis of active and passive modes in "deep listening," site-specific performance, online communications, and technological innovation. Oliveros offers a contemporary version of Mme. Blavatsky's syncretic, embodied performances. Opening her opera with Tibetan monks set the stage in an evocative way that once more re-imagined Tibet as a source code for spiritualist composition. Combining it with tropes of outer space, Oliveros brings its significations into its late twentieth-century form. She recycles the ancient texts within another other-worldly setting of science fiction. Rites of transformation play with iteration, machines with the live. The opera offers a finale of mid-century themes and strategies and heralds the performance traditions of the next millennium.

SCENE THREE: UNDER-MODERN: TRASH

Lowering the gaze from skies filled with saucers and aliens, and leaving the exclusive labs of science and performance, we can see the dark underside of the mid-century modern: the waste exuded from its techno-labs and their commodities. By the 1970s and 1980s, the clean machines of the mid-century had become ubiquitous. They were not only objects of the gaze, but transit-vehicles into techno and "outer" space. A techno-virtual was imagined as free from waste and wasting. Accreting the promise of earlier liturgical notions of the virtual, the new spaces were imagined as redeeming the promise of transcendence. Only the disenfranchised, who were not part of the corporate club, or the virtual class, were forced to remain in the abandoned spaces, spaces filled with the trash byproduct of the production of such transcendent technologies. For those exiled from such modes of transcendence, trash became an aesthetic as well as a practical tool for sustaining their living and performing habitats. Outside these privileged virtual spheres, something called the "environment" seemed to be literally wasting away. The environmental movement of the 1970s sought to make it clear that there was no "free" space, or boundless nature that could contain all of the human and industrial waste. Buckminster Fuller's famous proposition inverted the imagined transcendence of transit machines to a call for eco-responsibility: "We are all astronauts on a little spaceship called earth." In other words, the machine provides no "flight" from the environment; in fact, the spaceship is the earth.

One of the most influential new theorists of "space," David Harvey, has argued that irresponsible over-production of waste was a by-product of the call for the mastery of nature sounded by the Anglo-European tradition of Enlightenment philosophy and the "new" science. In this study, Goethe's *Faust* offers a dramatic paradigm of the shift from the shared subject of alchemical and Goethean science to a human subject who cuts the earth into canals, and fires up of the slag-producing furnaces of the nineteenth-century factories. At that point in history, nature became situated not only as the object of human will and need, but also as a space exclusively designed for the expression of the materialization of the human ego. (Harvey 1996: 122). Landscape paintings abounded, representing nature as a filter of the human imagination. Scaling the peaks of the Himalayas was a form of dominating them. Mountains simply measured human strength, endurance, and talent and sited its transcendence. By the end of the twentieth century, these same mountains have become a garbage dump of used oxygen tanks and other waste products of human endeavor.

From the perspective of the nineteenth century, Marx argued that the Enlightenment philosophers, who called for the mastery of the human subject, such as Descartes and Bacon, "saw with the eyes of the manufacturing period," understanding "the practical subjugation of Nature by Man" as a result of the altered form of production (quoted in Harvey 1996: 121). In other words, the philosophical and scientific systems worked together with the growth of industrial production and its capitalization, not only as business partners, but as co-producers of the notion of the dominant human subject. Both philosophy and industry required that nature be viewed as a space open to exploitation—a supplier. In the nineteenth-century novel, *Money*, Zola's protagonist celebrates "Speculation—why, it is the one inducement we have to live," comparing the new capitalization of such projects to bringing health to the body: "Yes! Fields will be cleared, roads and canals built, new cities will spring from the soil, life will return as it returns to a sick body. . . . " (quoted in Harvey 1996: 132). In contrast to the ascription of health-giving qualities to speculation, Marx wrote: "the dominion of private property and money is a real contempt for and practical debasement of nature" (quoted in Harvey 1996: 157). Near the end of the century, Chekhov staged these conflicting nineteenth-century attitudes toward industry and nature with the speculative clearing of the *Cherry Orchard*, on the one hand, and Dr. Astrov's utopic planting project in *Uncle Vanya*, on the other.

In contrast to the seeming riches that nature offered to nineteenth-century speculators, the twentieth century witnessed the beginning of a global crisis in the sustainability of these resources. By the end of the century, attention had shifted from Darwin's search for an "origin" of the species to concern for the extinction of many—and not from the operations of natural selection. The crisis in sustenance deepened as activists and scientists discovered that not only were the resources of land and water wasted, but new human technologies were actually wasting the supply of oxygen. Carbon dioxide emissions from industry, along with carbon pollution, were creating a "greenhouse effect" that altered the protective shroud of the entire earth and gave rise to global warming, a trend that would affect plant life, as well as all other species. Thus, new technologies were perceived as threatening life on a global level from the mid-century onward, from the atomic bomb, on the one hand, to global warming, on the other.

The result of the centuries-long degradation of sustainable conditions through human domination gave rise to a sense of something called the "environment," rather than "nature." The term "environment" suggested a space within which the human subject, among other species was located. In the late 1960s, and particularly in the 1970s, an international movement in support of sustainability, called environmentalism, took hold. As an international movement, it encouraged a responsibility for a shared space, a sphere beyond the boundaries of nation, or private property. The identification of such a sphere challenged how resources and waste should be regulated. The oceans, for example, particularly fragile sites for life and health, stretch among nations, but are owned by none. Supported by agencies growing up through the United Nations, the environmental movement needed nations to ratify its international treaties. Obviously, this movement found itself in conflict with those who wanted to assert property rights over profit-yielding territories and practices. Unfortunately, one of the nations most responsible for environmental degradation, the United States has denied ratification to several such acts, aligning national policy with the capital needs of industry.

However, the term "environment" still seemed to retain the traditional distinction between subject and object, imagining the environment to be something like a context, or an envelope of the subject. The movement grew to challenge this dyad of human/nature, to understand that "a human being is not a thing in an environment, but a juncture in a relational system. . . . " (Harvey 1996: 167). The term "biosphere" seemed to represent a more porous relationship among systems. The broad usage of the term evolved from the Biosphere Conference in 1968, organized by UNESCO, the World Health Organization, the International Union for the Conservation of Nature and Natural Resources, and other new international agencies growing up around the new crises. The conference concluded that "although some of the changes in the environment have been taking place for decades or longer; they seem to have reached a threshold of criticalness" (Caldwell 28). Thus, the return of a shared subject position among species and elements was catalyzed by the sense of a crisis in sustaining life on the planet. The 1972 United Nations Conference on Human Environment urged several new, international treaties for the protection of the biosphere.

Alongside the U.N. several political organizations were founded to intervene in destructive ecological practices using specifically performative means, such as Greenpeace, which has been campaigning against environmental degradation since 1971, and the Green Party, which first emerged in West Germany in the 1980s. In 1978, Greenpeace refitted a former fishing trawler, which, with a small crew, intervened in toxic dumping practices in the ocean, whaling, and seal hunts. Its media profile became so powerful that in 1985, it was bombed by the French government as it trespassed into the nuclear testing site at the Moruroa atoll. Its various interventions brought international press to reveal destructive practices at such ecologically damaged sites.

Although the movement now has identified many areas of sustainability that are critical, this section will focus solely on "trash." Returning to the ocean, for a

moment, as an international site for biosphere politics, the practice of trans-
porting and dumping waste through those waters has been at crisis levels for
several decades. An exposé published in the November 7, 1988 issue of *Newsweek*
revealed hidden practices of transnational illegal dumping. The article offers a
chilling account of ghost ships wandering the world's oceans filled with toxic
waste. As the article reports: "Off the coasts of Turkey, Haiti, Africa, the
Philippines—an armada of toxic ships is circling the world ... bearing the
poisonous waste of the industrial world to treatment facilities," some legal and
some illegal. As a prime example, it offers the story of the Bahamian-owned
vessel, Khian Sea, loaded with toxic incinerator ash from Philadelphia, which left
port in 1986 and then spent the next two years wandering the Mediterranean
and the Indian Ocean looking for a country that would accept the waste. At one
point, it dumped 4,00 tons of waste on a beach in Haiti. After being refused
entry almost everywhere, the ship was last spotted wandering the Indian Ocean
in 1988. Greenpeace suspects it has dumped the remaining waste into the ocean.
Cruise ships, however, are not required to have permits to dump their raw
sewage into the ocean, nor do they have to monitor or report what they have
released. A cruise ship with 3,000 passengers and crew produces 7 tons of
garbage and solid waste per day. They are pleasure ships for humans, poisoning
the waters of the world and thereby the fish and plants that live within them. To
coin Brecht's thought in his foreword to *Galileo*, they will be surprised to discover
that they, themselves, are even endangered by their practices.

Trash is piling up all around us. By 1996, nearly 210 million tons of trash—
about 4.3 lb. per person—was collected and disposed of by municipalities in the
U.S. In the Philippines, Metro Manila's 11 million residents generate 6,000 tons
of garbage every day. Only 4,000 tons are collected. Residents dump the rest
into rivers and waterways. In Kenya, a local women's group in Meru town is
working closely with the Meru Municipal Council to address dumping in the
Imenti forest. In the California deserts, massive illegal dumping has incited the
Cabazon Tribal Police and the Torrez-Martinez tribal authorities to begin
patrolling the areas to protect their sacred lands from becoming landfills. Israel is
reportedly dumping 10,000 tons of garbage per month in the West Bank; south
of Tulkarem City, the massive mound of garbage smolders day and night,
exuding lethal smoke into the surrounding area.

In the landfills, it is the machines of transcendence, computers and TV moni-
tors that compose the fastest-growing category of solid waste known as
"hazardous" waste. Their cyber spaces finally degrade into poisonous injections
of the groundwater. Their transcendent virtual spaces are actually degrading the
sustainability of life on the planet.

Queer and cyber trash

A performative resistance to such environmental wasting was mounted through a
redeployment of the term "trash." Reinvesting "trash" with cultural value and

re-animating its materials with the power of sustenance served as a performative resistance against the processes of waste. As a mise en scène, or as a practice, "trash" structured anti-normative representations of sex, gender, and property relations from the mid-1960s through the early years of the 1980s. This redeployment of "trash" compacted individual sexual practices with global environmental ones, in a time when radical changes were beginning to register in the cultural and social imaginary of space. If the mid-century modern fashioned gleaming, transcendent virtual spaces, the under-modern performed a transgressive embrace of their trash. Sets and costumes composed of trash, or garbage located gay drag performances in the 1970s, both in live performance and in underground film. Jack Smith, in his film and loft performances, staged interventions into the practices of capitalism, gender, and sexuality within a topology of trash. Trash, as a style of drag fantasy, glamorized the de-territorializing processes of gentrification and "white trash" denigration through the performance of "trashy" elegance by drag divas.

In spite of the "richness" of this tradition, by the turn of the decade into the 1980s, trash was disappearing from drag performances, signaling, by its absence, a shift in strategies of gay representation. At the same time as its disappearance in drag performance, new representations of trash were forming the cyberpunk fantasies of the megalopolis. The novels of William Gibson, Bruce Sterling, and others were set in underground communities, where the under-privileged dwelt within a habitat of re-constructed trash. Techno-trash, discarded by huge corporate conglomerates, provided a material advantage for the dispossessed, who could use it to hack their way in to the exclusive system of the corporate cyberspace.

These two very different registers of social gesture, the gay drag performance of the feminine gender, and the masculinized, heterosexist science fiction of cyberpunk both turned to trash for their carapace and, indeed, the incarnation of their alternative vision of desire and domain. Gay dragsters handed off trash to cyber-jacksters in a relay that imaged a major shift in social and material relations during that period. Trash housed first a feminized, then a masculinized representation of agency for those newly disenfranchised by the monumental socioeconomic changes of the period. Tim Jordan (1999: 145), in his book *Cyberpower*, summarizes that social change:

> A growing body of theoretical and empirical work in all areas of the social sciences argues that sometime in the 1970s a fundamental shift in the nature of society was initiated. At its simplest, this is portrayed as the third great shift in human society, from agricultural to industrial and now to informational societies.

This fundamental shift in production was accompanied by a new imaginary of virtual, performative spaces. For the disenfranchised, hacking into the virtual space of information could bring social agency back to those it had "trashed."

Queering trash

Stefan Brecht collected his reviews of underground performance in New York in the late 1960s and 1970s under the rubric of *Queer Theatre* (1986). The elements he identified in performance as producing "queer" also produce uses of "trash": drag performers wearing trashy costumes, with remaindered items composing the sets. The way trash works in these performances can be illustrated by the image of Charles Pierce doing his renowned drag version of Bette Davis, replicating her famous line from *All About Eve*: "What a dump!" Pierce's campy citation of Davis's line performs a kind of self-reflexive "dumping ground," where the movie industry's spectacular glamour is recycled in cheap costumes and on small stages. "Dump" ironizes the inversion of economic power that supports Pierce's performance. But, more importantly, Pierce actually recycles the devalued elements of the "dump" into cultural currency through his performance. By laminating his trashy live performance onto the recursive, technological loop of movie nostalgia, Pierce reclaims trash as a vivifying strategy, capable of producing cultural capital through underground performance.

In the 1970s, "trashy" performance recycled various elements of social and material detritus into new, desirable cultural artifacts. Charles Ludlam was the master of playing "trashy" drag roles that recycled high art, arguably culminating in his version of *Camille* (1973). Ludlam defined his Theatre of the Ridiculous as one which "takes what is considered worthless and turns it into high art" (Dasgupta 1998: 77). Ludlam re-invested the "worthless" with cultural value by making it seem to be the referent of the classical plays. In his work, "trash" inverts the value system by redirecting the signification of signs. Appearing as a cross-dressed Camille, in thrift store gown, he could retain the character of high art, but by playing her in an obviously "cheap" manner, he redirected the signification, thus re-investing the high in the "worthless."

The drag troupe known as Hot Peaches offered another strategy in relation to trash and signification: they actualized the trash. In their production of *The Magic Hype*, in 1973, Silicone Sally sang her lead song "Tacky Trash": "Get tacky, trashy/Do our thing/But make it sing. . . . Check out my brand new tits, they're silicone and plastic/ fan-tastic . . . I'm a superstar/Since my tits are what they are" (Brecht 1986: 120). Instead of playing on the change of referent, as Ludlam was doing, Silicone Sally actualized the referent of "trash," as she performed her own silicone-produced breasts. Silicone Sally celebrates the trashy effect of silicone as a transgender strategy. In thrift-store clothes, she seductively shakes the fakes. In this instance, trash is the effect produced by techno-enhancement procedures that use a synthetic material to simulate a "natural" one. Silicone Sally celebrates the synthetic version of the female body enabled by a new material in the design environment. Her performance of the plastic foregrounded new, medical technologies of gender as trash, like her thrift-store costume, that could perform a transgender identification.

Unfortunately, it was later discovered that these silicone implants could cause connective tissue disorders and they were banned by the FDA in 1992. While plastics do not degrade in the environment, posing a threat to its sustainability, they do degrade within the breast, polluting the body tissues. As we will see, when the focus of the gay community is turned to health matters through the onslaught of AIDS, the sense of trash will lose its playful potential.

Trash as dramatic universe: Jack Smith

Jack Smith is the queen of trashed space. Juan Suarez, in his book *Bike Boys, Drag Queens, and Superstars* describes the signature of Smith's work as "his interest in junk and debris" (1996: xiii). Here are some sample descriptions of Smith's mise en scène: Brecht describes the set of *Gas Stations of the Cross Religious Spectacle* (1971) as composed of "most of the junk in the middle of the floor [which] seemed the same as in the Christmas program" (1986: 15). In *Destruction of Atlantis*, a remake of Ibsen's *Ghosts* Smith played Oswald, "reading his lines from a tattered script, which he dropped onto the stage, along with handfuls of glitter, next to a pink hippo suspended in a pulley-operated basket, and toy monkeys in a wagon representing Pastor Manders, amidst other junk strewn around" (Hoberman 1998: 5–6). In *Ghosts*, Mrs. Alving was played by a man "who sat, swathed in scarfs [sic] and a thick black veil, inside a supermarket shopping cart" pushed on and off by a prop woman in a kimono and high wedgies. Smith's version of Mrs. Alving's mode of transportation was a shopping cart set adrift in the scrap heap of discarded commodities. Unlike Ibsen's specifically bourgeois mother, Smith's Mrs. Alving was unable to anti-up into the capital outlay of the "new." Instead, her habitat was someone else's discarded private property.

When asked about his sets composed of junk, Smith responded that, in part, his trash represented the effect of what he called "landlordism" (Suarez 1996: 208). Smith was repeatedly evicted from his lofts in Soho in the 1970s, forced to move to cheaper locations, and finally to the East Side, as the forces of gentrification took over Soho. His sets of junk were perversions of private property, signifying the temporary habitations of the homeless in an era of gentrification. Similarly in the Warhol-produced movie *Trash* (1970), the drag queen Holly Woodlawn assembles her wardrobe and her furnishings from the junk left on the sidewalk for the garbage trucks to haul away. Trash is her profession, her habitation, and her transgender fashion. Her major goal, her striving for upward mobility is to get on the welfare rolls.

Smith's junkscapes were cluttered and complex. Heaps of used commodities crowded the room. To make one's way through it required leaving the "straight path," to wander, turn, and twist through the junk. The indirection forced by the accumulation of garbage provides strategies of evasion and subterfuge. In cyberpunk works, as we will see, this trashy topology suggests an orientalist fantasy of the future Asia. It can be the "sprawl" of new Tokyo. For Jack Smith, it was a retro-utopia of Hollywood fantasias of "Araby." Smith emulated what he perceived as "Araby" with its complex of minarets and spires, winding ways, crowded streets, and endless mazes of back alleys, by creating tinseled mounds of trash, composed of a bathroom sink, hanging silk cloths, incense and brass pots. In Ron Vawter's reconstruction of one of Smith's "araby" performances, Vawter performs Smith as so obsessed with his numerous "oriental" costume effects, and the arrangement of the junk around him, that he fails to deliver his lines.[21] The accumulation of discarded commodities piled into the towers of the urban, decomposing the bourgeois dramatic worlds of Ibsen and others, reclaims waste as the exotic mise en scène of another world, a virtual space of glamour and intrigue. If the "new" science had successfully displaced the "Arab" ones in formulating a specifically European culture, Smith's "Araby" transmutated its surplus, its trash into a cultural capital of Arabian fantasies.

Smith's portrayals of cross-gender identification were as melancholy as the abandoned Mrs. Alving in a shopping cart. Apparently, "real" spectacular women were last seen through the lens of 1940s and 1950s Hollywood technology and could only be cited for effect. Drag Queens were the widows of cinematic women, mourning through trashy rites of return, picking their way through trash, and yet, revitalizing the cast-offs through their performances. At the same time, "real" men were going to the moon. Remember, the 1970s were ushered in by the landing of Apollo 11 on the moon. Both women and men were taking Bette Davis' "bumpy ride" on technology, in which gender was catapulted into the social space by machines. In his book *The Right Stuff*, Tom Wolfe wittily narrativized the melancholy crises of masculinity in the move from jet pilot to astronaut, as the agency of flight and landing were transferred from men to machine.

It is generally understood that this earlier form of drag performance did not continue as a central mode of gay performance in the 1980s. Its demise was due, in part, to the AIDS epidemic. The melancholic or playfully silly drag queen did not address the very real needs and resistances to the biomedical establishment and its regulations that were required to obtain greater research and distribution of medicine for the community. Melancholic citations of the cinematic undead did not serve a community dealing with those who were actually dying of AIDS. Instead, new forms were invented to perform AIDS activism, as David Roman so carefully archives in his book *Acts of Intervention* (1998). The end of this version of the drag queen was also the end of junk as her mise en scène. Trash was handed off from queer performers to a new form of science fiction.

Cyberpunk trash

In the early 1980s, cyberpunk took up junk as its setting. Trash became the landscape and megalopolis of high technology's radical dispossessed. The cyberpunk imaginary was both a form of fiction and a subcultural style, with its own 'zines and practices. Techno-junk was reclaimed not only as a habitat, but as a component of human corporeality, as one of the leading cyberpunk authors, Bruce Sterling explains:

For the cyberpunks . . . technology is visceral. It is not the bottled genie of remote Big Science boffins: it is pervasive, utterly intimate. Not outside us, but next to us. Under our skin; often, inside our minds. . . . Eighties tech sticks to the skin, responds to the touch: the personal computer, the Sony Walkman, the portable telephone, the soft contact lens. . . . The theme of body invasion: prosthetic limbs, cosmetic surgery, genetic alteration. The even more powerful theme of mind invasion: brain-computer interfaces, artificial intelligence, neurochemistry—techniques radically redefining the nature of humanity, the nature of the self.

(1988: xiii)

These hybridized cyberpunks lived in what Sterling called "interzones," where "the street finds its own uses for things." These are habitats constructed from the trash of the high tech (xiii). Here are a few descriptions of cyberpunk junk environments: In William Gibson's classic novel *Neuromancer* (1984), we read: "The door was a sheet of corrugated roofing . . . dense tangles of junk rising on either side. . . . The junk looked like something that had grown there, a fungus of metal and plastic. . . . " (1986: 47–48). In the short story *Freezone* by John Shirley we encounter: "the community that had grown up around the enormous complex of offshore drilling platforms" with "brothels and arcades and cabarets" on "derelict ships permanently anchored around the platforms . . . rusting hulks and shanty nightclubs" (1986: 141). In Bruce Sterling's *Islands in the Net* (1988), we discover Rasta hackers living in old, discarded supertankers as their cities, from which they hack into satellite communications.

In the world of trash cyberscapes, there is no modest, respectable middle class. The cyberpunk imaginary posits the emerging two-class system of high-tech corporate society: the corporate super-wealthy and the homeless vagrants with no means. For both drag artists and cyberpunks, the trash habitat represented the movement of private property up, up, and away into a virtual class, leaving only its junk behind. Celeste Olalquiaga, in *Megalopolis* relates the imaginary of this trashy future to an avoidance of death: "an apocalyptical fin de siècle as a melancholic appropriation—one that refuses to accept death, fetishistically clinging to memories, corpses, and ruins" (1992: 23). For Olalquiaga, then, the world of cyberpunk techno-trash, like the drag queen's recursive thrift store loop through screen divas denies death, or the signification of finality. But both are more than melancholy. Certainly, cybertrash exists in a world without ending, where, in *Neuromancer*, for example, the brains of corporate owners are kept in vats to run endlessly into the future. But the hackers in their habitats of trash are re-utilizing the remains these corporate, floating brains left behind to sustain their underground communities. And Smith's Mrs. Alving re-invests value in junk through performance. Trash, thus, reveals a radical potential for underground productivity.

Recursive as they were, the drag divas trashed the class relation that constructed femininity as bourgeois. Trashy transgender divas destabilized the traditional gender codes and class codes at once. In the cyberpunk subculture, gender appears as more traditionally stable in its codes, but totally different in its function. Gender becomes a component of the virtual displacement of the body. From Gibson's *Mona Lisa Overdrive* to his *Idoru*, the notion of a performer unties completely from a fleshly self. Instead, performers are commodity effects, projected through virtual means, as long as they have currency. They operate as people, in social relations, but are nothing more than compilations of popular images, or fandom. Performers, then, are the markers of the technological take-over. As they transmute into virtual markers, their only power of attraction is in the deployment of gender codes—specifically the feminine ones.

Biospheres and bioreserves

If these movements led to an embrace of the trashed environment, another movement signaled the retreat from it—the attempt to create a sustainable environment as a mise en scène. *Biosphere 2* could be imagined as one kind of a performance of these ecological fantasies. Built in 1991, just outside of Tucson, Arizona, the self-contained mini-world known as Biosphere 2 was designed to last for 100 years, testing "nature, technology and human endurance" (http://www.bio2.com/04_tour.html). It contains a one-million-gallon saltwater ocean, a rainforest, savannahs, a desert, and other types of "natural" environments within its walls. It recreates the natural world as a sealed-off stage of a biosphere environment. Likewise, the sealed missions, during which humans lived exclusively within the biosphere, could be considered as performances of survival. The first mission lasted from 1991–93, testing the ability of the participants to sustain themselves from its resources. Ironically, it was later revealed that Biosphere 2 was not, in fact, a project run by scientists, but by a cult-like theater troupe. So the sense of staging survival, which the biosphere suggests, was actually produced from a theater troupe. However, the biosphere is now operated through Columbia University, arguably a more scientific and possibly less performative project. This experiment may yield some important ecological knowledge, but it may also signal a retreat of the human from the biosphere of earth, in a future of wasted resources, or in future colonies on distant planets. Constance Penley terms the biosphere a "canned culture," arguing that such constructions are more about ideology than science.

To perform her critique, Penley contributed to the libretto of an "environmental opera" titled *Biospheria*, which premiered in San Diego in 2001. Audience members were outfitted in costumes similar to those worn during the sealed mission. Wearing headphones, they moved from site to site observing a sequence of live tableaux, and interacting with the performers, sets and objects as if within the biosphere. The soundtrack on the headphones included verbal excerpts from faux diary entries written by the people who supposedly endured the sealed mission along with computer-generated simulations of natural environmental sounds. Each site represented one historical moment in the lives of those who undertook the biosphere mission.

More fruitful for the future of the earth itself, biosphere reserves, launched by UNESCO in the 1970s, are areas of land set apart to encourage integrated environments. They are areas of conservation, research, and planning for an interrelated, mutually-sustaining ecology. These reserves already exist in Africa, Asia, Latin America, Europe and North America (http://www.unesco.org/mab/wnbr.htm). Perhaps they can be regarded as site-specific improvisations for the future, in sustainability and shared subjectivity.

SCENE FOUR: NEO-NATURE

While anxieties concerning new technologies prompted some to perform alien encounters and others to reanimate the trash they produced, still others re-imagined nature itself in terms of new technologies and virtual spaces. Geography, the measure of natural regions, became a virtual measure of spiritual power, distributed across continents, invoking a blend of indigenous traditions and UFO sightings. Central to this new virtual geography was the re-imagining and redistributing Tibet. Recalling the nineteenth-century investment in the Himalayas as a spiritual region, the twentieth-century moved Tibet into various virtual versions of it, from Hollywood films to the diasporic settlements of its spiritual practices. Ultimately, the virtual Tibet and its offspring produced a hybridized geographical and virtual space for consumption in postindustrial societies.

In the realm of technology, biogenetic engineering invented altered species and alternate methods of reproduction. A concern with ecology, the term that succeeded the environment and the biosphere, drove some activists to perform various interventions into the new research and development of these products. The production of "frankenfood," a term originating in the early 1990s to represent genetically-engineered crops inspired a new genre of performance known as "bioart" that aimed to resist these incursions into the ecological system.

Some examples of both kinds of performance are gathered here, from grassroots celebrations of virtual geographies to interactive performances of laboratory experiments. Unlike the transcendent impulses of the mid-century, or the recuperative ones of "trashy" performers, these performances seek to celebrate a virtual hybridity, on the one hand, and strategize against its genetic form, on the other.

Virtual Tibet

In the nineteenth century, Mme. Blavatsky created a paradigm of imagining Tibet, or the region of the Himalayas as the seat of avatars and esoteric learning. Imagining the geographical region of Tibet as a peak of transcendence and topography of the spiritual established a virtual space in which avatars could become embodied. The region's relative inaccessibility and theocratic system somehow inspired a Western imagination of it as composing a virtual, spiritual space.

In the twentieth century, imagining Tibet as a site of spiritual transcendence has inspired not only composers and performers in productions like the *Lunar Opera*, but also a spate of Hollywood movies, novels, spiritual practices, and actual pilgrimages. From such signature works as James Hilton's novel *Lost Horizon* in 1933 to the current books published by the Dalai Lama in the 1990s, the notion of Tibet as a spiritual realm has captured the imagination of postindustrial societies. Recycling Tibet, establishing a *Virtual Tibet*, as Orville Schell terms it, the invention of Shangri-La has overcome any "real" sense of the geographical site and its history and culture.

Today, the popular representation of the relations between China and Tibet has been made to signify the dialectic between a modernist, materialist, revolutionary state and an indigenous, independent theocracy. In one sense, the contest recalls the melodramatic dialog between spiritualists like Mme. Blavatsky and Darwinian science in the nineteenth century. Materialism is made to seem vulgar when set against high, spiritual offices, such as that of the Dalai Lama. Framing the China/Tibet relations within this particular narrative of conflict relates a modernist revolutionary takeover that has evacuated the mystic Tibet, driving it into a diasporic mode. If Marx and Engels included specters in their *Communist Manifesto*, the communist nation of China seems to be driving them out of Tibet. The image of conflict reads: revolution against reincarnation, hydroelectric power against rituals in hilltop monasteries, and women's rights against an exclusive, male lama-cracy.

The circulation of the conflict between China and Tibet inspires various kinds of popular performances that do not always distinguish clearly between religion, politics, and the virtual realm of popular entertainment. The punk Nina Hagen, with her group Trance Mission performed a "sacred cabaret" benefit concert and, resembling the rock concerts of the 1960s, a Tibetan Freedom Concert took place in Golden Gate Park in San Francisco with Smashing Punkins, Rage Against the Machine, and the Beastie Boys—band names that do not exactly resonate with Tibetan Buddhist beliefs. The Dalai Lama has visited Hollywood several times, making headlines in the *Los Angeles Times* that meld industry campiness with spiritual leadership, such as "Hollywood Elite Says Hello, Dalai" (Schell 2000: 46), while movies such as *Seven Years in Tibet* compete with *Kundun* for the Tibetan box-office effect. Bumper stickers reading "Free Tibet" can be seen around Hollywood, where various actors have entered the fray. On the one hand, the movie star Richard Gere has done much to support the cause of the Dalai Lama in the "free Tibet" movement for many years, co-founding the Tibet House in New York with Columbia Professor Robert Thurman (father of Uma); on the other hand, Steven Seagal, the martial arts director and actor has been investing a great deal of money and publicity into being deemed a *tulku*, or a reincarnation of a lama by some leading lama (Schevill 62). A clear distinction between celebrity status and *tulku/lama* status becomes indistinct when star-heroes of movies see themselves as heroes among the stars and when the Dalai Lama sits as an invited guest at industry dining tables. Just where Tibet is located becomes complicated by its representation in films, or its official representative in Hollywood. After all, *Seven Years in Tibet* was shot in the Argentine Andes and part of *Lost Horizon* in Ojai, California.

Outside of the Hollywood-effect, the influence of the Tibetan Buddhist tradition has inspired some Western, urban people to renounce their lifestyles and take on monastic or lamaistic practices. Taking Tibetan titles, such as Rimpoche, and names like Tenzin Palmo, and Pema Chodron, Western practitioners of "Tibetan" Buddhism have made themselves avatars, not only in the purely spiritual sense, but also as avatars of the virtual Tibet. The very nomenclature, "Tibetan" Buddhism is unique, as if there were Thai Buddhism, Japanese Buddhism, Northern Indian Buddhism, etc.

Western women have made a crucial intervention into the all-male tradition of hermits and leaders of monastic communities, creating a differently-gendered version of the avatar. Vicki Mackenzie's book *A Cave in the Snow* details the life of Diane Perry, who left her working-class neighborhood in London to live for years in a cave in the Himalayas. Taking the name Tenzin Palmo, she first traveled to India to study with a lama there. In 1973, she was one of the first Western women to receive full Bhikshuni ordination, after which she continued her apprenticeship in a monastery in the Indian Himalayas. After six years apprenticeship there, she determined to live as a Buddhist hermit-monk in a cave in the Himalayas. Even though women had typically never been encouraged to take on this highest form of meditation, Palmo insisted that she had earned the right to do so. Ironically, after several years, her retreat was ended only by the arrival of the local police, informing her that she would have to leave India because her visa was not in order. Once back in society, she organized a conference for Western nuns, finally raising enough funding through her lectures and teachings to open a nunnery and an international retreat center.

Deirdre Blomfield-Brown was born in New York City. Unlike Tenzin Palmo, who came from a working-class environment, she attended the exclusive Miss Porter's School in Connecticut and graduated from the University of California at Berkeley. In her mid-thirties she began her studies with a Tibetan lama. She received full Bikshuni ordination in 1981, taking the name Ani Pema Chödrön. She is now the director of Gampo Abbey, in Cape Breton, Nova Scotia, the first Tibetan monastery for Westerners. Pema Chödrön is arguably one of the most highly-regarded teachers of the Tibetan forms of meditation in the West. Her teachings combine stories from her own past with the traditional readings and her commentary. Both of these women, with profound dedication and long study have also helped to create a virtual Tibet. Like Mme. Blavatsky and Alexandra David-Neel before them, they have created a Western version of Tibetan Buddhist practices that they learned from their own Tibetan "masters."

If Tibet, the geographic location, has been somewhat evacuated of its traditions, virtual Tibets, designed to keep the traditions alive, have grown up in other countries. Founding study centers explicitly for Westerners, bridging the practice with examples and approaches more familiar to those living in the West, dedicated acolytes, such as these women have helped to construct the diasporic reception of Tibetan images and narratives that have grown up around the religion. However, teaching the classic writings in translation, through having read translated texts, extracting the teachings from the seasons of ritual practices, and creating an interface with Western social and political institutions, their teaching really invents a new meaning for the adjective "Tibetan" Buddhism. With references to some traditions once located in Tibet, now passed on by the exiled Dalai Lama and monks, the effects of memory, diaspora, and cultural difference transmutate these religious practices into a virtual sense of Tibet. An imagined Tibet empowers virtual referents and organizes a new form of avatar. The popularity of Tibetan Buddhism reveals how easily it seems to graft onto postmodern cultures that are saturated with new media technologies. After all, this religious diaspora gained much of its momentum and global attention during the same years as the expansion of the World Wide Web. The ease with which many practitioners move between Tibetan Buddhist practices and the technological virtual of the internet, the cellphone, and the computer game illustrates the growing relationship between the techno and the spiritual virtuals. The Buddhist tradition offers a vocabulary of terms and images that can illustrate or articulate experiences of the virtual, such as the avatar, spiritual and online, or modes of virtual communication, such channeling, or the internet. Tibetan images used for meditation, such as the complex, architectural Kalachakra mandala are not unlike images of electronic circuitry, and the imagined passage through the mandala, not unlike software applications. The overpowering realm of virtual simulation in postindustrial societies, with the accompanying sense of a retreating "real" can be imagined through the Tibetan Buddhist worldview of the veil of Maya, i.e. that life, itself, is an illusion. A synthesis of the ancient traditions with machinic technologies, in the grass-roots New Age imaginary and among high-tech designers now structures a virtual Tibet and its masters as a lens through which one might perceive the experience of the late twentieth-century techno-virtual.

Harmonic Himalaya effect

The virtual Himalaya effect has distributed practices of spiritual geography beyond those that use Tibet as a referent. Re-imagining rites associated with mountains as sources of spiritual strength has inspired neo-Mayan movements, which celebrate rites of transformation that imagine the Andes, and the neo-Olympian movement in Greece, which re-imagines the ancient rites of Zeus and Dionysus on Mount Olympus. One example that provides an insight into how these specific referents combine hybridized versions of geographical, traditional, spiritual, and technological imaginaries may be found in the celebration of the so-called "Harmonic Convergence" in 1987. A grassroots performance of time and transformation, politics, and spiritualism, the Harmonic Convergence was a response to a world-wide call for participation in meditations designed specifically to correct the continuation of aggression and warfare on the earth and to insure a future of peace. "Harmonic" referred to the hippie sense of "good vibrations," or the traditional "music of the spheres." Attuning meditation to temporal measure and geographic location was designed to alter the design for the future of the social.

The exact time of the performance, essential to its effectiveness, was derived from the Mayan calendar. In his book *The Mayan Factor* (1996), José Arguelles worked out his theories concerning the relationship of the mathematics of the Mayan calendar and harmonics, as exemplified by one chapter title "Calendar Harmonics." Based on his interpretation, Arguelles argued that the date August 16–17, 1987 marked the end of the Mayan period of the "Nine Hells." He saw the transition as the fulfillment of the prophecy of Quetzalcoatl, the feathered serpent god's vision known as the "Thirteen Heavens and Nine Hells." According to Arguelles, the date of the beginning of the first hell coincided with the arrival of Cortez in Mexico. Supposedly, that period of subjugation would end on this date in 1987—but only if the right vibrations were sent out into the universe.

The event called for 144,000 people to assemble at various "power centers" located on mountain tops. Performers converged at such diverse sites as Machu Picchu in Peru and Mount Shasta in California. On Mt. Shasta, several thousand people (some report as many as 3–5,000 participants) remained for those two days, practicing various forms of collective meditation. A mixture of UFO sightings, astrology, Native American rituals, and other traditions fed into the experience. Some of the participants experienced a climax of the Harmonic Conversion, similar to the resolution of Spielberg's movie, *Close Encounters* (1977), in which contact with aliens is produced by a tonal progression of intervals that the aliens then replicate and thereby make contact. Some descriptions of the Harmonic Convergence on Mt. Shasta also claim that the ceremonies concluded with attuned meditators being beamed up for extra-terrestrial travel.[22] As the SpiritWeb website describes it, the very purpose of the convergence was to provide "attunement to the planet and to the space brothers and sisters that make up the higher galactic intelligences which surround the planet Earth." (www.SpiritWeb.org). Thus, the mid-century performances of threatening alien contacts were inverted into a kind of welcoming ceremony, in which the denizens of virtualized earthly space and outer space could join together through harmonically-tuned meditations.

Arguelles, inspired by the huge success of his call for convergence, went on to argue for a rejection of the Gregorian calendar, imposed by the Spanish. As he interpreted it, the destruction of a "harmonic" Mayan time was completed by a Vatican calendar "reform" in 1582. He made a pilgrimage to Rome, to appeal directly to Pope John Paul II, inviting him to join in the calendar change, and, on behalf of world peace, to make further confession of the Church's historical errors. Arguelles's advocacy of the adoption of the Mayan calendar broke off into a neo-Mayan movement, which Arguelles later rejected. Nonetheless, the division of a time signature in these harmonics becomes literalized in the calendar, signifying, beyond specific convergences, a more auspicious organization of the temporal.

Critical Art Ensemble vs. Frankenature

In contrast to these spiritual imaginings, performances against so-called scientific "improvements" on natural "products" also call for convergences, but of a more critical, intellectually-informed set of practices. Neo-nature, to them, is a dangerous site of potential pollution. A collective of five artists, known as The Critical Art Ensemble (CAE) is dedicated to performing the intersections among art, technology, radical politics and critical theory. Since 1997, they have created various participatory performances as well as published numerous articles and books that critique biotechnologies. Their incendiary book entitled *The Molecular Invasion* records their latest interventions into biotechnical research. Their increasingly edgy experiments challenge the industrial food manufacturers and pesticide producers. In a time of dramatically increasing surveillance in the U.S., and a near-hysterical fear of terrorism, one of the members of the collective, Professor Steven Kurtz, was arrested for housing an alleged "bioterrorist lab" in his home. Kurtz's strictly performative experiment was perceived as a secret lab of biological terrorism, when, in fact, his experiments were designed to disrupt what he considers biological terrorism.

Performances by the CAE seek to intervene in the status of "transgenic" processes that alter the genetic make-up of organic plants in order to make them more susceptible to pesticides. CAE argues that unregulated for-profit research and untested results of genetic engineering create a dangerous practice of creating new genetic foods and releasing them out into the environment without understanding the full, ecological consequences of their alteration. Among other tactics, CAE proposes performances of "fuzzy biological sabotage" to bring attention to the unregulated research. The "fuzzy saboteur" makes situational decisions about how to encourage paranoia, provide inertia, or otherwise disturb corporate transgenic product development and distribution (CAE 2002: 100). One strategy in *The Molecular Invasion* consists of the release of mutant flies near biotech facilities. This "prank," as they call it, is intended to conjure paranoid fantasies among those living near research facilities that are growing these transgenic foods. They suggest that targeting a nearby restaurant for the release of mutant flies might make people take a more critical attitude toward the release of these foods into the ecology (103–104) (see also http://www.t0.or.at/cae/critical.htm). Considered as performance art, the release of the mutant flies continues in the tradition of site-specific performances that use performance to foreground the conditions of the site where they take place. The audience is composed of those who live or eat nearby, who notice the mutant flies and react in some psychic, or hopefully, activist manner. The performer is the "fuzzy saboteur," who mixes a scientific and a performative practice in the interest of a political agenda.

In addition to these "fuzzy saboteur" interventions, members of the Ensemble also create radical performances of transgenic effects that participate in the new form called "bioart." They perform what they call "contestational biology." As artists, they use bacteria, cell lines, plants, insects, and even animals as their media in order to intervene in the public perception of transgenics. For example, the art piece "Molecular Invasion" performs a resistance to the environmentally-destructive Monsanto products called RoundUp ready crops. These are transgenic foods designed by Monsanto to accept the weed-killer RoundUp. The Ensemble has been growing the transgenic seeds, experimenting with chemicals that would frustrate their RoundUp readiness. They invite the public to view their experiments and to follow their development. In this way, they make a scientific experiment into a public performance.

In a more illustrative piece, Beatriz La Costa, a member of the collective created the "Transgenic Bacteria Release Machine." This piece consists of a robotic game machine, which holds 10 Petri dishes. One dish holds a sample of a harmless strain of a recombinant e. coli bacteria, containing human DNA, while the others hold bacteria and mold samples from the nearby environment. Spectators push a red button, which spins the Petri dishes like a roulette wheel. A random stop, a mechanical arm opens the dish: a red light comes on if the transgenic dish was opened, green if local bacteria. The performance is actually the spectator's response to the possibility, or actuality of being exposed to transgenic material. This bioart work has appeared in several museums and art galleries around the world (see http://www.beatrizdacosta.net/machine.html).

Another sort of biotechnic performance practice is also developing followers; one that is formalist, rather than an activist, with more specious biopolitics. Eduardo Kac bioengineered an albino rabbit by splicing the green fluorescent protein (GFP) of a jellyfish into her genome. Under the lights, the rabbit glows green. Kac claims this effect as an art work. Medical ethicists and animal rights activists are incensed by the piece, foreseeing a future for human's pets genetically designed to entertain, or perhaps work as design accessories, without research into the long-lasting consequences for the organism.

In one sense, these various examples could be perceived as twentieth-century versions of the nineteenth-century science installations and natural history museums that made science into a spectacle. While they retain the pedagogical elements of the museums, they are designed to activate a response against the scientific and industrial alterations in genetic structures. In another piece, CAE actually performed a science class, replete with lectures, a lab, and illustrated skits. *Flesh Machine* played off of both the display of scientific materials and the teaching of them. Dressed in lab coats, the performers lecture and present performance sketches on eugenics. In the "lab" portion of the performance, audience members take part in actual experiments concerning alternative forms of reproduction. In addition, audience members take tests at various computers that assess their donor suitability for a range of possibilities, from surrogacy to cytoplasm. If they succeed, they receive a certificate of "genetic merit." Finally, they pass around a cryolized fetus that is "for sale." If no one buys it, it dies, thus acting out the market in living tissues.[23]

Doing Dolly: cloning and Caryl Churchill

Like the Critical Art Ensemble, Caryl Churchill's play, *a number* addresses issues of alternative reproduction. Churchill's play, however, is not an interactive performance, but a standard two-person play that stages the personal, psychological effects of cloning. Cloning is *the* iterative form of transgenic developments, in which a living organism can be exactly reproduced without traditional insemination. In 1997 a sheep named Dolly was successfully cloned. Using cells from an adult sheep's mammary glands, the scientists grew a tissue culture, then injected the nucleus from one of these cells into an oocyte, or unfertilized egg, zapped it with a small jolt of electricity, and planted it in the womb of a surrogate mother. Dolly's DNA matched exactly that of the mammary cells, making her a cloned copy of the donor ewe. Not only does this procedure recall Goethe's homunculus in a test tube, but for Frankenstein fans, it resembles the process of making the monster kicked to life by a bolt of lightning. Dolly's worldwide fame came from the successful creation of a living animal.

Dolly is a clone that does not proceed from a father, but, indeed from mammary tissue and oozyte. This reproductive traffic among females introduces an order of reproduction and repesentation outside the confines of Plato's, or Christianity's, or Derrida's, or Lacan's structural dependency upon the Father in the role of progenitor. If Christine Jorgensen's sex-reassignment surgery was like an atomic bomb at mid-century, as Stryker so wittily put it, Dolly offers a glimpse into a future order potentially beyond the Law of Church, representation, and Nature.

Ironically, Caryl Churchill's play *a number* (2002) stages the personal and social effects from human cloning in a dialogue between a father and his cloned sons. Churchill's history of writing feminist plays might suggest that this is a strategic irony, in settling a new iterative traffic among females upon the dislodged father-son model that has determined centuries of structural inheritance. In Churchill's play, the mother, the egg donor, is absent. The father is named Salter—only the condiment, but not the meat. Another historical irony of the play is that, although it treats a revolutionary scientific practice, *a number* stages no laboratory, no scientist, and none of the technological devices required for such a biotech achievement. Instead, it takes place in a domestic setting, with none of the special effects that technology has provided the contemporary stage.

Two of Salter's sons are named Bernard, signified in the text as B1 and B2 and the third is named Michael Black. The play opens:

> B2: A number
> Salter: you mean

B2: a number of us, a considerable
Salter: say
B2: ten, twenty

The dialogic style of sentence fragments runs throughout the play. Salter, the father, thrives on this form, fabricating/improvising positive potentials to salve the disturbed expressions by his sons. In this form, he works to absolve himself from his role as a damaging origin—a father caught in the act. The ambivalence this character creates around origins and effects resonates with the new, ungrounded role of the father in the cloning procedure. He claims no origin and thus no conclusion. His role seems limited to the decision to clone and the purchasing of the product.

In the beginning, Salter assures B2 that he was the original and the others were copies; that he was born in a "natural" manner and thus is the "real" son. In spite of his father's assurances, B2 is haunted by troubling intimations: "I got this impression there was this batch and we were all in it. . . . none of us was the original." B2 is melancholic because of the loss of the original, wondering if his copies are psychic duplicates as well as material ones. His mood is reminiscent of postmodern theorists of simulation, such as Jean Baudrillard, whose theories of copies seem dark and redolent with loss. Then Salter extends his narrative of origins to admit that there was an original son, who died. He adds that the mother was also dead and so the father wanted the son back, ordering one duplicate. Of course, the irony of one duplicate is not lost, here, in the narrative. Salter blames the hospital for illicilty making more copies—a process he claims he will contest. It is clear the father is adapting the story to the son's melancholy, unsettling any notion of a true origin, or motive. If the son is a duplicate, the father is duplicitous.

Next, B1 shows up, secure in the knowledge that he was the original, but disturbed that there are clones of him. B2's melancholic loss of the original is inverted in B1's violent response to the feeling that his originality has been mitigated by duplication. Churchill is putting individualism to the test, here, with its addiction to special status. However, B1 recalls several chilling, alienated instances in his childhood, including lying in his bed crying for, pleading for, finally shouting for, his father. It seems he did this every night and no one came. One cannot hail a father in the world of clones, no matter how one might plead or insist, but it seems that this break with the invocation of the father at the base of representation produces potential violence to all lines of inheritance: "B1: My brother . . . Has he got a child? Salter: No. B1: Because if he had I'd kill it." In the following scene, B2 reports that B1 has indeed been following him and ranting in an angry, frightening way. In scene 4, B1 reports having killed B2. Salter seems remorseful, but incapable of doing more than continuing to embellish his duplicitous narrative history.

Finally, Michael Black enters. He is seems happy and well-adjusted to the fact of his cloned duplication. He offers a positive account of transgenic trafficking: "We've got ninety-nine percent the same genes as any other person. We've got ninety per cent the same as a chimpanzee. We've got thirty percent the same as lettuce. It makes me feel I belong" (Churchill 2002: 50). So rather than playing the melancholic end of the original, or the violent break with individuality, Black celebrates the connective genetic web. Not only is individualism beside the point, to him, but the vitalism that has supported the special role of the human subject is happily dissolved by the genetic proximity of chimpanzees and lettuce. But his sunny outlook is dramatically darkened by the shade of his brother. Black's well-adjusted family life does not bring a happy ending to the play. The violence of B1 is still out there in the world, intent upon destroying the other clones.

Churchill's play does not engage any of the crucial ethical debates raging around cloning and other alternative fertilization practices, particlarly oppressive to poor women whose eggs are harvested for surrogate procedures. Since her play *Serious Money* explicitly engages with the social effects of new technologies in the stock market and international banking systems, it seems logical that she could take up the subject of cloning in terms of economics, but she did not. Activists are working to secure regulation for the harvesting of eggs for In Vitro Fertilization (IVF). Poor women undergo numerous instances of hormonal stimulation for the greater production of eggs exclusively for the market. Whereas women of means may purchase the eggs, poor women sell them, with great danger to their health, in order to survive. Activists in Europe have organized against these dangerous practices in Romania, for women providing eggs to the U.K. (see http://www.reprokult.de/trading_egg_cells.pdf for a manifesto).

Perhaps *a number* works in a manner similar to that of Churchill's recent play on transnational labor issues, *Far Away* (2000). There, the staging produces the dialectic of the visible and the invisible in terms of outsourcing labor. People working at creating fine headwear for the rich are portrayed as ideologically, not physically, blind to the band of enchained laborers that crosses the stage.[24] Perhaps it is the absence of women in *a number*, their invisibility, that makes the dramatic statement. The business of cloning may profit fathers, who seek sons without the intervention of a mother. Nonetheless, the play offers no image of the transgenetic traffic in eggs and cells that alternative reproduction processes are originating. The tensions among new biotechnologies, class, and gender remain outside the purview of the play, but foremost in the public eye of activism and national, state, and transnational regulating agencies.

Performances of neo-nature, then, may allow for grassroots strategies of reinventing the future, or of intervening in the bioindustrial alterations of food and human materials. A growing sense of a nature that can be produced through human endeavor, rather than stand as an alternative to it has motivated lively and even violent confrontations. The ongoing struggle against the development of "frankenfoods" has caused violent clashes between demonstrators and police at rallies against the WTO attempt to push the European Union into accepting them. Harvesting eggs in under-developed nations has inspired demonstrations around the world, and stem cell research is now a matter for the federal courts and the federal government. These few examples of performances concerning issues that will become definitive economic and ecological practices in the twenty-first century, only begin to suggest how to perform resistance to the new biotech transnational/industrial compound.

The avatar

The role of the avatar configures practices in the separate traditions of spiritualism, performance, and techno-experience. Moreover, it also configures their interface. Increasingly, these traditions have informed one another to create a figure for a navigational, agential device in a virtual space. In articulating the experience of these realms, the techno has invoked the spiritual, the spiritual the techno, and performance has invoked both to stage their encounters. Each tradition has provided strategies of representation that help to compose the figure of the avatar. Spiritual traditions offer notions of incarnation and rites of transformation; technologies provide the capability of audiovisual effects in a virtual space, and performance provides an order of action, or gesture that is somehow other than the "real." The virtual spaces the avatar inhabits are likewise particular to each tradition. The spiritual offers the sense of a transcendent space; the technological an immersive space, and the performative a characterological one. Spanning centuries from Sanskrit practices to online animations, the avatar continues to figure human subjectivity within virtual space.

As noted earlier, the avatar originated in the spiritual tradition. The Hindu belief that an incarnation of the god Vishnu dwelled on earth to aid humans in times of crisis inspired the figure of the avatar. In this study, the works and practices of Mme. Blavatsky offer an important Westernized revision of that term, making the avatar a "master" who comes and goes within the practitioner. The avatar incarnates, but through a human body that is not its own. Mme. Blavatsky's particular invention of the avatar has led to the more contemporary understanding of it as an incarnation that can occur only transitorily, can cohabit the subject without altering it, and can thus be constituted within the corporeality of the human. The spiritualist avatar is associated with virtual travel, encounters with the "other," and access to a virtual plane of information. Mme. Blavatsky's practice of the avatar has been cited as the origin of the New Age practice of channeling, informing a tradition of imagining a virtual "presence" in alternative practices that continue into the twenty-first century.

In grassroots traditions, the avatar has also been imagined in the form of an "alien" from another world. As an incarnation of navigation and agency in the unknown regions of outer space, the alien avatar subjectifies those regions and brings them into dialogue with people. The alien avatar eases the techno-hold on the imagining of "outer" space, imaging a form of contact. As aliens meet humans, the avatar compounds Hindu traditions with science fiction, with popular histories, and mediumistic effects to figure the search for access and understanding of the new and distant reaches of technology.

Within the new technospace of the internet, the avatar figures human participation online. The avatar animates movement in the online space, emulates contact, and offers a sense of agency. Just how the avatar signals the human within cyberspace combines elements from all of these traditions to make the new, electronic virtual seem familiar. While the basically commercial nature of the internet informs just how and what the avatar really signifies, the increasingly immersive experience of the virtual contrarily invokes notions of the transcendent derived from traditions of the spiritual.

The notion of performance plays a key role in constructing or imagining the avatar. Because the avatar is somehow different from the human, its actions only perform *as if* human. Whether considered as an actor on stage, who corporealizes a character, or as an online figure that represents the user at the computer terminal, the avatar's negotiation between the virtual space and the "real" one is through performance. It *acts* in a way that bridges known experience with the unknown: the familiar with the strange. The tradition of the avatar within rites and within the role of the actor is as an incarnation, foregrounding its corporeal functions.

This corporeal aspect of the avatar's representative nature leads some to assume that the crucial aspect of performance is still warranted by a "live" body. "Live" performance thus seemingly counters the influence of technospace and spirituality by performing an ontological resistance to virtuality. Peggy Phelan's oft-cited chapter "The ontology of performance: representation without reproduction" begins by hailing the "live" aspect of the performance as an original: "Performance's only life is in the present. Performance cannot be saved, recorded, documented, or otherwise participate in the circulation of representations *of* representations; once it does so, it becomes something other than performance" (1993: 146). Phelan then ties performance directly to the ontological status of the body: "Performance implicates the real through the presence of living bodies"(148). As treated earlier, Walter Benjamin referred to such claims for the live as "vitalism," a modernist version of a saint, for it rests on a special condition of the live that, he argues, was borrowed from the sacred: "Perhaps, indeed probably, it is relatively recent, the last mistaken attempt of the weakened Western tradition to seek the saint it has lost in cosmological impenetrability" (quoted in Hanssen 2000: 133). Somehow, then, the tradition of incarnation drives this notion of performance, even if, as in Phelan, the avatar actually incarnates an "absence" rather than a "presence." And, finally, the "real" is only a bipolar opposition to the virtual, thus signifying a realm, or order of things. The "live" necessarily evokes the virtual in its very resistance to it.

In *Liveness*, however, Philip Auslander counters that performance, or performing already belongs to the realm of the media. In some cases, it is embedded through prostheses such as microphones, or screens that magnify its proportions, and sometimes its "liveness" is a result of the success of its recursions, as in rock concerts that follow their recordings. Auslander characterizes Phelan's position as an anxious response to the "implosion" of the mediatized and the "live" in the latter part of the twentieth century: "As the mediatized replaces the live within cultural economy, the live itself incorporates the mediatized, both technologically and epistemologically. The result of this implosion is that a seemingly secure opposition is now a site of anxiety, the anxiety that underlies many performance theorists' desire to reassert the integrity of the live. . . . " (39). In other words, the electronic surround, the ubiquity of screens, and the prostheses of amplification already locate "liveness," as Auslander terms it, within the virtual. In that case, the "live" performer is always already an avatar.

Important here, is the way in which this debate between the "live" and the technological hinges on performance. Performing is already a form of gesture that is somehow abstracted from the "real" in spite of its warranting by actual bodies. What the Phelan/Auslander argument makes clear is that the kind of virtual space that registers performance is definitive of the composition of the avatar within it. The "live," which is associated with the "real" establishes the basis of Phelan's notion of performance, while Auslander perceives performance as an effect of mediatized space. As some performers straddle these two traditions, performing both "live" and onscreen in a single event, an interdependent sense of space is produced that houses their performance—one that virtualizes both the "real" and the techno in its combination. As the space of performance is virtualized, so is the performer, offering a version of an avatar that either incarnates, in the "real," or animates in the techno-virtual.

In the digital realm, the performer, or performing, as William Gibson narrativized in his novel *Idoru*, is simply an accretion of data in the binary code that drives various technologies—a "synthespian" as Gibson terms it, "a personality-construct, a congeries of software agents" (1986: 92). However virtual these synthespians, they nonetheless negotiate strategies of identity and identification. Identification with practices of gender, race, and sexuality are reproduced in virtual spaces, emulating traditions of racializing and sexualizing stereotypes. The codes do not remain unmarked, as they accrete into a figure, whose social attributes actually locate its appearance within the social surround. As we will discover, the synthespian, or techno-avatar can be a figure that breaks with an oppressive past, inhabiting a utopic virtual space, or it can be an oppressive, dark figure of social stereotypes.

This section will explore various exemplars of avatar construction to discover how they work to manage an interface among these various traditions. The section commences with a revitalization of the Faustian paradigm that was established at the beginning of the book. As traditionally, Faust serves as the moral figuring of the relation between the social, material, and the scientific. The figure of Faust can interpellate the subject into an ethical realm as if scientific discoveries extract a social price, or strike a social/moral bargain. Then a series of plays that script figures of leading scientists provide a characterological interface between the practice of science and the social through stagings of biographical data and psychological affect. Thus, scientists can be made into Fausts, or their own biographical avatars of the experiential and consequential effects of science. Musicians such as Sun Ra and Alice Coltrane reinvent themselves as racialized avatars of ancient and alien myths, who create audiovisual vehicles for travels into the virtual realm, inventing a reconfiguring of race as a synthetic product. Finally, a host of cyber avatars that perform various social identifications in the digital realm blaze a trail that leads, ultimately, to Lara Croft, the computer-animated avatar who "acts" on the digital platform of the Sony Playstation. The oscillation among these varied practices, will, hopefully, conjure an avatar in the mind of the reader, who can figure this vital intersection of discourses and traditions in contemporary experience.

Twentieth-century Fausts

Rocket science and satanism

One of the founders of rocket science obsessively experimented with both the invention of rocket fuel and the performance of satanic rites. John Whiteside Parsons, who would later become one of the co-founders of JPL (Jet Propulsion Lab) lived in a collective household in Pasadena that practiced Aleister Crowley's satanic rituals. Moving between the campus of the esteemed California Institute of Technology, and the collective house, Parsons worked to become officially recognized as a proper scientist and as an official representative of Crowley's sect. Daily, Parsons was experimenting with explosives that could kick a rocket out into space, dealing with highly unstable chemical compounds that sometimes accidentally exploded. At the same time, the sulphuric odors of Hell accompanied his rituals, leading him to seek equally explosive rites of the spirit. Parsons saw himself, then, as oscillating between scientific experiment and satanic rite, not unlike Faust.

In its earliest phases, rocket science was disparaged by many as simply a delusion, belonging only to science fiction fans, who read the stories in pulp magazines like *Amazing Stories* and watched movie serials like Buck Rogers. In one sense, this stereotype was not inaccurate. Some rocket scientists were among the legions of science fiction fans. Wernher von Braun, for instance, who led the development of rockets for the Nazis and later became a director of NASA, retained his subscription to *Astounding Science Fiction* during World War II, even arranging for its delivery to a secret drop in Sweden (Pendle 2005: 124–125). The Los Angeles Chapter of the Science Fiction League, begun in the 1930s, included several scientists in its membership, as well as sci-fi authors such as L.

Ron Hubbard, who later founded the Church of Scientology, and John Parsons. These practitioners and researchers did not adhere to a firm boundary between science as fiction as science as innovation. If rockets appeared only in fiction, then it was from there that these scientists would begin to imagine their designs.

Soon, Hubbard joined Parsons in the house of the satanic cult. For some time, they became obsessed with the practice of sex rituals with women in the cult in order to incarnate a female spirit named Babalon (Pendle 2005: 264–266). In this practice, we might see a version of the Gretchen story that appears in the midst of Faust's exploits. In 1950, they deemed the outcome of their Babalon rites as positive. They believed Babalon had become incarnated somewhere on earth. Soon after, Hubbard ran off with Parsons's wife and published, as an article in *Astounding Science Fiction* "Dianetics—The Evolution of Science"—the founding ideas for the Church of Scientology (Pendle 2005: 271). Thus, the beginnings of the development of rocket fuel, and of one of the most prestigious laboratories, JPL, which today leads in the development of the Mars probe and other forward-looking projects, was conjoined to the practice of satanic rituals and the founding of a church, whose moniker brings science and spiritualism together—The Church of Scientology—in this unique version of the Faustian paradigm.

Church of Science

The notion of a Church of Science brings together what have often been imagined as competing traditions in a unique institutional form. It's as if notions of the salvation or damnation of the spirit could be conflated with the health of the body. While faith-healing is an old tradition in many cultures, the Church of Science brings a more modernist version of it to the fore. Mary Baker Eddy founded the First Church of Christ, Scientist in 1879. Christian Science, as it is called, adopts a stance that regards the ontology of the body and the spirit as one, and claims that both sin and disease belong to an "unreal," order of things, since they were not created by God. Thus, the "real" body, which was created by God, can be cleansed of these unreal illnesses by practices of faith. Christian Science proceeds from readings of the Bible and a belief in Christ to practice a spiritual science on the body. Like the other nineteenth-century spiritualists, it imagines a resistance to the "new" science and even disallows its practitioners to consult medical doctors.

Scientology, in contrast, is founded on beliefs that mix allusions to the physical sciences with psychotherapy and science fiction. The basic text of Scientology is not the Bible, but Hubbard's science-sounding work *Dianetics: The Modern Science of Mental Health* (1950). At the core of the practice of Scientology is a form of psychotherapy called "auditing." In order to become "clear," participants pay for lengthy training sessions with auditors who use an e-meter, an "electro-psychometer," invented by Hubbard to combine electrical resistance with psychic processes. To begin with, these e-meters were claimed to be a scientific device, but later they were confiscated by the Federal Food and Drug Administration in 1963, which deemed them to be fake medical apparati. They are now claimed solely as "religious artifacts." The e-meter is an apparatus of mid-century making, like lie detectors and other institutional devices invented to trap the erring psyche in the time of shiny surfaces and retreating, secret interiorities. The e-meter provides a technological interface between religion and science.

The ritual of this church, then, is a form of techno-psycho-therapy, residing somewhere between Freud and Edison—the psyche and electricity. The ideological foundation of the e-meter rests on a narrative that sounds "amazingly" like science fiction. The final stages of auditing, open only to the most elite, involve auditing "body Thetans." Given the secrecy of Scientology, one cannot directly access their materials on this belief, but only the various narratives that circulate among disaffected members. The following account seems fairly representative. A very long time ago, "Thetans," originally related to Xenu, entered MEST (material-energy-space-time) to finally take up residence in human bodies. They are, then, both spiritual and alien avatars corporealized though human materials. "Thetans" were originally from a place called Xenu, who fled to earth. The e-meter is designed to awaken the Thetan, who has been trapped by engrams, which are something like Freud's notion of somatic memories. Thousands of dollars later, one might attain the level of "clear" (OT6, or "operating Thetan level 6"). The notion of "clear" derived from the function on a machine that "clears" its memory, so the status of "clear" means that the entrapping engrams are cleared. Buck Rogers, indeed. Yet thousands of converts claim resultant successes in drug rehabilitation, marital issues, employment crises, and other social discomforts. Scientology claims 3,000 churches in 154 countries and millions of practitioners, including leading movie stars such as Tom Cruise and John Travolta. Scientology has organized a wealthy and successful public profile. The claim to science and the technology of e-meters, combined with a sci-fi like history of the human species, offers a recycling of science and religion through the Faustian paradigm.

This cocktail of science and spiritualism, practiced by Hubbard and Parsons enjoyed various sorts of avatars: those who were self-proclaimed, such as Hubbard and Crowley, and those who were conjured up from the rituals, such as Babalon and Thetans. Mixing science with spiritualism created a shared virtual space of transcendence to define the experience of both new rites and new technologies. Recycling the Faustian paradigm provided a way to imagine the state of the practitioner within these virtual spheres as motivated by moral or anti-moral standards.

Heaven's Gate

Another Faustian figure, Marshall Applewhite, taking the name "Do," organized a cult around and through website production. The cult was known as Heaven's Gate, an apt signification of the spiritualist sense of the portal. "Do," along with other members of his cult committed suicide on March 26, 1997, in San Diego,

California. The local police discovered 39 bodies in an apartment, where the cult had committed collective suicide through the use of drugs, alcohol, and plastic bags used for suffocation. The cult claimed that they were joining an alien space-craft, which was trailing behind the Hale-Bopp comet. On their website, they explain how their avatar announced this decision: "The joy is that our Older Member in the Evolutionary Level Above Human has made it clear to us that Hale-Bopp's approach is the 'marker' we've been waiting for—the time for the arrival of the spacecraft from the Level Above Human to take us home to 'Their World'—in the literal Heavens."[1] Outer space was thus configured as a transcendent space, where post-humans would dwell after suicide. Suicide and space ships combine to offer travel out into the other spheres.

The cult produced a conflation of Christian images and those of science fiction to articulate their beliefs and goals. Their avatars were a compound of the two traditions: "We see fallen angels and space aliens as synonymous." Likewise, the sites where avatars exist reproduce this same mixture, as Do explains in a transcript from one of his videos:

> Now, I'm not trying to make a big deal over the means of transportation issue. For a spacecraft—belonging to the Level Above Human—is much more than a piece of transportation. It is a very valuable work station. It is commonly a place of service to the Level Above Human. These students that are leaving this kingdom level to go with me to my Father's Kingdom, to my Father's house, these will not go into houses on some planet like Earth, and reproduce, and have families and sit and watch television and make scrambled eggs. They're going to be genderless individuals, in service—full time—for whatever need the Level Above Human, the Kingdom of Heaven has for them. And the tools they use, the workstations that they use are spacecrafts—all sizes. . . . that size craft is best suited for whatever laboratory work or experimentation is going on.[2]

Spacecraft, scientific experiments, heaven, and gender are all mixed up here in a way that is typical to the later twentieth-century grassroots imaginary. Heaven and spacecraft combine with web worksites, avatars, and apparati. The avatar, in this case, is one who can negotiate the space travel and the space required for transcendence in one. A navigational device, the avatar corporealizes the web function of a link. He also moralizes it, making cyber-destinations into heavens and hells, not unlike the stage of the Morality plays.

Autopsies on those who died in the Rancho Santa Fe collective suicide revealed that some—including Do—had been castrated. These operations seemingly corporealized the "genderless individuals" who would work in outer space. Both male and female members of the Heaven's Gate group affected a unisex look, with buzz-cut hair and shapeless clothes. At first, this androgynous appearance led investigators to mistakenly identify all of the bodies as young men. The identification process was further complicated by the castrated bodies.

Remember, Goethe's Faust ascended the highest mountains to witness the ascension of the essential feminine. Through Goethe, gender ascended into a code through a gendered morality-tale, which imagined a new class of the virtual. These cult members, following the mid-century, highly-publicized medical reassignment of Christine Jorgensen, combined with some reception of feminist notions, and the religious practice of celibacy, associated ascension with a gender-neutral state. Gender remained key to ascendance as the Faust legend originally scripted, but, in this version, it was a state of gender-neutrality. Yet, also following in the sense of the constant, never-ceasing workforce first sighted by Shaw upon encountering Edison's workers, this ascension was to take their place through their worksite. So, with Nikes on their feet, wearing identical clothing, with surgically altered bodies, and a little change in their pockets, the Heaven's Gate web designers killed themselves in the hope of finding full-time employment somewhere behind the fleeting material body of the Hale-Bopp comet. They were set to perform "laboratory work or experimentation" in their spacecraft/workstations, as Do revealed, unhampered by families or TV.

The Mephistophelean Do led the cult members into a virtual world, presumably transforming them after death. As web designers, they were prepared to commit their designs of virtual space to a higher project. They already felt the sense of the portal to the virtual as something they could enter only through a transformed corporeality. The virtual space of the internet, in itself, was not transcendent, but inspired a vision of a transcendent space that would somehow emulate web design and somehow be more "real" in its effects.

Faust is Dead

Mark Ravenhill's play *Faust is Dead* (1997) is set at the time in the twentieth century when, as the text describes it, "reality ended and simulation began" (2001: 132). The transitory nature of the early Faust of Goethe, who lived in the real world, but could visit the virtual has been inverted. At the end of the twentieth century, Ravenhill sets Faust within a society of simulation, with only the death throes of the "real" remaining. The possibility for Faust to choose between the grace-filled real and the damned virtual is dead. Pete, a punk, urban version of Mephistopheles, can only bear experiences when looking through the lens of a camcorder. Even when Alain, the Faust-like figure, sucks him off, Pete watches through the lens, imitating the voice of a commentator. After orgasm, he says he didn't feel a thing. At another point, Pete and Alain sit in a circle of pills, taking them randomly to frame their experiences within a drug "high." Even the few shards of "real" experience remaining must be made to seem like simulations, set in the magic circle of a drug-induced, altered state.

Pete's father, Ravenhill's version of god, is chasing him in order to retrieve his computer disk that contains his software for the future—chaos—the inverted form of salvation. Pete and Alain move from place to place, in order to avoid the father. In various motel rooms, the have sex, go online and watch reruns on TV.

Even the simulations are mere reruns—iterations of themselves. Reports of the outside register only state and individual violence. The suggestion may be that the increase in violence is directly related to simulation, for in the simulated environment, it seems, one cannot feel anything. Violence serves as a simulation of feeling.

One day, Pete meets Donny online. Donny claims to have scarred himself with blades across the torso. Alain finds it beautiful as a sign of some corporeal "real" and wants to meet Donny. Pete asserts that Donny's a fake, insisting it's only ketchup on his wounds. Donny comes to the motel room, pleased that someone wanted to meet him outside of the online virtual. Pete challenges Donny to a cutting competition: Pete cuts his chest, but Donny slices his jugular and dies. Donny had planned this ahead of time, the Chorus advises, as part of his desire to be "really real." Finally, Pete shoots Alain, who is tired of running away, and eventually joins his father in the business of taking over the world. Alain is left alone in the hospital, until a virtual Donny somehow comes to comfort him.

Faust, Alain, may be saved in the end by Donny, a kind of Gretchen figure, but only to endure in the hellishly violent world of Pete and his father. There is no salvation into the real as long as simulation and random violence rule. This grand inversion of the real and the virtual, Ravenhill suggests, brings about the "end of man." In the violent contemporary world "after Belsen, sometime after Kennedy, sometime after MTV . . . man is no more" (138). By "man" the play seems to suggest humanity, the possibility for kind acts that are now made extinct, since the discovery that "we are no longer the subject but the object of forces" (138). Faust is dead because "man" is dead and the "real" is impossible. Nothing remains but Pete and his father, who distribute chaos and gratuitous violence across the globe.

Ravenhill scripts a version of the late twentieth century Faustian damnation. There is no longer any hope that technological devices will serve human or environmental needs. In fact, humans will be so alienated from the environment that they can only watch it onscreen. State and random violence run riot, without the experience of pain or pleasure. The virtual is a destructive, dangerous place, where its very virtuality requires violence for the simulation of experience. The play stages the quotidian results of such violence, among two individuals in a room. No space remains unperforated by it, no act beyond its unsensing, alienated borders. Rather than finding transcendence in the space of simulation, Ravenhill scripts a space of damnation.

Recycling the Faustian paradigm has meant, then, constructing a kind of register, either psychic, spiritualist, or political, for measuring the ecstatic or destructive qualities of the new virtual spaces imagined in the technological age.

Staging scientists

In contrast to staging discoveries of science as metaphysical contests, some playwrights have scripted semi-biographical portraits of scientists, in an attempt to script the social field of scientific research and development. These dramatic treatments deploy biographical and historical elements in order to figure contemporary crises in the interface between science and the social. The figure of the scientist is drawn to incarnate and personalize the social and ethical application of scientific discovery. Bertolt Brecht's *Galileo* used the astronomer to test the lens of perception, versions of Darwin tested the genealogy of human self-definition, and a portrait of Heisenberg measures the immeasurable possibility of nuclear disaster. In these plays based on scientists, the very mode of scientific investigation and its resultant discoveries become epistemologically and corporeally tied to the human figure of the scientist, providing a dramatic social frame for their research practices.

Perhaps it is the ethical frame of the portrait, or the traditional, liturgical notion of the scientist as what Haraway characterizes as "modest" that encourages these plays to excise considerations of sexual practices from their characterizations of scientists. Although Brecht emphasizes appetite and economics in his treatment of Galileo, there is no portrayal of sexual or romantic liaisons. Similarly, Wertenbaker locates Darwin on a ship without sexual fantasy or romantic letter-writing, Frayn treats Heisenberg as an intensely and singularly intellectual type, and Wilson creates an almost Puritanic staging of Einstein, in which there is almost no physical contact of any sort. So while the project of staging scientists seems to mean embodying scientific processes, the body is a celibate, singular one. The Faustian paradigm, which locates the lab or study in proximity to sexual ruination and virtual realms is frustrated by these modest, gentlemanly portraits of scientists as engaging in a form of *noblesse oblige*—parlor portraits of scientists.

Fleshy physics: Galileo

Although Bertolt Brecht first wrote *The Life of Galileo* in the late 1930s, he created a new version, the "American" version in 1945. Brecht was living in exile in Santa Monica at the time, reworking the play according to suggestions by the actor Charles Laughton, who was cast, by Brecht, in the title role. The play opened at a small theater in Beverly Hills in 1947. Brecht revised the play once more after his move to the German Democratic Republic, where he was working on a production of it by the Berliner Ensemble when he died in 1956. Thus, his work on the play spanned the mid-century years so central to both the ecstatic celebration of technology and the unleashing of its most destructive power. The play had first been sketched out during the Nazi invasions, the second version around the time of the Atomic Bomb, where it opened in New York as Brecht fled the country due to his Un-American Activities trial, and, finally, was slated for production in the new GDR. Laughton, by the way, closed the New York production, convinced by others that he was "playing into Communists' hands" (Brecht: xvi).

Derived from his understanding of the Marxist tradition, Brecht scripted scientific research in terms of the social and economic responsibilities of the scientist. The scientific apparatus, the telescope, is portrayed more as the catalyst for Galileo's moral and scientific dilemma than as an independent, isolated object, somehow free of ideological implication. Unlike the Expressionist *Adding Machine*, or *R.U.R.*, the apparatus itself is not portrayed with any dramatic agency, but only reveals the decision-making process of the scientist. Although Galileo's telescope, the scientific apparatus appears on stage, it only serves to throw focus onto the character of the scientist and his material situation. All claims for the autonomy of scientific apparati, or, indeed, discourse and research are regarded by Brecht as merely functions of bourgeois manipulation. In one of Brecht's drafts for a foreword to *Galileo* he notes:

> The bourgeois single out science from the scientist's consciousness, setting it up as an island of independence so as to be able in practice to interweave it with their politics, their economics, their ideology. . . . The research scientist's object is 'pure' research; the product of that research is not so pure. The formula $E = mc2$ is conceived of as eternal, not tied to anything. Hence other people can do the tying: Suddenly the city of Hiroshima became very short-lived. The scientists are claiming irresponsibility of machines. . . . Among other things, war promotes the sciences. . . . Obedience is the midwife of arbitrariness. . . . scientists get what they want: state resources, large-scale planning, authority over industry. . . .
>
> (Brecht: 220–221)

The socialist critique conjoins that which educational/scientific structures put asunder: the study of physics and the study of its ethics. Brecht deployed biography to dramatize the union. In what Brecht terms the "bourgeois" practice of "pure" research, the social effects of research become untied from the process. Revealing the ideologies of support or censorship that adjoin institutions such as the Church and the state, Galileo configures scientific research as not only supported by these institutions, but defined by their goals.

Brecht's adoption of the materialist critique is made flesh in the fulsome corporeality he assigns to the character of Galileo. Brecht imagines a fleshy, sensual scientist as the constitution of a material base of knowledge: "It is important that Galileo is not idealized. My Galileo is a powerful physicist with a big belly . . . a loud, fullblooded man with a sense of humor, the new type of physicist, earthly, a great teacher" who is "always gesticulating with his meaty hand. . . . " (my trans. Hecht 27). By "new type of physicist" Brecht is referring to the new Marxist view of the scientist, noting "Galileo of course is not a Falstaff: as a convicted materialist, he insists on his bodily pleasures . . . it is important that he works in a sensual way" (Brecht 1963: 28; my translation). Key to this fleshed-out version of the scientist is the compound of sensuality and work. Although Brecht portrays Galileo with a hearty appetite for food, he displays no sexual appetite. He lives alone with his virginal daughter, with no seeming liaisons. In contrast to the randy rocket scientist Parsons, these staged scientists are all de-sexed, as if making moral and ethical decisions are, somehow, still associated with the liturgical tradition of celibacy.

Brecht opens the play with the fulsome figure of Galileo stripped to the waist, washing his body, while devising ways around paying the milkman, and while also teaching young Andrea about the movement of the stars. The point is not to set a social, material context for scientific knowledge, but to situate forms of knowing across the social and economic fields that are isolated in more "bourgeois" representations. The nature of circles and straight lines are directly associated with practices of paying or not paying bills; while differing formulations of the solar system accompany the processes of washing and eating. While drying his naked torso, Galileo explains that the Ptolemaic system suited those who were social shut-ins, immobilized by structures of authority. His astronomy is based on corporeal needs and satisfactions and a celebration of the social. The organization of his research and his findings parallel social constructions.

While Brecht offers a correction to the binary represented by the bourgeois extraction of soul and mind from flesh, he also critiques the intellectual division that is scripted in the socialist film *Aelita* between the desire to know about Mars, characterized as idealistic, and the functional building of a dam. In an argument with The Little Monk, Galileo retorts: "We can't invent machines for pumping water if we're forbidden to study the greatest machine before our eyes, the mechanism of the heavenly bodies." For Brecht, it is not the function, or application of research that is integral to the socialist agenda, but the structure of knowledge. Pure research involves structures of knowing inherent to the application of it. Perceiving these structures, asking the broader questions trains the mind. The application will follow from the organizational principles of the research. These epistemological structures cannot be abstracted from materialist experience. Galileo continues: "The triumph of reason can only be the triumph of reasoning men. You describe your peasants in Campagna . . . How can anyone imagine that the sum of the angles of a triangle runs counter to their needs! But if they don't learn how to think, the best irrigation system in the world won't do them any good" (Brecht 1972: scene 8, 58). The scientifically-trained mind necessarily figures subsistence, while a simple focus on subsistence will not be able to figure its solution.

Galileo offers the method of empirical reason as the tool of liberation, in the tradition of the Enlightenment and of scientific socialism. However, Brecht's dramatic form embeds the deployment of such reasoning within argument and contradiction. The structure of the play itself adjusts the simple adherence to empirical reason to the changes in historical circumstances. Even though his foreword makes clear that Brecht was considering the moral implications of the dropping of the atomic bomb, he sets his dramatization of science in the historical period of the seventeenth century, at a time when bourgeois impulses could be observed in their break with feudalism, further attenuating the simple deployment of empirical reason. The play suggests that empirical reason may have a certain historically-specific function when moving out from feudalism, but a different one in the future that Galileo so often evokes, within the ascendancy of capitalism (Holmes 2002: 158–160). The play seems to ask if scientific reasoning, used in one way, could benefit the peasants in Campagna; how, in another, it could benefit those living in 1947.

The play *Galileo* asks the audience to consider how the rational and dialectical relations inherent in the materialist and epistemological conditions of empirical reason change its deployment and even its structure within different historical circumstances. In her study of reason (Vernunft) in *Galileo*, Ann Moss points out that in his later versions of the play, Brecht complicates the structures of critical reason with the deployment of shrewdness (Schlauheit). If empiricism and scientific apparati such as telescopes allow one to see what is "really there," it might not always be the wisest strategy to express it. In other words, something more and different may be required to engage with dominant ideology than empirical reason (Moss 1998: 139–141). Moss turns to the end of the play, where Galileo laments: "If only I could have resisted, if only scientists could have developed a Hippocratic Oath . . . a promise to use their knowledge only for the good of mankind!" (Brecht 1972: scene 14 94). Even though Brecht had embraced the liberative power of empirical reason, he saw that the outcome of such research could be used in various ways that were ultimately destructive (Moss 1998: 143). Thus, in itself empirical reasoning was not necessarily a positive force. This seemingly contradicts his other assumption that there is no division between the structures of research and its application. The contradiction remains in the play as essential to the problematic.

This contradiction is the dramatic movement of Brecht's Epic structure. Remember, Brecht was writing his Short Organum for the Theater at roughly the same time as he was working on Galileo, and his notion of how theater works is central to the structuring of his Epic plays. His sense of adherence to Enlightenment notions of reason and empiricism make for his more "scientific" stage. The scene titles offer a transparent language, one through which one might view the "real" appearance of things, as through Galileo's telescope. The scene titles imitate the traditional writing of history, of German *Wissenschaft* and of science. For example, the scene title for scene 3: "January 10, 1610: By means of the telescope Galileo discovers phenomena in the sky that prove the Copernican system. Warned by his friend of the possible consequences of his research, Galileo attests to his belief in human reason" (Brecht 1955: 22; my translation). However, the dramaturgical sense of the scene relies upon the audience perceiving the difference between this summary of the scene and historical and narrative irony. Brecht's stage apparatus imitates the scientific one: the audience can see all the workings of the stage apparatus, the lighting fixtures, etc. But the stage is designed for the audience to look at the apparatus, say, the telescope, rather than through it. Their distance from the stage lens allows them to situate what they see, in this scene for instance, Galileo's decision to go to Florence, believing in empirical proof and reason, and the knowledge that dominant forces of faith will ultimately defeat him. The irony in the vision before them, then, makes them consider the status of the Enlightenment claim to knowledge, which is removed from the materialist, historical dialectic.

In the final scene, Galileo's manuscript is smuggled out of the country, presumably to "enlighten" future scientists. Brecht took into account the world outside the theater, in which the audience participated. His plays were not intended to be viewed in isolation from it. Thus, the audience in 1947 knew about the uses of science that had led to the dropping of the Atomic Bomb and the destruction of Hiroshima in 1945. They knew where Einstein's research and the new physics had led. Today, the audience might associate the use of the telescope, or long-distance viewing with surveillance satellites. Today's audience is also aware of the founding of the GDR, where Brecht hoped to open Galileo, and its demise, with the fall of the wall. "Specters of Marx," indeed, fill their eyes, offering, perhaps a further ironic distance from the seemingly utopic promises of the social application of scientific reasoning. Thus, inspired by the contradictions that have formed the play, this critical audience might perceive how the continuing isolation of the structures of reason and contradiction in the practice of science, the continuing isolation of the practice of scientific research from the social, and the continuing failure to perceive the common structures in each has bound new technologies to threaten life on this earth, far greater than the subsistence needs of the peasants of Campagna. Agitated, on the one hand, by the pessimism of Galileo's final lament, in which science seems ultimately morally unredeemable and, agitated by the fatalistic optimism of the final scene, on the other, the audience may find a new urgency in reviewing, critically, the practice of scientific reasoning and research in our time and its situation within the social. Perhaps the audience member could even find consonance with the scientist as Brecht describes "him" in his foreword: "just when he has cut himself off from the people as the complete specialist, he is appalled to see himself once again as one of the people, because the threat applies to him too; he has reason to fear for his own life. . . . " (Brecht 1972: 222).

While the play agitates against any settled account of scientific reason, or of the relation of science to the social, it normalizes and stabilizes the masculinist aspects of science and the scientist. The descriptions Brecht offers of Galileo, with his big belly and meaty hand, the sound of his loud voice, the sight of his voracious appetite and of his naked upper torso are signs of an aggressive masculinity that stand in for the sensual, materialist base of the scientist. The scientist is unmistakably and essentially masculine, as is his work on instruments and the instrument itself. His poor daughter, Virginia, is made to look slow, and incapable of observation and reason, in contrast to the promising young (male) student, Andrea. Whereas Galileo teaches the young boy Andrea, when Virginia wants to look through the telescope, he treats her as if she is without any ability to understand it:

> VIRGINIA: May I look through it?
> GALILEO: What for? (Virginia has no answer) It's not a toy.

VIRGINIA I know, father.

. . .

VIRGINIA: Didn't you find anything new in the sky with it?
GALILEO: Nothing for you. . . . Go to your mass.

(Brecht 1972: Scene 3, 25–26)

In this way, Brecht's *Galileo* reveals the loss of the early liberative program for women within socialist thought that *Aelita* had depicted. The scientist, however much "he" may practice his scientific reasoning within the framework of dialectical materialism, once more resembles the patriarch. The gender and sexual politics of the changing social order are lost within the dramatization of scientific thought. Whatever the conditions of scientific reasoning, they are definitely practiced only by men.

Darwin

Previously, in the section on the nineteenth century, Darwin served as a figure for the scientific and social practices of determinism, but by the mid-to-late twentieth century, another reception of his work prevailed, organizing a central moral debate between the Christian versions of faith and empirical evidence. As in Brecht's figure of Galileo, the freedom of speech and thought would be tested by Darwin's portrait, but his findings also provoked a reaffirmation of the "divine" origin of creation.

The basic problem for the religious opponents to Darwin resides in how one interprets a text: the Bible. If the alchemists composed textual emblems to guide experiments, the religious adherents of creationism read the Book of Genesis as if a somewhat literal record of creation. They cannot accept the idea that the origin of various species, but most at issue, the human species, did not result from a divine source, but instead evolved over millions of years through the process of natural selection. Natural selection means that characteristics or varieties best suited to eating and mating would survive, reproduce, and evolve into the composition of future species—an idea that seemed to militate against the special, divine, vitalist notions of the human. From the perspective of the creationists, Darwin's theories emphasize a more random, almost accidental process of evolution rather than an embrace of God's design. Ironically, then Darwin is not viewed so much as a determinist as one who accepts a kind of random development over divine determinism.

The success of Darwin's theories, their later adoption by most biologists, made them even more significant as a representation of the divide between science and faith—particularly when taught in the public schools. In the United States, the controversy over teaching Darwin in the schools first became nationally and even internationally prominent in the so-called Scopes Monkey Trial of 1925. The ideas at issue in the trial still inspire legal controversy today. In fact, the debate between creationists and Darwinists forms a central platform of the fundamentalist religious and political movement in the U.S. in the early twenty-first century. In the original trial, John Scopes, a substitute high-school biology teacher in Tennessee was charged with illegally teaching Darwin's theory of evolution, in a state where it had been banned. The Tennessee law made it unlawful to "teach any theory that denies the story of divine creation as taught by the Bible."[3] William Jennings Bryan, who had lost a run for the Presidency several times, led the Fundamentalist Christian crusade against Darwin's theory of evolution and led the prosecution in the trial. Clarence Darrow, a known agnostic and "liberal intellectual" led the defense team for the American Civil Liberties Union (ACLU).

The trial itself was a kind of circus performance, with banners in the streets, lemonade stands along the way, chimpanzees, brought by the prosecution performing in side-shows, and tent communities of fundamentalist Christians surrounding the town. The courtroom was so packed, the officials were afraid the floor would fall through, so they moved the trial out onto the lawn, where over 5,000 people gathered to listen. Several radio stations transmitted the proceedings live. The vociferous applause by the audience sometimes seemed definitive in the success of the arguments, as if the performance overcame the legal arguments. Bryan made the case that to believe in evolution, particularly the origin of the human species as evolved from the "lower" mammals, was to go against the Bible, and by implication, God. The prosecution led off with a reading from the book of Genesis. At the apex of his defense strategies, Darrow called Bryan to the stand to question him on his method of interpreting the Bible. Darrow's case rested on whether Bryan did, in fact, read the text as literal. He asked Bryan about his reading of the whale eating Jonah, Joshua making the sun stand still, and, finally, if he understood that the earth was literally created in six days. To the point of creation, Bryan responded that he understood the days as eras, or periods of time. Once he had admitted any figurative understanding of the text, Darrow had won his point. Ultimately, however, the case was later tried on a technicality and dismissed from the Tennessee Supreme Court, leaving the issue unsettled.

In the present moment, 80 years later, the Department of Education for the state of Kansas is holding hearings that challenge the role of evolution in the state's school science curriculum. Once again, the theory of evolution is understood as a "bias against religion" (*Los Angeles Times*, June 5, 2005, A28). Local school boards in Georgia and Pennsylvania have recently voted to alter their science curriculum to include alternative creationist theories, the Ohio Department of Education has passed a measure ensuring teachers they can challenge Darwin's theory, and eight other states are considering such moves. While scientists continue to argue that subsequent research has proven Darwin's theories, the appeal to faith deems such evidence false. The new term for the opposition is "intelligent design" rather than creationism. The difference is that "intelligent design" does not name the designer, but only insists that there is one.

The play *Inherit the Wind* by Jerome Lawrence and Robert E. Lee was loosely based on the Scopes trial. The play opened on Broadway in 1955, in the era of the HUAC trials that had driven Brecht out of the U.S. Brecht was only one of many who were publicly interrogated about their communist sympathies and often condemned by association. The blacklisting was effectively a form of censorship, condemning many authors and their works to obscurity. In the play, the issue of science and religion was interpreted more as the issue of the freedom of thought/speech than the issue of scientific evidence versus faith-based tenets. In a scene based on trial records, the character playing Darrow speaks out against anti-intellectualism, conformity of thought, and fear of ambiguity. Darwinism, then, represented ratiocination rather than determinism, an attention to evidence rather than observation and the possibilities for change and mutation rather than iteration. Religious faith, in contrast, was represented more as an organizing principle for mob, conformist rule and untested hypotheses.

When the play became a Hollywood film in 1960, many of these issues remained, although the beginnings of the Civil Rights movement informed a portrayal of the South as "the Bible Belt," a provincial and intolerant region. One of the screenwriters was actually one of the authors who had been blacklisted by the HUAC, using the nom de plume Nathan E. Douglas, so the operations of McCarthyism were still informing the movie's portrayal of the issues. Both the play and the movie pit a moral individualist against a mob. Faith-based initiatives seem more like untested prejudice and adherents of Darwin more like those who can weigh evidence, test findings, and understand the exigencies of hermeneutics. This mid-century mobilization of science is made to seem like a liberal, free-speech version of a political platform.

Timberlake Wertenbaker's play *After Darwin* (1998) situates the figure of Darwin in a play within a play. Set on *The Beagle*, the ship Darwin took to the Galapagos, the dramatization of the familiar science/religion debate takes place between the creationist Captain of ship, Fitzroy, and his passenger, Darwin. This is the voyage that inspired Darwin's notion of natural selection. The play within the play consists, primarily, of the debates between the two men. However, Wertenbaker further frames the debate by alternating between this historical encounter and contemporary rehearsals for the play. The director is a refugee from Bulgaria, the playwright is an African American, and one of the actors is gay, thus situating the debate within other current social issues. Wertenbaker's context for the play within the play thus suggests that the perspective of social Darwinism somehow radiates out from the historical debate. The implied uses of science are the social applications of Darwin's basic assumptions—most obviously, the sense of the "survival of the fittest." But, unlike the traditional uses of social Darwinism, to support certain conservative agendas, it is used here as a critique of survivalism. Tom, the gay actor, is revealed as a kind of anti-intellectual, who is only out to succeed, taking whatever part he can get, without any real commitment to the ensemble or the ideas. Millie, the director, is trying to survive in London by "acting" English, thus, by adaptation. There are several debates among the four characters about social survival, until, after rehearsing a scene on the ship entitled "The Origin of the Species," Tom announces he has taken a part in a film and thus, will leave the play, making it impossible for it to open. Now the debate rages among the characters to test whose job will survive. Thus, the science/faith debate turns into one between a rather specific moral responsibility and economic survival, cast in the Darwinian notions of adaptation and "survival of the fittest." Evolution, historical periods, and memory interweave in the final dialogue as a set of "free" associations among the characters in the play within the play, the director, and the playwright:

> DARWIN: In considering the Origin of the Species, it is quite conceivable that a naturalist, reflecting on the mutual affinities of organic beings . . .
> MILLIE (director) "The Beak of the Finch."
> FITZROY: A puff of weather.
> DARWIN:—their geographical distribution, geological succession, and other such facts, might come to the conclusion that each species had not been independently created . . .
> MILLIE: "Darwin's Dangerous Idea."
> FITZROY: The dark side of his light.
> MILLIE: "The Mismeasure of Man."
> LAWRENCE (playwright): Blind kings, barren women, runaway children, and castaways peopled my childhood. . . . They became my ancestors, those loved figures carved from the crooked timber of humanity.
> FITZROY: Tolerance. . . .
> . . .
> MILLIE: The Origins of Virtue.
>
> (Wertenbaker 1999: Scene 7, 79–80)

Wertenbaker draws the figure of Darwin, the naturalist and scientific theorist, into a dialogue of childhood memories of failed antecedents, the historical carvings of African ancestors, expressions of tolerance, ambiguity, and rationality. The play seems to organize sympathetic resonances between the processes of science and evolution and the moral, social principles of tolerance and virtue. This set of associations is not unlike those in *Inherit the Wind*, but are spoken by the "others" in the social order, rather than the representatives of the law. The referents of the system of evolution are social rather than genetic.

Wertenbaker's staging of the scientist is distanced, in part, by its containment in the play within the play. Darwin himself provides a kind of origin for strategies of survival in the social realm. Thus, rather than focusing entirely on the decision-making events in the life of the scientist, Wertenbaker locates the historical contradictions of his findings within the production of the staged scientist. The findings and contradictions central to the historical Darwin leech out into the contemporary social structures that provide his representation.

Heisenberg

Michael Frayn's *Copenhagen* (1998) is based upon the historical encounter between two of the most important physicists of the early twentieth century, Niels Bohr and Werner Heisenberg, who met in Copenhagen in 1941 in the midst of World War II. These two had collaborated in their research during the 1920s, developing some of the key strategies in the new field theories. Now that the war was raging, it is provocative and puzzling to imagine why they would meet. The Germans had occupied Denmark and were beginning to consider how to handle the Jews there. Bohr was a half-Jewish Dane, so living at the edge of Nazi persecution. Heisenberg was a German nationalist, but not a member of the Nazi Party, who, nevertheless, headed the Nazi nuclear research program. He traveled to Copenhagen to meet Bohr. It is known that they went for a walk, possibly to insure a private conversation. However, the object of Heisenberg's visit was not recorded.

Copenhagen situates these two research scientists at the point in history when their work was being used for the creation of the weapon of mass destruction— the atomic bomb. Frayn cleverly applies Heisenberg's most renowned principle of physics, the Uncertainty Principle, to the moral and historical dramatization of this encounter. Did Heisenberg want to discuss the ethics of the development of the bomb with Bohr? Since the Nazis failed to produce the bomb, was it that Heisenberg deliberately sabotaged the building of it? Did Bohr withhold something vital to its development at the meeting? In the world of quantum mechanics, as developed by Bohr and Heisenberg, the so-called Copenhagen interpretation took up the debate as to whether matter is constituted by particles or by waves. What mattered in this new interpretation was not (as in classical physics) confirming the adequacy of a particular model by key experiments, but rather confirming probabilities in a large number of experiments without a coherent theory of why the phenomena occurred as they did. What was important was the mathematical result, not any clearer sense of an underlying reality or cause.

In the play, Heisenberg makes explicit the Uncertainty Principle in terms of social cause and effect. The two characters are discussing Bohr's habit of walking around the city, and compare that to the issue of whether electrons are waves or particles

> HEISENBERG: . . . Exactly where you go as you ramble around is of course completely determined by your genes and the various physical forces acting on you. But it's also completely determined by your own entirely inscrutable whims from one moment to the next. So we can't completely understand your behaviour without seeing it both ways at once, and that's impossible. Which means that your extraordinary peregrinations are not fully objective aspects of the universe. They exist only partially, through the efforts of me or Margrethe, as our minds shift endlessly back and forth between the two approaches.
>
> (Frayn 2000: 69)

Frayn wittily applies this principle to the encounter itself, leaving the audience with various possible explanations for the meeting, and thus, various interpretations of the morals of the characters and more, the morality of the situation of science at that point in history. Less deterministic than Brecht, in terms of moral and method, and, like Wertenbaker, situating the issues of science within a host of other social dilemmas, Frayn presents a compelling successor to Brecht and an apt reconsideration of scientific research near the end of the twentieth century. Like Brecht, he portrays the structures of the social in the scientific and vice versa. The character of the scientist figures this compound.

Staging the scientist, then, partakes in the Soviet tradition of situating science within ethics as well as the tradition of using scientific principles for interpreting social structures. The creation of the social sciences, "scientific" studies of social groupings and individuals entailed modeling the study of social and individual behavior after the methods applied to the study of the physical sciences. A belief in empiricism has shaped not only scientific research, but notions of history and psychology. Marx considered his approach to the study of economics as a determinative base for human organization to be scientific, inspiring the formation of something termed "sociology." Social Darwinism claimed to apply the laws of evolution to human genealogy, and, relativism borrowed Einstein's notion of the relations of time and energy to human systems of ethics. The discursive traffic between elements of scientific methods and philosophical, social studies has marked the peculiarly Western form of knowing.

In these plays, character functioned to depict this bridge between the unstable, ambiguous environment of decision-making and the certain, iterable environment of the laboratory. Jonson's *Alchemist* used character and motivation to destabilize the truth-claims of certain laboratory procedures, while these later plays situate the structures of scientific procedures as a basis for the dramatization of social debates. While the practice of staging science through the scientist proceeds throughout the twentieth century, another strategy was also invented. Rather than focusing on the figure of the scientist, it uses the theories of science for its form.

Einstein on the Beach

Philip Glass and Robert Wilson's *Einstein on the Beach* (Avignon, 1976 and New York 1984) treats Einstein not only as a figure in the production, but also makes use of the notion of field theory as a way to organize the overall composition of the piece. One might regard *Einstein* as a successor to Cage's *Variations V* in this sense, but with referents to the social realm. In the opera, an hermetic space similar to that in *Variations V* seems to envelop the performers, who rarely interact, but often move in close proximity to one another. However, unlike Cage, Wilson's performers are also proximate to thematic clusters of images. The production begs the oxymoronic description of a "minimalist spectacle," proceeding by image, but in the minimalist style. Wilson adopted the sense of opera more than lab, perhaps because of the more presentational and practiced nature of the production, or perhaps because it does make use of words and suggestions of scenes.

In *Einstein on the Beach*, three major images operate like Wagnerian leitmotifs: the train, the trial/prison, and a spaceship hovering over a field. One could imagine these images as referents to Einstein's biography: he used the metaphor of a train to explain one of his theories, the train was a nineteenth-century version of the spaceship, the spaceship represents Einstein's theories of space, and the trial is the moral trial of the discoveries that led to the atomic bomb. Moreover, the use of image as organizational principle suggests Einstein's own metaphorical processes in thinking about space through the image of falling elevators and the like. These referents hover around the images as other referents hover around the gestures of the performers and the words in the text. But the field of isolatable, unrelated images and gestures destabilizes any sense that there is a particular referent tied to any sign on stage, creating instead a field of possible referents that hover, but never really land. Yet, if the images do not suggest Einstein, they do suggest science and invention. The effect of a field of indeterminant referents is heightened by large sections of text Wilson uses in the piece, which were written by Christopher Knowles, an autistic poet, whose writing combines wildly different terms in a non-linear

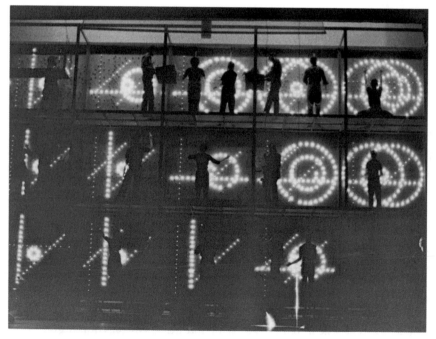

Figure 13 Final scene from Philip Glass's *Einstein on the Beach*, 1976.
Photograph: Theodore Shank

collage-like style. In this way, Wilson works within a semiotic field of meanings rather than a narrative line, or a symbolic rite. Although, unlike Cage and Cunningham, Wilson includes words alongside his dancers and images, the words are a more sonic and sculptural part of the composition than a discursive one.

The figure of Einstein, made up to resemble the familiar image and with wild, white hair, plays the violin midway between the orchestra and the stage. He is not constructed as a traditional character, as Galileo and Heisenberg are, but, instead, this animated citation of the persona of Einstein creates a musical and dramatic touchstone for the themes and images of the opera. He organizes a point of reference for both his notion of a field theory and the dramatic structuring of it.

Glass's music, a combination of acoustic, vocal, and electronic sounds is structuralist in a mode different from Cage's. Glass is not organizing a soundscape, as Cage had done, but a sequencing of rhythms and pitches that self-referentially point to their structural order. Repeated patterns of tone and rhythm cycle rather than develop any sense of progression. Withdrawing from allusion and expression, as Cage had done, the music points to its own structure rather than to that of the apparatus that produces it. Beginning the piece by counting out, in structure and in word, 1-2-3-4, the music suggests the mathematical basis of Einstein's work, or of the general discourse of science, along with the rhythmic sequence of the music itself. The organization of the music matches the compositional strategies of the overall production, with the repetition of images, and repetitive, isolated gestures in the choreography. As Wilson put it in an interview: "The play consists entirely of mathematical computations. Every gesture is counted out and the actors repeat them so often that in the end they become quite mechanical. The music and the rhythm in Einstein work like clockwork. The pencil movement was done exactly 64 times" (http://www.robertwilson.com/works/masterEinstein.htm). With the iteration of mathematical computations at its base, *Einstein on the Beach* does not invite indeterminacy, as Cage had done. The silences in the piece, the spaces between images and performers are not open ones, as in the Zen understanding of them, but isolable principles that create the sense of integers, numerical principles. These spaces are not the non-signifying closet of Cage, but the computational organization of integers.

While the semiotic space of referentiality does retain a certain indeterminacy within the space of the overall composition, sensing the strict control of director and composer and watching the obediently-replicated iterations of movement, suggest an almost Expressionist inkling of the oppressive and authoritarian nature of science and technology. Precise mathematical and mechanical iteration form the basis of dramatic. Yet the piece does not work to stage an oppressive environment. Instead, it is an opera that mimics modern or modernist science. The avatar of Einstein himself is radiant and white, ensconced in his own field of theories and metaphors that self-referentially, iteratively perform the nature of his research.

Cyber-Darwin

Following the practice of deploying the structure of a scientist's findings rather than "his" biography, digital artists are staging Darwin's research as a structure of software code rather than staging the scientist Darwin, or the life of Darwin. Uploading Darwin into the digital technosphere has meant replicating the evolutionary processes he described through software coding. Thomas Ray's *Tierra* (1998) simulates the concept of a wildlife reserve in the digital realm. Termed a "network-wide biodiversity reserve for digital organisms" the piece replicates the Darwinian codes of evolution in genetic codes run on computer calculations. Tierra is actually a source code that creates a virtual computer with a Darwinian operating system. The machine codes evolve by mutating, recombining, or reproducing their own operating code. The self-replicating machine code programs "live" as "digital organisms" in the network biodiversity reserve. Observors can actually watch the evolution of the programs through visualization software applications.

Galapagos (1997) by Charles Sims is named after Darwin's journey to the Galapagos Islands on *The Beagle*. The piece consists of an arc of 12 screens filled with computer-generated organisms. Viewers select an organism with which to interact by stepping on a sensor before it on the screen. This "unnatural selection" nominates the organism as a survivor, removing other organisms from the screen. The selected survivor then mutates and reproduces. Its offspring combines data from the parents with other randomly selected features.[4] This provides a witty version of "natural selection," by leaving the selection up to the viewer.

Darwin's "natural laws" are translated as control codes of data, visualized as color and form on the screen. The "natural environment" is cyberspace, the organisms are data and the laws are software codes. The deterministic elements in Darwin easily become translated as code, while random selection can also be coded into the programs. However, in the end, these artworks also reproduce "intelligent design," in that they are works of art with a creator who claims them as her or his own.

Avatars of synth-race

As noted before, science ties the coat of whiteness around its practitioners and its practices. These white-suited operators move in generally white environments as well. White walls signal antiseptic, carefully-extracted practices. The white costumes and sets of science participate in all of the cultural markings of whiteness. From the emergence of the "new" science, which sought to excise its Arab roots and establish an identification of empiricism and lab practices with some distinctly "European" identity, to twentieth-century iconic images of the predominantly white male scientists, the tradition of representing science as exclusively and distinctly "white" has continued for several centuries. In its ideological and symbolic functions, it carefully traces a lineage free of any of the techne associated with the Southern Hemisphere. These costumes, sets, and symbols of whiteness have provoked grassroots performances of specifically "other"-race-specific assimilations of their technologies and structures of identity. One particularly noteworthy practice is located in the production of music that melds synthesizers with jazz traditions. The combination of the affective nature of music with electronic sound production may be perceived as breaking down the strict barrier between science and spiritualism, providing a way to create new compounds of avatar and virtual worlds.

Kodwo Eshun's book *More Brilliant Than the Sun: Adventures in Sonic Fiction* assembles musical forms that combine ethnic cultural traditions with what he terms a mystic science. Eshun establishes the Afrodiasporic genres of hip hop, jazz, and scratch as "sciencemyth," a term that breaks with the binary of science and myth. Eshun claims these musical strategies organize a "myth-technology" that sets up "an interface between science and myth. . . . a continuum from technology to magic and back again." And magic, he argues, is just "another name for the future" (1998: 09[160]). The synthesis of science and myth enables a virtual space composed of the technics of the laboratory and the imagined relations of a myth. Eshun's creative compound of technology/magic/future opens up a new perspective on science, music and history. If the lineage of science is exclusive white, then even the genealogy must be reconfigured to accommodate racialized difference.

To this end, "Mythscience," or "Sonic Fiction," Eshun argues, creates a "discontinuum," or a break with history. Instead of playing within the familiar tropes of Eurocolonial histories, Sonic Fiction sets up an "AfroDiasporic Futurism" with "the force of the fictional and the power of falsity" to break with these oppressive histories and practices (00[-004-003]). Rather than as a form that recalls the traditional histories of an oppressed people, such as the Spiritual, or the Blues, this techno-music is understood as organizing a complete break with that past in order to imagine an alternative, empowered future life for its practitioners. Music produced through synthesizers and other techno-techniques of the sonic are perceived by Eshun to contradict the emotional affect, or religious sentiment claimed by the acoustic music tradition as the signifiers of an Afrodiasporic cultural tradition. For Eshun, the power of Afrodiasporic music does not reside in these melancholic affects, but in a technology that remixes, scratches surfaces, or researches sound through synthesizers and other electronic devices.[5] Music as a technology, however, does not belong to a rational, scientistic model. Instead, it operates by "flagrantly confusing machines with mysticism, systematizing this critical delirium into information mysteries" (09[161]). This futurism is outside a determining history, or an imagined linear development of a people's heritage. It offers the possibility to freely imagine social identifications and class structures.

Ultimately, in the Afro diaspora, this techno-music remixes and re-imagines the codes for "race." Eshun terms this process "synthrace." Synthesized race is a re-mix, or an electronically synthesized set of racializing principles that imagine racialized people as powerful, in-control citizens of a different order of things. Whereas, "singing the Blues" establishes the Afrodiasporic people as objects of a history of oppression, he argues, "synthrace" music creates its own, futuristic, Edenic world of special powers (09[160]). "Synthrace" technologies invest social relations with fictional rather than factual powers as instruments of change. In this powerful blend of mysticism, technology, and race, Eshun offers a brilliant adaptation of the nineteenth-century mystic sciences as a technology of deracializing, or racializing those in the diaspora. Rather than inheriting the Orientalist visions of a Mme. Blavatsky, on the mystic side, or the seemingly unmarked privileged relations to race that experimental music traditions offer, this technomusic is a synthrace technology for a radical remix of the codes through new technologies.

However revolutionary Eshun's notion of "synthrace" may seem, his argument is based on the traditional, even essentialist binary of acoustic/synthetic music, which relegates the acoustic to the realm of the traditional and natural, and the synthetic to the futurist and the technological. Ron Eglash, in "African Influences in Cybernetics" traces the construction of this binary though the 1960s, countering that "analog systems can achieve the same levels of recursive computation as digital systems; the two are epistemological equals" (1995: 19). Eglash claims the power of digital mixing and remixing for the acoustic. The point is important, Eglash argues, in considering African cultures, which, although analog, structure "complexities of recursion" (19–20). For example, Eglash claims fractal geometry in ancient North and Central African architecture, as an earlier "mythscience," arguing that these fractal forms had their base in Rosicrucian theories, and Egyptian architectonics. Thus claiming recursion for the analog and more, the tribal and the mystic, he divorces the function from its mechanistic associations that Cage, Oliveros and others in the experimental music tradition share.

Eglash cites examples of African American music-making that are similar to the ones Eshun uses in his book, but Eglash regards them as examples of "vernacular cybernetics," a form, he argues, common to many subcultures that freely assimilates scientific and technological advances for grassroots uses" (23). His argument fuses science with the vernacular, through the unlicensed borrowing of techno-tools by subcultures who have partial knowledges and abilities within the growing realm of a scientific virtual, but who assimilate its elements into their own cultural and social practices. Eshun, however, provides a radical version of Afrodiasporic technology through the digital/synthesizer technologies as part of an imaginary break with the past, on the part of an interested group, to serve their own "synthrace" purposes. Both arguments are resources for understanding how the structures of music in the Afrodiasporic tradition can be made to signify the social relations of "race" through technology. Perhaps if the analog or acoustic tradition can be perceived as a technology capable of recursive devices and of a myth-science conflation, it can be equally capable of signifying a break with traditions of oppression.

Sun Ra: Pharaoh from Outer Space

The titles of Sun Ra's albums reveal his own "synthrace" version of "myth-science:" *Rocket Number Nine Take-off for the Planet Venus* (1960), *The Solar-Myth Approach, vols. I&II* (1968), *Space is the Place* (1972), *On Jupiter* (1979), *Strange Celestial Road* (1980), *Beyond the Purple Star Zone* (1980), *Cosmo Sun Connection* (1984), and *Friendly Galaxy* (1991). These space themes expressed his performative approach to his particular mix of jazz and new techno sounds, which included the Theremin, the synthesizer and complex, improvisatory mixes of acoustic instruments. In the late 1960s, he began adding dancers and more outlandish costumes to his "arkestra," as he called it, creating a spectacle of his outer space "mythocracy."

Sun Ra saw himself as an avatar of a new world of potential power and social organization. In his performances, he appeared in different costumes to suggest his avatar aspect, sporting reflective capes, masks, headware with antenna-like protrusions, and jewelry with hieroglyphs that suggested those of ancient Egypt. He ritually renamed himself Sun Ra to represent the Egyptian god of the sun. The name itself constituted a break with the human-based genealogy and heritage of an oppressed history that Eshun interprets. As Ra records it: "it's a business name and my business is changing the planet. . . . and business is not family, nothing. . . . A business just happens, it's not born" (quoted in Szwed 1998: 84). Ra incorporated the master, the adept, and the incarnation of the god in the form of the Egyptian ruler. He represented the African's history in Egypt as the ruler, not as the slave. Ra traveled through space by means of the "audiovehicle," which he called his "Arkestra" devising the name from a combination of the term for the Egyptian god Ra's solar boat, the Ark of the Covenant, and from Black phonetics, "that's the way black people say 'orchestra" (Szwed 1998: 94). As Eshun phrases it, Sun Ra chose alien over alienation (157).

Sun Ra's sense of himself as an avatar from outer space extended beyond the simple formation of a stage character. In his early childhood, he recorded an alien abduction that took him to the planet Saturn and a return back to earth, filled with life-altering visions. For Sun Ra, the alien abduction was not a negative, medicalized fantasy, but one of positive change and new commitment. Mark Szwed, in *Space is the Place: Life and Times of Sun Ra* locates this abduction within specifically Afrodiasporic traditions, interpreting it as "less like a UFO story than a conversion experience and a call to preach in the Afro-Baptist tradition" (1998: 31). In other words, Sun Ra experienced a "calling" to his role of composer/conductor and jazz performer, which broke with the Christian tradition of his childhood and represented, instead, a baptism, of sorts, by aliens. Graham Lock, in his book Blutopia agrees with Szwed's association of the abduction with a kind of baptismal vision of purpose, quoting Sun Ra's own account:

> Anyway, they talked to me about this planet, and the way it was headed and
> what was going to happen to teenagers, and governments and people. They

Figure 14 Sun Ra from *Space is the Place*. Photograph: © 1972 Jim Newman

said they wanted me to talk to them. And I said I wasn't interested. So then they said I was the only one that could do this job. . . . They showed me [how] to be a ruler of the peoples. . . . We're going to teach you a kind of music that will talk in that type of language to them. They will listen.

(qtd in Lock 1999: 54)

It is important to note the connection to the tradition in Sun Ra's abduction story, but also to mark the originality and importance of the break with those traditions in his deployment of science fiction tropes. His composition, "Space is the Place" expresses the hope of this "outer" space:

Outer space is a pleasant place
A place that's really free
There's no limit to the things you can do

There's no limit to the things you can be
Your thought is free
And your life is worthwhile

(quoted in Lock 1999: 28)

Sun Ra's memory of alien transport marked the invention of his "Arkestra" and invested his music with more significance than simply aural entertainment. Somehow, with Sun Ra as avatar guide, the music could literally transport one to another world, where conditions are free and hopeful. Cannily building on the tradition of receiving music as otherworldy, or sacred, Sun Ra corporealized its tradition of virtuality with his own invented referents.

Along with his alien abduction, Sun Ra became preoccupied with visions of ancient Egypt in his youth. Szwed documents how the young boy became obsessed with the pictures and lore that surrounded the opening of the tomb of Tutankhamen at Luxor. In various interviews, Ra remembers poring over the photos in Life magazine when the tomb was discovered. Sun Ra's role as Pharaoh may have been a composite of those new discoveries and the rich heritage of "Negro Spirituals," which play off the relation of Egyptian slavery to that in the U.S. One of the most familiar spirituals hails Moses as liberator:

Go down Moses
Way down in Egypt land
Tell ole Pharaoh
To let my people go

Once understood as a melancholy recollection of oppression, later scholarship has revealed "Go Down Moses" as a political manifesto sung by the abolitionists, citing the activist third verse: "bold Moses said, 'If not, I'll smite your first born dead/Let my people go.'" Sarah Bradford's book about the famous activist Harriet Tubman Harriet: *The Moses of her People* argues that Tubman used this song as a coded message in the recruitment of people into the underground railroad. The call and response form of the song means that the repeated chorus, "Let my people go" was more activist than melancholic. Szwed also documents Ra's discovery of books written in the earlier half of the twentieth century that specifically linked African heritage to Egypt, typified by the titles *An Anthropological and Geographical Restoration of the Lost History of the American Negro People, Being in Part a Theological Interpretation of Egyptian and Ethiopian Backgrounds and Stolen Legacy, The Greeks Were Not the Authors of Greek Philosophy, but the People of North Africa, Commonly Called the Egyptians* (Szwed 1999: 69–71). Thus, blending together the images of Tutankhamen's tomb with music about liberatory avatars such as Moses in Egypt, and a sense of Afro-Egyptian "roots," Sun Ra composed his own "synthrace" avatar, blessed by aliens, African-American specific, and liberatory.

Ra's performances of this power translated traditional gestures into "spacey" ones, creating a performance vocabulary that invested science fiction tropes with ritual powers. This is not unlike some of the performances Ione created with Oliveros—in fact, as with their work, the use of techno sounds may have been more than an accompaniment to the idea for the composition. Sun Ra would come out before his Arkestra, in full space regalia of cape and headware with antennae, and walk ritualistically in counterclockwise circles, reminiscent of the African American "ring shouts." June Tyson, one of his dancers, reports inventing a space-age manner of walking with him, which was later replicated by Michael Jackson and known, tellingly, as the "moon walk," which became a a popular vocabulary of movement (quoted in Szwed 1999: 251).

Sun Ra's film *Space is the Place* narrativizes the various aspects of his avatar status and its relation to myth and social reality. At the beginning of the film, Ra makes a "Pharaonic" entrance, arriving from a "parallel future," in a retro-looking space ship. He says that he has come to deliver the promise of a creative future for African Americans. He then drives through the poor black area of Oakland, California, where, at that time, the Black Panthers had their headquarters. In an open convertible, he waves to the people, alongside one character who is wearing an Anubis-like mask, and another dressed as an alien. "I am the presence of the living myth," he announces. His dancers then perform a combination of robotic-type movements and orientalized versions of ancient Egyptian gestures. Ra informs the people in the street that he has chosen this particular planet as a possible place to resuscitate the black race, addressing a group of teenagers with large afros. One of the teenagers asks "How do we know you're real?" Ra responds: 'I'm not real, I'm just like you. You don't exist in this society. If you did, your people wouldn't be seeking equal rights. . . . So we're both myths. I do not come to you as reality. I come to you as the myth because that's what black [Camera cuts in close as he holds up a crystal to his face and stares at it] people are, myths." Ra then plays the synthesizer keyboard, accompanied by other musicians. He opens an "outer space employment area" in a boarded-up urban block. The film is campy, based on 1950s science fiction tropes, yet original in its politicizing of the Pharaoh from outer space and his connection to the ghetto. The healing power of his synthesizer is aimed directly at those most at risk for hopelessness—the young, the women, and the unemployed.

Throughout the film, Sun Ra competes with the dark, other side of African American identification. His arch-enemy in the film is portrayed as a pimp who drives a Cadillac and is brutal to his women, broadcasting a message of violence and hate. A violent scene in a brothel, where the pimp abuses his women is made to actually disappear through harmonic progressions of energy that Sun Ra applies to the scenario. It's as if Ra's music, his Arkestra could transport these women to safety and heal these violent, sexualized encounters. Ra's own sexuality and gender identification was complex. He seemed not to have any particular sexual liaisons and certainly did not construct his persona in any typical, masculinized way. His costumes were often flowing robes, accessorized with large, symbolic jewelry, worn with capes and headdresses. While he was not gay-identified, neither did he play the heteronormative, masculinist hero.

Sun Ra addresses the youth in the ghetto saying "I hate your absolute reality." For him, "reality" is simply the vain show of subjection, which they can evacuate through the synthesized outer space. This virtual space can interpellate its conditions into the ghetto, as if a utopic condition that could become immediately realizable. As an avatar of a Pharaonic "synthrace" Ra could perform, through the media of jazz and movement, how an alternative life might appear. Interpellating the crystal in the midst of an anti-racializing dialog, Sun Ra intimates emphasizes his power to move race from its historical determinants to rest in mystic powers. "If you're already a myth," he instructs, "why not embrace one of power and glory."

The combination of jazz improvisatory technique and the techno sounds of his later keyboards offered Ra the possibility of a composition that could break with traditional timbres and harmonies at once. Retaining the traditional instruments of jazz, such as the saxophone and the bass, he nevertheless encouraged his ensemble, including his singers, to move out and away from the traditional harmonic patterns and especially away from the repetitions. He was a master of the collapsed interval, somehow producing harmonies out of what first sound like dissonance. The effect is to produce a disjointed, but somehow related set of sounds. Yet, for example, in the documentary film, *Sun Ra: The Joyful Noise*, shot on a rooftop that resembles a landing pad, Sun Ra conducts the sound into a familiar crescendo, as he opens his arms to the heavens. With blue paint on his face and a cap with a wire-hanger-type antenna, he parades himself through the members of his Arkestra, as if inspiring their improvisations to reach more inventive levels. As the crescendo builds, so, too, do the wild dissonances, challenging the listener to discover the alternative pattern-building in the composition. Ra uses both the building-top and the crescendo to suggest the heights reminiscent of earlier romances with the Himalayas. These are urban heights, however, which also suggest the site of an antenna, or a launching pad.

Sun Ra reconceptualizes the alien abduction as an empowering visionary experience that led him to develop his own performance of the synthesized, musical and performative space of being outside oppressive, determinative structures. Moreover, he enacts an alien arrival as a helpful, empowering one, in which he, as the alien avatar, attempts to bring hope to people who feel oppressed. The dancing figures surrounding him promise a utopic space of celebration and creativity. For him, the virtual space of aliens could heal and inspire those caught in scenarios of violence. His witty, campy representations of science fiction and ancient Egyptian themes helped to translate them into the vernacular. His reconfiguration of electronic devices moves them out of the more privileged, exclusive, avant-garde tradition of electronic music.

Sun Ra represents an avatar of the techno that provides a race-specific, grassroots intervention into the reception of science as strictly rational and strictly separated from the affective arts. He brings together the major strands in this book, in terms of performing science and the virtual, combining the mystic with the rational and art with science. He represented virtual space as outer space, as space travel, and as the space produced by his Arkestra. Outer space was the site of his childhood abduction and his adult source. As his titles suggest, Space is the Place, which his music produced, from the planets Venus and Jupiter, to the "outering" of the ghetto. Sun Ra produced a unique and eccentric form of avatar, untied from other musical and mystical practices of his time.

Channeling New Age avatars

In contrast to Sun Ra's unique, eccentric performance of the avatar, channeling avatars has become one of the signature forms of New Age practices, located within a broad spectrum of techno-mystic practices. The very term "New Age" heralds a different form of spiritual practices in line with more "modern" living conditions. Growing out of the hippie movement, which embraced the "Age of Aquarius" as the dawning of a new age of peace and psychic powers, the New Age movement claims a reorganization of psychic powers and practices in accord with astrological temporalities. Reclaiming astrology within a new spiritual cosmology seems to reject all of the interventions theater and the new science made in the European displacement of the occult and Arab sciences. New Age practices provide an eclectic blend of beliefs and practices that are reminiscent of Mme. Blavatsky's Theosophy, including astrology, shards of Hinduism, Buddhism, Sufiism, and Christianity, rites of goddess worship, Wicca spells and other neopagan rites, yoga, energy work with crystals, aromatherapy, and various forms of contact with space aliens, to name only a few. In some cases, New Age practitioners adhere to a blend of all of these beliefs and practices. The relations among these different beliefs and practices are unclear and sometimes individually invented. The potential contradictions in belief systems seem to fade under the belief in a general sense of "spirituality." This ever-expanding syncretic set of beliefs accompanied the decades of intense globalization in the economic and political arenas, providing a metaphysical framework for the new amalgamations of transnational capital.

New Age practices combine fragmentary allusions to science and technology with spiritual beliefs. Many rites invoke a grassroots reception of the new physics, mimicking the flow of energy described in field theories and electromagnetic fields through work with crystals, feng shui, and New Age music. Alternative medical practices displace the power of drug industries and medical complexes by turning to older traditions of medicine such as Ayurveda and Chinese herbs and acupuncture, or through new healing rites with crystals and various forms of massage and body work. The insistence on "holistic" medicine, with an attention to a more integrated sense of the patient's body and psyche has greatly influenced the medical establishment in the past two decades.

Many of the arts have become reinvented within New Age practices, but perhaps the most successful has been New Age music. New Age music turns to both indigenous acoustic instruments and electronic ones, often combining the two. Thus, it brings together the mythic with the synthetic, as Sun Ra had done, but also with references, both instrumental and thematic to ancient indigenous musical practices. The New Age claim of the healing power of music is seemingly based on indigenous practices and the sense of "good vibrations" common to hippie culture and other twentieth-century receptions of the new physics. Similar to the works of Sun Ra, New Age albums locate these healing powers of music in the virtual space of outer space as a peaceful, bountiful, "heavenly" realm that listeners may inhabit. In fact, many of the New Age practices are aimed at creating this virtual space of peace, both individually and collectively. While this is an admirable aim, particularly in a time of wars and violent confrontations across the globe, its universalist claims have been perceived by many to be just another example of Anglo-American cultural and economic imperialism. The New Age claim to the indigenous, particularly the Native American traditions, has also been hotly refuted by some tribes as an imperialistic form of "white shamanism." Thus, the virtual realm of the Age of Aquarius may not only signify a grassroots reception of science and technology translated into alternative spiritual effects, but also reduplicate the basically white European project of those traditions.

The signature practice of avatars in the New Age is through channeling. Although many channelers hark back to Mme. Blavatsky as the "mother" of their invention, the contemporary practice began to flourish primarily in postindustrial, AngloEuropean countries beginning in the 1970s. Channeling flourished along with other New Age subcultures in the 1980s, becoming a widespread phenomenon throughout many countries by the 1990s. There are various accounts of the history of channeling, none received as "official." The practice seems to have garnered its first media reception in 1974 with the publication of the book *Seth Speaks* by Jane Roberts and Robert Butts. The authors claimed that "Seth," a very wise "unseen entity," offered advice about the nature of the universe, defining the soul as an "electromagnetic, energy field" that exists wihin a Platonic-like realm of the "Idea Potential." Seth dictated his treatise entitled "The Physical Universe as Idea Construction" through the channelers. Seth's physics offer this ontological insight: "we form ideas from energy, and make them physical" (quoted in Klimo 1998: 29–30). Thus, channeling began with a kind of mystic-science speak, combining familiar notions of electromagnetic fields and idiomatic usages of Einstein's energy-matter exchange with everyday notions of Platonic idealism. This New Age avatar, then, does not appear in the context of ancient Himalayan traditions, as in Mme. Blavatsky, but in the context of techno-science. As we have seen, ever since Edison's experiments with communications, the electromagnetic surround has articulated a luminous, spiritual plane to spiritualist subcultures.

The very term "channeling" implies a spiritual practice that understands itself through the structures of the media. It's as if the channeler "receives" a signal from an avatar-transmitter. The term suggests that the invisible nature of possession is like "channeling" on television, or the radio, in which the listener/viewer tunes into particular broadcasts. One common definition of channeling describes it this way: "Channeling is a means of communicating with any consciousness that is not in human form by allowing that consciousness to express itself through the channel (or channeler)." The avatar then broadcasts a message through the medium of the channeler (http://www.summerjoy.com/JourneyChapter1.html). As the famous channeler Kevin Ryerson describes his channeling process: "The guides and teachers who speak through me are primarily energy, and I act not unlike a human telephone or radio receiver" (Klimo 1998: 43–44). The spiritual practice is articulated through a metaphor of sonic technologies, yet the actual medium is a corporeal one—the channeler's body. Channelers claim possession by various kinds of avatars, some from so-called ancient eras of earth history to some who are extraterrestrials. Their processes and allegiances vary: some offer solo performances, while others belong to associations; some have been financially successful, while others eschew financial reward; some channel their own unique avatar, while others tune into a more common, collective one. Channelers combine the corporeal and the live with the virtual in their reception of avatars.

Perhaps the phenomenon of channeling can best be understood through a brief description of some of its avatars, agencies, and practitioners. For example, the avatar "Michael," first appeared in 1970. Michael is a "group soul," a collective consciousness of 1050 essences who have finished all their lifetimes on Earth, cycled off the physical plane, and recombined into an Entity who now resides and teaches from the mid-causal plane" (http://www.NewAgeInfo.com). Whereas many channelers claim exclusive access to their spirit guides, charging upwards of $1,000 a session, "Michael" provides a more collective reception, with the different aspects in the Michael collective of souls appearing to different people (http://www.michaelteachings.com). There are individual channelers of Michael, a book of the Michael Teachings, and The Michael Educational Foundation. Michael is, by now, a tradition of avatar appearance. In contrast to the collectively-channeled avatar, other channelers run a profitable business based on their exclusive talents. J.Z. Knight is one of the most popular and well-known channelers in the U.S. Knight channels a 35,000-year-old male, Cro-Magnon warrior called Ramtha, who speaks in the lower register in an archaic tongue with sentences such as "Woman, beautiful entity, what say you?" By 1986, Knight had engaged a staff of fourteen, who began to organize semi-monthly seminars, brochures, and tapes. The average seminar drew 700 attendees, paying $400 apiece (Klimo 1998: 41). Later, Knight was able to charge more than $1,000 to participate in one of her sessions. Likewise, the Sedona Circle, located in Sedona Arizona, one of the power centers, both metaphorically and commercially of the New Age movement, is a powerful association of channelers that publishes a nationally distributed magazine, manages a publishing company for books in the field, and runs a marketing company for products associated with the practice (Klimo 1998: 98).

The celebrity who has been immensely effective in popularizing channeling is Shirley MacLaine. MacLaine is a very successful Hollywood actress, who lends her fame as a movie star to her books and films that record her New Age discoveries. In 1987, ABC carried a mini-series based on MacLaine's book *Out on a Limb*, which depicts various encounters with the virtual that MacLaine has enjoyed, from Hollywood to Peru. In the film, the famous channeler Kevin Ryerson can be seen channeling two different avatars in MacLaine's home in the star-studded beach community of Malibu. MacLaine claims that she filmed him in an actual trance and asked his two avatars, John and Tom to repeat what they said in the original session with her. They agreed to perform. The avatar John uses the pronouns "ye" and "thee," denoting the historical period in which he lived as an "Irish/Scottish pickpocket." He speaks in a dialect vaguely reminiscent of those regions. The pickpocket tells Shirley that she and the man she loves were husband and wife in Atlantis and that her husband worked with extraterrestrials there. MacLaine seems heartened to learn that her new liaison has a validating history of connection and that it was closely related to the reception of ETs. The compound of Irish/Scottish roots, the mythical Atlantis, and information concerning a romantic attachment is not unusual in avatar reception.

The surplus value of self that is signified through the transnational marketing of celebrities takes on a spiritual form. So the movie star Shirley MacLaine, an avatar of the entertainment industry consorts with other powerful avatars who are stars in their own media, the bodies of New Age celebrities of spiritualism. The grassroots movement offers celebrities to perform their own social power as spiritual and it also opens the way for those outside the industry to become players in the technological surround of listening and watching. A certain intimate agency may be acquired during these channeling sessions that celebrate the affect rather than the function of the unseen and complex modes of these proliferating technologies.

Two modernist terms, then, dominate the cultural imaginary at the end of the twentieth century: New Age and new media. They are proximate in representation and affect. The postindustrial surround of electronic and microwave technologies of broadcast and contact, such as radios, TVs, cellphones, and ipods is emulated through grassroots practices of virtual space and avatars. A syncretic lifestyle emerges that mixes up spiritualism with science, claiming spiritual effects from various technologies and scientific effects of corporeal practices. At the same time, new media experiences of the virtual cyberspace begin to be articulated through spiritualist terms. The internet practices of avatars and virtual space inspire the users to turn to spiritual traditions to articulate their cyber-experiences.

Composing the cyber-avatar

In *The Pearly Gates of Cyberspace* Margaret Wertheim records descriptions by Virtual Reality designers that represent the VR experience as a spiritual one. Wertheim quotes at length from a speech by Mark Pesce, a codeveloper of VRML—the Virtual Reality Modeling Language. Pesce delivered the keynote to a conference of virtual reality software designers. The speech refers repeatedly to VR as the "Holy Grail" that constitutes "the object of desire. . . . of all mystics, witches and hackers for all time. . . . " The invention of VR is characterized as "The revelation of the grail. . . . the common element in our experience as a community" (1999: 253). Wertheim then turns to Kevin Kelly, a writer for the central magazine of the cybercommunity—*Wired*. Kelly claims to perceive "soul data" in silicon. The VR developer Jaron Lanier understands "the Internet as a syncretic version of Christian ritual," and the VR animator Nicole Stenger claims that VR "revealed a state of grace to us, tapped a wavewlength where image, music, language and love were pulsing in one harmony" (254). It seems that even the designers of VR, when immersed in the virtual techno-space that offers no sign of its production experience its synthetic convergence as a kind of religious ecstasy. Pesce situates hackers among witches and mystics, Kelly finds soul in silicon and Stenger experiences a kind of New Age "harmonic convergence" within its space. From the grail to hippie harmonics the experience seems to suggest that something "divine" is revealed or structured by the space of Virtual Reality. Wertheim's longer argument locates the representation of technology's virtual space within an historical development that begins with medieval, religious constructions and continues to figure the "pearly gates" of celestial space as within the cyber-imaginary.

Certainly, transcendence is an experience often attributed to the virtual cyberspace across many critical and entertainment platforms. Recalling the Futurist celebration of machines treated in the early section of this Act, we can observe a century-old tradition of masculinist ecstasy that accompanies the invention of new technologies. Yet the virtual space of the internet and Virtual Reality seems especially well suited to notions that the user has ascended into a more elevated condition. The movie *The Lawnmower Man* (1992) portrays a simple gardener who becomes a digitized god flowing through the internet. *The Matrix* (1999) nominates a character with the mythical name Morpheus, who consults the Oracle to learn that another character, Neo, is The One. These films encourage viewers to understand cyberspace as a meta-space fueled by lofty, mythical struggles concerning the future of the entire "human race." They link the religious quest with their narrative structure. Dungeons and Dragons, one of the first and most popular multi-user role-playing games began, as early as the 1970s, to configure mythical battles, imbued with medieval sorcery and a lingering sense of the quest for the grail.[6] This game and others like it, which were popular with players who later became involved with online MUDs, encourage users to imagine a link between online gaming strategies and heightened semi-spiritualist quests. In fact, in surfing the web one can experience multiple configurations of these mythical sites, wandering like the later Faust through medieval, classical Greek and Christian virtualities. The user's body, as in William Gibson's novel *Neuromancer*, the founding novel of cyberpunk fiction (where, in fact, the term cyberspace might have originated) is portrayed as denigrated "meat" compared to the bright lights of the cyber-virtual. Gibson's notion that uploading oneself into the cyber transcends the conditions of corporeal "meat" captures the assimilation of notions of transcendence associated with the cyber. The so-called "real" world is dull by comparison, offering few opportunities to save the human race, appear as various powerful avatars, and play with few consequences. One might imagine an easy correlation between this often-violent heroism and the rise of a militarized imaginary in U.S. culture.

This ascription of a transcended state to the subjects of cyberspace has led to an assimilation of the term "avatar" to represent their online image. Since "avatar" is a Hindu term for the incarnation of the god, the term seems to suggest that online characters participate in some process of manifestation understood through spiritual concepts. If the space is somehow celestial, so are its inhabitants. There is no definitive history of the use of the term "avatar" in the digital realm. One fairly inclusive article by Sean Egan suggests various origins of usage. In 1985, the term "avatar" was used in the personal computer game Ultima IV, where the goal of the game was to become "The Avatar." In later versions of the game, "Avatar" became the player's visual on-screen persona, which she could customize in appearance. However, Egan reports that "the 'bible of avatars for the geek community,'" at least according to Adi Sideman, CEO and Founder of Oddcast, Inc., a leading creator of avatars and avatar solutions, is Neal Stephenson's 1992 classic novel *Snow Crash*, "another story about hackers negotiating cyberspace." In the novel, Stephenson defines avatars in this way: "The people are pieces of software called avatars. They are the audiovisual bodies that people use to communicate with each other in the Metaverse (the virtual reality internet)." Egan proffers Ananova, the world's first virtual newscaster as the first online avatar. Ananova appeared in 2000, designed to deliver the latest news over the internet and on mobile devices. Constructed to resemble a 28-year-old, green-haired, British woman, this 3D avatar illustrated a full range of facial expressions and seemed to move "naturally" (http://imediaconnection.com/content/6165.asp).

In the past two decades or so, many sites have provided avatar experiences for the users. One of the earliest was "Habitat," developed by Lucasfilm in 1985: subscribers entered "regions" in the Habitat world as cartoon-like avatars, moving around using the Commodore's joystick. By typing simple commands they could pick up objects, read books, and talk to other avatars, with words displayed in a cartoon bubble above the avatar's head. AlphaWorld, The Palace, and Worlds Away offered not only avatars available for adoption by users, but the ability to design the environment in which they lived. Today, there are multiple sites where users may find avatars ready for their use in chat rooms and other interactive sites: Yahoo! Avatars, AOL SuperBuddies, ICQ Devil Factory, hotavatars, avatarity, deviantart, etc. At sites like Friendfinder.com, singles can flirt in the virtual world with FlashChat, which allows chatters to use three-dimensional avatars. As a teaching device, SPEAK2Me.net displays a female avatar named Lucy, who helps Chinese-speaking people practice their English. One can now even buy an avatar on eBay.

Critical treatments of the avatar offer various definitions of its composition and usage, but perhaps one of the clearest and most representative may be found in Jennifer Gonzalez's article "The Appended Subject." The title of the article suggests that the avatar serves as an online subject that represents an appended user. Gonzalez defines the avatar as "an object constituted by electronic elements serving as a psychic or bodily appendage, an artificial subjectivity that is attached to a supposed original or unitary being, an online persona understood as somehow appended to a real person who resides elsewhere, in front of a keyboard" (2000: 27–28). For Gonzalez and the majority of other critics and users, the avatar constitutes an identificatory fantasy of appearance online, often constructed with elements of fashions from the corporeal world, including industrial logos, Japanese anime, MTV images, Gen X fashions, movie stars, and Comix. Gonzalez lists avatar options as "simple grids of images (scanned photographs, drawings, cartoons) arranged thematically as movie stars or 'avamarks,' soft porn models or 'avatarts,' muscular men, or 'avahunks,' trouble-makers, or 'avapunks,' cats, dogs, Native Americans . . . happy faces, Hula dancers, space aliens, medieval knights and corporate logos" (2000: 28).

If we accept, as do Gonzalez and others, that the avatar serves as the online representative of the user, does that imply that cyber-avatars function in a manner similar to masks? Is the user an actor and the avatar her mask? After all, the definition of mask depends similarly on the opposing term of actor to mask, indicating some "presence" behind the mask. Indeed, the sense of a subject behind a mask is what Judith Butler nominates as the definition of performance against her concept of performativity.[7] Lurking behind the mask, then, is the "actual presence" of someone whose identity has been either altered or represented by the mask. Some notion of the "real," or the "natural" is required to delineate the function of mask as the techne of performance. In both cases, actor to mask and user to avatar, the action is understood as a performance. The medium of exchange between the corporeal and the virtual, then, is performance. "All the (cyber) world's a stage. . . . "

This notion of the avatar offers a prime example of performing science in the late twentieth century. The screen, often understood through cinematic terms, can also be seen as a version of the proscenium stage, with the avatars as its actors. The user is performing software functions within narratives and characterological images of transcendence as a form of entertainment and social contact. The "metaverse" as Stephenson hailed it, informs the "real" in terms of psychic and social investments in web activities.

The avatar as credit

Understanding the avatar as a representation of the user subjects the form to a critical scrutiny of identificatory processes and masquerade. Utopic visions of a sphere where cross-gender, cross-class, cross-ethnicity, and even cross-species identifications abound, juxtaposed to warnings against any belief in the possibility of "free" play within the historical significations of social differences. Yet both of these positions still agree that avatars are, somehow, performing versions of social identities and relationships in cyberspace. Notions of "self," volition, or agency, and attributes of social organization seem to compose the look and action of the avatars. Although this is the received notion of the avatar, I cannot agree with its semiotic suppositions. As I have argued more fully in my book *The Domain-Matrix*, many of these attributes are specific to an earlier form of entrepreneurial capitalism and do not reflect the contemporary, corporate structuring of social relations.[8] Following upon my earlier analysis, I would argue here that, given the corporate commercial take-over of what were once public domains of the social and the cybersphere, their sign systems no longer refer to a social "real." In other words, the avatar has ceased to serve as the representative of the user.

The digital artist and educator Victoria Vesna accounts for avatar usage in terms of the corporate profit motive. Vesna recalls that "investment in Web based communities really only started with the introduction of graphical user interfaces." In other words, the yield of greater profits from internet activities was directly tied to the image-based interface of the web. Since the avatar is an image-based form of user activity, Vesna foresees its functions as the key profit-making device in the future of the web. To support her argument, Vesna notes that by the year 2000, avatar-filled chat rooms were already generating 7.9 billion hours of online use and one billion dollars in advertising revenue. Vesna also cites a prediction that Apple Computer Chairman John Sculley made in October 1996, at the Earth to Avatar Conference in San Francisco, that avatars will become "a driving force shaping the economics of this industry" (http://telematic.walkerart.org/telereal/notime_vesna.html). These observations suggest that the production of avatars and spaces designed for their use is actually driven by a profit, not a performative motive. The avatars are not perceived as masks for user's performances, but as lures to entice people to remain online in the space of e-commerce. The profit motive of production displaces the user's imagined sense of the avatar as representing herself online, resignifying it as a function of e-commerce.

Toby Howard, at the University of Manchester explains that until now, the technologies used by most operators of virtual worlds have been proprietary and mutually incompatible. The older form of entrepreneurial capitalism that organized privately-owned and individually-structured spaces on the internet must give way to a corporate topology. In order to derive even greater profits from avatar usage, new standards are necessary to link existing, different multi-participant environments into an "electronic landscape" that will span the entire Internet. The internet will become a unified topology for avatars, which can then move from site to site, hopefully shopping with greater ease (http://www.cs.man.ac.uk/~toby/writing/PCW/vrml3.htm). Some designers have already formed Universal Avatar Standards (UAS). Their goal is to organize a secure site for investment, reasoning that "until there is some common definition of an avatar and universality of movement between spaces on the Internet, it seems unlikely that any VRML company can hope to make serious money. Because standardization renders identity in fixed and accountable form, the connection between the user's physical self and bank accounts will not be confused" (http://vv.arts.ucla.edu/publications/thesis/official/earth.htm).

These regulations understand the vital link to be between the avatar and the user's bank account, not the user's processes of social and psychic identification. The hope of these regulator/designers of avatars is to fix avatar identity as a stable link to the user's economic profile. The link could also contain data concerning the user's relations to various commodity fetishes through a history of her online purchases. The user's identity, then, is composed of patterns of consumerism. Note that the anxiety about the regulation of avatars does not concern issues of racism, or homophobia, but activities that could destabilize credit. In order to further secure the economics of the cyber avatar, a recent partnership was formed between NASA, a national agency, and TGraphco Technologies, a corporate one. They have joined forces to develop a product called Digital Personnel. TGraphco Technologies, Inc. (G-TEC) has acquired the exclusive worldwide rights to a patent that makes it possible to create photo-realistic animated humans as avatars for e-commerce and e-support applications. Digital Personnel is a human-image animation computer system that manipulates stored images of a person's facial movements in response to phonemes (the smallest units of speech). The result is photo-realistic animation of a person speaking, presumably in the secure space of a corporate/national transaction (http://vv.arts.ucla.edu/publications/thesis/official/earth.htm).

Within this analysis, then, the avatar appears as an animation of credit. Its referent is a secured line of credit for use in e-commerce. Now we have come full circle from studies at the beginning of this book of virtual and economic value in alchemy and gold and Goethe's Mephistopheles of paper money. Economic value and the virtual have circulated through mystic cosmologies, on the one hand, and through the apparatus of theater and science, on the other. As the theater and Edison sought to copyright theatrical and technological invention, the materials of value became more and more ephemeral. The guiding principles of intellectual property, the virtual product of value, have been challenged by digital (re)production and distribution. Ownership of virtual products is impossible to maintain in digital reproductions and downloads. Ironically, however, the digital has also assimilated economic value into its own virtual space, animating its functions through an avatar—an image adapted from spiritualist traditions.

Logo-centric avatars

Credit lines may constitute the future referents of the online avatar, but the completion of that project of signification is some years away, as the designers above inform us. At this time, the "extreme makeover" of cyberspace and its avatar is still underway, bringing along prior uses of the avatar, while remaking its significatory structures. The revision depends on new advertising trends that refashion notions of space and agency. Naomi Klein's book *No Logo* offers an exhaustive study of new corporate advertising practices that recreate significatory relations between people/space and products. Klein begins by tracing the corporate "branding" of individual products: "the first task of branding was to bestow proper names on generic goods, such as sugar, flour, soap, and cereal . . . Logos were tailored to evoke familiarity and folksiness" (2001: 6). Enter Uncle Ben, Aunt Jemima, and Old Grand Dad, who signified rice, flour, and whiskey. In a sense, they served as advertising avatars—imagined representatives of people in a simulated space. Their referents, however, were not actual people, but products. As corporate branding became more sophisticated, actual people began to stand in for the corporate logo, rather than a single product. These person-alized logos signify products, or more, the conglomerate behind products. On television, Magic Johnson's referent is Nike. Digitally-altered animals can stand in for products, such as a talking Chihuahua for Taco Bell, and McDonald's can extend its referent through any number of toys that resemble familiar cartoon characters. A looser, broader association is made between the advertising avatar and the referent. Magic Johnson may signify a tennis shoe designed for playing basketball, but more, he signifies the many products produced by Nike and their relative status across the complete line of sportswear. In fact, the logo for Nike has successfully displaced the word. The simpler and more design-reflexive the icon, the more sophistication is lends to the product line. The referent of the signifier, then, be it the image of Magic Johnson, or the logo begins to float across an entire line of products, their class appeal, and their function. As we can easily observe, Nike products are not worn just for playing sports. The online avatar circulates amidst these advertising practices.

The new virtual arena that advertising has organized also impacts the corporate structuring of cyberspace. Product placement is the method of inserting the product into an environment rather than into an ad. According to Klein, this practice began in the 1980s by placing logos or products within movies, novels, video games, and other so-called cultural venues. Cars in films or the repeated use of a particular kind of car associated with a film or TV hero is actually a placed ad for the car. The newer term for this strategy is "product integration," meaning that an even subtler insertion of the logo or product, better integrated into the narrative or symbolic structure of its environment has been developed.[9] This practice has extended into inserting the logo or product line into actual civic and cultural spaces, spawning what the *Wall Street Journal* identified as the "experiential communication" industry. "Experiential communication" refers to branded hotels, theaters, theme parks, and even little villages where people can live alongside fantasy rides. Together, these sites offer a topography of "experiential communication" as the social space of advertising. Within these social spaces, the brands loop back into their own worlds through synergies of entertainment and products, creating, as Starbucks calls it, "a brand canopy" (in Klein 2001: 148). Brands, then, Klein argues, "are not products but ideas, attitudes, values, and experiences. . . . the lines between corporate sponsors and sponsored culture have entirely disappeared" (2001: 30). Klein writes that this practice is "now used to encompass the staging of branded pieces of corporate performance art . . . " (12).

Cyberspace, or the World Wide Web, shares in the creation of a brand canopy, or a topography of "experiential communication" of corporate logos and products. Although there are other institutional sites within the WWW and even some so-called "free" sites launched by individuals or social communities still exist, the major environment of the web is permeated by corporate advertising and ownership. This space also induces a sense of the experiential as part of product enhancement, or "corporate performance art," with the avatar as its performer. Within this environment, the avatars take on fashions, or celebrity identities for their construction. These avatars have proceeded from Uncle Ben and Aunt Jemima, operating in a manner similar to logos to stand in for a corporate entity or product. They are gendered, raced, and sexualized in order to operate successfully as a fetish image within the logo culture. Marks of social identities, then, serve to create the seductive qualities of the logo-centric avatar that competes with other avatars for focus. The avatar does not referent the user, but the logo. Its seductive qualities serve to compete for focus with other online objects within the competitive, commercial, corporate topography of the cybersphere.

The digital diva: Lara Croft

Chat rooms and computer games are filled with avatars resembling a hyper-sexualized, scantily-clothed, fashionable, young "woman." This "digital diva" is a representation of feminine gender codes used to articulate the interface between the anterior sense of the private and the live in the figures of the new, corporate virtual systems. The diva helps to promote forms of interaction that seem familiar and enticing in the new cyberspace. Her success is derived from the advertising surround. Jean Kilbourne, a scholar of advertising, emphasizes that the average person in the United States is bombarded by 3,000 ads per day. Kilbourne notes that many of these ads create what she terms a "synthetic sexuality"—one that designates a certain body type, gestural system, and fashion sense as sexy (Kilbourne 2000/2001: 55). In these ads, the referent of the image of the sexualized woman is not sexuality; on the contrary, sexuality is the referent for a product line, or more, a corporation behind various product lines. Hyperfeminized avatars, then, do not represent the sexy user, as they seem to do; instead, these divas perform the allure of the digital platform that operates as their stage. They circulate among the other logos, as if at some sort of social event, acting out corporate and technological effects as seductive and even as sexual. Lara Croft offers a prime example of this kind of digital diva.

For those few who may not know, Laura Croft is the protagonist of the computer game Tomb Raider. Begun in the mid-1990s, the original game has

Figure 15 Lara Croft Tomb Raider: Legend © 2006 Core Design Ltd. Lara Croft,
Tomb Raider and the Tomb Raider logo are trademarks of Core Design Ltd.
Eidos and the Eidos logo are trademarks of Eidos. All rights reserved.

now extended into six sequels and two movies. In the narrative of the game, the avatar Lara appears as a "white," upper-class, British independent woman, who is off on adventures in the Third World. The backstory tells us that Lara was educated in private Swiss schools, that she survived a plane crash in the Himalayas, where she was traveling on a ski vacation, and that this experience turned into a "tomb raider," hiring out to reclaim lost artifacts in search of adventure. Lara is scantily-clad with a hyper-feminized gym body, sexy, but tough, bearing weapons and using martial arts in her arsenal against the Other. In her story, we find the by-now familiar elements of the Himalayas, ancient documents, mystic powers and the independent woman. However, in this animated version, the social referents of these symbols are privilege, competition, combat, and hyper-sexuality.

In the game, Lara is viewed from behind, suggesting to some that she represents, or works for, the game player. Thus, she seems to partake in the more traditional sense of avatar and user. Many feminist treatments of Lara replicate the traditional focus on the user's identificatory processes, debating her subject/object status for the mostly male players, who both desire her and identify with her. Many also emphasize that her personal fortitude is designed to appeal to young female players, who identify with her gym body and independent spirit. However, Lara may also be viewed another way. Launched at roughly the same time as William Gibson's novel *Idoru*, Lara's function as a virtual celebrity finds consonance with the Japanese form of the Idoru. In Gibson's novel, the celebrity is a hologram constructed at a node of massive information where her music videos flow together with her fan activity (1996: 178). In an online interview, Gibson refers to an actual online Idoru, which inspired his novel *Kyoko Date* (1996) (http://www.salon.com/weekly/gibson3961014.html). Arguably the first virtual idol, composed of 40,000 polygons by the Japanese music promotion firm Hori Productions, Kyoko Date has a complete backstory, pin-up photos, and a fan club. She even released a relatively successful single in 1996 (http://www.wdirewolff.com/jkyoko.htm and http://www.geocities.com/gnenosong/galleria_kyokodate.html). Thus, Lara joins ranks with other digital divas, who exist only as celebrity animations, who provide a backstory and attract fans in the same way that "real" celebrities do. These virtual divas are corporate pixilations that produce fan effects. Obviously, these digital divas offer several advantages to the industry. They can appear and disappear according to their market value. They never age and never cause any social embarrassment.

Lara Croft is a phenomenally successful version of the cyber-celebrity. Some suggest that she is actually only a "virtual commodity," designed to sell the products lines with which she is associated (http://www.gamestudies.org/0202/kennedy/). But Astrid Deuber-Mankowsky, in her book *Laura Croft: Modell, Medium, Cyberheldin*, offers a different version of how the avatar of Lara Croft, a "synthesized sexuality" serves as a diva hostess for the cyber-corporate-sphere. Through an exacting history of the image and the technology, Deuber-Mankowsky arrives at the conclusion that Lara Croft functions not as a character, a *Spielefigur*, but as a *Werbefigur*, an ad.[10] According to Deuber-Mankowsky, the composition

and function of Lara serve to perform the imaging power of the 32-bit platform
and the 3-D graphics card. She is the sexy diva that attests to the imaging power
of the Sony Play Station. In other words, an avatar of a heterosexualized, white
woman offers a ground for the imaging of the new convergence of filmic and
digital possibilities that made the game *Tomb Raider* popular. Lara represents the
high level of 3-D simulation that the successful upgrading of the computer platform and graphic card allowed in the construction of the game. Her figure
makes the technological platform seductive and entertaining. Accompanied by
realistic sound effects and a musical score, Lara lures users into the system,
keeping them in cyberspace, welcoming them into the exigencies of the software.
Codes of whiteness and gender converge in the figure of Lara to create an
alluring and powerful image of new technologies at work in the world.

The virtual Lara was made flesh in the movie version of the game *Lara Croft:
Tomb Raider* (2001) and *Lara Croft Tomb Raider, Cradle of Life* (2003) starring
Angelina Jolie. The animated Lara determines the character played by Jolie. The
advertising surround, then, moves its avatar hostess through the various sales
venues, hoping that each will lend its selling power to the other. Through the
avatar, a brand canopy is formed, to borrow the phrase from *No Logo*, in which
the hyper-sexualized female figure will seduce user/buyers into the commercial
foundations of the cybersphere. Tomb raiders of another sort, these user/buyers
buy their way into a space of artifact/commodities, following their avatar-guide,
Lara, who exudes desire, competition, and pleasure in her very composition.
Eventually, her treasure will be revealed as the Playstation itself, the machine that
makes her run.

Waitingforgodot.com

Performative resistances against these commercial practices also occur on the
web. Adriene Jenik and Lisa Brenneis created an online performance piece
that ironizes the space of chatrooms and the avatars who haunt them.
Waitingforgodot.com premiered at the Third Annual Digital Storytelling Festival
in Colorado in September 1997. *Waitingforgodot.com* takes place in a chat room
at a site called The Palace.[11] The title imitates a website address, notably a .com,
or commercial address rather than an institutional or personal one. In the chat
room, where avatars roam and users seek chat-mates, two roundheads appear,
reciting their version of some of the most familiar lines from Beckett's play.
They do not announce their performance as such, but, as a piece of cyber-street
theater, they simply perform in a public space. In fact, *Waitingforgodot.com* could
be perceived as a new kind of street theatre in the cybersphere, erupting in
social spaces where people pass through, or hang out. It offers a witty commentary on people hanging around in chat rooms with nothing to do or say and
nowhere to go. Rather than demonstrating unique and complex new software
applications, the piece was performed using the Palace visual chat software,
available to all visitors, demonstrating the equal access politics of the Desktop

Theater. Easy to use, the software requires limited bandwidth, and no unusual amounts of RAM, hardware upgrades, or specialized technical knowledge (Jenik 2001: 99).

The performance is a provocation that reveals how avatars seem to resemble people, but actually do not. In Beckett's play, the two tramps represent a minimalist, existential version of Everyman. Beckett's characters are literally Everymen, in a world of men, retaining stable gender referents in his play.[12] In contrast, *Waitingforgodot.com* deploys images derived from pacman video games and happy-face logos, which seem to suggest characters unmarked by gender. Even though they are colored the familiar yellow of the happy face, the color bears no reference to "race." Instead, the yellow face suggests "happiness"—an emotional quality cut off from any particular cause or action. The "happy" faces represent a free-floating happiness, born of the security and privilege of a secured space for the virtual class. Everyperson, then, or better, "Everysignifier," is a cartoon image, which was developed by the computer game industry and corporate ads to signify as socially neutral and virtually happy. The two floating heads are literally severed from referents to corporeal existence. Their unmarked status is part of the strategy of this performance.

As is evident in the accompanying illustration, these neutral "performers" are quite unlike the other avatars hanging out in the chat space, which are marked by hyper-gendered characteristics and subcultural styles. "Palace Princess" offers a scantily-clad female figure without a head, while "Hedge Witch" and "Jen"

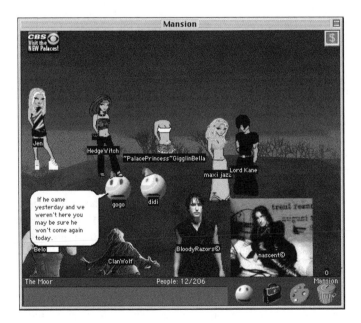

Figure 16 Waitingforgodot.com

portray young, hip, seductive fashions. Those choosing to appear as male offer more Punk or Gothic versions of "self," identified as "Bloody Razor" and "Clan Wolf." They are fully clothed, signaling masculinity thorough their bold looks out to the screen, or the tough violence suggested by their names. Interestingly, in this example, the masculinized avatars are composed of photos, while the feminized ones are cartoon-type characters. It is important to remember that this illustration represents an accidental grouping, merely archiving a moment in a chat room. The avatars, then, reveal a characteristic array of hyper-gendered features in their composition. The roundheads, in contrast, take focus through their distance from these identificatory structures.

Waitingforgodot.com not only performs the boredom and sameness of the chatroom, but also foregrounds, by its distance from the average avatar, how avatars work. They are simply composites of fashions, effects of consumer desire, collated along with fragments of celebrity and subcultural styles. Actually, they refer only to their own collage of consumerist effects, competing with one another for focus in the chat room.

Stelarc

The Australian digital/live performance artist Stelarc provokes the accepted relationship between the techno-avatar and the "real" with such mottos as "the body is obsolete." Stelarc's online avatar seems to signify ambivalently, referring both to Stelarc himself and, self-reflexively, to the avatar in cyberspace. Yet his manifesto-like writings on his website call for a break from the real, evoking the transcendent sense of the cyber as removed from the "meat." He calls for an end to the body: "It is time to question whether a bipedal, breathing body with binocular vision and a 1400cc brain is an adequate biological form. It cannot cope with the quantity, complexity and quality of information it has accumulated; it is intimidated by the precision, speed and power of technology and it is biologically ill-equipped to cope with its new extraterrestrial environment. . . . We are at the end of philosophy and human physiology. Human thought recedes into the human past" (http://www.stelarc.va.com.au/obsolete/obsolete.html). To Stelarc, the regime of the "real" is past and its agent, the "live" body requires uploading into techno forms in order to enter the future. The exigencies of the cyber determine the capacities of agency, forming their own techno-genetics of being.

Stelarc's projected invention of the Movatar reveals how he imagines an avatar that overcomes, even determines the structures of the physiological "real." The ironic inversion of the project is to reverse the flow of motion capture technology. Generally, motion capture translates the movement of a "live" body into its animation as a 3-D computer-generated virtual body. Its application in the movie industry has made films like *The Mummy*, or *Lord of the Rings* into box office successes. Stelarc's Movatar project would reverse that process, working from a virtual body to animate a living one. For example, the Movatar would express its emotions by appropriating the facial muscles in a human body, rather than visa versa. The human body thus becomes the avatar and the virtual Movatar the user. However, in motion capture, there is actually no referent to the body anyway. As David Saltz points out, the referent of motion capture is not motion. Saltz emphasizes that even though the virtual avatar moves as the body moves, there is no actual physical trace of the body that is loaded up into the virtual; instead, there is only pure information, with no "indexical link" to the original. In fact, as Saltz explains, "Motion capture does not record an image at all. It only analyzes the motion itself. . . . one can apply the data acquired in a motion capture session to any number of virtual bodies."[13] Thus, a dance by Bill T. Jones could become the movement pattern of an animated character, such as a frog, or appear as a graph, or as raw numbers. Noting that "motion capture" is a misleading term, Saltz asks "What exactly does motion capture capture?" The record of the movement is pure digital information.

Stelarc's conceptual art piece moves in the direction of Saltz's analysis, forsaking the body for the techno effect. But the Movatar project does not perform pure digital information. It still retains its agglutination into a figure, an avatar. Thus, Stelarc's reversal of the virtual/digital divide retains the notion of performance and mask, in which the avatar uses the human to perform. Still, its inversion of the flow from avatar to human revises that link, making cyberspace the place, as Sun Ra might have said (http://www.stelarc.va.com.au/).

The other avatar: neo-minstrels meet Cyber-Vato

Although the referent of the cyber-avatar may be the logo, and, finally, a line of credit, it uses the markings of race and gender to form an image that seems to represent the human. Human-interest takes on a different meaning, in terms of the cyber avatar. It means the qualities of the human that might draw interest to the avatar—find focus in the online field. As Uncle Ben stood in for rice, markings of ethnicity stand in for online corporate advertising as well. These racializing features draw from the dominant archive, or memories of race, thus reproducing the negative stereotypes of the past in the new cybersurround. In so doing, the painful, but powerful tradition of social stereotyping informs the construction of the avatars. At the same time, canny interventions against the dominant codes of race and sex perform online resistances to the oppressive practices. The "coloring" of avatars derives from the late twentieth-century practice I call "neo-minstrelsy."

The neo-minstrel effect has been charted by various playwrights and directors throughout the twentieth century, laying the groundwork for the perception of the online avatar as a form of minstrelsy. A brief review of some of these works reveals the different ways minstrels are depicted as continuing to inform racializing attitudes. Spike Lee's millennial movie *Bamboozled* (2000) charted minstrelsy as entertainment at the turn of the new century, while Velina Hasu Houston's play entitled *Waiting for Tadashi* (2002) staged an historically-based portrait of inter-racial identification through minstrelsy. Spike Lee's film concerns a TV executive who becomes successful by producing a new series called "Mantan: The New Millennium Minstrel Show." Lee seems to suggest that the current enthusiasm for black performance in mass media entertainment is just another form of the minstrel show. Houston's play concerns a young boy who is born of an African American G.I. and a Japanese mother, shortly after WWII. The young Tadashi experiences prejudices within both the African American and the Japanese communities because of his "hybrid" identity. To signal how being identified as "black" forces Tadashi to perform his ethnicity, Houston stages a minstrel act, complete with historical make-up and costume.

Looking back over the past few decades, we can discover numerous examples of a critical use of minstrelsy in contemporary performance. As early as 1958, Jean Genet wrote a play, *The Blacks: A Clown Show*, that made use of a kind of reverse minstrelsy. At the beginning of the text, Genet writes: "One evening an actor asked me to write a play for an all-black cast. But what exactly is a black? First of all, what's his color?" Instead of writing a play about blacks, Genet staged a reverse minstrelsy, in which an all-black cast plays out two predetermined "white" rites. Cast members don white masks to portray the colonists in Africa. With a similar theme, Caryl Churchill, in her play *Cloud Nine* (1979) sets the first act in a Victorian household in colonial Africa. Churchill specifies that a white actor should play the African colonial servant, but expands the cross-casting to include a man in drag who plays the mother, and a doll which stands in for the daughter, who is literally to be "seen, but not heard." Churchill cross-cast each of these roles to illustrate how race and gender are only constructed roles assigned to people as part of their oppressive conformity to the agenda of colonialism. Churchill also includes compulsory heterosexuality as part of this oppressive regime.

Although each of these plays takes on a transnational or colonial theme, neo-minstrelsy has also been used to critique practices within the United States. In 1967, the San Francisco Mime Troupe performed *The Minstrel Show or Civil Rights in a Cracker Barrel*—a show produced during the years of the Civil Rights Movement that used black face and minstrel routines to represent the legal prejudices against blacks in the voting process and other social and civil rights. And in 1981, The Wooster Group performed the controversial *Route 1 and 9*—a minstrel, black-face version of *Our Town*. *Our Town* purports to portray the quintessential "American" small town. By playing a lewd, contemporary version of some of the key scenes in the play in black face, The Wooster Group pointed to the "whiteness" implicit in Thornton Wilder's play and his puritanical vision of America as innocent, white, middle-class, and Protestant.

Internet performances of neo-minstrelsy incorporate some of these strategies and invent others. One of the most cynical and interventionist versions of neo-minstrelsy appeared in 1994, when Guillermo Gómez-Peña and Roberto Sifuentes infiltrated cyberspace as "cyber-immigrants" or what Gómez-Peña calls "cyber-wetbacks" (2005: 53). Along with the Native American performance artist James Luna, Gómez-Peña and Sifuentes opened the "Ethno-Cyberpunk

Trading Post and Curio Shop On the Electronic Frontier," which served as an installation in the Diverse Works Gallery in Houston, Texas with a simultaneous website and online performance. Their "Ethno-Cyberpunk" trading post traded in ethnic identities both in the gallery and on the internet. Roberto Sifuentes played Cyber Vato, a "robo gang member," and the other two played "el Postmodern zorro" and "El Cultural Transvestite," among other roles. Visitors to the website sent in images, sound, or texts about how Mexicans, Chicanos and Native Americans of the 1990s should look, behave, and perform. The artists then reproduced these stereotypes to represent ethnic identities online. In other words, these artists only reproduced stereotypical notions of how Chicanos and Native Americans seem to appear, in order to compose their avatars, or the online representatives of these members of ethnic communities. Lisa Nakamura coins the word "cybertype" to refer to these racialized stereotypes in cyberspace: "Cybertypes are the images of race that arise when the fears, anxieties and desires of privileged Western users . . . are scripted into a textual/graphical environment that is in constant flux and revision" (2002: 6).

Gómez-Peña went on to publish *ethno-techno* (2005), a collections of essays, performance pieces, and manifestos that include his sense of the pervasive power of technospaces in determining individual and social forms of racialized identifications. In a performance piece entitled "Millennial Doubts" he asks:

> Should I cross the digital divide west
> and join the art-technological cadre?
> How?
> Alter my identity through body-enhancement techniques,
> Laser surgery, prosthetic implants,
> And become the Mexica Orlan?
> A glow-in-the-dark transgenic mojado?
> Or a postethnic cyborg, perhaps?
> . . .
> Maybe I should donate my body
> To the MIT artificial intelligence department
> So they can implant computer nacho chips in my *&^%^76%78
> Implant a very, very sentimental robotic bleeding heart
> And become the ranchero Stelarc?
> What about a chipotle-squirting techno-falo jalapeno
> To blind the migra when crossing over?
> Or an 'intelligent' tongue . . . activated by tech-eela?
> You know, imaginary technology
> For those without access to the real one.
> I mean, I'm arguing for an obvious fact:
> When you don't have access to power
> Poetry replaces science. . . .

(Gómez-Peña 2005: 212–213)

Using the characteristic Latino-American idiom of Spanglish, a combination of English and Spanish, Gómez-Peña intervenes in the lingo of technology and art that is familiar to critics in the field. "Mexicanizing" the mechanical, he foregrounds the whiteness embedded in the techno-imaginary. A kind of reverse minstrelsy occurs here, as he strategically inserts nachos and tech-eela into computer chips and prosthetics. His conclusion, like much of the material in this book, renders such an idiomatic imagination of the technoscape as a strategy of the dispossessed, in which "poetry replaces science." While Gómez-Peña delivers an empowering, invasive discourse of technoadvances, the impression remains that the actual production and distribution of such techno-wares are limited to the privileged few, who are not racialized and ethnicized subjects.

In the past few decades, numerous strategies of representation have been used to depict racialized or ethnicized subjects. So the question becomes why these performers, playwrights, and moviemakers are taking up minstrel forms at the end of the twentieth century and the beginning of the twenty-first—particularly in the new media? Certain similarities between this era and the mid-nineteenth century, when minstrel shows were invented demonstrate a shared social crisis. In his book on minstrelsy, *Love and Theft*, Eric Lott locates the beginning of minstrel shows in the 1840s, during the depression that followed the panic of 1837 (1993: 137). According to Lott, the new consolidation of industrial capital caused high unemployment among the laboring classes. During industrialization, these minstrel shows, depicting "happy" slaves singing and dancing on the porch of the old cotton plantation, played out nostalgia for pre-industrial times (148). But this nostalgia for the time of the "happy old slave," did not operate through iden-tification with the slave. Minstrel shows were the product of white entertainers in the northeast, who portrayed black, slave culture in the "old south." Represented as lusting after a good time, the blacks were represented as unruly and uncivi-lized. The depiction of their behavior as unruly served two functions: to render the agrarian past as less structured and more fun than the new industrialized time, and to identify unruly behavior as specifically "black." Lott cites reviews of the minstrel shows that describe a "savage energy," with performers whose "white eyes [were] rolling in a curious frenzy" (140). He notes that when these performers cross-dressed as women, they portrayed the black women as enor-mous, gorging themselves on both food and sex. So lewd and lascivious behavior accompanied the "strummin' on the old banjo."

Lott suggests that the social function of these minstrel shows was to displace anxieties over new industrialized forms of production and their requirements for new skills, which resulted in massive unemployment in certain sectors. By encouraging racist and sexist prejudices, the enjoyment taken in the minstrel show displaced the uneasy sense of competition among whites for low-level employment in the northeast onto contempt for blacks in the "old South." This form of working-class entertainment thus consolidated the audience, through their laughter, as "whites" (137). Further, their "white" masculinity was shored up by the sexist rhetoric and the portrayal of heterosexual relationships as ones in which women were subordinate to men. Economically and socially threatened by the new skill sets and practices of industrialization, these working-class white men were drawn to a form of entertainment that based its humor and fun on the subordinate roles of the Other.

Many of the anxieties around new technologies in the 1840s may also be identified within the current digital age. In the digital age, which arguably began in the 1980s with the invention of the internet, the "upload" of economic prowess and employment possibilities into the electronic sphere has caused similar kinds of anxieties among workers. New electronic technologies are the basis for new forms of production. New skill sets are replacing old ones, while many kinds of companies and forms of employment are disappearing. Skills with new technologies and software are required for everything from job skills to personal communication and entertainment. In this way, the latter half of the twentieth century is not unlike the latter half of the nineteenth. Both witnessed the development of a new form of production and hence of new economic structures. During both periods, anxiety around employment, envy for the newly-enfranchised class, and competition among white working class sectors in the economy forms could be allayed by forms of entertainment that operated through stereotypes of black masculinity and female lasciviousness, or as the popular media phrases it today, sex and violence. Although their construction is no doubt complex at this time, part of their function, as in the mid-nineteenth century is to mask economic anxieties with stereotypes that promise to initiate us into the world of the successful. Gómez-Peña's term "cyber wetback" wittily captures the sense of those who are disenfranchised in the new cyber state, sneaking across its borders to find better-paying jobs and hopefully join the new "virtual class."

The problem of how to mark race in cyberspace is a complex one, involving strategies of recognition, both of an unmarked "white" identification and variously marked ethnic and racialized modes. An anthology entitled *Race in Cyberspace*, edited by Beth Kolko, Lisa Nakamura, and Gilbert Rodman, treats several of these different practices. Beth Kolko, in her discussion of LambdaMOO, observes that cyberspace is forming, both structurally and through its content "representative norms and patterns, constructing a self-replicating and exclusionary category of 'ideal' user. ... " (2000: 218). Kolko reviews how LambdaMOO allows users to enter numerous specifics about themselves, from favorite websites to gender, but offers no category for race or ethnicity. Kolko suggests that the user must somehow force an ethnic marking into the system by choosing a name with those specific associations, or by linguistic style, or by ethnic references Thus, the assumption is that the user is, by default, "white," the traditional unmarked category. (216). Yet, Jennifer Gonzalez questions how these markers, when inserted, can escape becoming merely "decorative features" (2000: 29). How can one determine when these elements may be serving an identificatory function for the user, who somehow "is" Latino, say, or when they are simply elements of play, or fashion? "Hood" fashion is widespread across many cultures, who emulate racialized markers as part of seeming "with it." Finally, would it matter whether the user who was manipulating these signs were actually Latino or not? These questions indicate the complicated and often obtuse ways in which race is represented on the web.

Lisa Nakamura, in *Cybertypes*, notes that some websites, such as NetNoir and Latino Link encourage a positive kind of ethnic identification. Unfortunately, NetNoir was hacked and defaced several times in the late 1990s, with the hackers claiming reverse discrimination on the part of the website, which indicates the kind of contested environment the web displays around the markers of ethnicity. The website has ceased to exist anymore, but offered an early example of organizing through an ethnically specific site. Latino Link is still up and running, at this date, dedicated to Latino youth and even offering Hispanic scholarships. But Nakamura continues to discuss the many other websites that participate in the new corporate style of "coloring" induced through advertising strategies by such influential institutions as Worldcom, a telecommunications conglomerate. These ads are part of the cyberfield of images and attitudes that stretches through cinema and computers games to the internet. These ads create what Nakamura insists is an "aestheticized and commodified racial diversity" (2002: 117). Her example is the Generation D series which shows people with multiple skin colors and ethnicities accompanying this narration: " I was born into a new generation . . . Generation D. It isn't about a country, it isn't about a culture, it's about attitude" (118). One problem, Nakamura argues, is that these representatives can, in no way, suggest "hybridity." Instead, they iterate the sense of an integral identity that is racialized. Racial categories are both iterated and seemingly transcended in such ads. These "technopeople of color," as she labels them, are, in the fact of both their stereotyped identity and their transcendence, the appropriate avatars of race in cyberspace: "Their color distinguishes them as appropriate facilitators of intercultural software handshaking" (118). They represent the falling away of borders, the end of the indigenous, the corporate, global cyberworld.

Nakamura's sense that race becomes both marked and transcended, an empty fashion online is part of a more major recession from social referents. As the frame of the real recedes from what are called immersive technologies, so, too, does its power as a referent. Cyberspace, then, stages a theatre of masks without actors. It organizes a space in which the signs of identification are merely self-referential, signifying the corporate space of the internet rather than the social world of the user. From this perspective, neo-minstrelsy may be understood as a transitional phase. Its set of identificatory needs are necessary to slowly wean the user from the old cultures of "liveness," as Auslander put it, to the new immersive technologies of digital, corporate dealings. Perhaps the masks of neo-minstrelsy mark not only ethnicity, but also the last stand of "live" users, who wield such technologies as tools of self-representation before being swallowed up into their logo displacements.

Transgender avatars are **Virtually Yours**

Several times throughout this study, transgender identities have been marked as part of the cultural imaginary concerning new technologies. Susan Stryker's reference to "Christine Jorgensen's Atom Bomb" articulated the mid-century panic around gender assignment that the story of Jorgensen's transsexual operation conjured up alongside fears of nuclear disaster. Jorgensen became a mid-century icon, or avatar of the destabilizing processes biomedical technologies wreaked on the gender regime. The anxieties surrounding medical gender reassignment, argues Connie Samaras, inspired abduction narratives that imagined alien egg harvesting and other sex/gender operations.[14] Aliens were the avatars of medically-altered humans, who disturbed identities rooted in the normative regimes sex and sexuality. In contrast to abduction narratives created by those who were distant from sex reassignment surgeries, some transgendered artists have begun to perform their multiple and sometimes vexed gender identifications in relation to the cybersphere.

The play *Virtually Yours*, composed and performed by Kate Bornstein at the now-defunct Josie's Juice Bar in San Francisco in 1994 and later published in the anthology *O Solo Homo*, stages transgender desire and vexation as taking place in and around an interactive computer game. The title *Virtually Yours* confounds desire and the virtual in a way that signals the dilemma in the plot. The play begins with Bornstein lit by the light of the computer screen. She narrates how she, a transsexual male-to-female lesbian is struggling with her girlfriend's decision to become a female-to-male heterosexual. What worries Bornstein is the fact that their lesbian relationship would turn into a heterosexual one, when the sex reassignment surgery that rendered the social definition of Bornstein as female would render her lover male. Bornstein listens to a phone message from her girl-soon-to-be-boy-friend, telling her that she should play the new computer game *Virtually Yours*.

The girl/boy friend never corporeally appears in the play, but appears only as a voice recorded on the answering machine. The telephone, after all, was the first instrument of virtual interaction to really penetrate domestic spaces, delivering a sense of a technology of the intimate. In "The Telephone and its Queerness," Ellis Hanson considers various erotic uses of the telephone, insisting that phone communication is "a mechanism of fantasy and pleasure," a site of perversions, and erotic behaviors, from the private cooing of couples, to the completely commercialized performance of phone sex (1995: 37). Hanson insists that through the telephone, "desire makes brazen its age-old love affair with capital," where these phone-borgs are "chips in the integrated circuit," which confuse "the conventional distinctions between human and machine, desire and commerce" (1995: 35). In Bornstein's piece, the phone messages are played back on the answering machine, so the contact is even less direct, processed by the recursive looping of tape. The phone voice, then, is the site of both the object of desire and the anxiety of being "cut-off." The lover is already a virtual one,

Figure 17 Kate Bornstein in *Virtually Yours*. Photograph: Dona Ann McAdams

whose messages are already from the past. Thus, the lover is a virtual effect, the second order representation of a virtual presence.

Bornstein takes her lover's advice and begins interacting with the virtual avatar of the computer game. The game avatar, who is also represented by only a voice, resembles a therapist, who is working with Bornstein as a patient. The game avatar listens to Bornstein's desires and fears and then constructs virtual characters who represent aspects of her problems. Thus, in the one-woman show, the "live" Bornstein also plays the cyber avatars that represent her problems within the game. The plot structures a complex linking of characters, who upload Bornstein's psyche into virtual performances. The apparatus of theater thus becomes an effect of the computer, in terms of the dramatic set-up. As Bornstein proceeds through her cyber avatars, the complexity of gender identifications causes the avatar of the game to finally suffer a "memory overload." As the system breaks down, it hails various pop cyber avatars, including Scotty from *Star Trek* and Dave from *2001: A Space Odyssey*. Apparently, the bipolar logic of the computer, which matches the bipolar gender system, breaks down with the complexities of transgender partnership. The game avatar begs Bornstein to play another game, because "Once the game is over and the players have left the field, who am I?"

Although this plethora of virtual avatars is somehow warranted by Bornstein's "live" body, it is important to remember that her "natural" body has been perforated by surgical operations and hormonal injections, producing it as "an operationalized surface effect achieved through performative means, " as Stryker (1999) describes it. The transsexual body displaces what Stryker calls "inner secrets," or the psychological, mental processes of internality with "internal secretions," proffering "estrogen and testosterone as deep truths of the body," rather than Freudian paradigms. The dramatic set-up of the performance, then, runs the axis of technology and desire through reconstructed transsexual bodies, parlayed through phone lines, and finally adjusted through a computer game.

Yet Bornstein, the live performer directly interacts with members of the audience, setting up a paradigm of the theatrical apparatus. In one sense, then Bornstein performs the triumph of the "live" bodily regime, which she reinforces with the use of revealing costumes and seductive play with the audience. Although she performs her location as somewhere within medical technologies and virtual systems, the "live/corporeal" performer still runs the show. In effect, Bornstein "channels" technology, rather than the reverse. In the terms of s/m, which she invokes, she "tops" the process of virtual interactivity, suggesting that the corporeal representation of identificatory processes is still too complex to be entirely situated within virtual technologies. The computer game breaks down when it tries to parse the transmogrifications of the material. The "live" avatar contradicts and overcomes the recursive looping of computer games, or telephone messages.

Bornstein is a longtime denizen of internet societies, using her computer expertise and long experience in cybercommunities to craft much of her work.

Along with *Virtually Yours*, she published the novel *Nearly Roadkill: An Infobahn Erotic Adventure*, co-written with Caitlin Sullivan. The novel consists of a long series of emails that record chat room encounters between two users, who have enjoyed many sexual encounters using different personae and gender roles. Eventually, the two begin to suspect that they have met numerous times, playing together in various chat rooms as different cyber-avatars. In their chats, they use the familiar techno terms of "Hir" and "ze," to displace the personal pronouns that, in traditional language, signify stable gender roles. The online writing is necessarily performative, since it is an online sexual affair, so they utilize the emoticons of physical expression, such as {{{}}}} which means hugging, or ::hugging you:: caps for shouting, etc. They also write descriptions of settings where their cyber encounters take place, with familiar gestures, such as ::soft carpet of needles, sunlight filtering through trees:: and ::kicking the leaves ahead of me as I walk:: (Bornstein and Sullivan 1996: 107). Although these encounters are not accomplished through animated avatars, but through written forms, the novel still attempts to narrativize these ur-avatar sexual encounters in a world where gender roles and sexual practices are fluid. The sense here, is the embrace of the internet as the playful space of masquerade. Avatars are representatives of gender-free, gender-morphing performances.

Bornstein's medically-altered body and gender performance is thus located somewhere between the "live" play of *Virtually Yours* and the computer-style textual play of *Roadkill*. Crafting a complex exchange of the attributes of gender and sex, Bornstein both celebrates the masquerade of the virtual and stages its failure. Likewise, the "live" both serves as a contradiction to the virtual and as a laminate of it. Gender and sex, the operative functions of desire and identity formation are virtual, anyway, she seems to imply, only codes like the others that can be set in the play mode. Yet there is something melancholic inscribed in the work—a site of loss. As Bornstein encourages the audience to play with her, she both implicates them in her world of virtual exchange and turns to them for solace, when it fails to satisfy.

Transgender express: the Brandon website

The Brandon website constructed a virtual space where users could "trans" gender and technology as they navigated the site. The website was designed to perform the representations of transgender bodies as well as the social violence against those bodies. Navigating the website created "cyber Brandons" as Jordy Jones, one of the designers who constructed it explained. At present, the website is only available in an archived form, so the interactive elements described here no longer play. Still, the images and history are available at http://www.brandon.guggenheim.org. The name for the website was derived from the life and death of Teena Brandon, known in transgender circles as Brandon Teena. Brandon Teena was a twenty-one-year-old who lived his adolescent life as a man, making a spectacle out of his success in dating good-looking girls in small towns in the Midwest. In 1993, he was brutally raped and murdered by two men who discovered "he was a girl," as they put it. His murder prompted a national move for protection rights by several agencies, and numerous activists. The murder trial was covered by national and international news agencies and attended by activists from around the world.

While the website alludes to the historical evidence surrounding Brandon Teena's death, it is not a website about Brandon. The web project leader, Shu Lea Cheang, a noted underground filmmaker, created a very complex website that linked discovery, rape, murder, transsexuality and gender through intricate navigation devices. It is neither obvious nor easy to traverse the site, nor are its significations always direct in their referents. Each navigation is unique— forming a cyber-Brandon along its path.

One page within the site is identified as the Big Doll, designed by a noted female-to-male transgender designer and activist Jordy Jones. The Big Doll, itself a secondary term of reference, provides a flashing glimpse of the techno-discourse of the gendered and sexed body in the late twentieth century, constructed through the lens of transgender discourse. On this page, one could encounter fifty images from different sources and with different content—all referring somehow to the social practices and institutions around transgender identifications. Some frames reveal fragments of subcultural bodies marked by tattoos, scarification, piercings, and prostheses such as dildos; others record the violent reception of these practices in newspaper headlines around Brandon Teena's death and legal proceedings, still others archive medical/physiological/

Figure 18 Big Doll, http://brandon.guggenheim.org

biological discourses of gender and sex, including anatomical sketches, and even close-ups of botanical genitals like pistils and stamens. The cyber-Brandon-user animates these images by navigating along framed spaces laid out like comix—those underground books of images that inform much of the visual composition on the web.

However, unlike comix, these frames do not delineate narrative incidents in a storyline; instead, they organize image fields that morph from image to image. Each frame includes several images that, together, constitute multiple "dolls," or compositions of identification. The images of bodily practices and newspaper headlines cohere as a field of allusions organized by subcultural and dominant codes from the gender/sex regime. A cyber Brandon is composed by the user who is familiar with the intersection of these codes, traversing the allusions to compose the "flickering signifier" of the particular cyber-Brandon that the doll represents. Traversal by the mouse animates these image morphings, and, as the user begins to put together a field of identification through a recognition of how these body practices, the Brandon trial, and medical technologies inter-relate, a cyber-Brandon is formed, or rather, is performed.

A page entitled "Roadtrip" organizes a history of transgendered people in the image of a highway. With art design by Jordy Jones and script by Susan Stryker, "Roadtrip" provides images of historical transgendered people that appear as if splattered on the highway, like roadkill, as the mouse drives along it. The mouse moves up the screen, following the yellow line, as if driving along a highway. There are traffic signs and other effects as well. When clicked upon, the history of these figures appears. The site includes Herculine Barbin, a nineteenth-century French hermaphrodite, whose life is discussed in the work of Foucault and celebrated in a play by Kate Bornstein; Jack Garland, born the daughter of the first Mexican consul to San Francisco in the early twentieth century, who lived his life as man, and the cross-dressed Venus Extravaganza from the film Paris is Burning. The cyber-Brandon "trips" through this part of the site, once again forming an archive of reference. As Peggy Shaw, put it, when playing a cross-gendered Stanley Kowalski in the play Belle Reprieve: " I'm so queer I don't even have to talk about it. I'm just . . . parts of other people all mashed into one body . . . I take all these pieces and I manufacture myself . . . When I'm saying I fall to pieces, I'm saying Marlon Brando was not there for me, James Dean failed to come through. . . . " (1996: 177) Like Shaw, the cyber-Brandon is constructed through traversing the images of Herculine, Jack, and Venus, but, to reverse Shaw's phrasing, this roadtrip offers the process of "coming to pieces."

Now, it may be that the cyber-Brandon created through navigating this website also "plays" some of these images in the flesh. In fact, in order to follow the complexity of significations throughout the website, s/he (ze) must have somehow acquired a familiarity with the practices they reference. S/he (ze) may be a practitioner of some of the bodily rites, such as piercing, or scarification, or more, s/he (ze)may inject his or her body with hormones, or more, have under-gone sex reassignment surgery. If so, a certain process of mimesis might take

Figure 19 Roadtrip, http://brandon.guggenheim.org

place in the formation of the cyber-Brandon. The person before the computer screen may experience something like a mirror effect, although perhaps only momentarily. The website, then, would organize an empathetic link between user and site. The cyber-Brandon would be a product of affect and recognition.

Yet the performance or composition of the cyber-Brandon occurs only through the animation of these images created by the movement of the mouse, combined with the user's identificatory processes. While identification is formed through allusion and metonymy, both social and eccentric processes, the movement of the mouse is a disciplined motion, controlled by the design of the images as well as that of the mouse itself. The choreography of the mouse is dull and repetitive. The cyber-Brandon performs, then, through a kind of dis-association between manual gesture and psychological identificatory processes. Unlike theatrical techniques that seek some kind of consonance between bodily gesture and internal state, the cyber Brandon is composed by the disciplined, repetitive motion of the mouse in contrast to the metonymic and indirect floating, if you will, of the sign for self. The solitary, disciplined body of the cyber-Brandon provides a stark contrast to the "live" performing body of Kate Bornstein, for example, in *Virtually Yours*. Bornstein reveals the plenitude of her womanly transgendered body, interacting directly with the audience, pulling them into performing her scenarios. The cyber-Brandon sits at the computer screen, scrolling through images.

Nonetheless, many critics and practitioners lend the language of the body and of the "live" to such screenic interactions. As Jordy Jones put it, "new cultural life forms are beginning to appear out there."[15] His notion of a "cultural life form" in cyberspace provides a brilliant composite of biology, culture, and technology. Beyond the sense of a cyber-Brandon, as an effect of a specific website, a "cultural life form out there" captures the sense of an avatar more independent and organic than the simple effect of navigation. "Out there," to Jones, imagined through the world wide web, is a worlding space—a global or interstellar space. In fact, by referent and production, the Brandon website is international. The referent, Brandon Teena, was from the Midwestern U.S. The site was first housed at the Banff Centre, an influential Canadian centre of new projects which combine virtual systems and art. The website project leader, Shu Lea Cheang, is from Taiwan, educated in the U.S. and well-known for her interethnic films. But more, the site became linked to several other institutions that arranged for it to become an international performance site, or rather a magnet site for performances of national and international issues linked to transgender politics.

The Brandon website was the first website to be hosted by the Guggenheim Museum in New York, which announced Brandon as "a one year narrative project in installments." It was also linked to events located on a Dutch site, the Society for Old and New Media, and to the Harvard Institute on the Arts and Civic Dialogue, directed by the playwright and performer, Anna Deavere Smith. Smith's organization used the site to stream a multi-site public event, in August 1998. The event, called "Brandon's Virtual Court System," took place at the Harvard Law School. Using documents based on real and cyber sexual assault cases, Shu Lea Chang and the theatre director Liz Diamond created a courtroom drama. Five actors from the American Repertory Theatre played the roles of the victims, with legal scholars playing the jurors. In other words, a performance of an international virtual "court of law" sat in session, streaming through a website that structured transgendered identifications. First-rate legal scholars performed as jury and actors as victims in mock trials of actual cases concerning sexual assault. This virtual court may offer what the actual courts do not, in equity and understanding. It may rehearse a change in the juridical and social systems of gender and sexual codes.

Notes

Introduction

1 My thanks to Jason Farman for alerting me to this game.

Prologue

1 See my work on Hrotsvit von Gandersheim in *Feminism and Theater* (Case 1988).
2 For a full, illustrated history of the "New Forest" see Cooper http://www.hants.gov.uk/newforest/history/history2.html. The webspace is supported by the Hampshire Country Council.

Act One

1 These documents are reproduced online at http://levity.com/alchemy/corpherm.html.
2 The Alchemy website provides an impressive number of manuscripts, illustrations, interpretations, interactive discussions, laboratory apparati, and notes toward experiments http://www.levity.com/alchemy.
3 For a discussion of Newton and the crisis in recoining, see White 1997: 260–263. For a full history of the coin in England, see Ross 2002 http://www.friesian.com/coins.htm; and Davies 2004 http://www.ex.ac.uk/~RDavies/arian/amser/chrono7.html.
4 For Knights Templars, see Malcolm Barber's *The New Knighthood* (1994), and also for convents and works on the abbess of Quedlingburg.
5 http://www.newtonproject.ic.ac.uk/
6 Dobbs notes that in the Keynes MS. 18, Newton records his preparations for the star regulus and his notes toward his essay on it (1975: 176).
7 http://www.alchemywebsite.com/rpvision.html
8 For a fuller description of this plan, reproduced from Newton's manuscripts, see White 1997: 159.
9 See Dobbs on Sendivogius' theory of sperm (1997: 157–158).
10 See Dollimore, *Sexual Dissidence* (1991), for a full treatment of subjectivity in the early modern; also Greenblatt's *Renaissance Self-Fashioning* (1980).
11 This argument is fully developed by R.L. Smallwood (quoted in Martin 2000: 394–395).
12 See the beginning of Foucault's *The History of Sexuality* (1980).
13 Ironically, in 1999, a project designed by Edward Said and Daniel Barenboim to bring together Palestinians and Jews into an orchestra as a project in cooperation opened in Weimar with the name "The West–Eastern Divan Orchestra."
14 From a letter by Abbott Johannes Trithemius, 1507 (quoted in Binswanger 1994: 2).

15 quoted in http://www.alchemylab.com/paracelsus.htm.
16 Goethe's scientific writings were published and translated into English by D.E. Miller in 1998. His most important influence on esoteric practices was on Rudolf Steiner, the founder of Anthroposophy, who in the first few decades of the twentieth century combined Goethe's science with Rosicrucianism and Blavatskyian Theosophy. A collection of phenomenological studies, *Goethe's Way of Science* was published in 1998; *Goethe's History of Science* in 1991; *The Wholeness of Nature* in 1996 (see Seamon and Zajonc 1998; Fink 1991; Bortoft 1996).
17 This translation is my own and is looser than some.
18 The Homunculus is a prescient figure in many ways. The seemingly advanced state of the virtual in the twentieth and twenty-first centuries still requires a body. In a study of today's virtual, cyberspace, Sandy Stone notes that a body is still required to "warrant" the subject position. Even on the internet, the avatar is secured by the sense of a body lurking somewhere outside of the screen (Stone 1995: 182). Like paper money, the floating signifier of subjecthood still relies on the warranting of corporeality. On the other hand, contemporary scientific projects of creating life and reason through cloning and artificial intelligence complicate the relation to corporeality. The strands of DNA, those emblems of being and time, have been decoded providing a site for the alteration and re-production of life. Corporeal functions are being replicated through manipulations of codes, producing a reasoning, remembering intelligence unattached to the human body—Articifical Intelligence. It seems the Enlightenment project of living purely through reason, as a result of reason, like the Homunculus, is still "alive" and well in the early twentieth-first century.
19 See Mellett 2000 at http://www.southerncrossreview.org/6/goethe.htm.
20 See "Goethean Science Methodology" on the web page for the Scottish School of Herbal Medicine http://www.herbalmedicine.org.uk/rootpages/Goethean%20 Paper.shtml.

Entr'act

1 In November of 2001, Duke University School of Law held a conference on the public domain. They published and uploaded papers from the lectures. This source has guided almost all of this discussion. See http://www.law.duke.edu/cspd/history.html.

Act 2

1 I will continue to use the appellation "Mme." Blavatsky throughout this examination in order to indicate her eccentric self-identity.
2 See, for example, Lita De Alberdi's *Channeling: What it is and How to do it* (2000). She refers to Blavatsky as the source in her brief history (7).
3 In *Madame Blavatsky's Baboon*, Peter Washington identifies the astral light as a common term in the nineteenth-century for the source of divine dictation. He compares it to Joseph Smith's claims about the source of the *Book of Mormon* (1993: 50–51).
4 At this point in time, however, when Hindu nationalism represents a hegemonic, ultra-conservative force, it is important to remember how it emerged, then, as a progressive movement against colonialism and a force toward the founding of the independent nation of India.
5 There is ample evidence of the role of Hinduism in the formation of the nation state, but one book I found helpful was K.N. Pannikar's *Culture, Ideology, Hegemony* (1995).
6 The online avatar raises a similar question: is the online avatar a mask of a "real" user whose "presence" is, somehow, acting online, or is it simply a part of a complete simulation—merely another empty cipher in the veil of cyber-maya?

7 See Mme. Blavatsky, *The Mahatma Letters to A.P. Sinnett* (1997).

8 See Parama Roy's study of heterosexist, masculinist discipleship of religion and nationhood in her fine study of Margaret Noble and Vivekananda in "As the Master Saw Her" (1995).

9 In the late twentieth century, these traditions, although popular in the U.S. and Europe, still maintain their gender-specific notions of spirituality. See, for example, Vicki Mackenzie's *Cave in the Snow* (1998), the story of Tenzin Palmo, an Englishwoman, perhaps the first woman to attain the status of enlightened monkhood in the Himalayan cave practices. She later appealed to the Dalai Lama to change the gender-specific practices of the theocracy.

10 See Washington 1993: 52.

11 Alexandra David-Neel briefly explains *tulkus* in *The Secret Oral Teachings* (1967: 104). She takes up the subject at length in her *With Mystics and Magicians in Tibet* (1937).

12 For a full examination of the rite, see *Kalachakra Tantra*, trans. Jeffrey Hopkins (1999).

13 In the nineteenth century, it was common practice to subsume various sects under the rubric of "Hindu," as Parama Roy discusses in "As the Master Saw Her" (1995: 113–114).

14 See Chapter 3 of *Mapping an Empire* (Edney 1997) on the institutions for mapping all of British India.

15 Washington reports that she was "massively stout," weighing 17 stone (1993: 33).

16 My thanks to my research assistant Jason Farman for his excellent research into Blavatsky's phenomena and the theatrical context. Lydia Thompson and her British blondes brought the first leg show to New York in 1868.

17 See the website for the Canadian Theosophical Association at http://www.theosophical. ca/TibetanInitiate.htm for the complete documentation of this letter.

18 Derrida wrote the treatise after the fall of the wall, thus using the double appearance/ disappearance of communism as a further troping of the spectral.

Act 3

1 This simple, perhaps overly-simple explanation is derived from Stephen Hawking's summary in *A Briefer History of Time* (2005).

2 Sokel, in his introduction to one of the only English translations of these plays, uses this term. It has become familiar in the teaching of the texts as well.

3 Elsewhere, I have argued for the vampire as a figure for appearance of lesbians in the system of representation. I think the work there amplifies this article's focus on gender rather than sexual practice. See Case (1991).

4 Interestingly, Bram Stoker served as secretary to the eminent actor/manager Henry Irving. The term secretary derives from the Latin "keeper of secrets." It had a more prestigious connotation for men in the Victorian era, when it suggested privy knowledge within the realm of public or governmental service. See *The History of the Secretarial Profession* on the official website of Professional Secretaries: www.iaap-hq.org.

5 For the complete program, see http://www.nodanw.com/shows_p/pinsneedles.htm.

6 A good translation of the complete article published in *Le Figaro* and the manifesto can be found online: http://www.futurism.org.uk/manifestos/manifesto01.htm 05/04/05.

7 For the complete manifesto and the translation of several of the plays, see http://www.cis.vt.edu/modernworld/d/futurist.htmlt 05/04/05.

8 In 1972, Heiner Mueller's play *Cement*, opening in the Berliner Ensemble, took this story as a classic base in the Socialist aesthetic to be revised and somewhat deconstructed.

9 Perhaps sensing the dangerous future for constructivists, Exter left Russia the year of the film's release to live the rest of her life in Paris.

10 The film is now available on DVD, produced in 1991 by Kino International and distributed by Image Entertainment. It is an excellent copy.

11 See Lynn Spiegel's excellent work on TV, the domestic and gender, in her several articles, such as " The Suburban Home Companion: Television and the Neighborhood Ideal in Postwar America" (1992). Or my own earlier work in *The Domain-Matrix*.

12 Although O'Neill finished the play in 1941, it was not released for production until 1956, when it opened on Broadway. Tennessee Williams' *Suddenly Last Summer* opened on Broadway in 1958.

13 The lavish production of *The King and I* opened on Broadway in 1951; *The Sound of Music* in 1959.

14 See http://www.filmsite.org/inva.html/7.5.05; http://www.gadflyonline.com/11-26-01/film-snatchers.html/7.5.05.

15 Interview with Schneider on documentary video of *Rockaby* in rehearsal with Billie Whitelaw. Produced by D.A. Pennebaker and Chris Hegedus, SUNY Program for the Arts.

16 See her interview at http://www.arts-electric.org/articles0203/020516.oliveros2.html/7/11/05.

17 The tape is distributed by the Cunningham Dance Foundation.

18 I do not pretend to fully understand these notions and particularly not within physics. For a relatively simple discussion of it, however, see Steven Weinberg's "What Is Quantum Field Theory and What Did We Think It Is?" http://xxx.lanl.gov/PS_cache?hep-th/7/16/05.

19 The SCUM Manifesto may be found at various websites, including http://gos.sbc.edu/s/solanas.html; http://www.churchofeuthanasia.org/e-sermons/scum.html; http://www.womynkind.org/scum.htm.

20 My thanks to Catherine Lord for this bit of research.

21 A video recording is available of Ron Vawter's *Roy Cohn/Jack Smith* distributed through Strand Releasing.

22 See http://www.spiritweb.org/Spirit/harmonic-1987-yashah.html.

23 For a fuller treatment of CAE, see Rebecca Schneider's article "Nomadmedia:On Critical Art Ensemble" (2000).

24 Thanks to Linda Kintz for a her brilliant treatment of this play in her paper at ATHE, 2005.

Act 4

1 Although the original website no longer exists, an uncut mirror site of the original, http://www.webcoast.com/heavensgate.com/ may still be maintained. If not, try a more recent archival site: http://www.rickross.com/groups/heavensgate.html/07/24/05.

2 This quotation is taken from the archived website materials.

3 See http://www.law.umkc.edu/faculty/projects/ftrials/scopes/evolut.htm /7/14.05 for a full description of the legal issues in the trial.

4 For a fuller description of these pieces see Christiane Paul's *Digital Art* (2003).

5 Ron Eglash, in "African influences in Cybernetics," makes a similar claim for "scratch," but also argues for rap music as "a newly spliced code; a mutant reprogramming of the social software" (1995: 24).

6 First published in 1974, *DnD* has enjoyed more than 20 million players and generated more than one billion dollars in revenues.

7 See "Critically Queer" (1993: 258–308).

8 See, especially, the section entitled "Bringing Home the Meat," which traces the commodification of social relations.

9 For an excellent description of these various strategies along with illustrations, see http://money.howstuffworks.com/product-placement.htm/printable

10 Unfortunately, for some, Deuber-Mankowsky's 2001 monograph is in German, but the translation should soon be available from University of Minnesota press.

11 For a complete discussion of desktop theater, see Adriene Jenik's "Keyboard Catharsis and the Making of Roundheads" (2001: 95–112). To access the archived performances, go to leda.ucsd.edu/%eajenik/main/files.

12 On the point of gender, see James Knowlson (1996: 610):

> [Beckett] felt very strongly that the characters in his plays were either male or female and that their sex was not interchangeable. There were many requests, sometimes fervent personal appeals made directly to him, for women to be allowed to play the male characters in *Waiting for Godot*. Beckett (or his agents) always turned them down, though he himself showed signs of wilting several times under the intense emotional pressure that was brought to bear on him.

13 I am referring to a paper David Saltz submitted to an ASTR seminar in 2002 entitled "The Ontology of Motion Capture."

14 See the Samaras (1997) article cited earlier "Is it Tomorrow or Just the End of Time?"

15 Jordy Jones and Susan Stryker came to U.C. Davis, November 1999 to give a public presentation of the Brandon website. They navigated the site and spoke at length about the ramifications of its construction. Much of what I have gleaned from the site has been guided by their remarks at this time.

Bibliography

Agamben, Giorgio. *The Open*. Trans. Kevin Attell. Stanford: Stanford University Press, 2002.

Alchemy Web Site, The. Ed. Adam McLean. 5/2/2005. http://www.levity.com/alchemy.

Amrine, Frederick. "The Metamorphosis of the Scientist," in *Goethe's Way of Science: A Phenomenology of Nature*. Eds. David Seamon and Arthur Zajonc. Albany, NY: State University of New York Press, 1998. 33–54.

Arguelles, José. *The Mayan Factor: Path Beyond Technology*. Santa Fe, New Mexico: Bear and Company Publishers, 1996.

Auslander, Philip. *Liveness: Performance in a Mediatized Culture*. London, New York: Routledge, 1999.

Baker, Ian. *The Heart of the World*. New York: Penguin Press, 2004.

Barber, Malcolm. *The New Knighthood: A History of the Order of the Temple*. New York and London: Cambridge University Press, 1994.

Beckett, Samuel. *Krapp's Last Tape. Collected Shorter Plays*. New York: Grove Press, 1984. 53–63.

—— *Proust*. 6th ed. New York: Grove Press, n.d.

—— *Rockaby. Collected Shorter Plays*. New York: Grove Press, 1984. 271–282.

Bernal, Martin. *Black Athena Vol. I: The Afroasiatic Roots of Classical Civilization*. New Brunswick, New Jersey: Rutgers University Press, 1987.

Binswanger, Hans Christoph. *Money and Magic: A Critique of the Modern Economy in the Light of Goethe's Faust*. Trans. J.E. Harrison. Chicago and London: University of Chicago Press, 1994.

Blair, Ann. *The Theater of Nature: Jean Bodin and Renaissance Science*. Princeton: Princeton University Press, 1997.

Blavatsky. *Collected Writings*. 15 vols. Boris De Zirkoff. Madras: Theosophical Publishing House; Wheaton, Illinois: Theosophical Press, 1950.

—— "Force of Prejudice." *Collected Writings*. Vol. 11. 1889. 333–340

—— *Isis Unveiled*. Ed. Boris de Zirkoff. Wheaton, Illinois: Quest Books, 1994.

—— "Magic" from *The Dekkan Star*, Poona, March 30, 1879. *Collected Writings*. Vol. 2. 31–39.

—— *The Mahatma Letters to A.P. Sinnett*. Facsimile of 2nd edition. Theosophical University Press, 1997.

—— "Misconceptions," from *Revue du Mouvement Social*, September 1887. *Collected Writings*. Vol. 8. 70–73.

—— "An Old Book and A New One" in *Collected Writings. The Theosophist*. I:3 (December, 1879) 70–89.

—— "Precipitation" from *The Theosophist*, December–January, 1883–84. *Collected Writings*. Vol. 6. 118–123.

—— *The Secret Doctrine*. Vol. II (*Anthropogenesis*). Pasadena, CA: Theosophical University Press, 1999.

—— "Transcendental Physics" from *The Theosophist*, vol. II, No. 5, February, 1881. *Collected Writings*. Vol. 3. 14–20.

—— "What of Phenomena?" from *Lucifer*, February 1888. *Collected Writings*. Vol. 9. 46–50.

Bornstein, Kate and Caitlin Sullivan. *Nearly Roadkill: An Infobahn Erotic Adventure*. New York and London: High Risk Books, 1996.

Bortoft, Henri. *The Wholeness of Nature: Goethe's Way of Science*. Edinburgh: Floris Books, 1996.

Boyle, James. "The Second Enclosure Movement and the Construction of the Public Domain." *Law and Contemporary Problems* 66 (2003): 33–74.

Brecht, Bertolt. *Aufzeichnungen zu Leben des Galilei*. Ed. Werner Hecht. Frankfurt: Suhrkamp Verlag, 1963.

—— *Leben des Galilei*. *Versuche*, heft. 14. Berlin: Suhrkamp Verlag, 1955. 7–102.

—— *Life of Galileo*. Trans. Wolfgang Sauerlander and Ralph Manheim. In *Brecht: Collected Plays, vol. 5*. Eds. Ralph Manheim and John Willett. London: Methuen, 1972. 1–95.

Brecht, Stefan. *Queer Theatre*. New York and London: Methuen, 1986.

Brown, Laura. *Fables of Modernity: Literature and Culture in the English Eighteenth Century*. Ithaca: Cornell University Press, 2001.

Butler, Judith. "Critically Queer." *Glq: A Journal of Lesbian and Gay Studies* 1:1 (1993): 258–308.

Cage, John. *Silence*. Wesleyan University Press, 1973.

Caldwell, Lynton Keith. *International Environmental Policy: From the Twentieth to the Twenty-first Century*. 3rd Ed. Durham and London: Duke University Press, 1996.

Čapek, Karel. *R.U.R. and the Insect Play*. Oxford: Oxford University Press, 1961. 1–104.

Case, Sue-Ellen. *Feminism and Theater*. New York: Methuen, 1988.

—— "Tracking the Vampire," in *differences* 3: 2 (1991): 1–20.

—— *The Domain-Matrix: Performing Lesbian at the End of Print Culture*. Bloomington: Indiana University Press, 1996.

Churchill, Caryl. *a number*. London: Nick Hern, 2002.

—— *Faraway*. New York: Theatre Communications Groups, 2000.

Clark, Jerome. *The UFO Book: Encyclopedia of the Extraterrestrial*. Detroit: Visible Ink, 1997.

Cooper, Graham. "New Forest History: 1189–1681." 2004. Hampshire City Council. 5/2/2005. http://www.hants.gov.uk/newforest/history/history2.html.

Cottrell, Alan P. "The Resurrection of Thinking and the Redemption of Faust: Goethe's New Scientific Attitude," in Seamon, David and Arthur Zajonc, eds. *Goethe's Way of Science: A Phenomenology of Nature*. Albany, NY: State University of New York Press, 1998.. 255–275.

Cranston, Sylvia. *HPB: The Extraordinary Life and Influence of Helena Blavatsky*. New York: G.P Putnam's Sons, 1993.

Critical Art Ensemble, *The Molecular Invasion*. New York: Autonomedia, 2002.

Daniel, Norman. *The Arabs and Medieval Europe*. London: Longman, 1979.

Dasgupta, Gautam. "Theatre and the Ridiculous: A Conversation with Charles Ludlam," *Theatre of the Ridiculous*, ed. Bonnie Marranca and Gautam Dasgupta Baltimore: The Johns Hopkins University Press, 1998. 77–91.

David-Neel, Alexandra. *My Journey To Lhasa*. Boston: Beacon Press, 1986.

—— *The Secret Oral Teachings in Tibetan Buddhist Sects*. San Francisco: City Lights Books, 1967.

—— *With Mystics and Magicians in Tibet*. Middlesex, England: Penguin Books Ltd., 1937.

Davies, Roy and Glyn. "A Comparative Chronology of Money: Monetary History from Ancient Times to the Present Day." 2004. 5/2/2005. http://www.ex.ac.uk/~RDavies/arian/amser/chrono7.html.

De Alberti, Lita. *Channeling: What it is and How to do It*. San Fransisco: Weiser Books, 2000.

Derrida, Jacques. *Specters of Marx*. Trans. Peggy Kamuf. New York: Routledge, 1994.

Deuber-Mankowsky. *Lara Croft: Modell, Medium, Cyberheldin; das virtuelle Geschlecht unde seine metaphysischen Tücken*. Frankfurt: Suhrkamp, 2001.

Diamond, Elin. *Unmaking Mimesis: Essays on Feminism and Theater*. London and New York: Routledge, 1997.

Dobbs, Betty Jo Teeter. *The Foundations of Newton's Alchemy*. Cambridge: Cambridge University Press, 1975.

Dollimore, Jonathan. *Sexual Dissidence: Augustine to Wilde Freud to Foucault*. Oxford: Clarendon Press, 1991.

Edison, Thomas Alva. *The Diary and Sundry Observations of Thomas Alva Edison*. Ed. Dagobert D. Runes. New York: Philosophical Library, 1948.

Edney, Matthew H. *Mapping an Empire: The Geographical Construction of British India, 1765–1843*. Chicago: University of Chicago Press, 1997.

Eglash, Ron. "African Influences in Cybernetics." In *The Cyborg Handbook*. Ed. Chris Hables Gray. New York and London: Routledge, 1995. 17–27.

Eshun, Kodwo. *More Brilliant Than The Sun: Adventures in Sonic Fiction*. London: Quartet Books, 1998.

Esslin, Martin. *Mediations: Essays on Brecht, Beckett, and the Media*. Baton Rouge: Louisiana State University Press, 1980.

Fink, Karl J. *Goethe's History of Science*. Cambridge: Cambridge University Press, 1991.

Foster, Barbara and Michael. *Forbidden Journey: The Life of Alexandra David-Neel*. San Francisco: Harper and Row, 1986.

Foster, Susan Leigh. "Closets Full of Dances: Modern Dance's Performance of Masculinity and Sexuality," in *Dancing Desires*. Ed. Jane C. Desmond. Madison: University of Wisconsin Press, 2001. 147–207.

—— *Dances That Describe Themselves*. Middletown, Connecticut: Wesleyan University Press, 2002.

Foucault, Michel. *The History of Sexuality*. New York: Random House, 1980.

Fowell, Frank and Frank Palmer. *Censorship in England*. London: Frank Palmer, 1913.

Frayn, Michael. *Copenhagen*. New York: Anchor Books, 2000.

Fuller, Jean Overton. *Blavatsky and her teachers: An investigative biography*. London: East–West Publications, 1956.

Gibson, William. *Neuromancer*. New York: Ace Books, 1986.

—— *Idoru*. New York: G.P. Putnam's Sons, 1996.

—— *Kyoko Date*, 1996.

Goethe, Johann Wolfgang. *Faust*. Kommentiert von Erich Trunz. Hamburg: Christian Wegner Verlag, 1965.

—— Trans. and intro. Walter Arndt. Ed. Cyrus Hamlin. New York/London: W.W. Norton, 1976.

"Goethean Science Methodology." *Scottish School of Herbal Medicine*. Ed. Alan Kerr. 2005. 5/4/2005. http://www.herbalmedicine.org.uk/rootpages/Goethean%20Paper.shtml.

Goldman, Wendy Z. "The 'Withering Away' of the Family," in *Russia in the Era of NEP*. Ed. Sheila Fitzpatrick, Alexander Rabinowitch, Richard Stites. Bloomington: Indiana University Press, 1991. 125–143.

Gómez-Peña, Guillermo. *Ethno-techno: Writings on performance, activism, pedagogy*. New York and London: Routledge, 2005.

Gonzalez, Jennifer. "The Appended Subject: Race and Identity as Digital Assemblage." In *Race in Cyberspace*. Eds. Beth Kolko, Lisa Nakamura, Gilbert Rodman. New York and London: Routledge, 2000. 27–50.

Goodall, Jane. R. *Performance and Evolution in the Age of Darwin*. London and New York: Routledge, 2002.

Greenblatt, Stephen. *Renaissance Self-Fashioning: From More to Shakespeare*. Chicago: University of Chicago Press, 1980.

Haggerty, George. "Psychodrama: Hypertheatricality and Sexual Excess on the Gothic Stage," *Theatre Research International* 28:1 (2003). 20–33.

Hall, Manly P. *Paracelsus, His Mystical and Medical Philosophy.* Los Angeles: Philosophical Research Society, 1964.

Hanson, Ellis. "The Telephone and its Queerness," in *Cruising the Performative.* Eds. Sue-Ellen Case, Philip Brett, and Susan Leigh Foster. Bloomington: Indiana University Press, 1995. 34–58.

Hanssen, Beatrice. *Walter Benjamin's Other History.* Berkeley, Los Angeles, London: University of California Press, 2000.

Haraway Donna. *Modest_Witness@Second_Millennium.FemaleMan_Meets_OncoMouse: Feminism and Technoscience.* New York: Routledge, 1997.

Harvey, David. *Justice, Nature, and the Geography of Difference.* Oxford: Blackwell Publishers, 1996.

Hawking, Stephen. *A Briefer History of Time.* New York: Random House. 2005.

Hayles, N. Katherine. "Voices Out of Bodies, Bodies Out of Voices." *Sound States: Innovative Poetics and Acoustical Technologies.* Chapel Hill: University of North Carolina Press, 1997. 74–96.

Hegge, Hjalmar. "Transcending Darwinism in the Spirit of Goethe's Science: A Philosophical Perspective on the Works of Adolf Portmann." http://www.anth.org/ifgene/hegge.htm#por1. 7/9/2003. 5.

Heitler, Walter. "Goethean Science," in David Seamon and Arthur Zajonc, eds. *Goethe's Way of Science: A Phenomenology of Nature.* Albany, NY: State University of New York Press, 1998. 55–69.

Hermes Trismegistus. "Corpus Hermeticum." http://levity.com/alchemy/corpherm.html.

Hoberman, J. "The Theatre of Jack Smith," *Theatre of the Ridiculous*, ed. Bonnie Marranca and Gautam Dasgupta Baltimore: The Johns Hopkins University Press, 1998. 1–11.

Holmes, Thom. *Electronic and Experimental Music: Pioneers in Technology and Composition.* New York and London: Routledge, 2002.

Irigaray, Luce. "The Forgotten Mystery of Female Ancestry." *Thinking the Difference: For a Peaceful Revolution.* Trans. Karin Montin. New York: Routledge, 1994. 89–112.

Irigaray, Luce. *The Speculum of the Other Woman.* Trans. Gillian C. Gill. Ithaca, NY: Cornell University Press, 1985.

Jenik, Adriene. "Desktop Theater Keyboard Catharsis and the Masking of Roundheads." In *TDR: The Drama Review* 4:3 (2001) 95–112.

Johnson, Mark L. "Embodied Reason" in *Perspectives on Embodiment: The Intersections of Nature and Culture.* Eds. Gail Weiss and Honi Fern Haber. London: Routledge, 1999. 81–102.

Jonson, Ben. *The Alchemist.* Edited with introduction and critical apparatus by F.H. Mares. Manchester: Manchester University Press, 1967.

Jonson, Ben. "Mercury Vindicated from the Alchemists at Court." In *Ben Jonson Selected Masques.* Ed. Stephen Orgel. New Haven: Yale University Press, 1970. 129–137.

Jordan, Tim. *Cyberpower: The Culture and Politics of Cyberspace and the Internet.* London: Routledge, 1999.

Josephson, Matthew. *Edison.* New York: McGraw-Hill, 1959.

Jung, C.G. *Flying Saucers: A Modern Myth of Things Seen in the Skies.* Trans. R.F.C. Hull. New York: MJF Books, 1978.

Kaiser, Georg. *Gas.* (In the original German) Berlin: Ullstein Theater Texte, 1978.

Kaiser, Georg. *Gas I.* Trans. Herman Scheffauer. New York: Frederick Ungar Publication, 1973.

—— *Gas II.* Trans. Winifred Katzin. New York: Frederick Ungar Publication, 1972.

Kalachakra Tantra, trans. Jeffrey Hopkins. Boston: Wisdom Publications, 1999.

Katz, Jonathan. "John Cage's Queer Silence; or, How To Avoid Making Matters Worse," in *Writings Through John Cage's Music, Poetry, and Art*. Eds. David W. Bernsetin and Christopher Hatch. Chicago: University of Chicago Press, 2001. 41–61.

Kilbourne, Jean. "Synthetic Sex." *Ms. Magazine*. Dec 2000/Jan 2001.

Kittler, Friedrich. *Draculas Vermächtnis*. Leipzig: Reclam Verlag. 1993.

——— *Gramophone, Film, Typewriter*. Trans. Geoffrey Winthrop-Young and Michael Wutz. Stanford, CA: Stanford University Press, 1999.

Klein, Naomi. *No Logo*. London: Flamingo, 2001.

Klimo, Jon. *Channeling: Investigations on Receiving Information from Paranormal Sources*. Berkeley: North Atlantic Books, 1998.

Knowlson, James. *Damned to Fame: The Life of Samuel Beckett*. New York: Simon & Schuster, 1996.

Kolesnikov, Mikhail. "Russian Avant-Garde and the Theatre of the Artist" in *Theatre in Revolution: Russian Avant-Garde Stage Design 1913–1935*. Ed. Nancy van Norman Baer. London: Thames and Hudson, 1999. 84–95.

Kolko, Beth. "Erasing <\\>@> race: Going White in the (Inter)Face." In *Race in Cyberspace*. Eds. Beth Kolko, Lisa Nakamura, and Gilbert Rodman. New York and London: Routledge. 2000. 213–32.

Lange, David. "Reimagining the Public Domain." *Law and Contemporary Problems* 66 (2003): 463–484.

Lansbury, Coral. "Melodrama, Pantomime, and The Communist Manifesto" in *Browning Institute Studies*, vol. 14 (1986). 1–10.

Lessig, Lawrence. *Code and Other Laws of Cyberspace*. New York: Basic Books, 1999.

Lindsay, Jack. *The Origins of Alchemy in Graeco-Roman Egypt*. London: Frederick Müller, 1970.

Lock, Graham. *Blutopia*. Durham and London: Duke University Press, 1999.

Lott, Eric. *Love and Theft: Blackface, Minstrelsy and the American Working Class*. Oxford: Oxford University Press, 1993.

Lukacs, Georg. *Goethe and his Age*. Trans. Robert Anchor. London: Merlin Press, 1968.

Mackenzie, Vicki. *Cave in the Snow*. New York: Bloomsbury Publishing, 1998.

Mao Tse-Tung. "On Contradiction" in *The Wisdom of Mao-Tse-Tung*. New York: Kensington Publishing Corporation, 2002. 43–90.

Marinetti, F.T. *Poupées Électriques*. Paris: E. Sansot & Co. 1909.

Martin, Mathew. "Play and Plague in Ben Jonson's *The Alchemist*." *English Studies in Canada* 26:4 (December 2000): 393–408.

Marx, Karl and Frederick Engels. *The Communist Manifesto: 150th Anniversary Edition 1848–1998*. Intro. by Robin D.G. Kelley. Chicago: Charles H. Kerr, 1998.

Mellett, Tom. "Goethean Science: Bringing Chaos to Order by Looking Phenomena Right in the 'I'." *Southern Cross Review* 6 (2000). 5/2/2005. http://www.southerncrossreview.org/6/goethe.htm

Metlitzki, Dorothee. *The Matter of Araby in Medieval England*. New Haven: Yale University Press, 1977.

Middleton and Dekker, *The Roaring Girl*.

Morse, Margaret. *Virtualities: Television, Media Art, and Cyberculture*. Bloomington: Indiana University Press, 1998.

Moss, Anne. "Limits of Reason: An Explanation of Brecht's Concept of *Vernunft* and the Discourse of Science in *Leben des Galilei*" in *German Monitor No. 41* Atlanta: Rodopi, 1998. 133–147.

Nakamura, Lisa. *Cybertypes: Race, Ethnicity, and Identity on the Internet*. New York and London: Routledge, 2002.

Negri, Antonio. *Marx Beyond Marx: Lessons on the Grundrisse*. London: Pluto Press, 1991.

Nietzsche, Friedrich. *The Birth of Tragedy*. Trans. Shaun Whiteside. New York: Penguin Books, 1993.

The Newton Project. Imperial College London. 2005. 5/2/2005. http://www.newtonproject.ic.ac.uk/

Ogden, Dunbar. *The Staging of Drama in the Medieval Church*. London, Cranbury, NJ, and Mississauga, Ontario: Associated University Presses, 2002.

Olalquiaga, Celeste. *Megalopolis: Contemporary Cultural Sensibilities*. Minneapolis: University of Minnesota Press, 1992.

Pannikar, K.N. *Culture, Ideology, Hegemony*. London: Anthem Press, 1995.

Parrinder, Geoffrey. *Avatar and Incarnation*. Oxford: Oneworld Publications, 1997.

Paul, Christiane. *Digital Art*. London: Thames & Hudson, 2003.

Pendle, George. *Strange Angel: The Otherworldly Life of Rocket Scientist John Whiteside Parsons*. New York: Harcourt, 2005.

Perloff, Marjorie. *The Futurist Moment*. Chicago: University of Chicago Press, 1986.

Peters, Julie Stone. *Theatre of the Book 1480–1880*. Oxford: Oxford University Press, 2000.

Phelan, Peggy. *Unmarked: the politics of performance*. London and New York: Routledge, 1993.

Pilling, John. *Beckett Before Godot*. Cambridge: Cambridge University Press, 1997.

Ravenhill, Mark. *Faust is Dead*. In *Mark Ravenhill: Plays:1*. London: Methuen Drama, 2001. 93–140.

Roach, Joseph. "The Artificial Eye: Augustan Theater and the Empire of the Visible" in *The Performance of Power:Theatrical Discourse and Politics*. Eds. Sue-Ellen Case and Janelle Reinelt. Iowa City: University of Iowa Press, 1991. 131–145.

—— *The Player's Passion: Studies in the Science of Acting*. Newark: University of Delaware Press, 1985.

The Roaring Girl and Other City Comedies. Ed. James Knowles. Oxford: Oxford University Press, 2001.

Roman, David. *Acts of Intervention*. Bloomington: Indiana University Press. 1998.

Rose, Mark. "Nine-tenths of the Law: the English Copyright Debates and the Rhetoric of the Public Domain." *Law and Contemporary Problems* 66 (2003): 75–88.

Ross, Kelly L. "British Coins before the Florin, Compared to French Coins of the *Ancien Régime*." *Proceedings of the Friesian School*, Fourth Series. 2002. 5/1/2005. http://www.friesian.com/coins.htm.

Roy, Parama. "As the Master Saw Her." *Cruising the Performative: Interventions into the Representation of Ethnicity, Nationality, and Sexuality*. Eds. Sue-Ellen Case, Philip Brett, and Susan Leigh Foster. Bloomington and Indianapolis: Indiana University Press, 1995. 112–129.

Ryan, Charles J. *H.P. Blavatsky and the Theosophical Movement*. Point Loma, California: Theosophical University Press, 1937.

Said, Edward W. *Orientalism*. New York: Vintage Books, 1979.

Samaras, Connie. "Is it Tomorrow or Just the End of Time?" *Processed Lives: Gender and Technology in Everyday Life*. Eds. Jennifer Terry and Melodie Calvert. London: Routledge, May 1997. 199–214.

Schell, Orville. *Virtual Tibet: Searching for Shangri-La from the Himalayas to Hollywood*. New York: Metropolitan Books, 2000.

Schneider, Rebecca. "Nomadmedia: On Critical Art Ensemble" in *TDR: The Drama Review* 44:4 (2000) 120–131.

Seamon, David and Arthur Zajonc. Eds. *Goethe's Way of Science: A Phenomenology of Nature*. Albany, NY: State University of New York Press, 1998.

Seltzer, Mark. *Bodies and Machines*. New York and London: Routledge, 1992.

Shanahan, John Henry. *Stages of Knowledge: Theater and Laboratory in Seventeenth-and-Early Eighteenth-Century England*. Diss. University of Michigan, 2002. Ann Arbor: UMI, 2002.

Shaviro, Steven. *Doom Patrols: A Theoretical Fiction About Postmodernism*. New York/London: High Risk Books, 1997.

Shaw, Peggy. *Belle Reprieve* in *Split Britches: Lesbian Practice/Feminist Performance*. Ed. Sue-Ellen Case. London: Routledge, 1996. 149–183.

Shirley, John. "Freezone." In *Mirrorshades*. Ed. Bruce Sterling. New York: Ace Books, 1986. 139–177.

Smith, Jack. "The Memoirs of Maria Montez, or Wait For Me At the Bottom of the Pool." *Film Culture*. No. 31 (Winter, 1963–64) 3–4.

Sobchack, Vivian. "Breadcrumbs in the Forest: Three Meditations on Being Lost in Space" in *Carnal Thoughts: Embodiment and Moving Image Culture*. Berkeley: University of California Press, 2004. 13–35.

Southern, R.W. *The Making of the Middle Ages*. New Haven: Yale University Press, 1963.

Spiegel, Lynn. "The Suburban Home Companion: Television and the Neighborhood Ideal in Postwar America" in *Sexuality and Space*. Ed. Beatriz Colomina. Princeton: Princeton Papers on Architecture, 1992. 185–217.

Steiner, Rudolf. *A Theory of Knowledge Implicit in Goethe's World Conception*. Trans. Olin D. Wannamaker. New York: Anthroposophic Press, 1968.

Sterling, Bruce. *Islands in the Net*. New York: Ace Book, 1988.

—— *Mirrorshades: The Cyberpunk Anthology*. New York: Ace Books, 1988.

Stone, Allucquere Rosanne, "Split Subjects Not Atoms; Or, How I Fell in Love with my Prosthesis" in *The Cyborg Handbook*; eds Chris Hables Gray, Heidi Figueroa-Sarriera, and Steven Mentor. New York: Routledge, 1995 (393–406).

Strindberg, August. *Inferno* in *Inferno, Alone, and Other Writings*. Ed. Evert Sprinchorn. Trans. Derek Coltman and Evert Sprinchorn. Garden City: Anchor Books, 1968. 117–283.

—— Preface. *Miss Julie*. In *August Strindberg Miss Julie and Other Plays*. Edited and Translated Michael Robinson. Oxford: Oxford University Press, 1998. 56–68.

Stryker, Susan. "Christine Jorgensen's Atom Bomb: Transsexuality and the Emergence of Postmodernity" in *Playing Dolly*. Eds. E. Ann Kaplan and Susan Squier. New Brunswick and London: Rutgers University Press, 1999. 157–171.

Suarez, Juan. A. *Bike Boys, Drag Queens, and Superstars*. Bloomington: Indiana University Press, 1996.

Symonds, John. *Madame Blavatsky: Medium and Magic*. London: Odhams Press, Limited, 1959.

Szwed, John F. *Space is the Place: The Life and Times of Sun Ra*. New York: Da Capo Press, 1998.

Taussig, Michael. *Mimesis and Alterity: A Particular History of the Senses*. New York: Routledge, 1993.

Tavel, Ron. "Maria Montez: Anima of an Antediluvian World" in *Flaming Creature: Jack Smith His Amazing Life and Times*. Eds. Edward Leffingwell, Carole Kismaric, Marvin Heiferman. New York: Institute for Contemporary Art/P.S. 1 Museum (catalog). 88–103.

Taylor, Timothy D. *Strange Sounds: Music, Technology and Culture*. New York and London: Routledge, 2001.

"A Tibetan Initiate on World Problems." Canadian Theosophical Association. Reprinted from "The Occult World" 1883 with a Foreword. 5/1/2005. http://www.theosophical.ca/TibetanInitiate.htm.

Tierney, Thomas F. "The Preservation and Ownership of the Body" in *Perspectives on Embodiment: The Intersections of Nature and Culture*. Ed. Gail Weiss and Honi Fern Haber. New York: Routledge, 1999.

Treadwell, Sophie. *Machinal*. London: Nick Hern Books, 1993.

Trunz, Erich. "Anmerkungen des Herausgebers" in *Faust*. Munich: C.H. Beck, 1976. 461–682.

Vesela, Pavla. "The Hardening of Cement: Russian Women and Modernization" in *NWSA Journal* 15.3 (2003) 104–123.

von Gunden, Heidi. *The Music of Pauline Oliveros*. London: Scarecrow Press, 1983.

Washington, Peter. *Madame Blavatsky's Baboon*. New York: Shocken Books, 1993.

Weheliye, Alexander G. "'Feenin': Posthuman Voices in Contemporary Black Popular Music." *Social Text 71*, 20:2 (Summer 2002). 21–47.

Wertenbaker, Timberlake. *After Darwin*. Woodstock, Illinois: Dramatic Publishing, 1999.

Wertheim, Margaret. *The Pearly Gates of Cyberspace*. New York: W.W. Norton, 1999.

White, Michael. *Isaac Newton: The Last Sorcerer*. Reading, Mass.: Addison-Wesley, 1997.

Wiles, David. *A Short History of Western Performance Space*. Cambridge: Cambridge University Press, 2003.

Zajonc, Arthur. "Goethe and the Science of His Time" in David Seamon and Arthur Zajonc, eds. *Goethe's Way of Science: A Phenomenology of Nature*. Albany, NY: State University of New York Press, 1998.15–30.

Zilliacus, Clas. *Beckett and Broadcasting*. Abo Finland: Abo Akademi, 1976.

Index

Page numbers in *Italics* indicate references to figures and illustrations.

Actors 8–10, 28, 39, 50–52, 53–55, 56, 60, 71, 83, 89, 91, 92, 103, 109, 110, 114, 153, 164, 172, 179, 184, 195, 199, 210, 214, 222, 225n.4; Actor training 2, 50, 141; Techniques 51, 54, 71–72, 83–84

Advertising 106, 109, 200, 202–3, 206, 207, 209, 214; Brand canopy 57, 202, 203, 206; Commercials 107; *see also* Logo(s)

Adding Machine, The 89, 98–99, 173

Aelita: The Queen of Mars 108–10, 111, 112–14, 120, 174, 177

After Darwin 179–80

AIDS 148, 149

Alchemist, The 20, 27, 29–30, 54, *55*, 182

Alchemy 8, 9, 11–12 15, 16–50, 58, 74, 79, 80, 82–83, 85–87, 100, 137, 177, 201, 223n.1–2; Alchemists 3, 11, 17–30, 32–33, 35, 40, 52, 58, 71, 73, 79, 83, 86, 177; and character 27–34; and chemistry 17, 19, 21, 22, 28, 32; and code 21–24, 26, 27, 31; Egyptian 15, 18, 20, 33; Elixir of life 20, 79; Emblems 17, 22–24, 25, 87, 177; Esoteric Tradition 15, 18, 20, 24, 26; and Faust 17, 24, 27, 32–49, 85; Furnace of 11, *16*, 17, 21, 28, 29, 43, 48, 143; and gender 26–27, 30–32; and gold 9, 19–21, 23, 26, 30, 34, 35, 80, 201; History of 15–18; and Islam 15, 17–18, 32, 33; Monetary value 19–21, 38, 79; Occult science 15, 17–19, 21; Old science 11, 12, 20, 31, 82; and Paracelsus 33–35, 46, 73; and performance 15, 20, 27–34, 38, 39; and philosophy 17–21, 23, 26, 27, 31, 33, 34, 38, 40, 79; *see also* Goethe; Newton

Aliens 82, 87, 89, 98, 119–24, 135, 141, 142, 152, 156, 163–64, 166, 168, 169, 188–93, 195, 196, 199, 215; Abductions 87, 89, 120, 122, 123, 156, 188–90, 192, 193, 215; Alien avatar 163–64, 168, 192, 215; And Sun Ra 166, 188–90, 192; *see also* Heaven's Gate; UFOs

All That Fall 124–25

Anarchy/Anarchists 72, 103, 107

Androids 100, 101, 105–6

Anthroposophy 49–50, 224n.16

Archer, William 71, 72, 84

Architecture 9, 49–50, 70, 112, 113, 115, 131, 155, 187

Astral Light/Astral Plane 60–64, 68, 70, 122, 224n.3

Astrology 17, 18, 33, 34, 156, 193

Atoms 74, 75, 84, 136

Atomic bomb 87, 116–17, 120, 143, 159, 172, 174, 176, 181, 183, 215

Avant-garde 5, 108, 116, 192

Avatars 2, 3, 47, 58, 62–66, 78, 79, 86, 88, 89, 101, 103, 118–19, 121, 152, 154, 155, 163–69, 184–222, 224n.18, 224n.6

Ballard, J.G. 105

Barnum, P. T. 60, 72, 73

Barron, Louis and Bebe 132

Baudrillard, Jean 105, 160

Bausch, Pina 103

Beckett, Samuel 5, 116, 123–28, 206–7, 227n.12; and Tape 5, 116, 123–28; *All That Fall* 124–25; *Krapp's Last Tape* 5, 125–28; And Proust 124–25; *Rockaby* 127–28, 141; *see also* Waitingforgodot.com

Bell, Alexander Graham 80; *see also* telephone

Bell Labs 133
Benjamin, Walter 10, 23, 126, 164
Bergson, Henri 124
Bhagavad Gita 62
Bioart 152, 157–59
Biospheres 87, 88, 144–45, 151–52;
   Biosphere 2 151; *Biopsheria* 151
Biotechnology 157–62; *see also* Frankenfood
Blavatsky, Helena 5, 6, 21, 50, 58–77, 80,
   85, 122, 140, 142, 152–54, 163, 187,
   193, 194, 224n.1; and Astral Light/
   Astral Plane 60–64, 68, 70, 122,
   224n.3; and avatar 62–67, 69, 152,
   163, 194; and gothic 75–77; and
   gender 63–66, 69; and grassroots
   performance 68–69, 71, 76; "Hindu
   man" 62–70, 81; *Isis Unveiled* 60–62;
   And Indian nationalism 64, 70; and
   "phenomena" 59, 64, 69–77, 80; *The
   Secret Doctrine* 65, 66; and Tibet 60–62,
   66–70, 140; virtual Tibet 67, 152–55;
   and Strindberg 85; *see also* Theosophy
Blitzstein, Marc 97
Bohr, Niels 181
Booth, Edwin 70
Bornstein, Kate 215, *216*–18, 220, 222;
   Nearly Roadkill 218; *Virtually Yours* 215,
   216–18, 220, 222
Brandon website, The 6, 218–*19*, 220–21,
   222
Breaking the Code 119
Brecht, Bertolt 13, 145, 172–77, 179, 182;
   Life of Galileo 145, 172–77; Short
   Organum for the Theater 175
Buddhism 65, 66, 70, 74–75, 136, 138,
   140, 153–55, 193
Burroughs, William 98

Cabinet of Dr. Caligari, The 91
Cage, John 6, 116, 130–39, 182, 184, 187;
   0'00" 130; *Cartridge Music* 130–31; And
   Einstein on the Beach 182, 184; And
   "experimental" music 131, 132, 135–
   36, 187; Homosexuality 137–38;
   Imaginary Landscape No. 1 130; *Variations
   V* 132–*4*, 135–38, 141, 182; and Merce
   Cunningham 132, 137–38, 139, 184;
   Silence 135; Silence as virtual space 135;
   Tape compositions 116, 133, 138; And
   Zen Buddhism 136–37, 184
Camp 5, 115, 147, 153, 191, 192
Čapek, Karel 99–101

Capital/Capitalism 5, 42–45, 48, 52, 79,
   80, 87, 90, 95, 101, 102, 104, 108, 113–
   15, 141, 143, 144, 146, 147, 148, 175,
   193, 200–203, 212, 215
Castle Spectre, The 76, 78
Cement 109, 225n.8
Censorship 32, 52, 60, 109, 138, 173, 179
Channeling 5, 66, 88, 155, 163, 193–96,
   217; channeling water 44, 48
Character 4, 5, 9, 13, 27–34, 39, 43, 45,
   47–49, 54–56, 63, 72, 80, 84 88, 90, 92,
   100, 102, 106, 107, 111, 124–28, 164,
   166, 173, 179–82, 184, 188, 198, 205–
   9, 217; Motivation 13, 27–31, 40, 49,
   54, 168, 182, 200, 221
Chat Rooms 198, 200, 203, 206–8, 218
Cheang, Shu Lea 219, 222
Chekhov, Anton 143
Chekov, Michael 50
Christianity 7–9, 11, 17, 32, 37–40, 45, 58,
   60, 61, 85, 159, 169, 177–78, 188, 193,
   197
Christian science 167
Churchill, Caryl 159–61, 210; *Cloud Nine*
   210; *Far Away* 161; *A number* 159–61;
   Serious Money 161
Class 1, 56, 78, 81, 106, 111, 113, 136,
   137, 150, 154, 161, 186, 199, 202, 205,
   210, 212, 213; *see also* virtual class
Classification 11, 13–14, 72; *see also*
   taxonomy
Cloning 159–61, 224n.18
Code 2, 3, 21–24, 26, 27, 31, 44–48, 67,
   71, 72, 84, 87–92, 116–19, 121, 125,
   127, 128, 137, 138, 142, 150, 151, 165,
   170, 185–87, 190, 203, 206, 209, 218,
   220, 222, 224n18, 226n5
Cohn, Roy 117
Cold War 117–19, 121, 137
Collective 18, 43–45, 53, 90, 97, 108, 111,
   114, 121, 128, 130, 140 141, 156–58,
   166, 169, 194, 195
Colonialism 61, 63, 64, 66, 70, 151, 186,
   210, 224n.4
Coltrane, Alice 166
Communism 77–79, 107, 109, 113, 117,
   118, 121, 122, 153, 172, 179, 224n.18
Computers 4, 6, 66, 87, 107, 112, 116–19,
   128, 145, 150, 151, 155, 158, 164, 166,
   170, 185, 198, 200, 201, 203, 206–8,
   211, 212, 214, 215, 217, 218, 221, 222;
   Computer Games *see* Games

Copenhagen 87, 181–82
Copyright 52, 53, 57, 201
Corporeality/corporealization 5, 8, 31, 47,
    59, 60, 62, 63, 65, 66, 68, 69, 73, 92,
    120, 123, 125–27, 163, 164, 168–74,
    190, 195, 196, 198, 199, 207, 215, 217,
    224n.18
Counterfeits 19, 20, 22, 30, 31, 34, 38, 41,
    45, 72
Crash 105, 107
Creationism 177–79
Critical Art Ensemble (CAE) 157–59; *The
    Molecular Invasion* 157–58
Croft, Lara *see* Lara Croft
Cryptography 87, 117–19, 138
Cults 3, 88, 151, 166–70
Cunningham, Merce 132, 134, 135, 137–
    39, 184
Curie, Marie and Pierre 76–77
Cyberpunk 146, 149–51, 197, 210–11
Cyberspace 2, 49, 57, 88, 89, 107, 145,
    146, 164, 185, 196–203, 206, 208, 209–
    11, 213, 214, 222
Cyborg 89, 105, 108, 211

Dalai Lama 61, 67, 153, 155
Dance 8, 29, 47, 97, 116, 131–35, 137,
    138, 184, 188, 191, 199, 209
Darwin, Charles 5, 6, 11, 21, 50, 66, 71,
    72, 83–85, 88, 100, 143, 153, 172, 177–
    80, 185; and Blavatsky 5, 21, 50, 66,
    153; and Creationism 177–79; Cyber-
    Darwin 185; *After Darwin* 179–80; *The
    Expression of the Emotions in Man and
    Animals* 71, 83; and Naturalism/
    Naturalist Acting 71–72, 83; and
    Scopes Monkey Trial 177–79; Social
    Darwinism 179, 182; *see also* Evolution
David-Neel, Alexandra 68, 74–75, 136,
    154, 225n.11; *The Secret Oral Teachings in
    Tibetan Buddhist Sects* 74–75; *My Journey
    to Lhasa* 74
Da Vinci Code, The 88
Davis, Bette 147, 149
Decoding 21–24, 88, 111, 116, 118–20,
    224n18
Decoder rings 2, 88, 118
Deep Listening 130, 141, 142; *see also*
    Oliveros
Derrida, Jacques 77–79, 159, 225n.18
Der Sturm 91
Descartes 20, 143

Dianetics 167; *see also* Scientology
DNA 88, 100, 122, 158, 159, 224n.18
Double Indemnity 93
Dracula 56, 95
Dracula's Legacy 95–96
Drag 65, 146–50, 210
Dunham, Katherine 97
Dynamism 11, 31, 104, 109

eBay 3, 198
Ecology 1, 13, 35, 43–45, 48, 57, 83, 103,
    144, 151, 152, 157, 162
Economics 1, 3, 5, 8, 12, 14, 19, 21, 22,
    30, 34, 35, 41–43, 48, 52–54, 61, 79,
    80, 89, 99, 100, 104, 108, 110, 112–14,
    146, 147, 161, 162, 165, 172–74, 180,
    182, 193, 194, 200, 201, 213
Ecstasy 42, 44, 89, 105, 107–8, 114, 171,
    172, 194, 197; *see also* Transcendence;
    Violence
Eddy, Mary Baker 167
Edison, Thomas 2, 6, 70, 73, 77, 80–82,
    92–95, 130, 131, 168, 170, 194, 201
Egypt/Egyptian 3, 15, 18, 20, 33, 64, 140,
    187, 188, 190–92
Einstein, Albert 6, 23, 70, 75, 86–88, 115,
    136, 172, 176, 182–84, 194; *relativity* 86,
    87
Einstein on the Beach 70, 86, 172, 182–3, 184
Electric Chair 2, 93–4, 95, 128, 131
Electric Dolls 105–6
Electricity 93–95, 105–6, 108, 114, 118,
    130–33, 153, 159, 167–68; hydroelec-
    tric power 108, 114, 153
Emblems 10, 17, 22–24, *25*, 28, 32, 39, 55,
    75, 87, 102, 118, 121, 177
Embodiment 3, 26, 62–66, 69–70, 81, 86,
    89, 96, 116, 121, 141, 142, 151, 152,
    172, 208; *see also* Corporeality
Empire 13, 41, 44, 48, 58, 67–68, 71, 138
Empiricism 17, 22, 35–38, 43, 47, 61, 64,
    66, 72, 73, 75, 108, 124, 136, 146, 174,
    175, 177, 182, 185
Engels 77–79, 113, 153; *The Origin of the
    Family, Private Property, and the State* 113
Engineer 44, 69, 90, 100–103, 108–14,
    119, 128, 131–33
Enlightenment, The 58, 68, 87, 142, 143,
    174–76, 224n.18
Environment(s) 10, 24, 43, 45, 46, 49, 75,
    83, 97–99, 104, 109, 114–16, 118, 125,
    130, 131, 134–35, 137–38, 142, 144–

48, 151, 152, 154, 157, 158, 171, 182, 184, 185, 198, 200, 202, 203, 208, 214; Definition of 144

Environmentalism 57, 142, 144; *see also* Ecology

Eshun, Kodwo 186–88

Esoteric practices 15, 18, 20, 24, 26, 31, 33, 35, 49, 63, 65, 70, 81, 118, 121, 141, 152, 224n16

Ethics 26, 34, 87, 88, 114, 119, 158, 161, 168, 172–74, 181, 182

Ethnicity 7, 32, 115, 186, 199, 209–14, 222; Cross-ethnicity 199; Markers of 209, 214

Eurythmy 49–50

Everest, Mt. 68

Evolution 12, 50, 71, 72, 83, 84, 100, 106, 127, 169, 177–80, 182, 185

Experiments/Experimentation 9, 17, 21–24, 26–29, 32–34, 38, 39, 45, 70, 71, 73, 77, 84, 85, 95, 99, 100, 105–6, 108–9, 123, 128, 130–40, 151, 152, 157, 158, 166, 169, 170, 177, 181, 187; Experimental Music 128–40, 187; Experimental Plays 105–6, 108–9

Expressionism 5, 89–109, 114, 128, 130, 173, 184

Expression of the Emotions in Man and Animals, The 71, 83

Exter, Alexandra 109–10, 114, 225n.9; *see also Aelita*

Factories 13, 80, 89, 98–102, 105, 108, 109, 111, 113, 143

Fascism 97, 102–4, 107, 181; And Futurism 107

Faust/Faustian 2, 3, 24, 27 32–49, 58, 77, 79, 85, 88, 91, 99, 165–68, 170–72, 197; Puppet plays 27, 33–34; *see also* Goethe

Faust Is Dead 170–71

Federal Theater Project 97

Feminism 1, 5, 138–41, 159, 170, 205

Fetish 126, 127, 150, 201, 203

Fidelity 127–31

Fields/Field Theory 2, 3, 10, 27, 61, 82, 86, 87, 90, 131–37 174, 181–84, 193, 194, 209, 214, 220, 226n.18

Fission 24, 87, 101

Frankenfood 157–58, 161–62

Frankenstein 159

Frayn, Michael 172, 181–82

Freud, Sigmund 69, 124, 126, 168, 217

Furnace 11, *16*, 17, 21, 28, 29, 43, 48, 143

Futurism 89, 104–8, 114, 130, 186, 187, 197, 225n.6; Definition of 105; *Futurist Manifesto* 104–5; Futurist Moment 104; 'Futurist Synthetic Theater' 106; And gender 104–5, 107; *see also* Marinetti

Galileo 20, 88, 172–77, 184

Games and Gaming 4, 6, 107–8, 116, 155, 158, 197, 198, 202–7, 214, 215, 217; *Dungeons and Dragons* 197, 226n.6; *Grand Theft Auto* 4; *The Sims* 4; *Tomb Raider* 203–6

Garrick, David 54–5, 56

Gas 100–103

Gaze 10, 11, 69, 103, 115, 142

Gender 1, 5, 6, 9, 26–27, 30–34, 45–49, 59, 63–66, 69, 74, 84, 88, 95–96, 99, 101, 104–5, 109, 113, 116, 120, 123, 127, 137–40, 146–51, 154, 159–61, 165, 169, 170, 176, 177, 191, 199, 203–10, 212–22, 225n.9, 227n.12; and alchemy 26–27, 85; as code 26, 27, 31, 45, 47, 48, 84, 150, 151, 165, 170, 203, 206, 218, 220, 222; and Communism 113, 153; Cross-gender performance 9, 31, 64, 65, 69, 149, 199, 210, 212, 220; and *Faust* 45–50, 170; and Futurism 104–5; femininity 45–48, 137, 146, 150, 151, 203; Ideal feminine 47–48, 63, 84, 170; Masculinity 46–47, 66, 69, 71, 73, 99, 104–8, 137–38, 146, 149, 176, 191, 197, 208, 212–13, 225n.8; Masculinist transcendent 105, 107, 197; And money 46–50; *Roaring Girl* 27, 30–31; Strindberg 84–85l; Virtual gender 45; *see also* Blavatsky; Drag; *Machinal*; Transgender

Genet, Jean 210

Genetic engineering 152, 157–58

Geography 7, 60, 65–70, 74, 123, 152–56, 180; Geographical societies 67–68; *see also* Mapping

Geometry/Geometric 50, 64, 67–68, 70, 86, 90, 91, 109–13, 135, 187

Ghosts 47, 76–79, 145, 148; *see also* Specters, Spirits

Gibson, William 146, 150–51, 165, 197, 205; *Idoru* 151, 165, 205; *Neuromancer* 150, 197

Gladkov, Fyodor 109

Glass, Philip 70, 86, 182–84
Global Warming 143
Goethe 2, 5, 17, 20, 26, 27, 32–50, 52, 60,
  63, 67, 74, 79, 84, 91, 99–100, 142–43,
  159, 170, 201, 224n.16; delicate
  empiricism 35–37, 43; *Faust* 2, 20, 24,
  26, 27, 26–29, 32–49, 63, 80, 85, 88,
  91, 100, 142–43, 170; *Faust II* 32, 34,
  39, 41–48, 79; Goethean science 35–
  39, 49–50, 143, 224n.20; *Maxims and
  Reflections* 35–36; *Theory of Color* 36;
  Sayings 38; *West-Eastern Divan* 32
Goetheanum 49–50
Gomez-Peña, Guillermo 210–13; Cyber-
  wetbacks 210–11, 213; *Ethno-techno* 212;
  see also neo-minstrelsy
Gothic 49, 75–79, 95–96, 116, 208
Gramophone, Film, Typewriter 80
Grassroots 2, 5, 33, 41, 52, 58, 60, 76–77,
  85, 88, 89, 119–23, 134, 152, 155, 161,
  163, 169, 186–87, 193–96; and
  Channeling 77, 193–96; Harmonic
  Convergence 155–57; And UFOs 109,
  119–23, 163; *see also* Blavatsky
Gravity 20, 22, 86–87
Greenpeace 144, 145

Habitats 48, 142, 146, 148–50, 198; *see also*
  Environments
Hackers 150, 197, 198, 214
Hafez, Shams-od-Din Muhammad 32
Hamlet 76, 78
Hamletmachine 103
Harmonic convergence 5, 155–57, 197
Haraway, Donna 72–73, 105, 120, 172
Hawking, Stephen 58
Heaven's Gate 168–70
Hegel 37
Heisenberg 87, 172, 181–82, 184
Helen of Troy 46, 47, 63
Hermaphrodite 31, 65, 220
Hermes Trismegistus 15, 19
Hermetic 19, 24, 26, 73, 182
Heterosexuality 45, 64–66, 146, 206, 213,
  215; Compulsory Heterosexuality 210;
  Heteronormativity 64, 101, 191;
  Heterosexism 146, 225n.7
Himalayas 60, 62, 63, 66–69, 143, 152–54,
  192, 194, 205, 225n.9; *see also* Tibet
Hinduism 62–70, 81, 163–64 193, 198,
  224n.4–5, 225n.13
Hogarth 54–56

Hollywood 2, 101, 103, 110, 148, 149,
  152–54, 179, 195, 196
Homosexuality 117, 137–39, 146–49, 179,
  191, 215; Homophobia 138, 201
Homunculus 46–47, 63, 99–100, 159,
  224n.18
Hot Peaches 147
House Un-American Activities Committee
  (HUAC) 117, 172, 179
Howard, Thomas 93, *94*
Hubbard, L. Ron 166–68, *see also*
  Scientology
Hybridity 127, 150, 152, 155, 210, 214

Ibsen, Henrik 148–49; *Ghosts* 148
Idoru 151, 165, 205
Identity/Identification 9, 15, 17, 18, 26,
  27, 29–31, 36, 43, 55, 65, 83, 92, 98,
  117, 139, 140, 147, 149, 165–66, 169,
  185, 186, 191, 199–201, 203, 205, 208–
  15, 217–21, 224n.1
Improvisation 51, 54, 55, 60, 128, 130,
  136, 138–42, 152, 160, 188, 192
Industrialization 43–44, 80–81, 92, 99,
  100, 104, 143–45, 212–13;
  Postindustrial society 88, 155, 196
Inherit the Wind 179–80
Intellectual Property 52–57, 87, 201
Intelligent Design 178, 185; *see also*
  Creationism
Interface 23, 63, 70, 75, 89, 90, 119, 150,
  155, 163, 165, 166, 168, 172, 186, 200,
  203; Graphical User Interface (GUI)
  200
International Ladies' Garment Workers'
  Union (ILGWU) 96–97
Internet, The 2, 4, 21–22, 46, 62, 57, 61,
  88–89, 108, 140–42, 155, 163–64,
  170–71, 196–203, 205–14, 217–18
Invasion of the Body Snatchers 122
Ione 139–40, 191
I, Robot 101
Isis Unveiled 60–61, 62
Islam 15, 17–18, 32–34
Iteration 9, 11, 12, 17, 20, 31, 33, 51–55,
  60, 64, 85, 93, 96, 116, 123–31, 135,
  142, 159, 171, 179, 182, 184, 214

Jenik, Adriene 206–7
Job 91–92
Johns, Jasper 133
Jones, Inigo 28

Jones, Jordy 5, 218–20, 222
Jonson, Ben 20, 27–32, 34, 40, 53, 55, 182;
    Masques 28–29; *Mercury Vindicated from
    the Alchemists at Court* 28–30; see also
    The Alchemist
Jorgensen, Christine 116–17, 120, 159,
    170, 215
Jung, Carl 120–21, 136; And the *Book of
    Changes* 136; *Flying Saucers: A Modern
    Myth of Things Seen in the Skies* 120; And
    UFOs 120–21
Junk *see* Trash

Kaiser, Georg 100–102
Kalachakra 66, 155
Kalidasa 39
Keynes, John Maynard 20–21
Kittler, Friedrich 80–82, 95–96; *Dracula's
    Legacy* 95–96; *Gramaphone, Film,
    Typewriter* 80–82
Klüver, Billy 133
Knights Templars 20
Kokoschka, Oskar 91–92
Koot' Hoomi Lal Singh 63, 66, 67, 69, 73;
    see also Blavatsky
Krapp's Last Tape 5, 125–28
Kunst und Gemüse 103

Labor 9, 19, 38, 43–45, 57, 79–81, 89–90,
    92, 93, 96–104, 106, 108, 112–14, 161,
    212
Laboratory 1–3, 6, 9, 17, 21–23, 27–30,
    34, 39, 43, 45–46, 48, 54, 58, 60, 71–
    73, 80–82, 84, 85, 91–94, 99–102, 108,
    110–11, 115–16, 118, 120–23, 128,
    133–39, 142, 152, 157–59, 166–67,
    169–70, 172, 182–86
Lacan, Jacques 95–96, 159
LambdaMOO 213
Land Reclamation 43, 48
Language 11, 17, 24, 33, 36, 45, 58, 60,
    63, 77, 78, 80, 92–93, 95, 106, 119–22,
    175, 189, 196, 197, 218, 222;
    Computer language 196; Numerical/
    mathematical language 24;
    Performative language 78, 105;
    Translation 36, 60, 121; Untranslatable
    language 120, 122; As weapon 95
Lara Croft 3, 6, 89, 166, 203, *204–6*
Laughton, Charles 172
Lee, Spike 209–10
Lhasa 70, 74; *see also* Tibet

Licensing Act of 1737 51–52, 54
Liturgy/Liturgical drama 7–8, 27, 82, 142,
    172, 174
Liveness 11, 89, 103, 116, 126, 164–65,
    195, 203, 208, 214, 217, 218, 22
Locke, John 22, 46
Logo(s) 127, 199, 202–4, 207, 209, 214
Long Day's Journey Into Night 116
Lost Horizon 67, 153, 154
Ludlum, Charles 147
Lugosi, Bela 56
Lukács, Georg 37–38, 42–44, 47
Luna, James 210
Lunar Opera 5, 140–*1*, 142, 153

Machinal 89, *109*, 92–95, 96, 99, 128
Machines 1, 2, 31, 39, 77, 80, 81, 86, 89–
    90, 92–101, 103–8, 111, 112, 114–21,
    123, 126–33, 138, 141, 142, 145, 149,
    155, 158, 168, 173, 174, 185, 186, 197,
    206, 215
MacLaine, Shirley 195–96
Macready, William 71
Magic/Magicians 21, 41, 51, 52, 54, 73,
    79, 121, 132, 170, 186
Magic Hype, The 147
Mandala 24, 66, 121, 155
Manifestos 77–79, 104–7, 138, 153, 161,
    190, 208, 211; Communist Manifesto
    77–79, 153; Cyborg Manifesto 105;
    Dada Manifestos 105; Futurist
    Manifesto 104–7; S.C.U.M. Manifesto
    138; Surrealist Manifestos 105
Mao Tse Tung 12–14, 19, 28, 30, 37
Mapping 67–70, 86–87, 225n.14; *see also*
    Geography
Marinetti, Filippo Tommaso 104–7; *Electric
    Dolls(Poupée Électriques)* 105–6; *see also*
    Futurism
Markets/Marketing 19–20, 30, 34, 35, 80,
    95, 98, 100, 159, 161, 195, 196, 205
Mary Magdalene 8–9, 12, 45, 55
Mary, The Virgin 8–9, 12, 55
Marx, Karl 42, 45, 77–79, 143, 153, 172,
    173, 176, 182; *Communist Manifesto* 77–
    79, 153; *The Critique of Political Economy*
    79
Masculinity/Masculinist 46–47, 66, 69, 71,
    73, 99, 104–5, 107–8, 137–38, 146,
    149, 176, 191, 197, 208, 212–13; *see also*
    Gender
Mathews, Max 133

Maya 62, 155, 224n.6
McCarthyism 117, 179; *see also* House Un-American Activities Committee
Medeamaterial 103
Mediums 42, 73, 75–76, 81, 92, 115, 124–25, 164, 195, 199; Spiritualist mediums 73, 75–77, 81, 164, 195; *see also* Channeling
Melodrama 58, 71, 78–79, 89, 121, 153
Memory 75, 123–26, 150, 155, 168, 180, 209, 217
Mercury 18–21, 24, 26, 28–30, 34, 48, 49, 84, 87, 101
Mercury Vindicated from the Alchemists at Court 28–30
Metaphor 10, 23–24, 29, 57, 73, 75, 86, 106, 183–84, 193, 195; In alchemy 23–24, 29; Einstein's use of 75, 86, 183–84; Theatrical 10
Mid-Century modern 115–16, 119, 130, 135, 140, 142, 146, 156, 172, 179; Definition of 115–16
Middleton and Dekker 30–31; *The Roaring Girl* 27, 30–31
Military-Industrial Compound 5, 90, 100, 102–3, 107, 114, 118
Mimesis 6, 87, 90, 106, 220–21
Minimalism 115, 135, 182, 207
Minstrelsy 209–10, 212; *see also* Neo-minstrelsy
Mise en scene 87–88, 90–92, 114, 146, 148–49, 151
Misogyny 85, 104; *see also* Gender
Modernism *see* Mid-century modernism
Modest Witness 60, 72–73, 80, 81, 116, 120, 130, 135, 172
Money 18–20, 29–30, 34–35, 41–46, 51, 54, 79–80, 87, 99, 113, 143, 153, 161, 201; And alchemy 18–20, 30 41; Coins 19–20, 72, 223n.3; Credit 34–35, 42, 201, 209; Counterfeit 18–20, 30, 34, 72; Gold 9, 19–21, 23, 26, 30, 34–35, 42, 79, 80, 84, 201; And *Faust* 41–46, 201; Forms of 19, 51, 53 54, 80, 87; And Gender 46–50; Paper money 19–20, 34, 41–46, 48, 51, 54, 79, 80, 201; Patents as 51, 80; And theater 30, 34, 51–54, 161
Monroe, Marilyn 138–39
Moog, Robert 132
Müller, Heiner 103, 225n.8
Mumma, Gordon 133

Museums 2, 72, 88, 158, 222
Music 2, 4, 8, 9, 40, 82, 88, 116, 128–40, 156, 166, 184, 186–94, 197, 205, 206; Electronic music/electronic instruments 2, 88, 131–34, 139, 184, 186, 192–93; Experimental music 128–36, 140, 187; Music of the spheres 40, 156; New Age music 193; *see also* Cage; Oliveros; Sun Ra; Theremin
Mysticism 58, 60, 64, 66, 68, 77, 82, 85, 153, 186–87, 192–94, 197, 201, 205
Myth 7, 15, 29, 40, 46, 47, 50, 60, 67, 120–21, 124, 140, 166, 186–88, 191–93, 196, 197
Mythscience 61, 186–88
Myth-Technology 186

Nation/nationalism 26, 35, 42–44, 45, 53, 55, 57, 61, 63–64, 67–68, 70, 87–88, 95, 100, 101, 104, 108, 118–20, 144, 161–62, 181, 201, 224n.4–5
National Security Agency (NSA) 117–18
Naturalism (in acting) 70–71, 83–84, 125
Natural Selection 143, 177, 179, 185
Nature 10–13, 19, 27, 28, 31, 36–39, 43, 45–46, 48–49, 73, 84, 88, 99, 105, 136, 142–48, 151–52, 157–61, 217; Enclosure of 11, 13, 57, 151; Neo-nature 157–62; As theater 10–13; In *Faust* 38, 43, 45
New Age 24, 60, 88, 140, 155, 163, 193–97
New Forest, The 13, 223n.2
Newton, Issac 4, 6, 19–27, 32, 34–37, 39, 40, 71, 86, 223n.3; Alchemical writings 20–21, 27; And decoding 21–22; And gravity 20, 22, 86; And "new" Science 20; The Newton Project 4, 21; *Opticks* 20, 36; *Praxis* 21
Neo-Minstrelsy 209–14; *see also* Gomez-Peña; Race
Nostalgia 5, 57, 127, 147–49, 212

Occult 15, 17–19, 21, 26, 60, 61, 65, 67, 71, 75, 76, 81,193
Olcott, Colonel 65, 74, 76
Oliveros, Pauline 5, 128, *129*–31, 138–42, 153, 187, 191; "Deep Listening" 130, 141–42; *In Memoriam Nikola Tesla, Cosmic Engineer* 131 *Lunar Opera* 5, 140, *141*–2, 153; *Njinga The Queen King*; *The Return of a Warrior* 139; *Tape Delay* 128–29; *To Valerie Solanas and Marilyn Monroe In Recognition of*

Their Desperation . . . 138; San Francisco
Tape Music Center 128, *129*
O'Neill, Eugene 116, 226n.12
Opera 139–1, 151, 182–84; see also
Einstein on the Beach; Lunar Opera
Operating theaters 12, 55, 117
Orientalism 6, 15, 32, 39, 59–60, 63–64,
68, 113, 148–49, 187, 191
Origin of the Species 66, 71, 143, 180; *see also*
Darwin
Origins 4, 7–11, 13, 18, 32–34, 60, 65–67,
71, 98, 120, 133, 143, 160–61, 163,
164, 177–78, 180, 198–99; Of the
avatar 163, 198–99; And copies 4, 52–
53, 87, 160–61; Of European culture
18, 98; Of humanity 65–66, 71, 143,
177–78; Of theater 7–9

Paik, Nam Jun 133
Palmo, Tenzin 154, 225n.9
Panama Canal 43, 48, 143
Paracelsus 33–35, 46, 73; and Mme.
Blavatsky 73
Parsons, John Whiteside 166–68, 173
Patents 51, 80, 96, 98, 201; *see also*
Intellectual property
Pema Chödrön, Ami 154
Performance Art 98, 105, 140, 157–59,
182–85, 203, 208–15
Phenomenology 35–36, 49, 69, 78, 80, 82,
224n.16
Philalethes, Erenaeus 22–24, 26
Physics 3, 11, 23, 38, 49, 70, 72, 74–75,
76, 136, 173, 176, 181, 193–94
Pins and Needles 96–98, 99
Plague 20, 29–30
Pollution 88, 143, 148, 157; *see also* Waste
Print Culture 4–5, 61
Prostheses 89, 95, 115, 150, 165, 211–12,
219
Proust, Marcel 124–25
Psychology/Psychoanalysis 74, 83, 85, 95–
96, 120–21, 135, 138, 159, 166, 167–
68, 182, 217, 221
Public Domain 51–54, 56–57
Puppets 27, 33, 34, 106
Pythagoras 24, 64, 81

Quem queritis 7–8, 27, 32

Race/racializing 18, 62–64 75–76, 88,
105, 115, 116, 165–66, 185–93, 201,

203, 207–14; Racism 18, 105, 115, 201,
212; Synth race 185–93; *see also*
Ethnicity; Gomez-Peña; Neo-
minstrelsy; Sun Ra
Radio 2, 124–25, 133, 178, 194–96
Rauschenberg, Robert 133
Ravenhill, Mark 170–71
Realism 71, 108–10, 114, 124–25, 201,
206; Socialist Realism 108–10
Recursion 5, 82, 116, 123–28, 130, 147,
150, 165, 187, 215, 217; *see also*
Iteration; Tape
Recycling 123, 142, 147, 153, 168, 171
Reimann, Walter 91
Remembrance of Things Past 124
Reproduction 28, 101, 122–23, 125, 127,
152, 158, 159–62, 164; Digital 56, 201;
Human 101, 122–23, 152, 158, 159–
62; Of performance 164; *see also*
Cloning; Iteration; Recursion
Resources 21, 38, 42, 44, 75, 93, 107, 108,
123, 125, 143–44, 151, 173; Natural
resources 44, 107, 143–44, 151
Rice, Elmer 98–99; see also Adding
Machine
Ritual 8, 82, 121, 139–41, 153, 155, 156,
166–68, 188, 191, 197
Roaring Girl, The 27, 30–31
Robots 6, 89, 99–101, 103, 105, 122, 132,
158, 191, 211
Rockaby 127–38, 141
Rocket Science 166–67, 173
Röhrig, Walter 91
Romanticism 34, 60, 67, 76; *see also*
Gothic
Rome, Harold 97
Royal Society 21, 45, 72, 73
R.U.R. (Rossum's Universal Robots) 89, 99–
101, 122, 173
Ryerson, Kevin 195–96

Said, Edward 15, 17, 32, 223n.13
San Francisco Mime Troupe 210
San Francisco Tape Music Center 128,
129; see also Oliveros
Sankara 62
Sakuntala 39
Science Fiction 2, 22, 23, 60, 82, 100, 110,
132, 140, 142, 146, 149, 164, 166–69,
189–92; *see also* Cyberpunk
Scientology 167–68
Scopes Monkey Trial 177–79

S.C.U.M. Manifesto 138
Screens 87, 103, 112, 115, 116, 133, 134, 150, 165, 171, 185, 198, 199, 208, 215, 220–22, 224n.18
Seven Years In Tibet 153–54
Sewing Machines 96–98
Sexual Electricity 89, 105–6
Sexuality 5, 26–27, 31, 60, 64–66, 83, 91, 96, 99, 101, 105–6, 113, 116–19, 123, 137–38, 146, 165, 172, 173, 177, 191, 203, 205–6, 210, 215, 218, 222; *see also* Heterosexuality; Homosexuality
Shakespeare, William 54, 55, 78; see also Hamlet
Shaw, George Bernard 80–82, 170; And Edison 80–82, 170; *The Irrational Knot* 80; *Major Barbara* 81
Shaw, Peggy 220
Sifuentes, Roberto 210–11
Silence 96, 107, 126, 135–39, 184; *Silence* 135; *see also* Cage
Simulation 30, 55, 83, 88, 100, 105, 147, 151, 155, 160, 170–71, 185, 202, 206, 224n.6
Singer, Issac 96
Smith, Adam 44
Smith, Anna Deavere 222
Smith, Jack 146, 148–49, 150
Snyder, Ruth 93–*4*; see also Machinal
Socialism 102, 107–14, 173, 174, 177, 225n.8
Software 22, 46–47, 88, 89, 101, 103, 118, 127, 155, 165, 170, 185, 197–99, 206–7, 213, 214
Solanas, Valerie 138–39
Sound 2, 6, 77, 80, 92, 122, 124–36, 138, 140–41, 151, 184, 186, 188, 191–92, 195, 206, 211; Soundscape 6, 131–33, 138, 184; *see also* Music
Space 2–4, 9, 10, 13, 23, 24, 28–32, 39–41, 48–54, 57, 63, 67–69, 75, 82, 86–87, 90–91, 101, 103, 107, 109, 115, 125–34, 136–38, 142–44, 146, 148, 156, 163–65, 169, 171, 183, 184, 188–94, 197–203, 206–7, 214–15, 218, 222; Absolute Space 40–41, 87; Abstract Space 48, 109, 133; Corportate/commercial space 34, 57, 68, 88, 101, 146, 200–206, 214–15; Domestic space 29, 45, 75, 85, 89, 115–16, 122–23, 131, 159, 215, 226n.11; Embodied Space 66–70; Euclidean space 40, 68–

69, 90; And gender 29, 45–49, 66–69, 75, 92–96, 137–39, 149, 215–22; Interior space 38–40, 115, 135, 168; Meta-space 40, 197; Outer space 111, 123, 132, 140–42, 156, 163–64, 169, 188–94; Ownership of 13, 51–57, 68, 200; Performance Space 10, 34, 49, 51, 87, 88, 114, 128–34, 141–42, 165, 222; Performative space 4, 132–33, 138–39, 146, 192; Private vs. Public 11, 13, 51–54, 56–57, 200, 206; Social Space 31, 93, 107, 115, 141–42, 149, 165, 202, 206; Sound Space 130–31; Space-age 115, 191; Space-time 86–87, 168; Techno-space 3, 142, 163–64, 197, 211; *see also* Cyberspace; Mapping; Virtual Space
Spaceships 111–14, 142, 169–70, 183, 191; *see also* UFOs
Specters 35, 76–79, 104, 153, 176, 195; *see also* Ghosts, Spirits
Spirits 24, 33, 44, 76–79, 167; *see also* Ghosts; Specters; Spiritualism
Spiritualism 3, 58–60, 72–77, 82, 85, 88, 121, 135, 139–40, 142, 152–57, 163–64, 166–68, 171, 186, 193–97, 201
Starkey, George 22; *see also* Philalethes
Star regulus 22
Stasis 11, 12–13, 18–20
Steiner, Rudolf 49–50, 224n.16
Stein, Gertrude 76
Stelarc 208–9, 211
Sterling, Bruce 146, 149–50
Stephenson, Neal 198–99
Stoker, Bram 95, 225n.4
Strindberg 5, 6, 58, 82–85; And alchemy 58, 82–85; And gender 84–85; And naturalism 83; *Inferno* 82; *Miss Julie* 83, 84
Sun Ra 140, 166, 188, *189*–93, 194, 209; *Space is the Place* 191; *see also* Race
Surplus 42–45, 48, 96, 101, 149, 196
Surveillance 13, 87, 91, 114, 117–19, 157, 176
Sweatshops 96–98
Swedenborg 85
Synthesizer 132, 186–88, 191
Synthespian 165; see also Idoru

Tape 5, 82, 95–96, 98, 99, 116, 123–30, 133, 138, 215
Taxonomy 11, 14, 29; *see also* Classification

Taylorism 89, 92

Technology 1–5, 9, 28, 33, 45, 59, 61, 77, 80, 84, 86, 95 88–89, 95–96, 101–8, 112, 114–26, 132–35, 138, 142–52, 155, 157–65, 168, 171, 172, 176, 184–88, 191–97, 199–201, 203, 205–8, 211–22; Biotechnology 157–62; And the environment 88, 142–43, 151–52, 171, 176; And gender 105–8, 116–17, 147–49, 151, 161, 197, 203–6, 215–22; Immersive technologies 114, 138, 163–64, 197, 214; Medical technology 33, 103, 116–17, 122–23, 147, 193, 215–17, 219–20; Myth-technology 186; And power 89, 102, 104, 107, 117–19, 163, 172, 184; Technological virtual 3, 9, 46, 77, 80, 82, 88, 142, 114, 123, 125, 155, 165; Techno-space 3, 142, 163–64, 197, 211; Theater technologies 28–29, 77, 87–89, 103, 116, 125, 132–34, 159, 165, 186, 201; And whiteness 211–12, 214

Technophilia 105

Teena, Brandon 6, 218–22

Telephone 77, 80, 93, 102, 116, 150, 155, 195, 196, 215, 217

Telescope 2, *111*, 112, 173–76

Television (TV) 66, 89, 115–16, 118, 120, 133, 145, 169, 170, 171, 194, 196, 199, 202, 209–10, 226n.11

Temple of Solomon 24, *25*, 39

Temporality/Time 4, 23–24, 44, 86–87, 123–25, 127, 128, 136, 140, 141, 155–57, 178, 182, 193

Tesla, Nikola 131

Theater 2–3, 7–17, 20, 27–31, 34–41, 47–58, 60, 71, 76, 78–79, 81, 82–88, 90, 97, 106–9, 131–32, 140, 147, 151, 172–76, 193, 201–2, 206, 214, 217, 222; And change 8, 11, 13, 20, 27, 29; And gender 7–9, 45–47, 84–85, 107; As Laboratory 9, 28, 30, 39, 48, 108, 134; As lens 13–14; Licensing of 30, 51–52, 54, 55, 72; And money 9, 30, 34, 51–54, 78–79; And nature 10–13, 38; Rebirth of 7–9, 12, 35; Synthetic Theater 106–7; Theater and science 2–3, 7, 9–13, 15, 17, 27–31, 39, 48–49, 54–55, 58, 85, 193, 201; Theater of anatomy 12, 55; Theater spaces 10, 12, 30, 39, 49–51, 54, 97, 108, 109, 131, 151, 172, 202, 206, 222; Theaterical

technologies 28–29, 77, 87–89, 103, 116, 125, 132–34, 159, 165, 186, 201

Theosophy 64–67, 70, 76, 80, 193, 224n.16; *see also* Blavatsky

Theosophical Society 50, 61, 64, 69–70

Theremin 131–33, 188

Tibet 60–62, 66–70, 74–75, 136, 140, 142, 152–55

Tourism 41, 135; *see also* Travel

Transcendence 1, 3, 9, 10, 13, 32, 34, 37, 39–42, 47–49, 65, 74, 76, 83, 88, 104–8, 114, 120, 142–43, 145, 146, 152, 153, 163, 164, 168–71, 197–99, 208, 214; And aliens/outer space 120, 169; And cyberspace 197–99, 208; And Faust 32, 34, 37, 39–42, 47–49; And Mme. Blavatsky 65, 74; Masculinist transcendent 104–8; And technology 88, 104–8, 114, 142–43, 145, 197–99

Transformation/transmutation 7–9, 11–12, 18–20, 23–31, 34–35, 39, 43, 48–49, 54, 60, 64, 67–68, 70–75, 78, 79, 82–87, 100, **101**, 123, 142, 149, 151, 155, 163, 170; And alchemy 11–12, 18–20, 23–30, 34–35, 43, 83–85, 87, 101; And gender 9, 26–27, 31, 45, 64, 151, 217; Rites of 7–9, 20, 26, 30, 51, 60, 82, 142, 155, 163; And theater 7–9, 27, 29, 54 82–85

Transgender 6, 63–65, 74, 139, 146–48, 150, 215–22

Transgenic 157–61, 211

Transsexuality 116–17, 215, 217, 219

Trash 142, 144–51, 152

Travel 33, 34, 41, 47, 50, 63–65, 74, 113, 123, 156, 163, 166, 169, 188, 192–93, 205; And gender 63–65, 74, 154; Space 113, 123, 156, 169, 188, 192–93; Virtual 34, 41, 50, 163, 166

Triangle Shirtwaist Co. Fire 97

Treadwell, Sofie 92–95, 128, 131

Tubman, Harriet 190

Tudor, David 130–31, 133

Turing, Alan 118–19

Typewriters 92, 95–96, 99

UFOs 89, 119–23, 132, 140, 152, 156, 188

Utopia/Utopian 13, 31, 44, 101, 104, 112, 143, 148, 165, 176, 192, 199

Vampires 95–96, 225n.3

Vanderbeck, Stan 133

Variations V 132–*4*, 135–38, 141, 182
Vawter, Ron 149
Video Games *see* Games and Gaming
Violence 71, 79, 88, 89, 91, 100, 103–7,
    116, 138–39, 160–61, 171, 191, 192,
    194, 198, 208, 213, 218, 219
Virtual 2–4, 7, 9–12, 20, 27, 30–31, 34, 37,
    39–54, 57–63, 67, 70–71, 73, 77–82,
    85–88, 100, 114–16, 121–25, 127,
    131–32, 135–38, 140–42, 145–46,
    149–56, 163–66, 168, 170–72, 185–87,
    190, 192, 194–209, 213, 215–18, 222,
    224n.18; Definition 2; Techno-virtual 3,
    46, 142, 155, 165; Virtual community
    45; Virtual class 88, 142, 150, 170, 207,
    213; Virtual gender 45; Virtual plane
    41, 60–61, 121, 163; Virtual systems
    11, 203, 217, 222
Virtuality 3, 41, 77, 132, 141, 164, 171,
    190, 197
Virtually Yours 215, *216*–18, 222
Virtual Reality (VR) 3, 88, 138, 196–98,
    201
Virtual space 2–4, 7, 9–10, 27, 30, 34, 37,
    39–41, 45–48, 51–54, 57, 58, 63, 82,
    88, 116, 121, 125, 127, 131, 135–36,
    138, 142, 145, 146, 149, 152, 156,
    163, 165, 168, 170, 171, 186, 192,
    194, 196, 197, 200–201 206–8, 218–
    22, 224n.18; And gender 45–49;
    Silence as 135–36; Theater as 2–4, 10,

27, 34, 37, 40, 49, 51–54, 165; *see also*
    avatars
Visitatio Sepulchri 7–8, 12

Waitingforgodot.com 206–*7*, 208
Waiting for Tadashi 209
Waldorf Schools 50
War 10, 35, 42, 95, 101–2, 104, 106, 112,
    116–18, 121, 137–38, 156, 166, 173,
    181, 194, 210; Civil war(s) 95, 112;
    Cold War 116–18, 121, 137, 181; WWI
    102; WWII 121, 166, 181, 210
Warm, Hermann 91
Waste 48, 98–99, 103, 142–46, 149, 151;
    see also Trash
Websites 4, 5, 19, 22, 130, 140, 141, 156,
    168–69, 206–8, 210–11, 213–14, 217–22
Wertenbaker, Timberlake 172, 179–80,
    182
Wiene, Robert 91
Whiston, William 32
Whitemore, Hugh 119
Whiteness 115, 185–86, 206, 210, 212; *see
    also* Race
Williams, Tennessee 116
Wilson, Robert 70, 86, 106, 172, 182–84
Witches/witchcraft 9, 26, 33, 38–40, 44–
    47, 50, 197, 207
Wooster Group 210

Zen 136–37, 184; *see also* Buddhism

Related titles from Routledge

Performance and Evolution in the Age of Darwin:
Out of the Natural Order

Jane Goodall

Performance and Evolution in the Age of Darwin reveals the ways in which the major themes of evolution were taken up in the performing arts during Darwin's adult lifetime and in the generation after his death.

The period 1830-1900 was the formative period for evolutionary ideas. While scientists and theorists investigated the law and order of nature, show business was more concerned with what was out of the natural order. Missing links and throwbacks, freak taxonomies and exotic races were favourite subject matter for the burgeoning variety theatre movement. Focusing on popular theatre forms in London, New York and Paris, Jane Goodall shows how they were interwoven with the developing debate about human evolution.

With this book, Goodall contributes an important new angle to the debates surrounding the history of evolution. She reveals that, far from creating widespread culture shock, Darwinian theory tapped into some of the long-standing themes of popular performance and was a source for diverse and sometimes hilarious explorations.

ISBN10: 0-415-24377-7 (hbk)
ISBN10: 0-415-24378-5 (pbk)

ISBN13: 978-0-415-24377-3 (hbk)
ISBN13: 978-0-415-24378-0 (pbk)

Available at all good bookshops
For ordering and further information please visit:
www.routledge.com

Science and the Stanislavsky Tradition of Acting

Jonathan Pitches

Providing new insight into the well-known tradition of acting, *Science and the Stanislavsky Tradition of Acting* is the first book to contextualise the Stanislavsky tradition with reference to parallel developments in science. Rooted in practice, it presents an alternative perspective based on philosophy, physics, romantic science and theories of industrial management.

Working from historical and archive material, as well as practical sources, Jonathan Pitches traces an evolutionary journey of actor training from the roots of the Russian tradition, Konstantin Stanislavsky, to the contemporary Muscovite director, Anatoly Vasiliev. The book explores two key developments that emerge from Stanislavsky's system – one linear, rational and empirical, while the other is fluid, organic and intuitive. The otherwise highly contrasting acting theories of Vsevolod Meyerhold (biomechanics) and Lee Strasberg (the Method) are dealt with under the banner of the rational or Newtonian paradigm; Michael Chekov's acting technique and the little known ideas of Anatoly Vasiliev form the centre-piece of the other Romantic, organic strain of practice.

Science and the Stanislavsky Tradition of Acting opens up the theatre laboratories of five major practitioners in the twentieth and twenty-first centuries and scrutinises their acting methodologies from a scientific perspective.

ISBN10: 0-415-32907-8 (hbk)
ISBN13: 978-0-415-32907-1 (hbk)

Related titles from Routledge

Virtual Theatres:

An Introduction

Gabriella Giannachi

The first full-length book of its kind to offer an investigation of the interface between theatre, performance and digital arts, *Virtual Theatres* presents the theatre of the twenty-first century in which everything - even the viewer - can be simulated.

In this fascinating volume, Gabriella Giannachi analyzes the aesthetic concerns of current computer-arts practices through discussion of a variety of artists and performers including:

- Blast Theory
- Merce Cunningham
- Eduardo Kac
- forced entertainment
- Lynn Hershman
- Jodi Orlan
- Guillermo Gómez-Peña
- Marcel-lí Antúnez Roca
- Jeffrey Shaw
- Stelarc.

Virtual Theatres not only allows for a reinterpretation of what is possible in the world of performance practice, but also demonstrates how 'virtuality' has come to represent a major parameter for our understanding and experience of contemporary art and life.

ISBN10: 0-415-28378-7 (hbk)
ISBN10: 0-415-28379-5 (pbk)

ISBN13: 978-0-415-28378-6 (hbk)
ISBN13: 978-0-415-28379-3 (pbk)

Available at all good bookshops
For ordering and further information please visit:
www.routledge.com